References for the Rest of Us!®

COMPUTER BOOK SERIES FROM IDG

Are you intimidated and confused by computers? Do you find that traditional manuals are overloaded with technical details you'll never use? Do your friends and family always call you to fix simple problems on their PCs? Then the *. . .For Dummies*® computer book series from IDG Books Worldwide is for you.

. . .For Dummies books are written for those frustrated computer users who know they aren't really dumb but find that PC hardware, software, and indeed the unique vocabulary of computing make them feel helpless. *. . .For Dummies* books use a lighthearted approach, a down-to-earth style, and even cartoons and humorous icons to diffuse computer novices' fears and build their confidence. Lighthearted but not lightweight, these books are a perfect survival guide for anyone forced to use a computer.

"I like my copy so much I told friends; now they bought copies."
Irene C., Orwell, Ohio

"Quick, concise, nontechnical, and humorous."
Jay A., Elburn, Illinois

"Thanks, I needed this book. Now I can sleep at night."
Robin F., British Columbia, Canada

Already, hundreds of thousands of satisfied readers agree. They have made *. . .For Dummies* books the #1 introductory level computer book series and have written asking for more. So, if you're looking for the most fun and easy way to learn about computers, look to *. . .For Dummies* books to give you a helping hand.

2/96

by John R. Levine and
Margaret Levine Young

Foreword by Ted Nelson

IDG Books Worldwide, Inc.
An International Data Group Company

Foster City, CA ♦ Chicago, IL ♦ Indianapolis, IN ♦ Braintree, MA ♦ Southlake, TX

MORE Internet For Dummies®, 2nd Edition

Published by
IDG Books Worldwide, Inc.
An International Data Group Company
919 E. Hillsdale Blvd.
Suite 400
Foster City, CA 94404

Library of Congress Catalog Card No.: 96-75111

ISBN: 1-56884-606-1

Printed in the United States of America

10 9 8 7 6 5 4 3 2 1

2A/RV/QT/ZW/IN

Distributed in the United States by IDG Books Worldwide, Inc.

Distributed by Macmillan Canada for Canada; by Computer and Technical Books for the Caribbean Basin; by Contemporanea de Ediciones for Venezuela; by Distribuidora Cuspide for Argentina; by CITEC for Brazil; by Ediciones ZETA S.C.R. Ltda. for Peru; by Editorial Limusa SA for Mexico; by Transworld Publishers Limited in the United Kingdom and Europe; by Al-Maiman Publishers & Distributors for Saudi Arabia; by Simron Pty. Ltd. for South Africa; by IDG Communications (HK) Ltd. for Hong Kong; by Toppan Company Ltd. for Japan; by Addison Wesley Publishing Company for Korea; by Longman Singapore Publishers Ltd. for Singapore, Malaysia, Thailand, and Indonesia; by Unalis Corporation for Taiwan; by WS Computer Publishing Company, Inc. for the Philippines; by WoodsLane Pty. Ltd. for Australia; by WoodsLane Enterprises Ltd. for New Zealand.

For general information on IDG Books Worldwide's books in the U.S., please call our Consumer Customer Service department at 800-762-2974. For reseller information, including discounts and premium sales, please call our Reseller Customer Service department at 800-434-3422.

For information on where to purchase IDG Books Worldwide's books outside the U.S., contact IDG Books Worldwide at 415-655-3021 or fax 415-655-3295.

For information on translations, contact Marc Jeffrey Mikulich, Director, Foreign & Subsidiary Rights, at IDG Books Worldwide, 415-655-3018 or fax 415-655-3295.

For sales inquiries and special prices for bulk quantities, write to the address above or call IDG Books Worldwide at 415-655-3200.

For information on using IDG Books Worldwide's books in the classroom, or ordering examination copies, contact the Education Office at 800-434-2086 or fax 817-251-8174.

For authorization to photocopy items for corporate, personal, or educational use, please contact Copyright Clearance Center, 222 Rosewood Drive, Danvers, MA 01923, or fax 508-750-4470.

About the Authors

John R. Levine was a member of a computer club in high school — before high school students, or even high schools, had computers. He met Theodor H. Nelson, the author of *Computer Lib/Dream Machines* and the inventor of hypertext, who reminded us that computers should not be taken seriously and that everyone can and should understand and use computers.

John wrote his first program in 1967 on an IBM 1130 (a computer roughly as powerful as your typical modern digital wristwatch, only more difficult to use). He became an official system administrator of a networked computer at Yale in 1975. He began working part-time for a computer company, of course, in 1977 and has been in and out of the computer and network biz ever since. He got his company onto Usenet (see Chapter 9) early enough that it appears in a 1982 *Byte* magazine article in a map of Usenet, which then was so small that the map fit on half a page.

He used to spend most of his time writing software, but now he mostly writes books (including *UNIX For Dummies, The Internet For Dummies,* and *Internet Secrets,* published by IDG Books Worldwide) because it's more fun and he can do so at home in the tiny village of Trumansburg, New York. He also teaches some computer courses and publishes and edits an incredibly technoid magazine called *The Journal of C Language Translation.* He holds a B.A. and a Ph.D. in computer science from Yale University, but please don't hold that against him.

Margy Levine Young has used small computers since the 1970s. She graduated from UNIX on a PDP/11 to Apple DOS on an Apple II to MS-DOS and UNIX on a variety of machines. She has done all kinds of jobs that involve explaining to people that computers aren't as mysterious as they might think, including managing the use of PCs at Columbia Pictures, teaching scientists and engineers what computers are good for, and writing and cowriting computer manuals and books, including *Understanding Javelin PLUS* (Sybex, 1987), *The Complete Guide to PC-File* (Center Books, better known as Margy and her Dad, 1991), *UNIX For Dummies, The Internet For Dummies, WordPerfect For Windows For Dummies,* and *Internet FAQs: Answers to the Most Frequently Asked Questions.* Margy has a degree in computer science from Yale University and lives with her husband, two children, and chickens in Lexington, Massachusetts.

Welcome to the world of IDG Books Worldwide.

IDG Books Worldwide, Inc., is a subsidiary of International Data Group, the world's largest publisher of computer-related information and the leading global provider of information services on information technology. IDG was founded more than 25 years ago and now employs more than 7,700 people worldwide. IDG publishes more than 250 computer publications in 67 countries (see listing below). More than 70 million people read one or more IDG publications each month.

Launched in 1990, IDG Books Worldwide is today the #1 publisher of best-selling computer books in the United States. We are proud to have received 8 awards from the Computer Press Association in recognition of editorial excellence and three from Computer Currents' First Annual Readers' Choice Awards, and our best-selling *...For Dummies®* series has more than 19 million copies in print with translations in 28 languages. IDG Books Worldwide, through a joint venture with IDG's Hi-Tech Beijing, became the first U.S. publisher to publish a computer book in the People's Republic of China. In record time, IDG Books Worldwide has become the first choice for millions of readers around the world who want to learn how to better manage their businesses.

Our mission is simple: Every one of our books is designed to bring extra value and skill-building instructions to the reader. Our books are written by experts who understand and care about our readers. The knowledge base of our editorial staff comes from years of experience in publishing, education, and journalism — experience which we use to produce books for the '90s. In short, we care about books, so we attract the best people. We devote special attention to details such as audience, interior design, use of icons, and illustrations. And because we use an efficient process of authoring, editing, and desktop publishing our books electronically, we can spend more time ensuring superior content and spend less time on the technicalities of making books.

You can count on our commitment to deliver high-quality books at competitive prices on topics you want to read about. At IDG Books Worldwide, we continue in the IDG tradition of delivering quality for more than 25 years. You'll find no better book on a subject than one from IDG Books Worldwide.

John Kilcullen
President and CEO
IDG Books Worldwide, Inc.

IX
WINNER
Ninth Annual
Computer Press
Awards 1993

IDG Books Worldwide, Inc., is a subsidiary of International Data Group, the world's largest publisher of computer-related information and the leading global provider of information services on information technology. International Data Group publishes over 250 computer publications in 67 countries. Seventy million people read one or more International Data Group publications each month. International Data Group's publications include: **ARGENTINA:** Computerworld Argentina, GamePro, Infoworld, PC World Argentina; **AUSTRALIA:** Australian Macworld, Client/Server Journal, Computer Living, Computerworld, Digital News, Network World, PC World, Publishing Essentials, Reseller; **AUSTRIA:** Computerwelt, PC TEST; **BELARUS:** PC World Belarus; **BELGIUM:** Data News; **BRAZIL:** Annuário de Informática, Computerworld Brazil, Connections, Super Game Power, Macworld, PC World Brazil, Publish Brazil, SUPERGAME; **BULGARIA:** Computerworld Bulgaria, Networkworld/Bulgaria, PC & MacWorld Bulgaria; **CANADA:** CIO Canada, ComputerWorld Canada, InfoCanada, Network World Canada, Reseller World; **CHILE:** Computerworld Chile, GamePro, PC World Chile; **COLUMBIA:** Computerworld Colombia, GamePro, PC World Colombia; **COSTA RICA:** PC World Costa Rica/Nicaragua; **THE CZECH AND SLOVAK REPUBLICS:** Computerworld Czechoslovakia, Elektronika Czechoslovakia, PC World Czechoslovakia; **DENMARK:** Communications World, Computerworld Danmark, Macworld Danmark, PC World Danmark, PC World Danmark Supplements, TECH World; **DOMINICAN REPUBLIC:** PC World Republica Dominicana; **ECUADOR:** PC World Ecuador, GamePro; **EGYPT:** Computerworld Middle East, PC World Middle East; **EL SALVADOR:** PC World Centro America; **FINLAND:** MikroPC, Tietoverkko, Tietoviikko; **FRANCE:** Distributique, Golden, Info PC, Le Guide du Monde Informatique, Le Monde Informatique, Reseaux & Telecoms; **GERMANY:** Computer Business, Computerwoche, Computerwoche Extra, Computerwoche Focus, Electronic Entertainment, GamePro, I/M Information Management, Macwelt, PC Welt; **GREECE:** GamePro, Macworld & Publish; **GUATEMALA:** PC World Centro America; **HONDURAS:** PC World Centro America; **HONG KONG:** Computerworld Hong Kong, PCWorld Hong Kong, Publish in Asia; **HUNGARY:** ABCD CD-ROM, Computerworld Szamitastechnika, PC & Mac World Hungary, PC-X Magazine; **INDIA:** Computerworld India, PC World India, Publish in Asia; **INDONESIA:** InfoKomputer PC World, Komputek Computerworld, Publish in Asia; **IRELAND:** ComputerScope, PC Live!; **ISRAEL:** PC World 32 BIT, People & Computers; **ITALY:** Computerworld Italia, Computerworld Italia Special Editions, Lotus Italia, Macworld Italia, Networking Italia, PC Shopping, PC World Italia, PC World/Walt Disney; **JAPAN:** Macworld Japan, Nikkei Personal Computing, SunWorld Japan, Windows World Japan; **KENYA:** East African Computer News; **KOREA:** Hi-Tech Information/Computerworld, Macworld Korea, PC World Korea; **MACEDONIA:** PC World Macedonia; **MALAYSIA:** Computerworld Malaysia, PC World Malaysia, Publish in Asia; **MEXICO:** Computerworld Mexico, GamePro, Macworld, PC World Mexico; **MYANMAR:** PC World Myanmar; **NETHERLANDS:** Computable, Computer! Totaal, LAN Magazine, Macworld, Net Magazine; **NEW ZEALAND:** Computer Buyer, Computerworld New Zealand, MTB, Network World, PC World New Zealand; **NICARAGUA:** PC World Costa Rica/Nicaragua; **NIGERIA:** PC World Africa; **NORWAY:** Computerworld Norge, Computerworld Privat, CW Rapport Klient/Tjener, CW Rapport Nettverk & Telecom, CW Rapport Offentlig Sektor, IDG's KURSGUIDE, Macworld Norge, Multimedia World, PC World Ekspress, PC World Nettverk, PC World Norge, PC World's Produktguide, Windows Spesial; **PAKISTAN:** Computerworld Pakistan, PC World Pakistan; **PANAMA:** GamePro, PC World Panama; **PARAGUAY:** PC World Paraguay; **P. R. OF CHINA:** China Computerworld, China Infoworld, Computer & Communication, Electronic Product World, Electronics Today, Game Camp, PC World China, Popular Computer Week, Software World, Telecom Product World; **PERU:** Computerworld Peru, GamePro, PC World Profesional Peru, PC World Peru; **POLAND:** Computerworld Poland, Computerworld Special Report, Macworld, Networld, PC World Komputer; **PHILIPPINES:** Computerworld Philippines, PC Digest, Publish in Asia; **PORTUGAL:** Cerebro/PC World, Correio Informático/Computerworld, Mac•In/PC•In Portugal; **PUERTO RICO:** PC World Puerto Rico; **ROMANIA:** Computerworld Romania, PC World Romania, Telecom Romania; **RUSSIA:** Computerworld Rossiya, Network World Russia, PC World Russia; **SINGAPORE:** Computerworld Singapore, PC World Singapore, Publish in Asia; **SLOVENIA:** MONITOR; **SOUTH AFRICA:** Computing S.A., Network World S.A., Software World; **SPAIN:** Computerworld España, COMUNICACIONES WORLD, Dealer World, Macworld España, PC World España; **SWEDEN:** CAP&Design, Computer Sweden, Corporate Computing, MacWorld, Maxi Data, MikroDatorn, Nätverk & Kommunikation, PC/Aktiv, PC World, Windows World; **SWITZERLAND:** Computerworld Schweiz, Macworld Schweiz, PCtip; **TAIWAN:** Computerworld Taiwan, Macworld Taiwan, PC World Taiwan, Publish Taiwan, Windows World; **THAILAND:** Thai Computerworld, Publish in Asia; **TURKEY:** Computerworld Monitör, MACWORLD Turkiye, PC WORLD Turkiye; **UKRAINE:** Computerworld Kiev, Computers & Software Magazine, PC World Ukraine; **UNITED KINGDOM:** Acorn User, Amiga Action, Amiga Computing, Amiga, Appletalk, CD Powerplay, CD-ROM Now, Computing, Connexion, GamePro, Lotus Magazine, Macaction, Macworld, Open Computing, Parents and Computers, PC Home, PC Works, The WEB; **UNITED STATES:** Cable in the Classroom, CD Review, CIO Magazine, Computerworld, Computerworld Client/Server Journal, Digital Video Magazine, DOS World, Electronic, InfoWorld, I-Way, Macworld, Maximize, MULTIMEDIA WORLD, Network World, PC World, PUBLISH, SWATPro Magazine, Video Event, WebMaster; **URUGUAY:** PC World Uruguay; **VENEZUELA:** Computerworld Venezuela, GamePro, PC World Venezuela; and **VIETNAM:** PC World Vietnam 10/17/95

Dedication

Margy would like to dedicate this book to Jordan, an extraordinary guy.

John would like to dedicate this book to Tonia and to a player to be named extremely soon.

Acknowledgments

We'd like to acknowledge Jordan Young, who wrote the chapter on Windows 95; Douglas J. Muder, who wrote the chapter on Netcom; Arnold Reinhold, who wrote the chapter on privacy; and Carol Baroudi and Philippe LeRoux, who wrote the chapter on business on the Net. This is a much more interesting book because of their contributions.

We'd also like to thank our Internet providers: The Internet Access Company in Bedford, Massachusetts; LightLink in Ithaca, New York; and the Finger Lakes Technologies Group in Trumansburg, New York. Liz Walter at GNN provided valuable information, as did the whole crew on the IRC `#gnnchat`.

Mike Kelly provided terrific editorial support, as usual. Thanks also to the rest of the folks at IDG Books, with special consideration to Kelly Ewing, Bill Barton, Diane Giangrossi, Suzanne Packer, and Sherry Gomoll. And as ever, Lexington Playcare Center and Barbara Begonis provided the child-care without which this book would not have been possible (for one author, at least)!

Finally, thanks to all you smarties who have sent e-mail to us here at Internet for Dummies Central. If you have ideas, comments, or complaints about this book, e-mail us at `moreint2@dummies.com`. Also, visit our web site at `http://dummies.com` where we'll post any updates to this book.

(The Publisher would like to give special thanks to Patrick J. McGovern, without whom this book would not have been possible.)

Credits

Senior Vice President and Publisher
Milissa L. Koloski

Associate Publisher
Diane Graves Steele

Brand Manager
Judith A. Taylor

Editorial Managers
Kristin A. Cocks
Mary Corder

Product Development Manager
Mary Bednarek

Editorial Executive Assistant
Richard Graves

Editorial Assistants
Constance Carlisle
Chris Collins
Kevin Spencer

Production Director
Beth Jenkins

Production Assistant
Jacalyn L. Pennywell

Supervisor of Project Coordination
Cindy L. Phipps

Supervisor of Page Layout
Kathie S. Schnorr

Supervisor of Graphics and Design
Shelley Lea

Reprint/Blueline Coordination
Tony Augsburger
Patricia R. Reynolds
Todd Klemme
Theresa Sánchez-Baker

Media/Archive Coordination
Leslie Popplewell
Melissa Stauffer
Jason Marcuson

Project Editor
Michael Kelly

Editors
Kelly Ewing
William A. Barton
Diane L. Giangrossi
Suzanne Packer

Technical Reviewer
Dennis Cox

Project Coordinator
Sherry Gomoll

Project Coordination Assistant
Regina Snyder

Graphics Coordination
Gina Scott
Angela F. Hunckler

Production Page Layout
E. Shawn Aylsworth
Brett Black
Elizabeth Cárdenas-Nelson
Kerri Cornell
Dominique DeFelice
Maridee V. Ennis
Jill Lyttle
Jane Martin
Ron Riggan
Marti Stegeman

Proofreaders
Melissa D. Buddendeck
Gwenette Gaddis
Dwight Ramsey
Carl Saff
Robert Springer

Indexer
Steve Rath

Cover Design
Kavish + Kavish

Contents at a Glance

Cartoons at a Glance

By Rich Tennant

page 175

page 5

page 289

page 259

page 58

page 73

Table of Contents

Part V: Online Odds and Ends 289

Foreword

Geez, another edition already. Has it really been a year and a half? But *so much has changed!* Everybody's calling 1995, the year just passed, "the year of the Internet" — when the secret madness of computer people spread across the world like an exploding birthday cake. Now there are 10 million Internet users (some say 15 million) in America alone, and the expansion curve is going practically straight up.

The Internet, or Net, has changed radically. It went from black-and-white (originally with just keyboard commands) to a single unified hypertext system (called World Wide Web by its creator, Tim Berners-Lee, who has the nerve to tell me it was just a random name). Then the Internet went to Technicolor overnight under the mischievous pragmatic cobbling of young Marc Andreessen, who threw together the artful Mosaic program. Then, no longer welcome at the University of Illinois where he had achieved this wonder, he wandered west, fell in with good company, and wrought the Miracle of Netscape — a virtual coup d'état of the Internet, a company whose public offering shot into the billions.

Last year was the big change. To insiders, the era of personal computers was a replay. We went through the same old endless fascinations — programming tricks, business applications, operating systems, programs, languages, new chips, ho hum. But — bang — we're in a new new world.

"Internet machines" will soon be available cheap, with none of the complications of personal computers that you've gotten to know and hate. Only a year ago it seemed astonishing that 2 million pages of text were on the Net; now that number seems small. And it looks like everyone really *will* have a home page.

But counter to myth, all information still won't be free; only some of it. And there will still be information haves and have-nots — and copyright. Stay tuned.

Welcome to John and Margy's *MORE Internet For Dummies,* 2nd Edition, their fourth brother-and-sister book together. It is, of course, exactly the right thing to follow their excellent *UNIX For Dummies* and their phenomenally successful *The Internet For Dummies* (written with Carol Baroudi).

John is mischevous and clever and seems to know everything; Margy is clever and gentle and wise. Both are frighteningly competent. I'm terribly pleased to have the opportunity to write a foreword for them, because we've been friends for a very long time. I first met John and Margy in 1970, when they were members of the famous R.E.S.I.S.T.O.R.S. computer club of Princeton, New Jersey (Radically Emphatic Students Interested in Science, Technology and Other

Research Studies). The group was playful, zany, and clever. They ranged from age 12 to 16, but were doing professional-level work in computer languages and programming. The Levine home in Princeton was one of the warmest homes I have ever seen. Bob and Ginny Levine, the kind, trusting and astute parents of John and Margy, made it a kind of clubhouse where everyone was welcome.

For me, the Levine household became a home away from home. My excuse for hanging out in Princeton was that I was learning so much from the kids, but in fact it was also a place where my work was appreciated, as it was not yet appreciated in the Official Computer World. John was the know-it-all patrician of the club; Margy was warm and clever and eager. Both of them seemed to understand everything, but John managed to turn his insights into a constant stream of wisecracks.

With his glasses and curly hair, John bears a curious and unplanned resemblance to the academic-looking cartoon figure of the . . . *For Dummies* books, though the character preceded him in the series. (I had forgotten John had a Ph.D. till I looked over the previous volume — most Ph.D-encumbered friends don't let you forget it.)

John is a Class A wag, but his one-liners generally take a moment to understand. His dry delivery enfolds a pithy wisecrack like a fortune cookie. You can't laugh quickly because you have to unpack it. He was always like that. When he was 16, I was driving a car full of R.E.S.I.S.T.O.R.S. around Princeton. Boisterously they called out contradictory driving instructions. "I demand triple redundancy in the directions!" I barked. It was John who replied laconically, "Right up ahead you turn right right away."

The coolest subject of our day

Now the Internet is today's cool subject. Everybody wants in on the Internet because they hear it's important, but most people don't know what it is. However, as you insiders already know from the first book, *The Internet For Dummies,* the Internet is just a bunch of computers talking to each other, kind of. The Internet is not a Thing any more than the highway system is a Thing. You connect to the highway system by building a stretch of road from your house to any other piece of road that's *already* connected to the highway system; that makes the highway system include your piece of road as well. The Internet is like that. And like the highway, the Internet is there for the taking, awaiting your particular use. (Except that the asphalt is a data-sending procedure that makes sure the messages get back and forth.)

The hottest topics

Not only is the Internet a cool place, but all the hot topics are piling into it, like overheated people into a midsummer swimming pool. Everybody wants to get into interactive multimedia — ahem, the *correct* term is "hypermedia," which I coined thirty years ago — and everybody wants to produce interactive texts, movies, whatever, for the TV screen or computer screen (which will no longer be distinct from one another). The computer world is getting just like Hollywood, where everybody says he's a producer. As a matter of fact, the computer world isn't getting just *like* Hollywood, it's turning *into* Hollywood and vice versa — Hollywood itself is now treating hypermedia as its new frontier.

But the hypermedia are no longer just on disks that people buy. Till recently, many people have thought electronic media meant CD-ROM disks — but CD-ROM publishing isn't electronic publishing, it's publishing *plastic.* CD-ROM forces a pre-Columbian view of the world — when you get to the edge, you fall off. The limited size of the CD-ROM — 600 megabytes — means that much of the editorial effort is concerned with deciding what's in and what's out. And it's not connectable: every CD-ROM is absolutely separate from every other CD-ROM.

Whereas with *true* electronic publishing — that is, publishing *electrons, over networks* — there are no boundaries, there is no limit on size, nothing has to be left out. The publisher can keep filling up more disks up to any size, all available on-line; and you the reader/viewer can keep sending for the stuff indefinitely.

(Note that when the above paragraph was written a year and a half ago, it was sheer speculation. Nobody was publishing big things on the network, and few could imagine it — except a few of us who expected a vast anarchic electronic publishing network. Indeed, the growth curve — and the timing — were exactly what I predicted for the explosive growth of Xanadu in the 1990s. I got the events right, but the name wrong.)

So *true* electronic publishing has begun. World Wide Web is already a wildly successful network hypermedia publishing system. We will see many more that will make available media of every kind, across the world, under many different schemes of copyright and royalty. (Each of us seems to think he, she, or it has the answer to copyright. We shall see what works.)

But the politics of the net have now assumed center stage. We computer crazies thought the net would be a place of new freedom, but now our challenge is that some Bad Guys may try to take it away from us. One challenge is freedom of privacy. Some in government circles champion a police-state approach to monitoring the Net, claiming that they have a God-given right to spy on all communications so that users can *think* their communication is private — but the government can listen in at will.

But no actual criminal will submit to these restrictions; any high school kid can figure out a code that the government *can't* listen in on. What, then, is the point of some of these proposed cryptography laws? What the advocates of the Clipper Chip seem really to want are the laws that the chip was sneakily designed to impose on us — enabling laws that will make it illegal to aid and abet cryptography, enabling laws that will allow search and confiscation of computers, enabling laws that will allow search and confiscation of any private information and data by those suspected of actually trying to hide things in a way that the government cannot read.

And now governments say somebody else is under the bed. That latest bogeyman is the fear that children will — shhh! — be exposed to sexual materials on the Internet. Well, we let kids go to the *bathroom,* even though public restrooms may have sexual material scrawled on the walls. Some think that what the government is *really* trying to do is keep alternative sources of information from us.

Didn't a guy named Orwell talk about this quite a while ago? Welcome to the New Order. But we're getting smart about such things. This book is intended to help make you smart. New sources of information are what this book is about.

Wasting time

People ask me: Do you surf the Internet? Oh sure — the *old* Internet.

If your idea of fun is gossip columns, want ads, card catalogs, and graffiti, then the Internet is for you. A lot of Internet enthusiasts are people who apparently have nothing better to do than send and receive electronic chitchat and Hot News and look at silly cartoons all day long.

But actually I'm talking sour grapes here: The problem really is that all that Internet stuff is too interesting. You can throw your every waking hour into it. Don't go near it unless you're good at Tearing Yourself Away. Everybody's uncle and pet ferret is putting up a page on the World Wide Web, and looking at them is like eating potato chips. Once the bag is open, or the screen is on . . .

And e-mail can eat you alive. At three minutes a message (my own average), e-mail consumes hours of prime time a week. But I sure feel more in touch than I ever did before — even though I'm now working in Japan.

So welcome back to the sequel

New kinds of moving data, winds of data, are sweeping across the world. Eddies and gusts of data, hurricanes, cyclones of data. Now, John and Margy guide you with their warmth and wit through this wild and windy world.

Ted Nelson
Sapporo HyperLab
Sapporo, Hokkaido, Japan
January, 1996

Ted Nelson is best known for coining the terms hypertext *and* hypermedia *and for designing a worldwide network publishing system with automatic royalty in 1960, now called* xanadu *— soon, we hope, to become a reality.*

Introduction

More about the Internet? But we've written so much already! Are you sure you want to know more?

Actually, so much has happened in the world of the Internet over the last year that we have lots of new, exciting things to report on. More online services now offer access to the Internet, especially e-mail and the World Wide Web. Windows 95 has arrived, with some built-in support for the Internet. And the world of WinSock software for Windows machines has gotten better and better.

So welcome to *MORE Internet For Dummies!*

About This Book

This book covers lots of new stuff on the Internet, especially new ways for you to connect to it. If you are curious about the innards of the Net, we suggest that you browse Part I, "Behind the Scenes in NetLand." If you don't have an Internet connection yet, try reading Part II, "Getting Your PC a SLIP/PPP Account," and Part III, "Three More Entrance Ramps," to decide how to proceed. If you want to create your own pages on the World Wide Web, jump to Part IV, "Home Page, Ho!" And if you already use the Internet and want to get more out of it, skip directly to Part V, "Online Odds and Ends."

How to Read, or Not to Read, This Book

We think, of course, that this book is one of the finest ever written in the English language, so the most appropriate way to read it is to

- Set aside several uninterrupted hours.
- Find a comfy chair and a suitable beverage, such as (depending on your cultural background) a fine old Madeira, a double espresso, or a warm can of Diet Mr. Pibb.
- Savor each page of the book in turn.
- When done, rush out and tell all your friends to buy the book and read it the same way you did.

Unfortunately, in the hurly-burly of modern life, not everyone has the opportunity to read books in this fashion, so you can also read this book in any order you want, because the parts are largely independent of each other.

Conventions in This Book

When you have to type something, it appears like this:

```
Hello, Internet!
```

Type it in just as you see it. In many cases, you must use the same capitalization that we do. We tend to use small letters unless the program we are talking to insists on capitals. (Capital letters always seem like shouting to us.)

If you have to follow a complicated procedure, we spell it out step by step, with the stuff you have to do highlighted in **boldface**. We also tell you what happens in response and what your options are.

When choosing commands from menus, we write File⇨Exit when we mean for you to choose the File command from the menu bar and then choose the Exit command from the menu that appears.

Who Are We Talking To?

As we wrote this book, we assumed that

- You use the Internet, or are interested in doing so, but you don't want to turn into a nerd in the process.
- You have a copy of *The Internet For Dummies* (IDG Books Worldwide, Inc.) around somewhere. This book builds on the first book, specifically the third edition, and makes references to information that was fully covered there.

How This Book Is Organized

This book is split into five parts, each with its own theme. With few exceptions, each part stands on its own, so dip into the book as you see fit.

The following sections share what each part of the book contains.

Part I: Behind the Scenes in NetLand

This part includes general information about the Internet, including technical information for those who are so inclined. (Those who nod off at the thought of the innards of a network can just skip right over this part.) Chapter 1 contains a refresher course on the Internet, including a roundup of the services it offers.

Part II: Getting Your PC a SLIP/PPP Account

Here you find out how to connect your Windows PC directly to the Internet — not as a measly, lowly terminal but as a full-fledged Internet host computer. Having done so, you find out how to download, install, and use the most popular Windows Internet software for reading your mail, browsing through Usenet newsgroups, grabbing files, chatting, searching online databases, and reading the hypertext in the World Wide Web.

Part III: Three More Entrance Ramps

In *The Internet For Dummies,* 3rd Edition (IDG Books Worldwide, Inc.), we describe the top three online services (CompuServe, America Online, and MSN). In this part, we describe another three popular services — Prodigy, GNN, and Netcom. In each chapter, we describe how to get an account and how to use Internet services.

Part IV: Home Page, Ho!

If you're dying to have your own home page on the World Wide Web, or if you want to help your company, club, or church create Web pages, these chapters take you through the whole process, step by step.

Part V: Online Odds and Ends

Here are the interesting tidbits that we've been saving for those die-hard fans who are willing to read through both of our volumes about the Internet. We describe some lesser-known Internet services — IRC, telnet, and Gopher. You also read about how to keep your communications private on the Net, how to use the Internet effectively for business, and how to create your own domain name (like `dummies.com`).

Icons Used in This Book

This icon warns you that nerdy, technoid information is on the loose. Skip it if you don't like the looks of it.

When we describe a neat shortcut, timesaving step, or other cool little item, you see this icon.

If you need to follow a step-by-step procedure to get something done, this icon introduces the steps.

When you see this icon, you'll find the address of some fascinating information on the Net.

Heads up! Watch for falling data!

Talk to Us!

If you want to contact us with comments, questions, or complaints, send us e-mail at `moreint2@dummies.com`. In fact, if you just want to test that your e-mail program works, drop us a line — our computer responds automagically. Also, visit our Internet for Dummies Central Web site at `http://dummies.com` where we post information about and updates to all the . . .*For Dummies* books we've written.

Traditionalists can send snail-mail (you know, regular old paper mail) by using the reader response form in the back of this book. Although we read all the mail we get, we can't promise personal responses to every message.

Part I
Behind the Scenes in NetLand

"WHAT CONCERNS ME ABOUT THE INFORMATION SUPERHIGHWAY IS THAT IT APPEARS TO BE ENTERING THROUGH BRENT'S BEDROOM."

In this part . . .

The Internet is a happening place, and a lot's been happening recently. So it's time to get reacquainted and get back on the Net.

This part of the book starts with a reintroduction to the Internet — definitely a must-read chapter — followed by several chapters of unbelievably technical stuff, which you are invited to skip.

Chapter 1

Something Old, Something New

In This Chapter

- What's new on the Net?
- A short refresher course
- Some common Internet abbreviations
- What is client/server computing?
- Who's who — network names and numbers
- The Net's number one service — e-mail

Welcome to *MORE Internet For Dummies,* 2nd Edition, your all-singing, all-dancing Internet guidebook! We crammed this book full of stuff that either is new since we wrote *The Internet For Dummies* or that we just couldn't fit in the book.

Naturally, you've read and memorized *The Internet For Dummies.* So, starting on page 31 in the discussion of V.32bis modems we. . . . Ouch! What was that?

That was the editor slapping our wrists, pointing out that *MORE Internet For Dummies,* 2nd Edition, isn't one of those boring books for network weenies who enjoy memorizing TLAs (Three-Letter Abbreviations) — this book is for people who have a life and want to get something done. Oh, right, sorry.

What's New on the Net?

Instead, let's look at some new developments on the Internet. Here are the most exciting changes on the Net and what we have to say about them in this book:

- Your typical Internet user used to be a student or technical employee with an expensive workstation who got Net access from school or work. Today, most people come to the Net through independent providers or online services and usually pay $10 to $20 per month for access. We covered a lot of the online services in *The Internet For Dummies,* and we tell you about more of them here — Prodigy, Netcom, and GNN.

- As the World Wide Web has swept the online world, everyone has to have a home page, a Web page with overly personal information and pictures of your kids or your dog. (Even we do, at `http://www.dummies.com`, but neither of us owns a dog.) We've included a few chapters on how to make your very own home page.
- Microsoft Windows users have WinSock, a standard way of writing cool Internet programs that run equally well no matter what brand of underlying Internet software you're using. As a result, lots of excellent new Windows Internet software is available, most notably Netscape, and we spend several chapters looking at how you can get WinSock loaded on your Windows PC.
- New Internet applications are arriving on the scene, such as VRML and voice programs. VRML lets Web pages include 3-D images and animation, and the voice programs let you talk — really talk, with your mouth and vocal chords — to other people using the Net. After you have WinSock set up, you can try out VRML, voice, and other applications available from the Net.

The Internet has continued to grow faster than anyone expected, resulting in an explosion of new resources on the Net. You can find *long* books — we're talking 600 pages long — that list only Internet mailing lists. *MORE Internet For Dummies,* 2nd Edition, isn't one of those books (the only thing more boring than reading a book full of mailing list names is writing a book full of mailing list names), but we tell you where you can find lots of swell new stuff worth looking at.

A Brief Refresher Course

We cover the basics of Internetology in *The Internet For Dummies,* and that's where you should look for the real introductory material, such as explanations of what the World Wide Web, FTP, and Usenet newsgroups are. But in case a friend borrowed your copy of this must-read book, here's a short course in Internet Basics.

What Is the Internet?

The short answer is that the Internet is a bunch of computer networks all connected together. Several million computers all over the world are connected to those networks, and if you have access to one network, you have access to all the others. (In reality, the number of computers that let you connect to them and then do anything interesting after you're connected is a lot smaller, but a small fraction of a million computers is still a lot of computers.)

The Internet is a *peer-to-peer* network, which means that, in principle, every computer on the Net, from a tiny laptop to a behemoth supercomputer, is equal, and any computer can connect to any other computer. On a peer-to-peer network, any computer attached to the Net can offer services to anyone else, and many do. When you use an Internet service, the computer on the other end providing that service can be anything from a PC to a CM-5 supercomputer.

Deep down, the only thing the Internet does is to deliver data from one place to another. Interestingly enough, programs running on all the computers on the Net use that data delivery to provide useful (well, useful considering that computers are involved) services, such as electronic mail, remote file retrieval (FTP), and real-time networked versions of Dungeons and Dragons. In this book, we talk about the cool services that are available on the Internet. (For the extremely cool people who read . . .*For Dummies* books, only the coolest in computing will do.)

Too many abbreviations

Computer systems always have a lot of obscure abbreviations, and networks have even more abbreviations than regular computers do. Here's a quick rundown of the abbreviations you can't get away from on the Internet. (For a longer list, see the Glossary at the back of *The Internet For Dummies,* 3rd Edition.)

IP Internet Protocol, the scheme that gets a packet of data from one computer to another

TCP Transmission Control Protocol, the scheme that keeps track of IP messages in case some of them get lost

TCP/IP TCP and IP used together, the most common way that programs communicate on the Internet

DNS Domain Name System, a huge worldwide database that keeps track of the names of all the computers on the Internet

SLIP Serial Line Internet Protocol, data sent over a regular modem

PPP Point-to-Point Protocol, similar idea to SLIP, different details

CSLIP Compressed SLIP, another mutant version of SLIP

Serve that client

In business computer circles, client/server computing is considered to be really cool and totally advanced. On the Internet, we've been doing client/server computing for 25 years, only at first we didn't know that's what it would be called. Whoop-de-doodle. (Students of European literature may be reminded of the scene from Molière in which a character, newly apprised of literary styles such as poetry and prose, is astounded to discover that he's been speaking prose all his life.)

In fact, the idea of client/server computing is pretty simple. One computer (the server) has some resource available, like, say, a database. Another computer (the client) wants to use that resource, most likely because a human being wants to. Some sort of network connects the two computers.

The client sends a request to the server asking it to do something, and the server sends back the response. (If a human user is involved, the client generally presents the response to the user, perhaps after spiffing it up a little to make it look nice.) This dialogue repeats until the client is done.

On the Internet, all the swell stuff you can do is provided by servers — Web pages by Web servers, file transfer by file transfer servers, and so on. The program you actually run is considered the client, but it contacts the server automatically. In nearly all cases, the client/server business is either obvious (if you're logged into some other machine, that machine is the server) or irrelevant. The main case in which the client/server distinction is notably evident is when the client machine is working, but the server isn't. In that case, you tend to get not-very-helpful messages from the client program, along the lines of "No Route to Host," when it finds that it can't contact the server.

On some low-rent kinds of networks, (if we were naming names, Novell is one of the names we would name) some computers are permanently anointed as servers and the rest are clients. On the Internet, being resolutely egalitarian, any computer on the Net can take either or both roles. If the computer runs server programs, it's a server, if it runs client programs, it's a client, if it runs both, as many do, it can be both.

The clienthood and serverdom are a little (to put it mildly) obscure in two cases: electronic mail and the X Window system used on workstations to display stuff on-screen. In the case of electronic mail, when you send a message to someone, the recipient's machine is considered to be the server, and the sender's machine is the client, with the service being that the server graciously agrees to accept mail from the client (sender). If you think about it for a while, this scenario makes sense — think of the server as a mailbox into which you can drop letters. In the case of X Windows, the machine with the screen on which X is displaying its windows is considered to be the server, and the program that's doing the actual work and telling it what to display is the client. If this scenario seems backward, that's because it is, but it's too late to do anything about it.

Names and Numbers

Computers on the Internet, known as *hosts* (which we suppose makes us users *parasites*) are identified by names and by numbers. The numbers are written in four parts, something like

```
140.186.81.2
```

The names are written in two or more parts, like

```
xuxa.iecc.com
```

Every machine on the Net has a number. Machines connected to more than one network, which is fairly common for large systems, have a number for each network they're connected to, although which of those numbers you use doesn't matter.

Most machines on the Net have a name, which is easier to remember than the numbers, unless you are blessed with a most unusual memory. The connection between names and numbers is quite flexible, so a single host can have several names, and a single name can refer to several hosts (which is useful for a service with multiple machines where which of the machines you use doesn't matter). Quite a lot can be said about the structure of the names, but because you don't need to know anything about host names and numbers to use the Internet, we describe them in Chapter 2, where you can ignore the whole discussion.

Upper- and lowercase letters don't matter in host names, so `xuxa.iecc.com`, `XUXA.IECC.COM`, and `XuXa.IeCc.CoM` are all valid forms of the same name.

Basic Services

Here's a roundup of the basic services that most Internet hosts support. We discuss most of them in *The Internet For Dummies,* so we won't describe them in a lot of detail here.

Electronic mail and mailing lists

Electronic mail (e-mail) remains the number one service that people use on the Internet. All mail is sent to mail addresses, which look something like `moreint2@dummies.com` (that's us — drop us a line and tell us how you like the book). Each address has a name part that identifies the recipient, an at-sign (@), and a host part that identifies the host computer to which the message should be sent. Most addresses correspond to actual people, but many of them are other things:

- Mailing lists, which send a message to a whole slew of people
- Mail server robots, which automatically send back a response
- Gateways to other kinds of services, such as netnews (discussed in the section "Network news" later in this chapter)

Thousands of special-interest mailing lists are active on the Internet, and you can join them to exchange messages with people with interests like yours. The topics of lists can be quite specific — for example, one list is for dairy cattle, and a separate list is for beef cattle.

We discuss e-mail in detail in Chapters 6, 7, and 8 in *The Internet For Dummies,* 3rd Edition.

Remote login

The *telnet* and *rlogin* services allow you to connect to a remote host and then use that computer as though you were sitting at a plain-character terminal (one that can display only text, no fancy graphics) directly connected to the remote host. Telnet used to be a very popular service but has been eclipsed in the past few years as people have moved to the much zoomier World Wide Web.

You'll find a whole chapter about telnet in this book — it's Chapter 19.

File transfer

File Transfer Protocol, universally called *FTP,* lets you copy files between remote hosts and your own system. A common convention called *anonymous FTP* lets you use FTP to retrieve files from remote systems, even though you don't have accounts on those systems.

The Internet For Dummies, 3rd Edition, has a chapter about FTP (Chapter 10, actually). In this book, Chapter 9 describes how to use FTP to download and install software from the Internet using FTP.

Network news

Usenet, or *netnews,* is like a bulletin board system. Each item someone "posts" to netnews is passed from system to system until the message eventually goes to all the Usenet hosts in the world. The amount of news is enormous — 140MB per day and growing. To make sense of this flood, items are tagged with topics known as *newsgroups,* and users can look only at the newsgroups they're interested in, skipping the rest. Even within a single group, a lot of traffic occurs, enough that spending every waking minute of your day reading news is easy to do.

We describe Usenet newsgroups in Chapter 9 of *The Internet For Dummies,* 3rd Edition.

Really cool stuff

The coolest Internet services are the most recent ones, particularly Gopher and the World Wide Web. These services let you access a world of online information in ways so cool we won't even try to describe them in this chapter.

Chapter 20 in this book describes Gopher, and the World Wide Web is explained in Chapters 4 and 5 of *The Internet For Dummies,* 3rd Edition. We tell you how to create your own World Wide Web pages in Chapters 14 and 15 of this book.

Chatting live

Internet Relay Chat (IRC) lets Internet users all over the world enter into lively debates online. It's unfortunate that so much of the conversation on IRC brings new meaning to the word *banal.* See Chapter 18 to try it for yourself.

Odds and ends

A dozen other minor services are available on the Net. Most are useful only to computers and the weenies who love them, things like a service to get two computers' time-of-day clocks in sync, or one that lets various computers on an Ethernet network check their network addresses.

A few minor services are of use to humans:

- *Finger* lets you check on the status of a person or system.
- *Whois* looks up people in the official Internet directory. Whois would be a swell service except that the only people listed are the ones who run the various networks comprising the Internet. If you happen to be looking for one of those people (for example, the one of us who takes care of the computers is listed as JL7), Whois is quite handy. But the other 99.7 percent of the people on the Net are not listed.
- *Ping* checks to see if a remote system is alive at all.

And now — on with the Internet!

Chapter 2

A Look under the Hood

In This Chapter

- Packet switching
- How networks are hooked together
- SLIP, PPP, TCP/IP, and other protocols
- Zones, domains, and other stuff
- An unbelievable amount of nerdy terminology

This chapter contains gruesome details about how the Internet actually sends data from one place to another. You can skip this entire chapter and the next one, if you want. But we don't advise that you do because we think this stuff is interesting. The first few pages of this chapter even contain stuff that mortals may use in day-to-day Net work. (Hmmm, guess that means if you read the rest of the chapter, you must be an immortal.)

First, Get Organized

Well, okay, so more than three million computers are attached to the Internet, and you are looking for information on a particular host computer, like `www.yahoo.com` or `ftp.winsite.com`. How do you find the host computer you want? You can locate the host computer in two ways (nobody said this was going to be simple). Each machine on the Net is identified by a number and a name. First, we look at the numbers and then at the names.

Executive summary

The way that the numbers and names are assigned on the Internet is, unavoidably, fairly technical. So here's the short version, in case you'd rather save the full version for later.

- Each machine on the Net (called a host in Internet-ese) has a number assigned to identify it to other hosts, sort of like a phone number. The numbers are in four parts, like 123.45.67.89. You should know the host number of the computer you use most, but otherwise you can forget about the numbers.
- Most hosts also have names, which are a lot easier to remember than numbers. Dots separate the names' multiple parts, for example `chico.iecc.com`, the name of one of our computers. Hosts can have more than one name, but which name you use doesn't matter.
- Complicated rules control how names and numbers are assigned. But because you're not likely to be doing any of the assigning, you don't really need to know these rules.
- Each network in the Internet has rules about what kinds of network traffic (e-mail, terminal sessions, and other connections) it allows. You should know the rules that apply to the network(s) you use to avoid getting the network managers mad at you.

What's in a number?

Any computer of any kind, from the smallest to the largest, that is attached to the Internet is called a *host* (which must make us users parasites — yuck). Some hosts are giant mainframes or supercomputers providing services to thousands of users. Some are little workstations or PCs with one user. And some are specialized computers, like routers, which connect one network to another, or terminal servers, which let dumb terminals (or PCs running Procomm, Crosstalk, or the like) dial in and connect to other hosts. But from the Internet's point of view, all these things are hosts.

Each machine is assigned a host number, which is sort of like a phone number. Being computers, hosts like 32-bit binary numbers. For example, the number of one of our computers is

```
10001100101110100101000100000001
```

Hmmm. That number is not very memorable. To make the number slightly easier to remember, it's broken up into four 8-bit groups. Each group is then translated into a decimal equivalent. So our computer's number turns into

```
140.186.81.1
```

That number isn't a whole lot better, but at least humans can remember it for a minute or two.

How much should I care about these numbers?

By and large, you can get by without knowing any host numbers because, in most cases, you use the much more memorable host names described in "What's in a Name?," later in this chapter. Occasionally, though, the naming scheme breaks down. In such a case, writing down the following two numbers is helpful:

- The number of the computer that you use
- The number of a nearby computer to which you have access

If you can contact a nearby computer by number but not by name, you can reasonably conclude that your connection to the naming system has failed. If you can't contact a nearby computer either way, it's more likely that the network, or at least your network connection, has failed, quite possibly because you inadvertently kicked a cable loose. Oops.

Networks have numbers, too?

We're afraid so. Consider, for a moment, your phone number, which is something like 202-653-1800. In the phone number, the first six digits designate where the phone exchange is — in this case, Washington, D.C. The last four digits are a particular phone in that exchange. (Call it for a good time, by the way.)

Internet host numbers are also divided into two parts: the network number and the local part. (Remember, a lot of different but interconnected networks compose the Internet.) The local part is a host number on that particular network. In the case of the computer we mentioned, host number 140.186.81.1 means network number 140.186 and local host number (on that network) 81.1. Sometimes, for added confusion, people write out network numbers in four parts by adding zeros, like 140.186.0.0.

Because some networks have more hosts than others, networks are divided into three sizes: large, medium, and small. In large networks (Class A), the first of the four numbers is the network number, and the last three numbers are the local part. In medium networks (Class B), the first two numbers are the network number, and the last two numbers are the local part. In small networks (Class C), the first three numbers are the network number, and the last number is the local part.

The first of the four numbers tells you the network's class. Table 2-1 summarizes classes and sizes.

Table 2-1 Network Numbers and Sizes

Class Number	*First Number*	*Length of Net Number*	*Maximum of Hosts*
A	1–126	1	16,387,064
B	128–191	2	64,516
C	192–223	3	254

Great big organizations (or at least organizations that have a whole lot of computers) tend to have Class A networks. For example, IBM has network 9, and AT&T has network 12, so host number 9.12.34.56 would be at IBM, and 12.98.76.54 would be at AT&T. Medium-sized organizations, including most universities, have Class B networks. Rutgers University has network 128.6, and Goldman Sachs (an investment broker that must use a lot of computers to keep track of all the money it handles) has network 138.8. Class C networks are used by small organizations and sometimes small parts of large organizations. Network 192.65.175, for example, is used by a single IBM research lab. (Why doesn't it use the general IBM network number? Who knows?)

Some host and network numbers are reserved for special purposes. In particular, any number with a component of 0 or 255 (two numbers with great mystical significance to computers) is special and can't be used as an actual host number. (This statement is a slight exaggeration, but it's close enough for most purposes.)

Rules of conduct

Parts of the Internet have fairly firm rules of conduct. Depending on what part of the Net you are attached to, the rules may be more or less strict. The most restrictive rules were for the NSFNET, which prohibited all commercial activity. Regional networks have less restrictive policies, and commercial networks are less restrictive still. All reserve the right to boot you off for malicious or destructive conduct. Be aware of the rules that apply to your site and be prepared to honor them.

If you are on a less restrictive network and decide to use a more restrictive one — for example, you log on to a machine at an educational institution that uses the NSFNET rules — you are subject to the most restrictive rules of any network that you use.

Most networks require that users act in a way that doesn't adversely and unnecessarily affect other network users or users of other networks to which they are connected. Networks at educational institutions usually require, due to their tax-exempt status, that users of their network refrain from using the network for direct commercial advantage. This limitation typically means that ordering something over the Net or posting short "for sale" messages about used stuff you want to get rid of is okay, but advertising or taking orders for a business with which you are affiliated is not. Don't take our word for it, though — check out your network's rules before, rather than after, someone gets mad at you for breaking them.

Networking on the cheap

Early on, all the networks in the Internet were big industrial-strength networks that had permanent expensive adapters to connect their computers together. In the 1980s, a researcher at MIT was working on connecting then-new IBM PCs to MIT's network, and the thought occurred to him that you didn't have to use those expensive network adapters. PCs have cheap *serial ports,* originally designed to connect to printers and modems, but quite capable of carrying network data, so in about two minutes, he invented a *Serial Line Internet Protocol,* also known as SLIP. We've been stuck with SLIP ever since. SLIP makes a network out of two computers connected through a serial line. (The MIT guy didn't think SLIP was that great — the note he wrote describing SLIP calls it a *nonstandard* — but that didn't stop him from starting a rather successful company to develop and sell PC Internet software.)

Originally SLIP connections were *hardwired* — that is, a wire went directly from the serial port on one computer to the serial port on another computer, and the only way to change the network setup was to change the plugs. But serial ports connect just fine to dial-up modems, so with only a little extra twiddling, setting up a SLIP connection between two computers connected by modems and a phone line, even computers thousands of miles apart, became possible. This trick became wildly popular, and these days the standard way you connect your PC to your Internet provider is with a SLIP or SLIP-like connection. Because a SLIP connection is considered to be a network, it has a network number, and each of the serial ports on the end has a host number, at least while the connection is active.

What's the point!

After people realized that SLIP was here to stay, its shortcomings became impressively apparent. (For example, on a dial-up connection, SLIP doesn't offer any way for one end to check who the other end is, a security hole roughly the size of the Grand Canyon, which in practice has to be addressed with a variety of software Band-Aids.) The Internet powers-that-be got to work to figure out what a SLIP-like scheme should really do. They came up with the *Point-to-Point Protocol,* or PPP.

From a user's point of view, there isn't much difference between SLIP and PPP. They both do the same thing — transfer data over a serial line — and they both do so at about the same speed. But PPP is a zillion times easier to set up. If you have a SLIP connection, all the SLIP options have to be set up by hand before the SLIP connection starts. If you get anything wrong, the usual symptom is that the connection mysteriously hangs. PPP does *protocol negotiation,* in which the two computers have a little chat when they're first connected and automatically come up with the best usable set of options. Because the two computers set the options automatically, you don't have to, and a lot less can go wrong at setup time.

We return to the gory details of SLIP and PPP in the next chapter, but what we've told you is already more than you need to know to be able to use them.

Subnets, supernets, super-duper nets, . . .

This discussion is extremely technoid. Don't say we didn't warn you.

Frequently, an organization that has a single network number wants to set up its computers internally on multiple networks. For example, all the computers in a single department are usually attached together on a single network, with some sort of connection linking department networks together. (Both administrative and technical reasons exist for this arrangement, but we won't bore you with these details.) But adhering to the way the Internet was originally set up means that an outfit with 25 internal networks would have to get 25 different network numbers.

This need for multiple network numbers was bad news for several reasons. Every time a company wanted to set up a new internal network, it had to apply for a new network number. Even worse, the rest of the Internet world had to put that network number in their tables so that they knew how to route messages to it.

Clearly, something had to be done. That something is *subnets.* One network can be divided into pieces called subnets. On a subnet, part of what would normally be the host number now becomes part of the network number. For example, in our network 140.186, the third number in the host number is the subnet number. So for machine 140.186.81.1, the subnet number is 140.186.81, and the host number is 1. Subnets enable plenty of local networks to be installed. (Currently we use only 100 of the 254 possible subnets in that network.) As far as the outside world is concerned, they still only have the single network 140.186 to worry about.

In practice, all but the smallest networks are subnetted. Also in practice, you almost never have to worry about subnets. When your computer is first attached to the net, the guru who installs it has to set its *subnet mask* to reflect the local subnet setup. If the mask is wrong, you may have strange problems, like being able to communicate with half your company's departments (such as the even-numbered ones, but not the odd-numbered ones).

A few organizations have an opposite problem. They have too many computers for a Class C network (more than 254) but nowhere near enough to justify a Class B. (These days, the demand for network numbers is so great that getting anything bigger than a Class C is practically impossible.) In this case, the organization can get a block of adjacent network numbers and treat part of the network number as a host number, a process called *supernetting.*

The supernetted number is then invariably subnetted, an extra wart that we don't even start to consider. Supernetting is currently uncommon but will become more widely used as more companies put a lot of computers on the Internet. Like subnetting, you don't have to worry about the supernetted number unless someone screws up your system's configuration.

The final straw in this load of camel, er, whatever, is *Classless Internet Domain Routing,* invariably abbreviated *CIDR,* which is pronounced "cider." CIDR lets network managers treat groups of networks of whatever class like a single network. Again, you don't have to worry about CIDR unless someone screws up your system's configuration.

Multiple multiple numbers numbers

A final added confusion in host and network numbering is that some hosts have more than one number. The reason is actually quite simple: Some hosts are on more than one network, so they need a host number on each of the networks to which they are attached. If you need to contact a machine with multiple host numbers, which number you use doesn't matter.

What's in a Name?

Normal people use names, not numbers, so in a rare bow to normality, Internet hosts are usually referred to by name, not number. For example, the machine we have heretofore referred to as 140.186.81.1 is named chico. In the earliest days of the ARPANET, machines had simple one-part names, and a master list of names existed. The machine at Harvard was called HARVARD, for example. Simple names worked fine in a network with only 100 hosts, but with a million machines on the net, coming up with different names for all is kind of hard.

To avoid a crisis of naming creativity, the solution was to go to multipart names, a scheme grandly known as the *Domain Name System,* or DNS. Host names are a string of words (or at least word-like things) separated by dots. In the multipart regime, chico's real name is `CHICO.IECC.COM`. (The naming scheme was evidently invented by people WHO LIKE TO SHOUT EVERYTHING IN CAPITAL LETTERS. Fortunately, lowercase in host names is taken to be equivalent to uppercase, and henceforth we avoid shouting and put the names in lowercase.)

Zones, domains, and all that

You decode an Internet name from right to left, which may seem perverse. But reading a name backward turns out in practice to be more convenient than the other way around, for the same reason that we put surnames after first names. (In England, where they drive on the left, they write host names from left to right. Typical.)

The rightmost part of a name is called its *zone.* If we examine chico's full name, `chico.iecc.com`, the rightmost part is *com,* which means that this address is a commercial site (in the `com` zone), as opposed to educational, military, or some other kinds of zones we mention later in the next section.

The next part of chico's name, *iecc,* is the name of John's company, the Invincible Electric Calculator Company. (Yes, it's sometimes pronounced "yecch" — John should have picked a better abbreviation.) The part to the left of the company name is the particular machine within the company. This address happens to be a rather small company with only six computers, so chico's friends, milton, tom, ivan, astrud, and xuxa, are known as milton.iecc.com, tom.iecc.com, astrud.iecc.com, ivan.iecc.com, and xuxa.iecc.com.

Logic actually exists for the naming of chico and friends. They're named after our favorite Brazilian pop stars. Chico (pronounced *shee-ku*) is Chico Buarque, who's quite political. Tom (pronounced *tome*) is the late Antonio Carlos "Tom" Jobim, who wrote "Girl from Ipanema," best known in the U.S. from a soda pop ad 25 years ago. Milton is Milton Nasciemento, who's more lyrical and melodic. Ivan is Ivan Lins, who, after an early embarrassing "soul man" period, has found his niche with solid, popular, melodic pieces. Xuxa is Xuxa, who's sort of a cross between Madonna and Mr. Rogers. And Astrud is Astrud Gilberto, known in the U.S. for singing the original presoda-pop version of "Girl from Ipanema."

The host naming system is quite egalitarian. In it, iecc.com, a company with two employees, is right up there with ibm.com, a company with several hundred thousand employees. Larger organizations usually further subdivide machine names by site or department so that a typical machine in the computer science department at Yale University is called bulldog.cs.yale.edu. Each organization can set up its names any way it wants to, though in practice names with more than five components are rare, not to mention hard to remember and type.

If you type a simple host name with no dots, your local computer assumes that the rest of the name is the same as the computer that you're currently using. So if we're logged into milton and want to contact chico, we can simply refer to chico, and our local computer assumes that we mean chico.iecc.com.

Are you on the Internet, or aren't you?

The most popular Internet service is still electronic mail, and a lot of mail systems not directly attached to the Internet have indirect connections, using an intermediate system on the Net to pass messages back and forth. Originally, to send mail to these indirectly connected mail systems, you had to use strange and ugly mail addresses that involved lots of illegible and incomprehensible punctuation. Eventually the Internet powers-that-be arranged a special feature, *mail exchange*, or *MX*, host names to handle all this mail. For the purposes of sending mail, an MX name works like any other name, but for any other service, the host doesn't exist. For example, MCI Mail has a mail connection to the Internet, so you can send mail to users at mcimail.com. But because that's an MX address, you can't use the World Wide Web, FTP, finger, or other Internet services to contact mcimail.com.

The Twilight Zone?

Zones (the rightmost part of the host name) divide into two general categories: the three-letter kind and the two-letter kind. The three-letter zones are kind of set up by organization. You've seen `com` for commercial. Table 2-2 lists the rest of the three-letter zone names.

Table 2-2 Three-Letter Zone Names

Zone	*Meaning*
`com`	Commercial organizations
`edu`	Educational institutions
`gov`	U.S. government bodies and departments
`int`	International organizations (mostly NATO at the moment)
`mil`	Military sites
`net`	Networking organizations
`org`	Anything else that doesn't fit elsewhere, such as professional societies

In the United States, most Internet sites have names in one of the three-letter zones. Elsewhere, other countries usually use geographic names, which are discussed in the next section.

Where's Vanuatu?

Two-letter zone names are geographically organized. Each zone corresponds to a country or Other Recognized Political Entity. An official international standard list of two-letter country codes exists and is used almost but not quite unmodified as the list of two-letter zones. The country code for Canada is CA, so a host at York University in Canada is called `nexus.yorku.ca`. Each country's network administrators can assign names as they see fit. Some countries have

Is there a complete list of host names anywhere?

No. In principle, you should be able to go through all the systems where names are registered and enumerate them all. People used to try to do that, partly out of nosiness and partly out of an interest in collecting network statistics. They gave up after the Net had grown to the point that the collection program ran for over a week and still hadn't finished.

organization-level subdivisions; for example, a site at an Australian university is called `sait.edu.au`. Other countries assign names more haphazardly. A two-letter code exists for every country in the world, so a host whose name ends in `.vu`, for example, is in Vanuatu.

In the United States, few computers have names in the geographic U.S. zone, which is organized by city and state. Because I.E.C.C. was in Cambridge, Massachusetts, `chico.iecc.com` u sed to be known as `iecc.cambridge.ma.us`. (John hadn't named it chico yet, because at the time it was the only computer he had.) In the United States, the choice of geographic or organizational names is pretty arbitrary. If you have one or two machines, getting a geographic name is easier. If you have more computers, getting an organizational name, which lets you administer names within your organization yourself, is easier. (See Chapter 21 for the gruesome details of how names are registered.)

Table 2-3 lists common geographic zone names. Appendix A contains a full table of geographic zones.

Incidentally, Vanuatu, an island in the South Pacific, was formerly known as the Condominium of the New Hebrides. France and Britain jointly administered the island; when you arrived you had to state whether you wanted to be subject to French or British law. Now Vanuatu has a limited dial-up Internet connection, and we've gotten e-mail from there.

Other random zones

You may run into a few other zones and pseudozones. Even though the ARPANET, the Internet's predecessor, has been officially dead for several years, a few sites still, for historical reasons, have names ending in *arpa*. And as for machines on the UUCP and BITNET networks, you occasionally see names ending in *uucp* and *bitnet*. These zones aren't real, and hence names using them aren't really valid host names, but a lot of systems treat these names as special cases and route mail to them anyway. Any BITNET or UUCP site can arrange to get itself a real host name, so *bitnet* and *uucp* names are heading for well-deserved oblivion.

Table 2-3 Common Two-Letter Zone Names

Zone	*Country*
AU	Australia
AT	Austria (Republic of)
BE	Belgium (Kingdom of)
CA	Canada
CZ	Czech Republic
DK	Denmark (Kingdom of)
FI	Finland (Republic of)
FR	France (French Republic)
DE	Germany (Federal Republic of)
IN	India (Republic of)
IE	Ireland
IL	Israel (State of)
IT	Italy (Italian Republic)
JP	Japan
NL	Netherlands (Kingdom of the)
NO	Norway (Kingdom of)
RU	Russian Federation
SU	Former Soviet Union (officially obsolete but still in use)
ES	Spain (Kingdom of)
SE	Sweden (Kingdom of)
CH	Switzerland (Swiss Confederation)
TW	Taiwan, Province of China
UK	United Kingdom (official code is GB)
US	United States (United States of America)

Why the Post Office Isn't Like the Phone Company

Gruesome Detail Alert: The details of what goes on in the Net get a lot more gruesome from here on. You don't *need* to know any of the stuff in the rest of this chapter to use this book. But we still think these little details are interesting.

Enough of this administrative nonsense. We'll get back to the grotty details. What the Internet does, basically, is transmit data from one computer to another. How hard could that be? Well, it's not that hard, but it is fairly complicated.

The most familiar examples of information transfer in real life are the post office and the phone company. If you want to contact someone by telephone, you pick up the phone and dial the number. The phone company then arranges an electrical circuit from your phone to the phone that you're calling. You and the other person gossip until you're done, or if you're calling on a modem, your computer and the other computer gossip until they're done, and then you hang up, at which point the phone company releases the circuit. Then you can call someone else. At any particular moment, you can only have one call in progress over a particular phone line. (Yeah, you can use three-way calling, but that doesn't count.) This scheme is called *circuit switching* because a circuit is set up for the duration of the conversation. Well, the Internet doesn't work this way, so forget this nice little scenario. (Don't entirely forget it; we come back to simulated circuit switching later.)

The other model is the post office. If you want to mail a package to someone, you write the recipient's address and your return address and mail your goodies. The U.S. Postal Service doesn't have dedicated trucks from every post office to every other post office. (The post office may be inefficient, but it's not *that* inefficient.) Instead, the package is routed from your local post office to a central post office, where it's then loaded onto a truck or a train headed in the general direction and repeatedly passed from office to office until it gets to the recipient's post office, at which point the letter carrier delivers it to the door along with the rest of the day's mail.

The Internet works more like this second scenario. Each time a host wants to send a message to another host, either the recipient is on a network to which the first host is directly connected, in which case it can send the message directly, or else it's not. In that case, the sender sends the message to a host that can forward it. The forwarding host, which presumably is attached to at least one other network, in turn delivers the message directly if it can or passes it to yet another forwarding host. A message passing through a dozen or more forwarders on its way from one part of the Net to another is quite common.

You're probably wondering, "What kind of cretin would think the post office is a better model than the phone company?"

Don't be led astray by the analogy. The main complaints that people have about the post office are that it's slow and that it loses stuff. The Internet occasionally has both of these problems, but these problems are not as much of an issue as they are with paper mail. In the middle of a busy day, the Net can indeed slow down, though the time a message takes to be delivered is still measured in seconds. Losing stuff turns out not to be a problem in practice, for reasons discussed later in this chapter in the section "TCP: the Rocket-Powered Mailman."

All the world's a packet

Now take our postal analogy a step further. Say that you want to send a copy of the manuscript for your new and very long book to a close friend in the island nation of Papua New Guinea. (Papua New Guinea doesn't have many bookstores.) Unfortunately, the manuscript weighs 15 pounds, and the limit on packages to Papua New Guinea is 1 pound. So you divide the manuscript into 15 pieces, and on each package you write something like *PART 3 OF 15* and send them off. When the packages eventually arrive, probably not in the right order, your friend takes all the pieces, puts them back in order, and reads them.

The various networks on the Internet work pretty much the same way: They pass data around in chunks called *packets,* each of which carries the addresses of its sender and its receiver (those host numbers we talked about in this chapter). The maximum size of a packet varies from network to network, but is generally between 100 and 2,000 *octets* (Internet-speak for *bytes* or *characters*). A typical size is 1,536 octets, which, for some long-forgotten reason, is the limit on an Ethernet network, the most popular kind of local network. Messages that are too large for a single packet have to be sent as several packets.

One advantage the Internet has over the post office is that when Internet software breaks a large package of data into smaller pieces, putting the pieces back together is no problem. When the post office delivers something in small pieces, you are generally out of luck.

Defining the Internet protocols

The set of conventions used to pass packets from one host to another is known as the *Internet Protocol,* or IP. (Catchy, huh? Actually, the network is named after the protocol, not the other way around.) The Internet, quite simply, is the collection of networks that passes packets to each other using IP.

You can set up a network that uses IP but that isn't actually connected to the Internet. A lot of networks are set up that way in companies that want to take advantage of IP (which comes free with every UNIX workstation and now also with Mac System 7 and Windows 95). These inside networks are often called *intranets* and are often used to distribute information inside the company using e-mail, netnews, and particularly the World Wide Web (Netscape, Mosaic, and all that) the same way they're used to send information around outside.

In the past, many intranets weren't connected at all to the outside world or were connected only by a funky mail connection. In the last year or two, a lot of these disconnected networks have gotten hooked to the Internet. That's partly because the advantages of being on the Net have increased, and mostly because new commercial Internet vendors have made the cost of connection about a tenth of what it used to be. In many cases, a *firewall* computer monitors and controls the connections between the internal and external networks, but don't worry, it's a detail. (Oh, wait, this whole chapter is details. Well, a firewall is a particularly detailed detail.)

A lot of protocols are used in connection with IP. The two best known are *Transmission Control Protocol (TCP)* and *User Datagram Protocol (UDP).* TCP is so widely used that many people refer to it as *TCP/IP,* the combination of TCP and IP used by most Internet applications.

I'll build a gateway to paradise

To work, the Internet has to be able to pass packets from one network to the next so that packets can get routed from the network where they originate to the network of their destination. Three kinds of things (for lack of a better term) pass packets from one Internet network to another: *bridges, routers,* and *gateways.* Here's a quick rundown of the differences so that you can hold your own at nerd cocktail parties.

Bridges

A *bridge* connects two networks in a way that makes them appear to be a single, larger network. Bridges most commonly are used to connect two Ethernet local area networks. (An Ethernet physically consists of a long cable connecting all the machines on a network, and a single cable's length is limited.) The bridge looks at all the packets flying by on each network, and when it sees a packet on one network destined for a host on the other, the bridge copies it over.

Ethernet host numbers (which, of course, are different from Internet host numbers) are assigned by the serial number of the Ethernet card rather than by network number. The only way the bridge can tell what hosts are on which network is to build a big table listing all the hosts on each network, based on the return addresses on all the packets flying by on each network. It's a miracle that it works at all.

The good thing about bridges is that they work *transparently* — the hosts whose packets are being bridged do not need to be aware that a bridge is involved, and a single bridge can handle a whole bunch of different kinds of network traffic (like Novell Netware as well as IP) at the same time. The disadvantages of bridges are that they can only connect two networks of the same type, and that bridging fast networks that are not physically next to each other is very expensive.

Routers

A *router* connects two or more IP (that's the Internet Protocol) networks. The hosts on the networks have to be aware that a router is involved, but that's no problem for IP networks because one IP rule is that all hosts have to be able to talk to routers.

- A good thing about routers is that they can attach physically different networks, such as a fast, local Ethernet to a slower, long-haul phone line.
- A bad thing about routers is that they move packets slower than bridges do. Figuring out how to route packets requires more calculation than it does to bridge them, particularly when the networks are of different speeds.

Routers: the good, the bad, and the really bad

A hot topic among Internet weenies these days is Routing Policy. The Internet is, for the most part, *redundantly connected* — that is, you can get from one network to another in several ways. In the good old days, finding a route was relatively easy because the main goal was to find the shortest route to each known network. Only a handful of networks was around, so the *routers* (hosts that pass packets from one network to another) simply compared notes to figure out which one had the shortest route to where. If you wanted to be really fancy and if you had two equally fast routes to somewhere, you could monitor the amount of traffic on each route and send packets by the less busy route.

Things are no longer so simple. For starters, the number of networks of which a router has to be aware is no longer a handful (unless you have extraordinarily large hands). Over 20,000 different networks are attached to the Internet, and more are added weekly. Furthermore, the speeds of communication lines have increased much more quickly than have the speeds of computers used for routing, enough so that special hardware is needed to keep up with the networks that will be installed in the next few years.

Another issue is that political as well as technical distinctions exist among networks. The Commercial Internet Exchange (CIX), for example, has a router that only handles traffic for CIX members and their immediate customers. This means that some traffic can't be routed the most direct way, if the traffic isn't appropriate for one of the networks on that route.

Another wart on the face of routing is that many organizations have *firewall* routers that only pass certain kinds of traffic. Typically, firewall routers allow incoming electronic mail but not incoming remote terminal sessions or file transfers, in an effort to keep out ill-mannered users looking for security holes (and if you have a large enough internal network, a hole will certainly be found somewhere).

Lots of technical papers are published about advanced new routing schemes, policies, or whatever, each with a new three- or four-letter acronym. (OSPF and BGP are currently trendy, while RIP and EGP are passé. What they stand for doesn't matter.) Fortunately, you as a user can completely ignore the issue because as long as routers eventually get your packets to the right place, how they do so doesn't really matter.

A fast network can deliver packets a lot faster than a slow network can take them away, causing network constipation, so the router has to be able to tell a sending host to talk slower.

Another problem is that routers are *protocol specific* — that is, the way a host talks to an IP router is different from the way it talks to, say, a Novell router. This problem is now addressed by the router equivalent of a Ginsu knife that slices and dices every which way and knows about routing every kind of network known to humankind. These days, all commercial routers can handle multiple protocols, but usually at extra cost for each added protocol. Incidentally, this kind of router is usually pronounced *ROOter,* (except in Australia) because a *ROWter* is something you use in a woodworking shop.

Gateways

A *gateway* splices two different kinds of protocols together. If, for example, your network talks IP and someone else's network talks Novell or DECnet or SNA or one of the other dozen Leading Brands of Network, a gateway converts traffic from one set of protocols to another. Gateways are not only specific to particular protocols, but they are also specific to particular applications. The way you convert, say, electronic mail from one network to the other is quite different from the way that you convert a remote terminal session. Gateways are very difficult to do correctly, which is why Internet mail to or from a cc:Mail or other office mail system often arrives smashed — the gateway did it.

Mix-and-match terms

These terms are not cast in stone. The term *gateway* has often been used for what we here call a *router,* and things called *brouters* act like something halfway between a bridge and a router. Also, keep in mind that all the differences among bridges, routers, and gateways are based on software, so in some cases it's quite possible to make the same pieces of hardware into a bridge, router, or gateway by loading in software from different floppy disks.

TCP: the Rocket-Powered Mailman

We've established that the Internet works just like the post office, in that it delivers hunks of data (packets) one at a time. So what do you do if you want to "have a conversation," such as logging into a remote computer? Back to the postal analogy. Say that you're a chess player. Normal chess is played face-to-face with each player immediately responding to the other. Abnormal chess is sometimes played by mail with each player mailing moves to the other. Such games can take months to complete. But what if your mail were delivered by someone with rocket shoes who zipped each move to the other player within a fraction of a second? That would be a lot more like normal chess.

TCP (Transmission Control Protocol) is that rocket-powered mailman. TCP provides what looks like a dedicated connection from one computer to another. Any data you send to the other computer is guaranteed to be delivered, in the same order it was sent, as though a dedicated circuit were connected from one end to the other (the details of this process are explained in the next section). In fact, what TCP provides isn't really a circuit but a lot of IP packets. What TCP provides is a *virtual circuit.* But a virtual circuit is real enough for most purposes, which is why nearly every Internet application uses it.

TCP has to add quite a lot of glop to each packet to do its magic, which makes TCP somewhat slower than the underlying IP. A simpler protocol called *UDP (User Datagram Protocol)* doesn't make any promises about reliability. UDP uses much less glop, making do with whatever reliability IP gives it, for the benefit of applications that want to roll their own reliability features or that can live with the flakiness. (In local networks, IP usually delivers upwards of 99 percent of all packets correctly, even without TCP's help.)

Certify That Packet!

Make no mistake, the Internet shares with the U.S. Postal Service some inherent unreliability. The postal service has two schemes for ensuring that something is delivered: registered mail and return receipts. If you're mailing something of great intrinsic value, such as an original 45 RPM record of Bill Haley and the Comets' "Rock Around the Clock," you send the package registered. When you mail something registered, the clerk at the post office immediately puts it in a locked drawer. Each time the package is moved from one place to another, it's carefully logged and signed for all the way until the recipient signs for it. Registered mail is quite reliable but slow because of all the logging and signing. (Yeah, these days any sane person uses overnight express, but it turns out to be handled a lot like registered mail: Electronically scanning the bar code on the package label logs the package's progress. But we digress.)

The other scheme is used for certified letters that don't have any intrinsic physical value but contain an important message, typically a letter from your insurance company saying that it's canceled your insurance again. These letters are sorted and handled normally until they are delivered, at which point the recipient signs a card that is mailed back to the sender. If the sender doesn't get the card back in a reasonable amount of time, it sends the letter again.

Different computer networks use either scheme. A network scheme called X.25, used in commercial networks like Tymnet and Sprintnet, uses the registered model, with each packet carefully accounted for. There's even a protocol called X.75 that is used to hand packets from one network to another very reliably. X.25 works okay, but it's slow for the same reason that registered mail is slow — there's all that logging and checking at each stage.

TCP/IP is much more like certified mail. As IP routes each packet through the network, it does what it can to deliver it, but if some problem arises or if the packet is garbled on a communication line, tough luck — IP simply throws the packet away. TCP numbers each packet, and the TCP software on the two communicating hosts (but not on any intermediate hosts) tracks the packet numbers: Each tells the other what it has received and what it hasn't and resends anything that got lost.

This approach has two advantages over the X.25 approach. The end-to-end approach is faster and fundamentally more reliable because it doesn't depend on all the intermediate hosts, between the sender and the recipients, doing everything correctly. (We can report from considerable experience with X.25 networks that intermediate hosts often *don't* do everything correctly, causing annoying *connection resets.*) TCP/IP also enables networks to be built much more cheaply because routers can be much dumber. A router for TCP/IP need only understand IP, not TCP or any other higher-level protocol.

For a small network, you can build a perfectly adequate router out of a small computer and a few network cards. For example, all the Internet traffic to and from the network at I.E.C.C. used to pass through a router built out of an old clone 286 PC, which cost only $300. Worked fine.

Any Port in a Storm

The final topic in this survey of Internet Geek-speak is *ports.* In postal terms, port numbers are sort of like apartment numbers. Say that you want to communicate with a particular host. Okay, you look up its host number, and you send the host packets. But we have two problems. One problem is that a typical host has lots of programs running that can be having simultaneous conversations with lots of other hosts, so you have to find a way to keep the different conversations separate. The other problem is that when contacting a host, you need to tell it what sort of conversation you'd like to have. Do you want to send electronic mail? Transfer files? Log in?

Ports solve both problems. Every program on a host that is engaged in a TCP or UDP conversation is assigned a *port number* to identify that conversation. Furthermore, a large set of low port numbers is reserved (sort of like low-numbered license plates) for particular well-known services. For example, if you want to log into a host using the standard telnet service, you contact port 23 because that's where the telnet server is.

Connections to *client programs* — programs that use remote services — are assigned arbitrary port numbers that are only used to distinguish one connection from another. Servers, on the other hand, use well-known port numbers so that the clients can find them. Several hundred well-known (well known to Internet programming geeks, at least) port numbers are assigned. Hosts are under no obligation to support them all, just to use the correct number for those that they support. Some well-known numbers are pretty silly, like port 1025 for network blackjack games; others are very specialized, like port 188 for an implementation of the MUMPS database language. But they're there if you need them.

Usually you don't have to worry about port numbers, but there are a few cases when it's handy to know about them. When you want to use a conversational service on another computer, the usual technique is to use the telnet program to connect to port 23 on the remote computer and log in as a normal user. (See Chapter 19 for all the gory details.) But other ports provide services.

For example, a computer in Michigan offers a geography server (described in Chapter 22) that lets you look up any place name or zip code in the U.S. If you telnet to that computer on the standard port 23, you get an invitation to log in as a regular user. This isn't very useful, because you don't have any passwords for that computer. (If it makes you feel better, neither do we.) But if you telnet to port 3000 on the same computer, you're connected directly to the geography server. When you need to use a port other than the standard one to contact any service, that's noted in the service's description.

Actually, two separate sets of port numbers exist: one for TCP and one for UDP. But all of the well-known port numbers are assigned identically for both. For example, TCP port 23 is telnet, so UDP port 23 is also telnet for inattentive users who don't mind if some data gets lost.

ISO protocols: Trust us, they'll be great

The *International Organization for Standardization* (inexplicably known as *ISO*) has for many years been developing a set of communication protocols that was supposed to replace TCP/IP. ISO is an enormous international consortium of standardization groups, so it probably will not come as a big surprise to hear that it moves ahead at a rate that suggests that it is stapled to a rather arthritic snail.

A bunch of ISO standards are supposed to define various network protocols (we mentioned X.25 already), but they are in most cases slow, complex, and not well debugged (much like the group that is defining them), so nobody uses even the ones that exist unless they are forced to for political reasons. If someone tells you to forget all this unofficial and unsanctioned TCP/IP nonsense because ISO protocols will replace them all, nod politely and pay no attention. People who build actual networks use TCP/IP.

In fairness, the ISO's electronic-mail protocols have achieved moderate success. The mail transfer standard is called X.400 and is used in many places as a gateway protocol between mail systems. (You can find out about sending mail to X.400 addresses in Chapter 17 of *The Internet For Dummies,* 3rd Edition.) X.400 is in some ways better than Internet mail because you can use addresses similar to those you'd use for real postal mail, rather than often arbitrary login names as is more common with Internet mail. The standard for name-lookup service, X.500, is late and slow but looks to be widely adopted because the Internet has nothing like it. However, mail is the *only* place where ISO is getting much attention — its standards for file transfer and other applications were dead on arrival.

Chapter 3

You Made Us Do This: More Gory Details

In This Chapter

- Lots of technoid details about the innards of the Net
- Deep dark secrets about TCP, IP, and other unspeakable acronyms

Chapters 2 and 3 of the original edition of *The Internet For Dummies* had some fairly detailed descriptions of how computers communicate on the Internet. We figured that the information should be in the book, but that nobody would read it. One reviewer even complained that those chapters were a waste of paper that otherwise would have been healthy, living trees.

Well, our original conclusion was wrong. "More, more!" people demanded in their e-mail messages. Okay, your wish is our command. In this chapter, we look "under the hood" at some of the lower-level operations of the Net.

See that little guy with the glasses there? You'll be seeing him a lot in this chapter — it's the most technical one in the book. If you're not sure that you want to read all this tech stuff, check the upcoming executive summary, and you'll *know* you don't want to read it.

Executive summary of this chapter

There's a lot of detailed glop going on at the lower levels of the Internet. Big deal.

Feel particularly free to skip this chapter, unless you have a morbid need to know what's going on in the bowels of the Internet, or perhaps if you have a particularly stubborn case of insomnia.

Packets and All That

As we allege in a previous chapter, the Internet, stripped down to its skivvies, is two things:

- A way to move data from one computer to another
- A whole bunch of conventions, known in network-ese as *protocols,* about how programs use that ability to communicate with each other

For example, when you send electronic mail to someone over the Internet, your mail program and the mail program at the other end communicate using a convention called SMTP (the optimistically named Simple Mail Transfer Protocol) to transfer the message from your computer to the recipient's. SMTP, in turn, uses other protocols (TCP and IP, in particular, which we discuss in detail in Chapter 2) to handle some of the details of message transfer.

On the level

The workings of the Internet are complicated enough that nobody, not even the world class network geeks who designed it, can keep the whole business in mind at once. To make things understandable (at least by geek standards), it's traditional to divide the design into *levels* (sometimes, just to keep us all confused, also called *layers*). At each level, you sort of take all the lower levels for granted and only worry about what happens at your own level.

To take a somewhat strained example, imagine that you're making a tuna salad sandwich. The recipe says that you take bread, tuna salad, and mayo and make a sandwich out of them. At that level, the Sandwich Construction Level, you assume that you have the ingredients on hand. But at the next level down, the Sandwich Makings Level, you need a recipe for making bread, a recipe for tuna salad, and a recipe for mayonnaise. More likely you'd buy the bread and the mayo, but at the Sandwich Construction Level, that's a detail we can ignore. Well, enough of this example, we're getting hungry.

Exactly what the levels are in the Internet is a religious issue among network types, but here's a typical list, from highest to lowest:

- **Application level:** Two actual useful programs talking to each other, for example, the mail client program talking to the mail server program. Typical message: "Deliver mail item to `moreint2@dummies.com`." Each different kind of program (mail, file transfer, remote login, and so on) has its own protocol. The application-level protocol assumes that the next level down will take care of passing the messages reliably between the programs.

- **Transport level:** A program on one computer connected to another program on another computer, carefully making sure that everything the first program sends is received by the second program, and vice versa. Typical message: "We just received 14,576 characters of data from your program number 42. Urrp." The usual transport level protocol used in the Internet is called *Transmission Control Protocol,* or TCP. (Pretty creative naming, eh?) The transport-level protocol assumes that the next level down will take care of moving chunks of data from one computer to the other.
- **Internet level:** One computer sending a chunk (known as a *packet*) of data to another computer, which may or may not be on the same network. Typical message: "Send this packet to computer number 140.186.81.3, by way of computer number 127.45.22.81, which is on the same network that I am." The usual Internet-level protocol is called (now this is really, really creative naming) *Internet Protocol,* or IP. This protocol assumes that the next level down will take care of moving packets on the local network.
- **Link level:** Actually transferring data between two computers physically located on the same network. The connection may be an Ethernet, for computers connected in an office, or a phone line, for computers connected across town. Typical message: "Send this packet to computer number 127.45.22.81, which I can see across the hall."

Some people put another level below the link level to deal with the different physical ways that two computers can be connected, but enough is enough. One way to think of the flow of information is that it starts at the highest level, percolates down to the lowest level on the sending computer, across the actual network wires to the receiving computer, and then percolates back up from the lowest level to the highest.

What's a packet?

The fundamental item that the Internet slings around is a *packet.* A packet of what? Well, a packet of, er, stuff. One of the few notably consistent aspects of the Internet is that all data sent through the Internet is sent as packets. If you're logged into a remote computer and you press the Z key, that Z is packed up in a packet and shipped from your computer to the remote system. Its response is in turn packed into a packet (or several packets, if it's really long, because a single packet is limited to about 1,000 characters) and shipped back to your computer, where it's displayed to you.

A single packet contains

- Header bookkeeping stuff
- Even more header bookkeeping stuff
- Actual data (due to network megalomania, the actual data is optional)

Each network level adds its own header information to keep track of what's happening at its level. With the encrustation of headers, a packet can easily end up with more header than actual data, which isn't great (headers do take up space in memory and take time to transmit over network links), but that inconvenience is the price we pay for all the Internet's flexibility.

Down in the Links

We start in the basement of the Internet, the link level, which passes a packet from one computer to another on the same network. At the link level, two kinds of networks exist — the kind with only two computers and the kind with more than two computers. The kind with two computers is usually some kind of phone line with a computer at each end (including some rather exotic phone lines such as high-speed fiber optic connections that send 45 million bits per second). The kind with more than two computers is usually a local network, such as an Ethernet. The reason for the difference is quite simple: When your computer ships out a packet, if only one other computer is on the network, you don't need to worry about specifying the recipient. If several other computers are on the network, the link level has to make sure the packet goes to the right one.

Getting to the point

For phone line-style links (usually called *point-to-point links,* an amazingly normal term), you may think that to send a packet from one end to the other, all you need to do is ship it down the wire. After all, how's the packet going to get lost between one end of a phone call and the other? Well, the packet won't get lost, but plenty of complications are on the way.

- **Framing:** A 25-cent word that merely means that because you can't automatically tell where one packet ends and the next begins, you need a way to mark the boundary between them.
- **Error detection:** If a bird is sitting on the phone line or something, knowing when a message is corrupted is nice.
- **Multiprotocol support:** Say you have an expensive high-speed phone line connecting two branches of your company, and you have modern, efficient TCP/IP networks and other kinds of grungy, obsolete networks, like Novell Netware and Digital's DECnet. All the various networks (or, in network-ese, *network protocols*) sharing the phone line is nice.
- **Authorization:** If the connection involves one machine dialing up another using a modem and a regular phone line, and you have the least interest in security (which, admittedly, a lot of Internet sites don't) you can require passwords or something before you ship data to whoever just dialed in.

How we SLIPped up

The least complicated approach to handling these link-level complications is known as *SLIP,* Serial Line Internet Protocol, declared in its defining document to be an official "nonstandard." SLIP deals with most of the preceding issues by ignoring them. Errors in transmission? Tough. Multiprotocol support? Forget it. Authorization? Not our problem. (You may recall from a previous chapter that SLIP was designed in about two minutes on the back of a matchbook.) SLIP does at least handle framing, by defining a special character to put between packets so that you can tell where one packet ends and the other begins.

Despite its, er, technical shortcomings, SLIP has become quite popular, partly because, for a long time, the widely accepted way to connect computers to the Internet has been to use a regular phone line. SLIP actually works pretty well. Transmission errors aren't usually a problem because these days most modems do error correction automatically, so SLIP doesn't have to. Most systems with SLIP handle authentication somehow — usually your computer has to send a login name and a password, and only then does SLIP start. But SLIP suffers from a lot of slightly different versions, a topic we address up close and personal in Chapters 6, 7, and 8.

As the bits flow by, a packet of data as sent by SLIP looks generally like

```
CO hexadecimal (that is, a character containing binary 1100
          0000)
packet data, however long it is
CO
```

That is, the packet data is sandwiched between two special C0 characters. But what if a C0 is in the packet? No problem; in that case, you send two characters, hex DB and DC. But what if a DB is in the packet? Still no problem; in that case, you send a DB followed by a DD. But what if a DD is in the packet? Stop bothering us. (Well, in fact, those two substitutions turn out to be all that SLIP needs.)

One major mutant version of SLIP is called Compressed SLIP, or CSLIP, for short. A smart guy named Van Jacobson was looking at the data sent over a typical SLIP line and noticed that the header data in one packet was usually nearly the same as the header information in the preceding packet. So by simply sending the header differences rather than the whole header each time, the link got faster because less data overall was sent. This scheme, give or take a few details that aren't worth going into, is now known as CSLIP. CSLIP uses the same C0 framing as SLIP.

If you have a choice, CSLIP is always preferable to SLIP because it sends less data and, as a result, is faster.

On the backbone

As we've already mentioned about 400 times, the Internet is a collection of computer networks. Some networks are fast, long-distance ones (across the continent or across the Atlantic Ocean, for example) that have to be managed a little more carefully than your typical dial-up phone line. For one thing, building a modem that works at a million bps is tougher than building one that works at 14,000 bps. Also, when you have a network link that runs that fast, a lot of people are going to be depending on it, and those people will get really annoyed at you if you're in charge of the link and it fails. So you need network management tools sothatyoucantell, for example, how often a message sent from one end of the link arrives garbled. (Links often go slightly flaky in preparation for dying completely. It's like the cough that may develop into pneumonia.)

Furthermore, these fast links are often set up in groups so that if one fails, its traffic can be shifted to the others and, being long-haul links, they tend to be located all over the country. Because you can have dozens, or more, of these links all over the place, having technicians running to each end of each link to check whether it's okay is a mite inconvenient. So PPP supports *remote network monitoring,* an obvious idea that took about 20 years to think up, which uses the network itself to transmit network management information to a central site where a single set of technicians can manage the entire network. Large networks take management very seriously, and all have people monitoring the network 24 hours a day, 7 days a week, so central management has the important benefit that the network only needs one set of expensive all-night network managers.

PPP has an extremely complete set of network monitoring facilities, the details of which we spare you because the descriptions read like this:

"If true(2) then the local node will attempt to perform Magic Number negotiation with the remote node. If false(1) then this negotiation is not performed. In any event, the local node will comply with any Magic Number negotiations attempted by the remote node, per the PPP specification. Changing this object will have effect when the link is next restarted."

(*Magic Number negotiation* is a way for a system to check whether a link was wired wrong and the system ends up talking to itself. See, we told you didn't care about this stuff.)

PPP solves another problem for fast networks: Until PPP came along, no standard existed for fast Internet links. If a link was faster than SLIP could handle or the link was too important to put up with SLIP's cruddiness, manufacturers invented their own link protocols. If you had a Brand X router, a specialized computer that moves packets from one network to another, at one end of a link and a Brand Y router at the other end, you'd have to be sure that they could talk to each other. As you might expect, each router manufacturer would cheerfully point out that the easiest way to avoid compatibility problems was to buy all your routers from them, and each network did indeed tend to have all the same kind of routers.

PPP provides a standard link protocol that everyone is supposed to support, so eventually you should be able to plug any kind of computer into any network link. To our surprise, this idea actually works — when Internet for Dummies Central got its fast million bps phone line in late 1995, we plugged our PC into our end of the line, the people at the phone company plugged their computer into the other end of the line, we both told our respective ends to speak PPP, and packets started to flow as soon as we got the modem switches set right. Wow!

Getting to the point, for real this time

After a while, system managers and a few users started to get tired of dealing with SLIP's flakiness. So the Internet powers-that-be (formally known as the IETF for Internet Engineering Task Force) came up with a swell new industrial strength, all-singing, all-dancing replacement for the link level called *Point-to-Point-Protocol,* or PPP. (In fairness, PPP also solves other problems with high-speed lines. See the sidebar "On the backbone," in this chapter.)

PPP is a much more complicated protocol than SLIP. The definition of SLIP is only six pages, four of which contain only descriptive examples. The PPP definition runs to 66 pages, not counting the descriptions of all the network-management information, which are another 60 pages. PPP is built on top of a widely used low-level link handling scheme known as HDLC (Hierarchical Data Link Control, for what it's worth), which is what most fast modems used already. A typical packet sent via PPP looks like

```
7E (hex) Here comes a packet
FF (hex) required by HDLC
03 (hex) Also required by HDLC
00 21 (hex) This is an Internet packet actual data
   at last!
xx xx Frame Check Sequence (see below)
7E (hex) There went the packet.
```

The first three characters (7E FF 03) say that this packet is an HDLC message destined for whoever is at the other end of the link. Computers are fairly stupid, so they don't find that to be obvious. The 00 21 says that this packet is Internet data, not Novell, Appletalk, DECnet, Hairnet, or anything else. Then comes the actual data, followed by a Frame Check Sequence (FCS), and a final end-of-packet flag. The FCS, which is used to see if the packet was received correctly, is calculated by the sender by adding together the binary values of all the bytes in the packet. (This is a gross oversimplification, but the actual details would fill ten pages even more boring than this one.) The receiver makes the same calculation and should come up with the same FCS. If not, the packet got messed up on the way, so the receiver throws it away to avoid using corrupted data.

PPP has all sorts of configuration facilities so that when a PPP link first starts up, the two ends can have a nice chat, introduce each other, and nail down some last-minute details about the link, such as what is the largest packet it is willing to receive from the other. PPP includes optional compression like CSLIP; during the initial chat, the two ends can agree whether they want to use it.

Even though PPP is more complex than SLIP, it solves a lot more problems and works much better in the case of errors (phone-line glitches, garbled packets, and the like) than does SLIP. The automatic configuration also makes PPP a lot easier to set up. Given a choice among SLIP, CSLIP, PPP, choose PPP.

Through the ether

Compared to sending your packets over a point-to-point link, sending them over an Ethernet is a breeze. Framing and error detection, the first two problems that provoked people to write PPP, are handled automatically by Ethernet hardware. (Sounds too good to be true, doesn't it?)

Multiprotocol support is pretty much automatic as well. The only fly in this otherwise perfect ointment is *addressing*. Your typical Ethernet has 100 computers attached to it, so you need some way to tell which of the 100 computers the packet is intended for. An obvious solution is to put the Internet address of the destination computer at the front of the packet. Then as each packet flies by, only the computer with the correct address receives it, and the rest ignore it. This idea is indeed almost what they do, except for the minor problem that Ethernet has its own rules for addressing, and they're not the same as the Internet. Unlike Internet addresses, Ethernet addresses are much longer, 48 bits rather than 32, and they are assigned almost entirely at random. (Well, not quite; rules make sure that no two computers get the same Ethernet address, but other than that, addresses may as well be random.) So before your computer can ship a packet over the network, you must figure out the minor issue of what Ethernet address corresponds to the desired Internet address. If you're smart, you'll take our word for it when we say that there's a plan to handle that. Or, if you insist, read the sidebar about ARP, ARP, and RARP.

On the Internet Level

Enough of that link-level stuff, already. The link level handles the details of getting a packet from one computer to another on the same network. What happens when you need to send a packet of data to a host on *another* network? That's where the Internet level comes in.

The process of passing a packet from network to network until it gets to its final destination is known as *routing*. A packet that passes through 20 or even 30 hosts on its way from your computer to one on a far-flung network is quite common. For example, say we telnetted from a computer at I.E.C.C. to one of the systems at Delphi. The packet left our computer, passed through three small routers (two of which were old 286 PCs, quite adequate for low-performance routers) to our local network provider, through another two routers to SprintLink, the long-haul network we used, through about five routers taking the packet from Boston to New York to Washington, where there's a connection to MCI's long haul network, through another five routers or so, taking the packet to the connection to Delphi, through a router that connects all of Delphi's computers, and finally to the host at Delphi. The total distance the packet went was about a thousand miles and the trip took about $^1/_5$ second. Delphi was physically about a mile away from I.E.C.C. (we could walk to a grocery store downstairs from Delphi, in fact), but the network is fast enough that the extra detour doesn't really matter.

ARP, ARP, RARP!

ARP is the Address Resolution Protocol for Ethernet that figures out the hardware Ethernet address that corresponds to a software Internet address. ARP (considering that a network's involved) is amazingly simple — the computer that needs to know the address shouts, "Hey, what's the address for 127.45.32.11?" and the computer with that address shouts back, "I'm 9a374cdf9e32 on the Ethernet."

This process works because on an Ethernet you can *broadcast* a message, which means that the message is received by all the computers on that network rather than just one computer. In this case, the first computer broadcasts the question, then one with the right address broadcasts an answer, and the rest ignore both the question and the answer.

Adding the inevitable confusion to this pristine situation, we have *Proxy ARP* and *Reverse ARP*, or RARP. In Proxy ARP, a computer answers an ARP request with a message saying, "Send messages for that host to me, and I'll take care of it." Proxy ARP mostly helps hosts so dumb that they can't handle ARP themselves. Reverse ARP is for the benefit of diskless workstations. When a diskless workstation starts up, because it has no disk to load from, it has no software loaded and no idea of what its Internet address is. It loads itself up over the Net using something called BOOTP, the details of which we spare you. Then the workstation sends a RARP message saying, "My Ethernet address is 373db49c7e12, who am I?" A better-informed computer (which presumably does have a disk) looks up the newly-hatched machine in a list and sends back an ARP response saying what it is. This scheme makes it easy to have a network of a few dozen diskless computers, which are all physically identical except for their hardware Ethernet addresses, load them up with identical software (BOOTP handles that), and then use RARP to give them separate Internet numbers, which they need to work with the rest of the Internet.

Fortunately, ARP and RARP work largely automatically. If you're feeling inquisitive, on a UNIX system there may be a command called `arp` or `/etc/arp` that shows you the table of Ethernet and Internet addresses. On a PC or a Mac that's attached to an Ethernet, you can probably find the ARP table in the Status menu of your network software.

Take this packet and. . . .

Each time a host in the Internet receives an IP packet, it asks, "Is this one for me?" If so, great; the host passes the packet to the next higher level of software (usually TCP, which we discuss in the next chapter). If not, the host has to route the packet. Your typical Internet host is attached to only one network, and only one "gateway" machine on that network attaches the host to the outside world, so the host sends all packets for other networks to the gateway. For a host connected to more than one network, the routing is a little (or maybe a lot) more complicated. Indeed, the routing is complicated enough that in the network backbones, the high-speed links that connect the fastest networks, routing is done by dedicated routers, specialized computers that do nothing but fling packets from one network to another.

How many networks would a network network?

Back when the Internet was young and dinosaurs roamed the earth, routing seemed like a pretty simple problem. Only a dozen or so networks were in the Internet, so each computer could keep a little table listing each network along with the best route to that network. Then when a packet arrived, the computer could look up the network number of the destination (the network number is the first few digits of a host's address) and send the packet on its way.

That worked fine for a while, but now the Internet has become a victim of its own success. For one thing, the communication links have gotten a lot faster, and for another, about 30,000 networks are now in the Internet with more joining every day. These things both make routing a lot harder. In dinosaur days, the fastest network link ran at 56,000 bps, which seems fast to people, but is a snail's pace for a computer. These days, your typical network link runs at 1 million bps (known in telephone-ese as "T1"), and the backbone links are trading up to 45 million bps. (That's "T3." Nobody seems to know what happened to T2.) Because a typical Internet packet is about 1,000 bits long, in the old days a link could only handle about 50 packets per second, but T1 can handle 1,000 packets per second and T3 45,000 packets per second. We turn those numbers inside out to see how long the receiving machine has to handle a packet, measured in milliseconds ($^{1}/_{1000}$ second):

Line speed	*Packets/sec*	*Time/packet*
56,000	50	20 milliseconds
T1	1,000	1 millisecond
T3	45,000	.02 milliseconds

(Note to the arithmetically inclined: yes, we've rounded these numbers.)

The problem is that in 1 millisecond, a typical modern computer barely has time to look up a network number in a 13,000-entry table. In .02 milliseconds, it barely has time to notice that a packet has arrived, much less do anything with it. For the hosts in the network backbones, which really have to know where all of networks are and can't punt most messages to a gateway, expensive special hardware is needed that can look up routes quickly and send packets on their way.

Cough, cough, we seem to have congestion

As through routing weren't a severe enough problem (and it's pretty bad; lots of Ph.D. students have gotten theses out of routing problems, too) there's the related problem of congestion. If you think of network links as roads, imagine two two-lane roads funneling into a third two-lane road. If both of the incoming roads are full of traffic, there just won't be room for all of those cars on the outgoing one and traffic will back up. The standard solution to network congestion

Where does routing come from, where does routing go?

The astute reader may have noticed that we haven't said anything about where tables of routes come from. If only a handful of networks existed, skilled network managers could load the routes into the routers, updating the routes on the rare occasions when new network links were added. But, as we say in the computer biz, maintaining tables by hand doesn't scale well. Now that the Internet comprises 30,000 networks, it probably has 50,000 routers, and any size army of administrators can't keep them up to date. So instead, the routes are updated automatically.

In fact, even when the Internet was tiny, the routes were still updated automatically. A major goal of the projects leading to the Internet was to create networks that would continue to work if the links and routers failed. (The military, which funded the work, was worried about enemy attack, but the same techniques are just as useful when an errant construction crew cuts a buried cable, known puckishly as "backhoe fade.")

Every few seconds, each router on the Net sends messages to each of its neighbor routers (that is, other routers on the networks to which it is directly connected.) By comparing notes, the routers can figure out what's connected to which network and which way to send packets to each of the thousands of networks. Originally, routers just tried to minimize the number of hops a packet would have to take to get to its destination. That focus made sense when all network links were about the same speed, but now it's a lot quicker to take four hops on T3 links (the superfast 45 million bps kind) than one hop on an old 56,000 link. Political issues also exist. Some networks allow general traffic, and others only allow research traffic, and you can't route from one general network to another through a research network, no matter how fast the links are.

may surprise you: throw the extra packets away. The IP level is officially unreliable, which means that if a problem occurs during the delivery of a packet, the heck with it. That attitude may seem awfully antisocial, but it turns out to be the best solution, mostly because all the schemes to make the network reliable at this level are more trouble than they're worth. (You can make sure your data get delivered, but we get to those ways in the next chapter.)

When someone's packets get thrown away, the host that does the throwing away is supposed to send a special "source quench" message back to the sender, which tells it to talk slower. This message helps somewhat. But there's no question, at peak hours the Net can get awfully congested and slow, and the only solution is more and faster (and more expensive) network links.

A peek inside a packet

Every packet handled by IP has a *header,* a bunch of information stuck on the front of the packet that IP uses to keep track of the packet's progress through the network.

- **IP version number:** Always 4 — evidently Versions 1, 2, and 3 didn't make the grade
- **Header length:** Size of the IP information, as distinct from the actual data that IP is supposed to be sending
- **Type of service:** A hint that this packet should be sent faster or more reliably than normal
- **Total length:** Total size of the packet, including both the IP stuff and the contents
- **Identification:** A sequence number to help tell this packet apart from other packets of similar appearance
- **Fragment info:** See the sidebar "Aargh! I've been fragmented"
- **TTL:** Time to live, a freshness date saying how much longer this packet can be passed around before it gets stale and should be thrown away
- **Protocol:** The higher-level protocol (TCP, most likely) that uses this packet
- **Checksum:** Checks for scrambled or corrupted header info
- **Source addr:** IP address of the original sender
- **Dest addr:** IP address of the ultimate recipient
- **Options:** Every general's favorite features, things like "top secret" or "priority flash override"

Aargh! I've been fragmented

You may occasionally hear network propellerheads complaining about *packet fragmentation.* Each network in the Internet has a largest-allowed packet size, known as the *maximum transmission unit,* or MTU. The MTU on an Ethernet is about 1,500-characters, while the limit on a dial-up link may be only 500 characters. So what happens when a 1,500-character packet needs to be sent over a 500 MTU link? The packet gets broken up into pieces, called *fragments.*

Fragmentation is, from the point of view of network implementors, a pain in the neck. If a sender breaks a packet into three fragments, the receiver has to wait for all three fragments to arrive before it can reassemble the packet and send it along to the next network. And what if the fragments arrive out of order, which can happen for technical reasons? Or if one of the fragments gets lost? How long should the receiver wait before giving up and considering the whole packet to be lost? There's no good answer.

If you use network software that lets you set your own system's MTU (Trumpet WinSock, discussed in Chapter 7, is one) be sure to set it fairly low, like 500 or less, to avoid dreaded fragmentation.

Chapter 4

Even More Grotty Details

In This Chapter

- What's a circuit and why
- More about TCP
- The innards of packets
- A live example: sending mail using SMTP

You read Chapter 3, and you're still reading? Are you nuts? There's no accounting for taste, evidently.

In the last chapter, we established that the Internet, using the creatively named Internet Protocol (IP), is able to send packets of data from one computer to another, even when the two computers are on different networks in different parts of the world. But a single packet is rarely enough to say anything useful. (It's like saying "Hi" to someone, but not waiting around to hear an answer.) In this chapter, we look at the way the Internet uses packets, lots and lots of packets, to create conversations between two computers. (That's called the *transport* level of the net.) Finally, to show that you can make all this nonsense do something useful, we use the transport level to deliver an e-mail message.

Executive summary of this chapter

The lower levels of the Internet have even more detailed glop going on than we discussed in the last chapter. Big deal.

You don't have to read any of this chapter to follow the rest of the book or to use the Internet. In the unlikely event that you've read Chapter 3 and you're still interested in this stuff and/or your insomnia is still a problem, read on.

Controlling Those Transmissions

As we mention in Chapter 2, when you have a network connection between two computers, the most convenient kind of connection to have is known as a *circuit*. The most familiar example of a circuit connection is a telephone call. If we call you, after the connection is made, everything we say is transmitted to you, and everything you say is transmitted to us. (If this scenario seems obvious, that's because it is.) A circuit connection between two computers works the same way — everything one computer sends is received by the other and vice versa. When you dial in over the phone to a BBS or a UNIX provider, you have a circuit connection to the BBS or UNIX provider.

The Internet, on the other hand, doesn't have circuits. It has packets. So what's a circuit lover to do? You fake it, that's what you do. You take the stream of data that you'd like to send over a circuit to another computer, slice it into packets, number it, send it to the other computer using IP, and put it back together in numbered order. The result isn't a real circuit, but it's close enough that we can pretend it is and call it a *virtual circuit*. The scheme that creates these virtual circuits is known as Transmission Control Protocol, or TCP. Because TCP depends on IP to do the actual packet delivery, the two together are usually known as TCP/IP.

If Circuits Are So Swell, Why Not Use Them Directly?

In olden days, people did. IBM has its own network scheme grandly named Systems Network Architecture (SNA) which, when you make a connection, establishes a circuit through the network for the duration of the connection. But it turned out that the TCP/IP approach — with virtual circuits created atop a sea of packets, and only the computers at the ends of the connection worrying about the circuit stuff — worked a lot better.

The reason is that a network connection involves not just the two computers at the ends, but also all the computers in between that route the data from one network or piece of a network to another. In an SNA-like scheme, all the routers in the middle need to know about all the circuits that pass through them. (We oversimplify here, somewhat. Don't worry about it.) Having to know about circuits greatly complicates a router's job compared to the TCP/IP approach in which a router merely moves packets from one network to another, without regard to which virtual circuit each packet may be part of. In our network, for example, an ancient 1984-vintage 286 PC is quite adequate to route data from one network to another, even though hundreds of virtual circuits can be active at any time. If a 286 PC had to track each circuit, it probably wouldn't be up to the task.

The TCP/IP approach is also much more robust in the face of enemy attack (see the description of "backhoe fade" in Chapter 3). If a TCP/IP network link fails, but alternate links can get packets to the same place as the failed link did, a router need only send packets via the alternate links. The computers on the end don't even notice. When a lot of alternate links are available, sending different packets in the same virtual circuit via different links, depending on which is busier at the moment each packet arrives, is quite common. Even if one router fails, taking down all its links, the network still operates as long as alternate routes are around it.

In a network system with real circuits, on the other hand, each circuit that used a failing link needs to be identified and rerouted individually. This process is slow and error prone and is an administrative nightmare.

By the way, for more than a century, telephone calls have all been circuit switched, with the facilities for each call set up when the call is established, and dedicated to that call until you hang up. In recent years, even staid phone companies are climbing aboard the packet-switching bandwagon, turning your phone calls into lots of little packets of data, whipping them through the network at high speed, and turning them back into voice at the other end. The current telephone buzzword is ATM (an unhelpful acronym for Asynchronous Transfer Mode), which is actually high-speed packet switching for both voice and computer data.

TCP Takes Control

We've established (Still awake? Just checking.) that the job of TCP is to deliver data from one computer to another. TCP's job can be broken down into several parts.

- **Reliability:** Everything sent has to be received. We have to be prepared to send everything over and over again until the receiving end confirms that the message got there.
- **Sequencing:** Everything sent has to be received in the correct order. The sending computer's TCP slices the data into packets, and by the time the packets are routed through the network, they may be out of order. The receiver has to put them back into the correct order to avoid having the message this like received be. TCP assigns a sequence number for each data byte sent, and each packet identifies the sequence numbers of the data in that packet.
- **Flow control:** A fast computer sending to a slow computer can easily send data faster than the receiver can process it. To avoid network congestion (known in the extreme case as network constipation, ouch), the receiver sets a *receive window* that limits how fast the sender can send.

Living in duplex

A connection between two computers can be one-way, two-way, or, sometimes, both. (Strange but true.) In the interest of avoiding excess clarity, these possibilities are referred to as *simplex*, *full duplex*, and *half duplex*.

Say you're using FTP to retrieve a file from another computer. After you type your "get" command (or the equivalent click if you're using a spiffy full-screen FTP program), FTP makes a connection for the file's data, the data comes streaming across from the remote computer to your computer, and when it's done, that connection is closed. That's a simplex connection because the data flows only one way.

On the other hand, say you're using telnet to connect to a remote computer. Everything you type is immediately sent to the other computer, and everything it says is immediately sent back to you, with no particular synchronization between the two directions. You can, for example, type ahead of what the remote computer is reading, and it will catch up with your typing when it gets around to it. That's a full-duplex connection.

On the third hand (this lecture is evidently being given by a Hindu deity), in some cases the data flows in one direction for a while and then in the other direction for a while, flip-flopping back and forth. The classic example is if you're talking to someone — actually talking, no computers here — via a radio phone. One person talks and says "over" when finished, and the other person talks and says "over," and so on. (Incidentally, the terms *simplex* and *duplex* originally come from radiotelephony, the first place where the issue of one- versus two-way conversation arose, probably in the 1920s.)

When computers are talking to each other without pesky humans directly involved, for example, when transferring news or e-mail, half-duplex connections are the norm because they're easier for computers to keep straight than are full duplex. Simplex isn't usually adequate because you need a way to get errors and acknowledgments back in response to a message. (If you're wondering about FTP, it uses two connections, a half-duplex one for commands and messages, the ones you see when you type commands to FTP, and a separate simplex one for file data.)

For an excellent example of half-duplex communication, we recommend the old British World War II romantic comedy *I Know Where I'm Going* in which Wendy Hiller plays a gold-digging young Englishwoman who's heading for a remote Scottish isle to marry a rich old industrialist. While waiting for a storm to clear so she can take a boat to the island, Wendy instead falls in love with the impoverished but raffishly charming local nobleman. Several scenes show Wendy at the post office, talking via the half-duplex radio telephone to her industrialist, saying, "I miss you, darling, over," and so on. The nonhalf-duplex parts of the movie aren't bad, either.

What does the "Transmission" in Transmission Control Protocol have to do with the transmission in my car?

Nothing whatsoever. What did you expect?

Marching in sequence

The operation of TCP is, in principle, actually pretty simple. (In practice, it's utterly baroque, but most of the barocity comes from being prepared to handle errors and exceptional conditions.) Each byte of data sent over a connection has a sequence number. Say, for the moment, that the sequence number of the last data handled was 1000, and we're sending 100 data bytes per packet. So a packet we send contains data 1001–1100. When the receiver gets that packet, the receiver sends back an acknowledgment (ACK for short) saying, "I've received up through 1100, now send starting at 1101." The sender then can send 1101–1200.

If we waited for an ACK after each and every packet, we'd spend more time waiting than sending, so we're allowed to send several packets ahead of what's been ACKed. The number of data bytes we're allowed to get ahead is the *window* — and yes, people really do say "ACKed," even though they sound like Bill the Cat. If the window were 300 bytes wide, then we'd actually send 1001–1100, 1101–1200, and 1201–1300 before waiting for an acknowledgment. If we then receive an acknowledgment up through 1200, we can now go 300 bytes beyond that, so we can now send 1301–1400 and 1401–1500. When the network is working smoothly (which, surprisingly, it does most of the time), the data and acknowledgment messages arrive at roughly the same rate, so the data keeps flowing at a constant speed.

Could you repeat that, please?

What happens if we send data, and we never get an ACK? Or, more commonly, we've sent up through 1300, but we keep getting back ACKs only through 1100? That means a packet has gotten lost. (Remember, IP is allowed to throw away packets in case of a transmission error or lack of network link capacity.) What do we do now? Simple. We resend the lost data. Because we have ACKs through 1100, we resend 1101–1200 and 1201–1300. Eventually we get ACKs for the re-sent data (if not, we have to send the data yet again until we do), and we can resume passing more data to the other end. An essential rule for TCP is that the sender has to hang on to a copy of everything sent until the receiver ACKs it, because the data may have to be retransmitted.

Stereo networking

Adding a little more complication to this scenario (that's "a little," as in when your dentist says, "This may cause a little discomfort") is the full-duplex-itude of a TCP connection. If we have a connection between Boston and Geneva, data can flow both eastbound and westbound at the same time. So a separate set of sequence numbers and a separate window exist for each direction. In the interest of packet economy, each TCP packet can include both data and a sequence number for one direction and an acknowledgment and window for the other direction. A packet might say, "Here's bytes 5001–5100 of my data, I'm ACKing up through byte 97,000 of your data, and my window is 600 bytes." Even though the packets are shared, each direction is logically separate, so you can think of them separately, sharing packets only to save network overhead.

I feel congested, can you close the window?

To keep the network working well, each receiver needs to set a reasonable window. If windows are too large, senders may send packets so fast that the network becomes overloaded. But if windows are too small, senders spend most of their time waiting for ACKs, needlessly slowing down communication.

The traditional rule of thumb is that the window for a connection should be the amount of data that can be sent in the time it takes to make a round-trip on the network. For example, assume that you have a fast network that can transmit 100,000 bytes per second and that the time to send a packet to a distant host is 1/4 second. (These are fairly typical numbers.) So the round-trip time is twice 1/4 second, or 1/2 second. In 1/2 second, we can send 50,000 bytes, and a reasonable window is 50,000 bytes.

Now the black magic begins. If the network isn't congested at all, and no packets are ever lost to errors, you have found the perfect window size. But in real life, the network is always congested when you want to use it, and errors do happen. Detecting network congestion is fairly easy — the sender may receive "source quench" packets from a router that had to throw packets away, and the receiver may notice packets arriving less often than they would if the network were flowing freely. So you should shrink the window to slow down the sender and alleviate the congestion. How much should you shrink the window? Well, er, some. Lots of theories, but no accepted rules of thumb, exist, so there are no doubt lots of Ph.D. theses yet to be written on congestion control.

A related question is how long after you send a packet do you wait for an ACK before you conclude that you have to send it again? If the time is too short, you needlessly transmit data twice, wasting network capacity. (The recipient can tell from the sequence numbers that the second copy of the data is redundant, so the situation is handled correctly, but it's still a waste.) If the time is too long, you can end up waiting a long time until the sender finally gets around to retransmitting a lost packet. The traditional rule of thumb is that you should wait about twice the round-trip time, but there are lots of theories and upcoming Ph.D. theses here, too.

Socket to Me

So far we've considered how to handle one TCP connection (or virtual circuit) at a time. But on a real networked computer, you don't just have one connection, you have a whole bunch, potentially thousands on a large server system. TCP keeps connections separate by using *ports*.

If you think of a computer's Internet address as a phone number, the port is like an extension number. Any particular TCP connection runs from a particular port on one host to a particular port on the other host. A single port on a particular host can have multiple connections active as long as they are to separate ports on other hosts.

By convention, standard server programs use agreed-on low-numbered ports. For telnet, you connect to port 23, for FTP to port 21, for Gopher to port 80, and so on. On a UNIX system, the list of port numbers is in a file called `/etc/services`. On PCs, the list is usually in a file called services or services.txt in your network software directory.

When a client program wants to establish a network connection, it asks its system for an unused port, usually in the 1200 range, and then connects to the low-numbered port for the service it wants. When the connection is done, the client program gives its high-numbered port back to the system for later use.

Grotty Packet Details

For the masochists among you, here are the details of the header info that TCP puts on each and every packet it sends. Remember that TCP packets are sent inside IP packets, so the sender and receiver host addresses are already handled by IP.

- **Source Port:** the port number on the sender's machine
- **Destination Port:** the port number on the recipient's machine
- **Sequence Number:** the sequence number of the first data byte in this packet
- **Acknowledgment Number:** (optional) the sequence number of the next data byte this sender is expecting to receive

- **Data Offset:** the size of the TCP header so that the recipient can figure out where the actual data starts
- **Control flags:** special indicators like "reset this connection," "ACK number is present," and "end of data"
- **Window:** the size of the receive window, in bytes
- **Checksum:** a control total of all the data in the header, to be recalculated and compared by the recipient to detect scrambled packets
- **Urgent Pointer:** packets can contain "urgent" data that is delivered immediately to the recipient's program (In a telnet session, Ctrl+C may be considered an urgent message because it usually tells the server to interrupt what it's doing.)
- **Options:** miscellaneous junk, can include a hint to the recipient about a good maximum number of data bytes to send per packet

Isn't there an awful lot of header glop on each and every packet?

You bet. TCP is what's known as a *heavy-weight* protocol. A typical packet will have 40 bytes of TCP header and 20 or more bytes of IP header, which seems a wee bit top-heavy for a packet that may contain a single data byte representing a keystroke you've typed on a telnet connection.

The design of TCP/IP is cast in stone (three million computers will need to have their software updated when it's changed), but some gross hacks, er, advanced techniques, can cut down the header bloat. The most notable technique is Compressed SLIP, or CSLIP. This technique takes advantage of the fact that the headers in one packet tend to be very much like the headers in the packet that preceded it, so CSLIP usually just sends a single byte with a code for "same as last time." The original bloated headers are reconstructed by the recipient, which saves time over slow links (by not sending the bloat) but remains compatible with the rest of the TCP/IP world. PPP, the industrial-strength successor to SLIP, offers similar header compression.

By the way, when we said that TCP/IP is cast in stone, we were lying. The Internet is running out of IP addresses, partly due to profligate handing out of addresses in the early 1980s to people who didn't end up using them, and partly due to the Net growing a lot more than anyone expected. A new version of IP has been introduced that has much bigger addresses — 64 rather than 32 bits — and enough addresses to assign a separate one to every electron in the universe, which we presume will be enough. Fortunately, the old and new address schemes will be able to coexist for several years as everyone's host software is upgraded. But this new addressing scheme will make the header bloat problems even worse, because the IP header will grow from a minimum of 20 bytes to more like 30 or 40 bytes. We presume that yet more header compression will allow people on slow PPP links to avoid having all their packets become larger and take longer to send, but the details of that aren't even under discussion yet.

An opposing view: Keep it simple

For some purposes, TCP is severe overkill. There is, for example, a simple time service, where the sender sends a request asking, "What time is it?" and the recipient sends back a response with the time and date. Each message can fit in a single packet, so using TCP, which needs a minimum of five packets to start and stop a connection, to send one packet each way seems silly.

For those lean, mean, network applications, UDP, the User Datagram Protocol, is an alternative to TCP. UDP has ports like TCP to handle multiple programs on a single host and an optional checksum for error detection, but other than that, it doesn't do you any favors. If a program sends a UDP message, that message turns into one packet. UDP can be a lot faster than TCP because it sends fewer packets and the packets it does send are smaller.

UDP is used both for very simple applications, like time of day, and also for applications that do their own error-checking, so they don't need TCP to do it for them. The most important of these applications is NFS, the Network File System. Each NFS operation involves a client sending a request and the server sending back a response. Whether the responses arrive in the same order the requests were sent (they often don't, because NFS operations can take a lot longer than others) doesn't matter because NFS takes care of matching up a response with the corresponding pending request. NFS performance is extremely important (for many workstations, most or all of their disk operations are handled over the net via NFS) so small, fast UDP is just the ticket.

Let's Play Postman

For the grand denouement of this chapter, we look at the operation of an actual Internet application, the euphemistically named Simple Mail Transfer Protocol (SMTP). Mail programs use SMTP when sending e-mail messages on the Internet. Watch as SMTP delivers an e-mail message.

In an SMTP operation, the receiving machine is considered to be the server and the sending machine the client. To deliver a piece of mail, the sending machine opens a TCP connection to the server on port 25, where the receiving machine's SMTP server should be waiting to receive something. The communication between the two machines uses plain old lines of text.

The sender sends a sequence of commands, each of which is a four-letter word (usually spelled wrong, unless the word actually has four letters), perhaps followed by some parameters. The recipient sends back status messages. Each message starts with a three-digit number identifying the message so that dumb computers can use the numbers to figure out what's going on without having to try to read the text that follows.

Note: In the examples that follow, we use `S:` and `R:` to identify lines from the sender and from the recipient. Commands and responses appearing in uppercase are historically conventional, although today the commands can be upper-, lower-, or mixed.

Say we're sending a message from `aaron@aardvark.com` to `zeppo@zebra.org`. The sender, `aardvark.com`, makes a connection to the recipient's server at `zebra.org`. The first computer to speak after the connection is made is the recipient:

```
R: 220 ZEBRA.ORG Mail server version 123.4A ready
```

Then the sender sends a HELO (we already said these commands aren't spelled very well) to identify itself, and the recipient acknowledges it:

```
S: HELO AARDVARK.COM
R: 250 Hi, AARDVARK.COM, pleased to meet you
```

(Mail programmers have a sense of humor, too, sort of.) Then the sender announces a piece of mail is coming and who it's from, followed by a recipient (spelled RCPT) line, identifying who the mail is for:

```
S: MAIL FROM:<aaron@aardvark.com
R: 250 OK
S: RCPT TO:<zeppo@zebra.org>
R: 250 OK
```

If more than one recipient exists, more than one RCPT command can be used. Here's a command for an invalid address:

```
S: RCPT TO:<elvis@zebra.org>
R: 550 No such user here
```

The recipients having been named, the sender prepares to send the text of the message:

```
S: DATA
R: 354 Start mail input; end with <CRLF>.<CRLF>
```

Then the sender sends the literal text of the message, ending with a line consisting of a single dot:

```
S: From: aaron@aardvark.com
S: To: zeppo@zebra.com
S: Subject: lunch
S: Date: 14 Sep 1996 11:30:00 EDT
```

```
S:
S: How about lunch at Elsie's?
S: .
R: 250 OK
```

The OK response means the message has been accepted. That's it; a QUIT command wraps up the session.

```
S: QUIT
R: 221 Sayonara
```

You can actually send mail this way by telnetting to a host and typing very carefully. (No provision for correcting typing errors exists, because SMTP is intended for computers, not for humans.) As is common in computer-to-computer communications, this exchange is a half-duplex conversation. One side talks, then the other side, and then the first, alternately, until they're done.

Had Enough?

That wraps up our tour of the bowels of the Internet. Please remember to leave your hard hats at the exit and to wipe your feet on the way out.

If you're a glutton for punishment, the documents that define all of these protocols and many, many others, are available online. They are, as standard computer documents go, fairly readable, meaning they sort of make sense if you stare at them for a long time. The Internet documents are known, for some ancient reason, as Request For Comment documents, or RFCs. (You can comment all you want about TCP, IP, UDP, and SMTP, but it's about 12 years too late now.) Some RFCs define standards, some comment on problems with standards or propose changes, and many propose possible standards that never went anywhere. You can find RFCs at the InterNIC. The Web page is `http://www.internic.net/ds/dspg0intdoc.html`. Each RFC is numbered, and well over a thousand exist. A few RFCs that you may, maybe, want to look at are

rfc768	User Datagram Protocol (UDP)
rfc791	Internet Protocol (IP)
rfc792	Internet Control Message Protocol (source quench and all that)
rfc793	Transmission Control Protocol (TCP)
rfc821	Simple Mail Transfer Protocol (SMTP)
rfc822	Format of Mail Messages

Web pages and downloadable files with an index of all the RFCs and the RFCs that define actual Internet standards also are available.

The 5th Wave By Rich Tennant

©RICHTENNANT

"SINCE WE GOT IT, HE HASN'T MOVED FROM THAT SPOT FOR ELEVEN STRAIGHT DAYS. ODDLY ENOUGH THEY CALL THIS 'GETTING UP AND RUNNING' ON THE INTERNET."

Chapter 5

Resource, Resource, Who's Got the Resource?

In This Chapter

- A roundup of resource types and how to get to them
- Mysteries of mailing lists and reminders of news
- Nibbling on Gopher
- Strands of the World Wide Web

How many ways are available to get to Internet information, anyway? Roughly a zillion. Among the services are e-mail, Usenet newsgroups, telnet, FTP, Gopher, and the World Wide Web (WWW). A few items arrive in other hard-to-characterize ways. What's more, a great deal of overlap occurs among the various services. You can get to Gopher by way of the Web and telnet. Or you can get to FTP by way of Gopher, the Web, or e-mail. In this chapter, we summarize the ways to get to these different resource types, depending on which sort of hardware and software you have available. For each type, we list the ways in rough order of quality so that a fast and easy-to-use way is listed before a slow and painful one.

This chapter tells you exactly how each type of resource is described in technical Internet-ese, usually using things called URLs. You need to know this stuff to access the information we describe in the rest of this book.

Don't Hurl! It's Only an URL!

The World Wide Web brought us the extremely useful concept of *Uniform Resource Locators,* or *URLs.* A URL (pronounced *url* or *U-R-L*) is a simple and consistent way to name Internet resources. A URL consists of a resource type, a colon, and a location. In most cases, the location is two slashes, the host name where the resource can be found, a slash, and a name on that host.

Some typical URLs are

```
http://www.ncsa.uiuc.edu/demoweb/demo.html
```

and

```
gopher://wx.atmos.uiuc.edu:70/1
```

The first URL is a World Wide Web page, which is accessible by HTTP (the standard scheme the Web uses). The host name is `www.ncsa.uiuc.edu`, and the name on that site is `demoweb/demo.html`. The second URL is a Gopher directory that is on site `wx.atmos.uiuc.edu`, port 70, and the Gopher's name is `1`.

Table 5-1 shows commonly used URL resource types.

Table 5-1 Types of URLs

Type	*Description*
`gopher:`	A Gopher menu
`http:`	A HyperText Transfer Protocol document (that is, something in native WWW format)
`ftp:`	A directory or file on an FTP server
`news:`	A Usenet news item (unsupported by many WWW client programs)

Originally intended as a way for computers to pass around resource names, URLs also tell people about Internet resources, which is how we use URLs in this book.

Put Me on the Mailing List

E-mail mailing lists are the oldest way — and still one of the most popular — for people of like interests to get together on the Net. You send and receive messages from a mailing list in the same way you send and receive messages from individual correspondents. You can use mailing lists even if the only Internet service you have is e-mail (which is true for many people).

The basic operation of a list is simple: Any messages sent to the list are relayed to all the list members. Other people usually reply, which creates a sequence of back-and-forth comments in a running discussion. Different lists have different characters. Some lists are sociable, and other lists are quite formal. Some lists have a great deal of traffic — dozens of messages per day — and other lists go for weeks or months without a message.

Immoderation and indigestion

Some mailing lists are moderated, and some lists are digests (many are both). In a *moderated* list, messages are not automatically relayed but are given to a human moderator who weeds out the irrelevant messages and forwards the approved messages. Different moderators have different styles — in some lists, practically everything is approved, and in others, only a few messages are approved. Many lists are quite popular, and the moderator doesn't reject inappropriate messages, but rather acts as an editor who chooses the best submissions to create a high-quality list.

Some people grumble that moderators are petty fascists who choose messages to serve their own whims. Well, we (yes, *we* — one of your authors moderates a list on a technical computer topic) do pick messages to serve our own whims, but users who grumble the most seem to be the ones whose messages need to be weeded out.

Some moderated lists are really one-way mail distributors. That is, the messages on the list don't come from the subscribers, but from some outside source. One list relays National Weather Service hurricane announcements, for example, and all the messages on that list originate from the NWS. These announcement-only lists can be useful ways to get news by e-mail.

When a list sends out more than two or three messages a day, subscribers' mailboxes can fill quickly. A common way to lessen the mail overload is to collect all the day's messages in a single large message, known as a *digest,* which replaces the dozen little messages sent throughout the day. Some lists are available only in digest form, and other lists are available either way.

An open-and-shut case

Most mailing lists are *open,* which means that anyone can send in a message. Others are *closed,* which means that only people who subscribe to the list are allowed to send in messages. If you try to send a message to a closed list to which you don't subscribe, you get back an automatic response rejecting your message. Closed lists can sometimes be a pain: If the return address on your e-mail message doesn't exactly match your address as listed in the subscriber list, you can't send in a message. If your return address doesn't match your listed address (if your system manager changes the configuration, for example, and your address is improved from `gw@musket.mtvernon.va.us` to `George.Washington@mtvernon.va.us`), send a nice message to the person who manages the list and ask to have your new address added as one allowed to send in messages.

A few lists are open only to qualified subscribers, who apply to belong to the list. A Usenet moderators' list is limited to people who moderate Usenet groups, for example. If you apply to a list with such restrictions, the list manager will probably ask you to show how you qualify.

Mailing list wrangling

Be sure to remember the difference between the mailing list *manager address* you write to in order to get on and off the list and the *submission address* you write to in order to send messages to the list members. A common newbie mistake (and you certainly wouldn't want to be mistaken for a newbie) is to send a manager message to the list itself. Everyone doesn't have to know that you want to subscribe or unsubscribe to the list, so send the message to the manager address. This kind of mistake is particularly embarrassing because everyone on the list sees how you messed up. Don't make this mistake.

You get on and off mailing lists in three major ways. (You didn't think that getting off and on a mailing list would be simple, did you?) The ways depend on whether the mailing list is run by the LISTSERV program, the Majordomo program, or an actual human being. (You can tell by looking at the manager address; see if it's something like `listserv@something`, `majordomo@something`, or something else.) Fortunately, they're all easy to deal with.

LISTSERV

The most popular mailing-list maintenance software is LISTSERV. LISTSERV is a family of programs that automatically manages mailing lists, distributes messages posted to the list, adds and deletes members, and so on without the tedium of doing so manually. Originally written to run on giant IBM mainframe computers, LISTSERV has popped up on other kinds of computers. LISTSERV lists usually have names like SAMPLE-L. Remember that all management-type messages, such as requests to subscribe and unsubscribe, should be addressed to `listserv`, not to the list address.

You can tell when you are dealing with a LISTSERV mailing list because the manager address is similar to `listserv@something`.

To subscribe to a LISTSERV list, such as the `sample-l` mailing list on the Internet host `sample.org`, e-mail a message to `listserv@sample.org`, which contains the following line:

```
sub sample-l George Washington
```

The line contains `sub` (short for *sub*scribe), the exact name of the mailing list you are talking about, and then your real, human name. (Remember to substitute the list's real name in this example — and your name for George's — and send the message to the Internet LISTSERV host computer's real name.)

To get off the list, send to the same address a message containing the following line:

```
unsub sample-l
```

If the list has optional digesting (urp!), you can switch between getting daily digests (see "Immoderation and indigestion," earlier in this chapter) and individual mail messages by sending one of the following messages to the LISTSERV address:

```
set sample-l digest
set sample-l mail
```

The `digest` message gets you the daily digest, and `mail` gets you individual mail messages.

If you have trouble getting on or off a LISTSERV list, you can contact the postmaster at `OWNER-SAMPLE-L@sample.org` (which is the list name prefixed by `OWNER-`).

After you're on the list, send messages to subscribers by mailing to the list name, not to LISTSERV (`SAMPLE-L@sample.org`, for example).

Majordomo

Originally a LISTSERV wannabe, Majordomo is not the automatic mailing-list manager that people like the best. However, Majordomo has escaped LISTSERV's annoying IBM-isms, such as the TENDENCY TO PUT EVERYTHING IN UPPERCASE and LISTSERV's limitation of names to eight characters. To get on or off a Majordomo list, send a message to `majordomo@sample.org` (using the actual host name, of course, rather than `sample.org`).

You can tell when you are dealing with a Majordomo mailing list because the manager address is similar to `majordomo@something`.

To subscribe to a list, send the following message:

```
sub name-of-list
```

To unsubscribe, send this message:

```
unsub name-of-list
```

Unlike with LISTSERV, with Majordomo you *don't* put your real name after the list name on the `sub` command. Majordomo regards whatever you type after the list name as the mailing address to use, not the message's return address, which can come in handy if your mail system puts a bad return address on your outgoing mail.

To contact the human manager for a Majordomo list, send mail to `owner-name-of-list@sample.org`, the same way you do with LISTSERV.

Manually maintained lists

A fair number of lists are still maintained manually by humans. To subscribe or unsubscribe to these lists, you send a message to the list maintainer asking to be added to or deleted from the list. For manual lists, you concoct the maintainer's address by adding `-request` to the list name; so for a list named `sample`, the maintainer's address is `sample-request@whatever.org`.

Humans, not being computers, sometimes leave their keyboards to eat, sleep, or otherwise have a life. (Hard to believe, isn't it?) For a manually maintained list, therefore, the maintainer can take a couple days to act on your message. We can tell you from experience that sending lots of extra messages to the maintainer doesn't get you attention any sooner, and any attention you *do* get is probably not the kind you want.

URLs for mailing lists

Unlike the other types of resources listed in this chapter, you can't get to a mailing list's contents via Gopher, FTP, or the World Wide Web. A URL for a mailing list doesn't exist.

For more information on mailing lists, see Chapter 8 in *The Internet For Dummies*, 3rd Edition (IDG Books Worldwide).

Usenet Newsgroups: The World's Biggest Bulletin Board

The largest volume of public information and misinformation comes flooding in through Usenet newsgroups, which currently run an astonishing 100MB per day. Usenet is a system of thousands of distributed bulletin boards. The only reasonable way to read the news is with a newsreading program such as `trn`, `tin`, or `nn` on a UNIX system, or Trumpet or WinVN on a PC. (See Chapter 9 in *The Internet For Dummies,* 3rd Edition, for information about reading Usenet newsgroups.)

Almost any system, except those systems that handle only mail, provides a news program (or if you're using a PC with SLIP or PPP, provides a news server for your local news program). If you're unaccountably stuck in a news-free environment but can telnet out to other systems, you can try telnetting to `cyberspace.org` or `launchpad.unc.edu`, two systems that provide limited public access to news. World Wide Web browsers provide access to Usenet news also. Because none of the Web browsers we've seen handle topic threads (groups of articles that — allegedly — deal with similar topics), accessing Usenet news is a slow and painful way to read more than about four articles in a sitting.

Subscribing to a newsgroup

When you find out about an interesting newsgroup, tell your news program to present the newsgroup to you. To subscribe to a group you haven't read in the past, follow the appropriate step in this list (we list instructions for each of the most common newsreading programs in use):

- trn **users:** At the newsgroup selection level, press **g** and type the newsgroup name.
- nn **users:** At the menu listing newsgroups, press **G** and type the newsgroup name.
- tin **users**: At the screen showing newsgroups, press **g** and type the newsgroup name.
- **Trumpet users:** Choose Group Subscribe from the menu and then choose the group you want from the list of unsubscribed groups.
- **WinVN users:** Simply scroll down to the group and double-click the group's name.

News by way of e-mail

Some Usenet groups are also available by e-mail. The group comp.dcom.telecom is the same as the e-mail list telecom@eecs.nwu.edu and the group comp.compilers is the same as the LISTSERV list compil-l@american.edu. Anything that appears in the group is mailed to the list and vice versa. Every few weeks, a message posted to the newsgroup news.lists contains a list of groups available by e-mail.

If you're at a site where you can read news but can't post to the site, you can send Usenet articles by e-mail by using the following public mail-to-news gateways:

- One gateway, at Digital Equipment in Palo Alto, California, is decwrl.dec.com. To submit an article to a newsgroup, mail the article to the group name with .usenet@ decwrl.dec.com added to the end. To submit an article to the rec.travel newsgroup, for example, mail the article to rec.travel.usenet@decwrl.dec.com.
- The other gateway, at the University of Texas, is cs.utexas.edu. A newsgroup's mailing address is the group name with periods changed to hyphens (rec-travel@cs.utexas.edu, for example).

Although possible, sending messages to groups you can't read is really tacky. (This type of message usually ends, "Please send me e-mail because I don't read this group.") If you're interested in a group's topic, find a way to read the group. For all you know, your point has been made three times a week for the past year, or someone answered your question yesterday.

URLs for newsgroups

Newsgroups use a URL that starts with *news:*. A newsgroup URL is useful if you want to use a Web browser to read newsgroup articles. The URL for a newsgroup looks like the following:

```
news:news.group.name
```

For example, the `rec.gardens.orchids` newsgroup is called

```
news:rec.gardens.orchids
```

Telnet: The Next Best Thing to Being There

Telnet is the classic service that lets you log in to other computers on the Net. Telnet's more interesting services are provided on nonstandard network ports (the standard telnet port is number 23; anything else is nonstandard). If you use a UNIX-based system, run telnet by giving the host name and, if it's nonstandard, the port number, as in the following:

```
telnet martini.eecs.umich.edu 3000
```

Occasionally you see a telnet address written as a URL, as in the following:

```
telnet://martini.eecs.umich.edu:3000/
```

You need the address in this URL format if you want to use a World Wide Web browser program for telnetting.

For more information on telnetting, see Chapter 19.

FTP: Files Delivered to Your Door

FTP (*File Transfer Protocol*) is a way of sending files from one Internet host to another. A computer that stores files for transfer is called a *file server,* or *FTP server.* To get the files, you run an *FTP client program.* On UNIX shell systems, the FTP client is called (strangely enough) ftp. If you use WinSock programs, you can use your Web browser or an FTP program. WS_FTP is a good shareware WinSock FTP client program. Most Internet software suites (such as Internet Chameleon) come with an FTP client program.

You don't need an account on many FTP servers in order to grab their files. Instead, you can use *anonymous FTP,* in which you use the username *anonymous* and your e-mail address as your password. Here's how:

1. **Start your FTP program by typing a command or clicking an icon (depending on the antiquatedness of your computer).**
2. **Connect to the server.**
3. **Log in by typing** anonymous **as your username and typing your e-mail address as the password.**
4. **Change to the directory that contains the files.**
5. **Set binary mode (unless it's a text file).**
6. **Get the file.**

Refer to Chapter 10 in *The Internet For Dummies,* 3rd Edition, for details about FTPing.

Let's face it, though: FTP is getting kind of long in the tooth. . . . Fortunately, two convenient — sneaky even — ways to get to FTP are available: Gopher and the Web.

Gophering to FTP

Many FTP servers are also Gopher servers. (The extra software required for a Gopher server can usually be added by a student in an afternoon, so what the heck.) The presence of files called `.cache`, which Gopher uses to speed up some retrievals, is a frequent clue that you have both an FTP and Gopher server. If you see files with the name `.cache`, you can be pretty sure that a Gopher server is lurking nearby. (See "Going for Gopher," later in this chapter for more on Gopher.)

In any event, seeing whether you can retrieve files with Gopher rather than with FTP doesn't hurt. On heavily loaded FTP servers, Gopher is often faster because fewer people use Gopher to retrieve files by using Gopher than by using FTP. You can also try name guessing. If an FTP site is called `ftp.std.com`, for example (that's the FTP server for our friends at The World, an Internet provider in Boston), a pretty good guess is that `gopher.std.com` is the Gopher server. See "Going for Gopher" for suggestions on how to use your Gopher program to connect to a particular Gopher host.

The Web meets FTP: URL that file

The World Wide Web, which we discuss in more detail in "Web Walking Wisdom," later in this chapter (and also in Chapter 4 of *The Internet For Dummies,* 3rd Edition), has built-in features that make the Web a good way to get files from

FTP servers. Any public FTP server has a Web URL that lets you look at the available directories and files. If the FTP server is called `sample.com` and the directory you want is `/pub/samplefiles`, the URL is

```
ftp://sample.com/pub/samplefiles
```

If you give this URL to your Web-browsing program (such as Netscape, Mosaic, WebSurfer, or Lynx), the program automatically takes care of the details of logging in to the server, retrieving directories, and so on. Conversely, if someone gives you this URL and you don't have a Web browser, don't worry @md you're not stuck. Fire up your FTP program, connect to `sample.com`, move to the `/pub` directory, and retrieve `samplefiles`.

Going for Gopher

Yet another system of organizing information on the Internet, Gopher is described in more detail in Chapter 20. Lots of Gopher pages are available (partly) because Gopher is a highly advanced information-retrieval system (but mostly because the Gopher server software is free and not hard to set up).

Gopher meets the Web and gets the URL

The following line shows the URL for a typical Gopher item:

```
gopher://akasha.tic.com:70/11/bruces
```

This line tells you that the host is `akasha.tic.com`, port 70 (the standard Gopher port, so you could have left out the port number) and that the host's pathname is `11/bruces`. Who knows exactly what `11/bruces` means, but if you ask Netscape or Mosaic to show this URL to you, they can find it. As with any URL, you can give this entire Gopher-type URL directly to a Web-browsing program, which scrounges up the menu for you.

You can also use a URL with a Gopher client, but surgery on the name is required first. The host name and port number are perfectly okay, but the path needs work. The problem is that Gopher items have types that are internally remembered as single digits and letters. Most notably, a Gopher menu is type 1, and a plain file is type 0. In a URL, the first character in the path part (the part after a single slash) of the URL is the item type (in this case, 1). So our earlier URL example refers to a Gopher menu (the first 1) whose actual path is `1/bruces` (the rest of the path). You type **1/bruces** for your Gopher path.

You can usually get away with leaving out the path on Gopher URLs. In almost every case, an empty path gives you the main Gopher menu for the server, and you can go through a few menus to find the item you want more easily than you can unscramble the path by hand.

UNIX Gopher

You can tell a Gopher program on a UNIX-based Internet system which Gopher item you want to see. Follow the `gopher` command that you type with the path, host, and port. To start at the Gopher menu discussed in the preceding section, you type `% gopher -p 1/bruces akasha.tic.com 70`.

If the path is empty (frequently the case for Gopher URLs), you can leave out the `-p` part. If the port is number 70, you can leave that number out also. To start at the top-level Gopher menu on the host in our example, you type `% gopher akasha.tic.com`.

Web Walking Wisdom

The World Wide Web is by far the coolest thing mortal Internauts can use. Unlike the other programs we mention, Web browsers use URLs directly.

What do you do if someone tells you the URL of a cool Web page or if you find a URL listed in this book? What you do varies a little depending on which Web program you use. Here are some hints for using Netscape and Mosaic, the most popular Web programs.

Getting to a URL by way of Netscape

Using Netscape, simply type the URL into the Location box near the top of the Netscape window and then press Enter. Netscape shows you that URL. Easy!

Getting to a URL by way of Mosaic

If you use any of the many Mosaic versions, choose File⇨Open from the menu. In the Windows version, you can also click the little open folder near the top of the window. In the UNIX version, you can click the Open button at the bottom of the window. No matter which version you're using, you type the URL in the window that pops up and then press Enter or click OK.

We often find URLs in Usenet messages we're reading. Lazy typists can find ways to avoid typing by copying and pasting the URL out of the news message, which saves time and is more accurate than retyping the URL. Here are a few ways:

- On UNIX, if you are reading Usenet news by using `trn` or another newsreader in an `xterm` window, use the mouse to select the URL (that is, move the mouse pointer to the beginning of the URL, press and hold the first mouse button, move to the end of the URL so that the URL is highlighted, and release the mouse button). Then move the pointer to the type-in box in the Mosaic Open pop-up window and press the middle mouse button. A friendly gnome types the selected URL into the window.
- In Windows, if you are reading Usenet news by using Trumpet or another newsreader, select the URL by using the mouse and press Ctrl+C to copy the URL to the Windows Clipboard. Then switch to your Web browser, choose File⇨Open, and press Ctrl+V to paste the URL in the window. Then click OK or Open to fetch the URL.

World Wide Web by telnet

If you don't have a Web browser such as Netscape, Mosaic, or Lynx available locally but you can telnet to other systems, telnet to a public Web system (see Table 5-2). Public Web systems don't let you view all the spiffy embedded graphics, but they're better than nothing. When asked to log in, type **www** as your username.

Table 5-2 Web Servers You Can Telnet To

Where	*Name*
New Jersey	`www.njit.edu`
Kansas	`lynx.cc.ukans.edu`
Switzerland	`info.cern.ch` or `telnet.w3.org`

Web pages by mail, for the desperate

If you simply can't find a Web browser and you can't telnet, try an e-mail server. Using the Web by e-mail is like playing chess by mail. To retrieve a Web page, send an e-mail to `listserv@info.cern.ch`. The text of the message should contain a line saying `SEND`, followed by the URL, as shown in the following example:

```
SEND http://www.w3.org/hypertext/DataSources/bySubject/
          Overview.html
```

(This Web page contains a list of Web servers, by the way.)

You may think that, because the Web gives you access to pretty much every resource on the Net, you can use the Web to retrieve giant binary files, read Usenet groups that aren't available at your site, and otherwise suck down gigabytes of data. Don't. The same thing has occurred to the people who run the Web server at W3 (the World Wide Web Consortium), and if people start abusing the mail server, it will go away. You can't get giant files anyway because each response is limited to 1,000 lines of text.

Don't Simply Take Our Word

Throughout this book, and especially in Chapter 22, you can find the URLs for information we find useful on the Net. But the Internet is growing like crazy, and new resources appear literally every day. Existing resources move or get shut down. The Internet is a moving target.

The Usenet group `comp.infosystems.announce` contains only announcements of new Internet resources, almost all of which are new Web pages or other resources, such as Gopher menus, you can use by way of the Web. This group is strictly moderated so that no extraneous messages appear. Messages are posted only once or twice a week, so monitoring the group doesn't take much time, and all sorts of interesting new stuff appears there.

Another good idea is to use a Web index or search service, such as those listed in Chapter 22, to find the information you are looking for.

Part II

Getting Your PC a SLIP/PPP Account

The 5th Wave
By Rich Tennant
©RICHTENNANT
IT'S FRICASSEE OF PYTHON WITH FRIED ANTS AND CRISPY GRASSHOPPERS.
YOU'RE GETTING RECIPES OFF THE INTERNET AGAIN, AREN'T YOU?

In this part . . .

If you use a PC and run Windows 3.1 or Windows 95, the Internet is a happening place. This part of the book talks about how to get your PC onto the Net in a whole new way so that it's actually a *full-fledged node* on the Internet. Once you do that (as described in Chapters 6 and 7 for Windows 3.1 and Chapter 8 for Windows 95), you can use spiffy new Windows-based programs to read your e-mail, browse through Usenet newsgroups, and surf the Web. No more ugly, outmoded, character-based programs for you!

And the best thing is that most of this fancy new software is available for downloading right off the Net! Some of it is free, and some is *shareware,* which means that you can try it before you pay for it, and the cost is very reasonable. Chapter 9 tells you how to download and install software from the Internet, and Chapter 10 describes cool programs you'll want to try.

Chapter 6

Getting Your Windows 3.1 PC on the Net

In This Chapter

- What are SLIP and PPP, and why do you care?
- What you need to connect to the Internet
- Installing SLIP and PPP software
- Telling your software about your Internet provider
- Making the SLIP or PPP connection
- What to do if your connection doesn't work
- Pinging another computer

Online services are easy to get started with but can be expensive if you use them for more than a few hours a month. UNIX shell accounts are boring — you can't use all the new snazzy graphical software, like Netscape. (If your Internet provider runs TIA or SLIRP, your shell account can pretend to be a SLIP account; see the sidebar "Shell users, don't despair; TIA is here.") So in this chapter, we talk about SLIP and PPP accounts, the coolest way to connect to the Net over the phone. We concentrate on software for Windows 3.1. This chapter helps you get the software you need (a shareware program called Trumpet WinSock), and the next chapter explains how to install and run it.

The three ways to get your computer on the Net are

- **Sign up for an online service.** In *The Internet For Dummies,* 3rd Edition, we describe how to sign up for and use America Online, CompuServe, and Microsoft Network. Part III of this book describes Prodigy, NetCom, and GNN.
- **Sign up for a UNIX shell account with an Internet provider.**
- **Sign up for a SLIP or PPP account with an Internet provider.**

In this chapter, we explain how to get your computer on the Internet by using a SLIP or PPP account and the Trumpet WinSock shareware TCP/IP package. We chose Trumpet WinSock because it's freely available shareware (we thought you'd like that). After you are connected, we describe how to use FTP, the program you need in order to get other WinSock programs from the Internet. In Chapter 9, we talk about how to get software from the Internet itself, and in Chapter 10, you find descriptions of other nifty Windows-based software your SLIP connection allows you to use, including programs for reading your mail, reading newsgroups, and browsing the Web.

Mac users, stop right here. You already have most of the software you need to connect to the Internet, because System 7.5 comes with MacTCP. Upgrade to System 7.5 to get it, or get a book about Macintoshes and the Internet that comes with a diskette. Windows 95 users need to go to Chapter 8.

What Are SLIP and PPP Again?

In case you took our advice and skipped all that technical stuff in Chapters 2 and 3, we'd better explain what SLIP is. Here are the three incomprehensible acronyms you need to know:

- *SLIP (Serial Line Internet Protocol)* allows your PC to connect to the Internet, not as a terminal, but as a full-fledged member of the Net, at least while your computer is on the phone to its Internet provider.
- *CSLIP (Compressed SLIP)* is the same idea as SLIP, but it's a little faster.
- *PPP (Point-to-Point Protocol)* is a fancier system that does more or less the same thing.

Because these three protocols are identical for our purposes, we refer to them all as SLIP. (If you care about the differences, which you probably don't, see Chapters 2 and 3.) All three are versions of IP (Internet Protocol), the underlying part of TCP/IP (Transmission Control Protocol/Internet Protocol), the way that all computers on the Internet communicate with each other. And all three are cool because many network operations are much simpler when your own computer is on the Net instead of acting as a terminal to someone else's big computer — programs running on your own computer can do much nicer sound, graphics, and animation than a terminal can.

The really cool thing about TCP/IP software is something called WinSock. *WinSock* (which stands for *Win*dows *Sock*ets — don't you love these names?) is a standard way for Windows programs to work with SLIP and PPP accounts. If your TCP/IP software does WinSock, you can run any WinSock application, such as Eudora for reading e-mail, Free Agent or News Xpress for checking out newsgroups, and Netscape for browsing the World Wide Web. Remarkably, many of the best WinSock applications are available for free on the Net.

SLIP and e-mail — a digression

When you use SLIP to communicate with your Internet SLIP provider, your lowly PC becomes a full-fledged node on the Internet. That is, your PC is now a *host* computer. This elevated status may entitle your PC to a name. For one PC, for example, we chose the name of our favorite five-year-old, `meg`. The full network address of your PC is its host name, followed by the name of your Internet provider. For example, we use a local provider, TIAC (The Internet Access Company), whose Internet address is `tiac.net`. So the address of the PC is `meg.tiac.net`. Not all providers assign host names to SLIP users, and some assign boring names like `slip247.gorgonzola.net`, but your SLIP account works just fine anyway.

The PC is not on the Net all the time, however — when the computer is turned off, for example, or not connected to the SLIP provider. Normally, incoming Internet mail is delivered directly to the recipient's computer. (See Chapter 2 for the gory details.) But when a PC is not connected to the Net, what happens to incoming mail? Do you really have to keep your computer on the phone 24 hours a day just to get your mail?

A good question, and we're glad you asked. No, you don't. SLIP Internet providers receive your mail for you and hold on to it until you next log in, at which point you can move your mail to your own computer. As long as your SLIP provider's computer is connected all the time (and you have a pretty poor provider if it's not), mail flows unimpeded.

This arrangement means that, as far as the rest of the Internet can tell, your mailbox is on your Internet provider's computer, not on your own PC. Your e-mail address is usually your login name, followed by an at sign (@), followed by your provider's address. We have a login called `margy` on TIAC, for example, whose address is `tiac.net`. So mail can come to `margy@tiac.net`. (But don't send us mail at that address — you get better results from `moreint2@dummies.com`, which connects you to *Internet For Dummies* Central, which is in fact on the Net continuously.)

A bunch of WinSock-compatible TCP/IP Internet connection packages are available for DOS and Windows. (See Chapter 21 in *The Internet For Dummies,* 3rd Edition, for a list.) All packages support WinSock, and most support SLIP and PPP. If your Windows computer is already set up with software that connects you to a SLIP account, you are in luck. Luckily, all WinSock programs work the same no matter which connection software is running underneath. So if you already have a WinSock-compatible SLIP or PPP connection, skip the connection part of this chapter and Chapter 8 (which is about Windows 95) and go to Chapter 9.

When you are online with your Internet SLIP provider, your computer is *on* the Net. Conversely, when you hang up with your provider, your computer drops off the Internet. If someone wants to look at a Web page that you store on your own computer and you're not on the phone, your page doesn't appear. Not staying online all the time isn't a big problem for most people — see Chapter 14 for where to store your Web pages.

SLIP connections are easy enough to use, but they can be tricky to set up. Installing and setting up TCP/IP software require entering lots of scary-looking numeric Internet addresses, host names, communications ports — you name it. If this subject makes you nervous, consider getting our book *The Internet For Windows For Dummies Starter Kit* (written by us and published by IDG Books Worldwide, Inc.), which comes with TCP/IP and WinSock software that sets up your SLIP account and automagically does all the configuration work for you. (You can use the book's software free for 30 days, and then you pay a modest charge to register it permanently after that.)

Still with us? Right now may also be a good time to find a local Internet expert and ask for help in getting your TCP/IP software and SLIP connection set up. Having in hand a plate of cookies, particularly freshly baked ones, when you ask for help is never a bad idea.

Getting a SLIPped Disk

Okay, you are raring to go. What are the steps you need to follow? And what hardware and software are you going to need?

The big picture, SLIPwise

To get your Windows PC set up for SLIP or PPP:

1. **Arrange for a SLIP or PPP account from a local provider.**

   In the section "Who Will Provide?" later in this chapter, we give you ideas for how to choose one.

2. **Get the basic TCP/IP software loaded into your computer somehow, either from a disk or over the phone.**

   Use the software your SLIP provider gives you, if any, or follow the instructions in "Tuning In to Channel 1," later in this chapter, to get Trumpet WinSock by downloading it from a BBS named Channel 1®.

3. **Type about a thousand setup parameters.**

   Don't worry — we tell you what they are.

4. **Crank up your TCP/IP program and fiddle with it until it works.**

After doing so, you can go on to load the swell applications described in Chapter 10.

Have you got what it takes?

Hardware- and softwarewise, here's what you need to cruise the Net:

- **A modem that connects your computer to a phone line.** The faster, the better. Try to get a modem that talks at 9600 bps (bits per second), 14.4 Kbps, or even 28.8 Kbps. Otherwise, things are going to be sluggish.
- **A phone line (you probably guessed that).** Make sure that your phone line doesn't have call-waiting. If it does, you need to type ***70** or **1170** at the beginning of your provider's phone number to tell your phone company to turn off call-waiting for this phone call.
- **TCP/IP software that does SLIP or one of its variants.** We tell you how to get this software in "Tuning In to Channel 1," later in this chapter. Chapter 7 explains how to install it and get connected to your new Internet account.
- **Software for getting your mail, reading newsgroups, and so on.** We talk about these things in Chapter 10.
- **A SLIP or PPP account with an Internet provider and a bunch of technical information about the account (described in the next section).**

If your PC is on a local-area network, things get confusing. You have to talk to your network administrator to find out how to get connected to the Internet, with or without SLIP. Rather than connect your individual PC, your network may use a gateway to connect the entire local-area network to the Internet.

Who Will Provide?

To use WinSock software, you need a SLIP or PPP account. (Actually, you may be able to use a UNIX shell account; see the sidebar "Shell users, don't despair; TIA is here." Some online services can work with WinSock, too, like America Online, CompuServe, GNN, and Netcom.) Dozens of national Internet providers have phone numbers all over the U.S., and hundreds, probably thousands, by now, of regional and local providers have phone numbers in limited areas. Be sure to find a provider that

- Offers SLIP, CSLIP, or PPP accounts
- Has a phone number that is a local call for you so that you don't have to pay long-distance phone charges
- Has reasonable phone support
- You can afford (otherwise, you never use it!)

Can online services do it?

Some online services let you use WinSock software. So if you already have an online account, consider using it for running Netscape, Agent, and that other cool WinSock stuff. Here's the rundown on the major online services:

- America Online works with WinSock software. Go to keyword **WinSock** to find out what to do. We describe using America Online with WinSock software in Chapter 13 of *The Internet For Dummies,* 3rd Edition, too.
- CompuServe works with WinSock software. You have to use its NetLauncher software, described in Chapter 12 of *The Internet For Dummies,* 3rd Edition.
- Prodigy can't work with WinSock software (at least not as of early 1996).
- Netcom can support WinSock software — see Chapter 12. Its NetCruiser software can even search your disk for WinSock programs that you have installed.
- GNN works fine with WinSock software. We explain how to use GNN in Chapter 13.

Where to look for a provider

To find an Internet provider

- Look in your local newspaper, especially in the business pages.
- Ask friends what providers they use.
- Ask the reference librarian at the local public library.
- Find someone who has an online account, and go to the following Web site, which contains a huge listing of Internet providers by area code:

```
http://thelist.com/
```

Chapter 20 in *The Internet For Dummies,* 3rd Edition, contains more information about how to find an Internet provider.

When you open your account, ask your Internet provider if it has software you can use. Many providers give you a disk containing a nice set of freeware and shareware software for connecting to the Net, along with instructions.

Shell users, don't despair; TIA is here

If you have a UNIX shell account, you may be able to get it to act like a SLIP or PPP account. Talk to your Internet provider's support folks and find out if they can run TIA, The Internet Adapter. TIA makes a shell account pretend to be a SLIP account so that you can use all the neat WinSock software we talk about in Chapter 10.

If your Internet provider has never heard of TIA, tell it to e-mail InterMind at `tia-host-pricing@marketplace.com`.

Another package called SLIRP does much the same thing as TIA, so if your provider supports that package, you can also do SLIP.

Ask your provider

Before you can use a TCP/IP program to connect to your SLIP or PPP account, you need a bunch of scary-looking technical information. Ask your Internet provider for this information and write it down in Table 6-1:

Table 6-1 Information about Your SLIP Connection

Information	*Description*	*Example*
Your domain name	The name of your Internet provider's domain. It looks like the last part of an Internet address and usually ends with `.net` or `.com` (in the U.S., anyway).	`dummies.com`
Your communications port	The communications port on your own computer to which your modem is attached, usually COM1 or COM2. Even if your modem lives inside your computer and doesn't look as though it is connected to a port, it is.	COM1
Your modem speed	The fastest speed that both your modem and your Internet provider's modem can go. If your modem can go at 9600 or 14.4 Kbps, for example, but your Internet provider can handle only 9600 bps, choose 9600 bps. Conversely, if your modem can do only 2400 bps (which will seem really slow when you get connected), choose 2400 bps	14.4 Kbps

(continued)

Table 6-1 *(continued)*

Information	***Description***	***Example***
Your modem	The kind of modem you have. Actually, WinSock packages are only dimly aware of the details of different kinds of modems. A regular PC-type modem is probably similar enough to a Hayes model to fool the programs we're using here.	Hayes
Phone number	The number you call to connect to your Internet provider, exactly as you would dial it by hand. If it is long distance, include the *1* and the area code at the beginning. If you have to dial 9 and pause a few seconds to get an outside line, include *9,,* at the beginning (each comma tells your modem to pause for about a second, so stick in extra commas as needed to get the timing right).	1-607-555-1234
User name	The name on your account with your Internet provider, also called a *login* name.	`myoung`
User password	The password for your account.	friedrice
Start-up command	The command your Internet provider should run when you call in. Your Internet provider can tell you this command. If the provider starts SLIP right away when you log in, you may not need a start-up command, so you may be able to leave this entry blank when the time comes to type it in.	SLIP
Domain name server (DNS) address	The numeric Internet address of the computer that can translate between regular Internet addresses and their numeric equivalents (between `dummies.com` and `205.238.207.67`, for example). Your Internet provider should give you this address.	`123.45.67.99`

Information	Description	Example
Interface type	Exact type of interface used by the provider. The three choices are SLIP, CSLIP, and PPP. Trumpet WinSock handles only SLIP and CSLIP. If your software and provider handle it, use PPP; the next-best choice is CSLIP; and the worst (but still okay) choice is SLIP.	PPP
MTU	Some providers limit the sizes of individual packets of data sent over the SLIP link, the *maximum transfer unit (MTU)*. If your provider has an MTU, it lets you know.	
Your own numeric Internet address	Your PC's own numeric Internet address Although it is for your computer, you get this number from your Internet provider. Some providers issue you a number each time you call, in which case they don't give you a permanent number.	`123.45.67.89`
Your own host name	The name of your computer. Most Internet providers don't give each user's computer a name, but if yours does, make it short and spellable, and perhaps cute.	`meg`

Where Does All This Software Come From?

You can find a TCP/IP program that connects your computer to the Internet using a SLIP or PPP account in several places:

- **Your Internet provider may offer the program on a disk.** That's certainly the easiest way to get it. If your Internet provider gives you software, use it. That way, when you call for help, your provider knows what to do (one hopes!). But note that the software your provider gives you is probably shareware — which means that you are honor-bound to send a donation to the author if you use it. See the section "Doing Your Part" in Chapter 10.
- **Your Internet provider may make the program available from a shell account.** You use Windows Terminal (or a better terminal program, such as Procomm, if you have it) to download it.

- **You can get the program from a BBS.** We've arranged with Channel 1, a large BBS in Cambridge, Massachusetts, to make the basic files for Trumpet WinSock (a widely used shareware WinSock-compatible TCP/IP program) available at no charge. Calling Channel 1 and downloading the software is a bit of a hassle, but if you don't have another way to get it, Channel 1 gets you off the ground. (If you are in the Boston area, consider using Channel 1 for your Internet provider, too!)

The programs you need

Assuming that you plan to use the shareware Trumpet WinSock program, you need three programs to get going:

- **Trumpet WinSock is the actual TCP/IP connection program.** You can follow our instructions to get the software from Channel 1. If you get a copy from your Internet provider, the program may be contained in a file called `TWSKnn.ZIP` (where *nn* tells you the version of Trumpet WinSock). On Channel 1, the file is named TWSK21F.EXE (for version 2.1). If a later version comes out, the filename may contain a different number.
- **An FTP program, which you can use for transferring other programs from the Internet.** Chapter 10 in *The Internet For Dummies,* 3rd Edition, describes how FTP works. Any FTP program will do. If you use Channel 1 to get your software, you get a freeware program called WS_FTP, stored in a file named WS_FTP16.EXE.
- **A ping program, which is a little program that tests your Internet connection.** Ping isn't absolutely necessary, but it's very useful when you are getting your SLIP or PPP account set up. Trumpet WinSock comes with a ping program, which is darned nice.

Matching up your WinSocks

You may have available full or sampler versions of commercial Windows TCP/IP packages from vendors such as NetManage's Chameleon or Frontier's SuperTCP. Windows 95 comes with its own WinSock — see Chapter 8 for instructions on how to use it.

If you have one of these products available, you may as well use that package rather than Trumpet WinSock because the commercial versions tend to be somewhat better supported and sometimes faster. Part of the charm of WinSock is that it is an actual standard, so no matter which version of WinSock you have, you can install and run the other WinSock applications we describe.

What if I'm already on a network?

If your PC is already connected to a network via a modem, you can still use Trumpet WinSock to communicate by way of SLIP. Just be sure that no other program is trying to use your modem at the same time as Trumpet WinSock does.

Configuring Trumpet WinSock to use a real Ethernet network rather than a modem is also possible, but the instructions for doing so are, unfortunately, way beyond what we can print here. The details depend on the type of network, the particular brand and model of network card installed in your computer, and what (if any) other network software is already installed.

Whoever runs your existing network is the right person to talk to, to find out whether also installing Trumpet WinSock makes sense.

A home for your programs

Before you begin filling your computer's disk with network software, you have to make a directory in which to put these new programs. You can use this directory for the programs you download in this chapter in addition to useful little programs you find on the Net. In Windows File Manager, move to the directory in which you want to create the new directory (probably the root, a.k.a. C:\), and choose File⇨Create Directory. In the rest of the book, we call it C:\INTERNET.

If you don't already have one, you should also make a directory for storing things temporarily. You need the directory when installing the software you are about to download from Channel 1. We recommend calling the directory C:\TEMP.

Tuning In to Channel 1

Here's how to download (copy) the TCP/IP software from a BBS called Channel 1. If you have a computer and a modem (which you need to connect to the Internet, after all), you can dial Channel 1 and download the latest versions of the TCP/IP software for free. (Note: Channel 1 has provided, as of this book's printing, a menu so that, by following the rest of this section, you have easy access to this software.)

We assume that your Windows computer is plugged in and turned on, as is your modem (if it's the kind of modem with its own on-off switch), and that they're connected. If not, consult *Modems For Dummies* (by Tina Rathbone and published by IDG Books Worldwide, Inc.), which discusses the secrets of modems in far more detail than we can do here.

If you already have the requisite files on disk, you can skip the next section on downloading them from Channel 1.

Channel which?

Begun in 1985 and holder of the cyberspace trademark for the first of 5 billion channels, Channel 1 of Cambridge, Massachusetts, is one of the oldest and largest bulletin board systems in the world. In this age of the Internet, Channel 1 now provides its members Internet e-mail, a Web browser, and a huge collection of freeware and shareware programs to download. It also provides design, site-creation, and hosting services for personal and business Web applications.

For more information on Channel 1's Internet services, contact Channel 1 at Channel 1, P.O. Box 338, Cambridge, MA 02238, at `info@channel1.com`, or call 617-864-0100.

Running a terminal program

To call Channel 1, you need to use a terminal program, like Windows Terminal. (If you have a terminal program you prefer, go ahead and use it.)

1. **From the Accessories window in the Program Manager, run Windows Terminal, the World's Most Generic Terminal Program.**

   (To be fair, it's the World's Most Generic Windows Terminal Program.) If you have another terminal program you like better, feel free to use it.

2. **From the Terminal menu, choose Settings⇨Phone Number and set the phone number to something appropriate (1-617-354-3230, if you have a 14,400 bps modem, for example). Then click OK.**

   See the sidebar "The many phone numbers of Channel 1" for a list of phone numbers you can use. If you have to dial something special before the number (a 9 for an outside line, for example), put it before the number. If you're making a long-distance call, change the Timeout field from 30 to 60 seconds.

3. **Choose Settings⇨Terminal Emulation and be sure that it's set to DEC VT-100. Click OK again.**

   The DEC VT-100 is a kind of ancient computer terminal that Channel 1 is prepared to talk to, so your PC pretending to be one is a good idea.

4. **Choose Settings⇨Terminal Preferences and set the Terminal Font to Terminal. Click OK again.**

   If you don't, some BBS menus are unreadable.

5. **Choose Settings⇨Binary Transfers and be sure that Kermit is selected. Click OK when you have done so.**

   If you are using a better communications program than Windows Terminal, select ZMODEM if possible, otherwise YMODEM, and otherwise Kermit.

The many phone numbers of Channel 1

Any large BBS has a zillion phone numbers. If you want to download the software from Channel 1, you have to use at least one of these numbers. (In case it's not obvious, use the number that corresponds to the fastest speed your modem can handle.) If you happen to be a local call from Cambridge, Massachusetts, you can leave out the 1-617.

14,400 bps	1-617-354-3230
28,000 bps	1-617-349-1300
USR Dual Standard modems	1-617-354-3137

Channel 1 is a busy place, and you may occasionally get a busy signal or no answer. Don't worry — just call back.

6. **Choose Settings⇨Communications and be sure that the parameters are set appropriately for your modem. (See Figure 6-1.) Then click OK to save the settings.**

   The Baud Rate (really bits per second) should be 19200, unless your modem runs at 2400 bps or slower, in which case you should use the actual modem speed. Flow Control should be set to Hardware, Connector should be COM1, unless your modem is attached to a different port, and Carrier Detect should be checked.

   If you don't know what you are doing, leave these settings alone and proceed. Maybe everything will work (cross your fingers!).

7. **Choose Settings⇨Modem Commands to check what kind of modem the program thinks you have.**

   You see the Modem Commands dialog box. If you have a modem that works like a Hayes modem (most do), click Hayes in the Modem Defaults box. Don't click OK yet — the next step uses the Modem Commands dialog box, too.

8. **If your phone line uses click rather than tone dialing, change the Dial Prefix from *ATDT* (short for Ahoy There, Dial the Telephone) to *ATDP* (short for Ahoy There, Dial the Phone). Then click OK.**

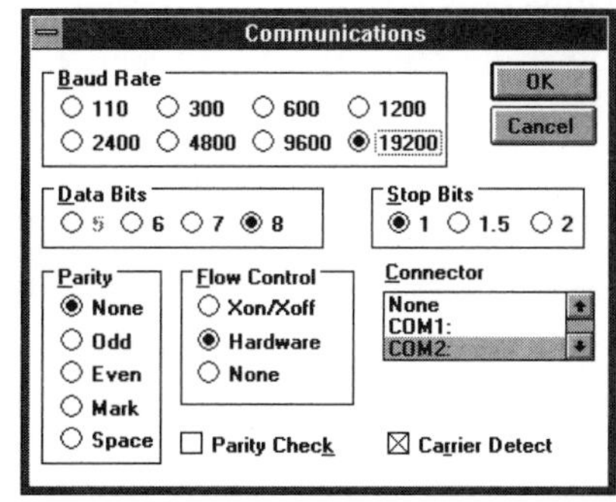

Figure 6-1: Tell the Windows Terminal program how to talk to your modem, if you dare.

At this point, saving the setup parameters is smart so that you don't have to do all this again if you have to call back.

9. **Choose File➪Save As and name your configuration CHANNEL1.TRM.**

   The next time you use Windows Terminal, you can choose File➪Open and double-click CHANNEL1, and all the settings are restored.

   Finally, you are ready to call Channel 1 and log in.

Note: If you want to call Channel 1 again later, run Terminal and choose File➪Open to open the CHANNEL1.TRM configuration file. Poof! All your terminal settings are ready to use.

Making the call

You're ready to dial the phone and connect to Channel 1. You need about 1MB of free disk space to store the file you're going to download. You also need about 10 minutes (or more, depending on how fast your modem is) to connect and transfer the file.

1. **From the Windows Terminal menu, choose Phone➪Dial.**

   Terminal dials the phone and connects to Channel 1. If it doesn't, check the phone number. If your modem has a speaker, what you hear should give you a clue about what went wrong. (Did you need a 9 to dial out? Forget the area code? Get a busy signal?)

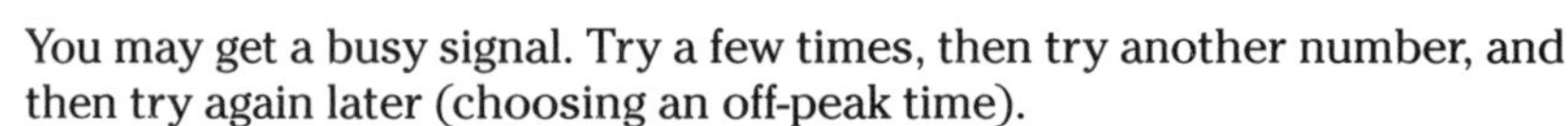

   You may get a busy signal. Try a few times, then try another number, and then try again later (choosing an off-peak time).

   When you connect, Channel 1 gives you a list of languages in which you can work.

2. **If you find English adequate for your computing needs, press Enter. Then you're asked whether you want color prompts. Press Enter again for No.**

   (Color prompts are cute, but they're slow.)

   Finally you're asked for your first and last names.

3. **When asked for your first name, type** internet dummies **and press Enter.**

4. **If you're asked something like *Scan Message Base Since 'Last Read'?* press** N.

   You see a list of files, like the list in Figure 6-2. Your list may be different because Channel 1 may update the files or add new ones to the list.

5. **Press the number for downloading Trumpet WinSock and then press Enter.**

   The option is probably item 1 on the menu, but if Channel 1 changes the list, it may not be.

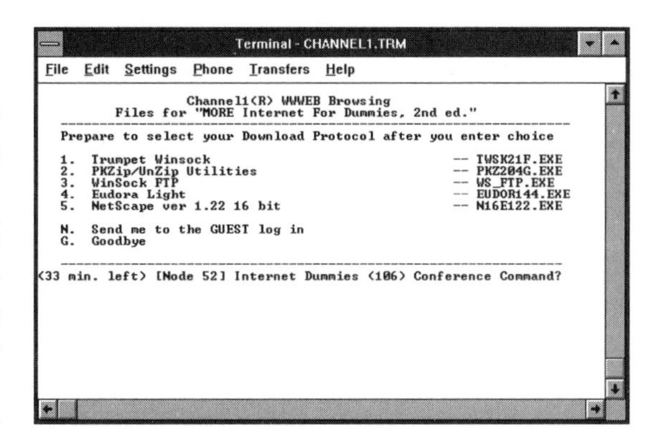

Figure 6-2: Channel 1 has a menu of files just for readers of this book!

6. **When Channel 1 asks for the protocol type for the transfer, press** K **and then press Enter.**

   That is, tell Channel 1 that you want to use the Kermit protocol. If you set your terminal program to use XMODEM, press **X**. For YMODEM or ZMODEM, press (you guessed it) **Y** or **Z**.

   Channel 1 should tell you a few things about the file, such as how long downloading takes, and then say something like

   ```
   , Sz* @-#Y1~^
   ```

   which means "hello" in Kermit-ese.

   If you need to interrupt the file transfer, press Ctrl+X.

7. **Note the name of the file Channel 1 is sending you, which appears on a line that begins *File Selected.***

   You're going to need to know the filename in a minute.

8. **Choose Transfers⇨Receive Binary File.**

   You see a dialog box that you can use to tell Terminal where to store the file you are about to receive.

9. **Choose the directory you want to put the file in (use the directory you usually use for storing files temporarily, which is usually called C:\TEMP) and a filename (use the same one it already has).**

   The filename for Trumpet WinSock is something like TWSK21F.EXE. Be sure to use the EXE filename extension for the file because it's an executable file (as you see in the next chapter).

   The file begins arriving. Look at the Download Time line to see Channel 1's estimate for how long the file will take to transfer. The time should be just a few minutes. Don't worry — the transfer is free — although you do have to pay long-distance phone charges, unless you live in the Boston area.

Windows Terminal displays a bar at the bottom of the window saying that it's downloading the file, with a counter that begins counting the amount of data received. The warnings that Kermit is slow are indeed true, so downloading is a good time to run down the hall for a cup of coffee or other beverage of your choice.

When the downloading is done, you see the message `Transfer successful, Internet`. (Channel 1 thinks that your first name is *Internet* and your last name is *Dummies* because of the way you logged in. Don't sweat it.)

10. **Press Enter to continue.**

    You see the same menu you saw after step 4.

11. **Repeat steps 5 through 10 to download WS_FTP, a file transfer program for use on the Internet.**

    Name the WS_FTP program file using its Channel 1 filename, which is something like WS_FTP16.EXE (that is, the Windows 3.1 *16-bit* version of WS_FTP).

    You're finished downloading the vital stuff.

12. **If you live close to Boston and you don't mind spending another half hour online with Channel 1, you may want to download Eudora (an excellent e-mail program) and Netscape (a Web browser), too.**

    If you are paying long-distance charges, skip these programs. You can download them later over the Internet (Chapter 9 tells you how to do so). Chapter 10 describes Eudora, Netscape, and lots of other cool software you may want to try.

13. **Press** G **for Good-bye to hang up.**

14. **Leave Windows Terminal by choosing File⇨Exit.**

Now you've got the Trumpet WinSock program and an FTP program, which you use in Chapter 10 for downloading other interesting programs. Nice work — in the next chapter, we install 'em!

Chapter 7

Sound the Trumpet WinSock!

In This Chapter

- Installing Trumpet WinSock and Trumpet Ping
- Making the SLIP or PPP connection
- Pinging another computer
- Installing WS_FTP, your friendly FTP program

This chapter describes how to install Trumpet WinSock, a program that allows your Windows 3.1 machine to connect to a SLIP or PPP account from an Internet provider. If this sounds like what you want to do, but you skipped Chapter 6, back up and read Chapter 6 now.

If you followed the instructions in Chapter 6, you now have the software you need to get connected to your SLIP or PPP account. You either got them by downloading them from Channel 1, or you got similar files from your provider. Before you can use the files, you have to unzip them and install them. Don't worry — doing so is much easier than the stuff you did in Chapter 6.

If you got the software from Channel 1, you've got these two files (the filenames may be slightly different, if you have more recent versions that the ones we list):

TWSK21F.EXE	Trumpet WinSock Version 2.1
WS_FTP16.EXE	WS_FTP, the FTP program (this is the version for Windows 3.1)

A note to people who skipped Chapter 5 because they have a floppy disk with software: Follow your provider's instructions for installing the program.

Installing Trumpet WinSock and WS_FTP

Here's how to install Trumpet WinSock and WS_FTP from the files you downloaded from Channel 1. You'll end up with an icon for each program in Windows Program Manager.

1. **In Windows File Manager, move the files into your C:\INTERNET directory, or wherever you've decided to store Internet software.**

   That is, move the files if they aren't already in that directory.

2. **Still in File Manager, double-click both of the filenames you downloaded.**

   Double-click them one at a time, if you know what we mean.

   The files you downloaded are named TWSK21F.EXE and WS_FTP16.EXE, or similar names. Each file automagically self-extracts, which means that the compressed files contained in each file pop out.

   Next, create a program group in Windows Program Manager for the icons for your Internet programs to appear in.

3. **In Windows Program Manager, choose File⇨New, click Program Group, and click OK.**

   You see the Program Group Properties dialog box.

4. **In the Description box, type** Internet Software **or whatever you want to call the new program group. Then click OK.**

   You see a new, blank program group in Program Manager.

5. **Create an icon for Trumpet WinSock by dragging the TCPMAN.EXE filename from File Manager to the program group you just created.**

   To make this work, you need Program Manager and File Manager open at the same time, and the new program group must be visible. When you drag the filename to the new program group, a lovely little trumpet icon appears.

   The icon is called *Tcpman,* which means TCP (the communications protocol you're going to use) Manager. You can rename the icon *Trumpet,* if you like, by selecting the icon, pressing Alt+Enter to display its properties, and editing the name.

6. **Create an icon for the Trumpet Ping program by dragging the TRUMPING.EXE filename to the new program group.**

   You see a little PING icon entitled *Trumping.* (Sounds like you're going to be playing bridge.)

7. **If you want easy access to the Trumpet help file, create an icon for it by dragging the filename TRUMPWSL.HLP to the new program group.**

   You see a question-mark icon.

8. **Create an icon for WS_FTP by dragging the WS_FTP.EXE filename to the new program group.**

   You see a new icon that shows a power cord being plugged in. Yes, you've got power now!

Cool! You've got a bunch of new icons, looking very official in Program Manager, as shown in Figure 7-1.

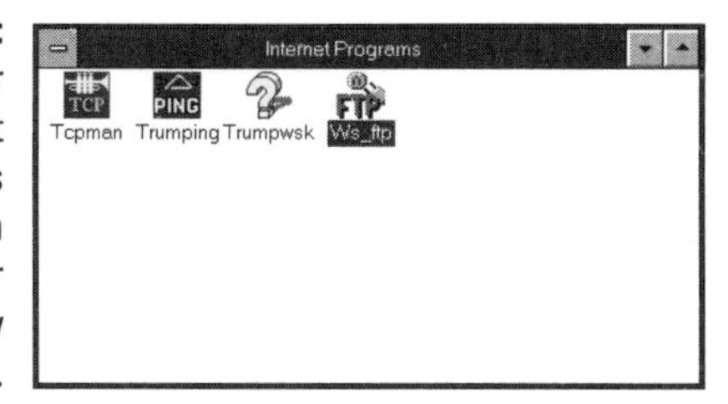

Figure 7-1: Here is your Internet Programs group with icons for your new programs.

This all seems awfully complicated

By this time, you're probably wondering whether all this clicking, typing, and installing will ever end and whether a simpler way perhaps exists.

The answer to the first question is yes, it will end. This stuff is a pain in the neck to get set up, but after it's set up, it's actually pretty easy to use — two or three clicks to start a network connection and later another two or three clicks to shut it down.

The answer to the second question is, um, well, yeah, it could be considerably easier. A nice full-screen setup program should prompt you through the standard questions. (Although, in defense of Trumpet WinSock, we have installed many commercial TCP/IP packages, and most of them aren't a heck of a lot better.) So for the moment, you just have to keep slogging.

Telling Windows Where to Find the Program

The directory containing Trumpet WinSock must be on your *path,* that is, on the list of directories in which DOS and Windows look for programs. To edit your path

1. **Run Windows Notepad.**

   Its icon is usually in the Accessories program group in Program Manager.

2. **Open the file C:\AUTOEXEC.BAT by choosing File⇨Open and choosing the filename.**

   This file contains DOS commands that are run automatically when you start your computer.

3. **Find the line that begins with the word *path* and add the following to the end of it:**

   ```
   ;c:\internet
   ```

   That is, type a semicolon at the end of the existing path statement and type the pathname of the directory that contains Trumpet WinSock. If you put Trumpet WinSock in a directory other than C:\INTERNET, include the name of the directory where you stored it.

   Don't type any spaces in the path command. DOS is very stupid about dealing with spaces.

4. **Choose File⇨Save to save your updated AUTOEXEC.BAT file.**

5. **Choose File⇨Exit to leave Windows Notepad.**

6. **Exit from Windows and reboot.**

Now DOS and Windows can find the Trumpet WinSock program files, as well as any other program files you store in the same directory.

Telling Trumpet WinSock Where Your Modem Is

Trumpet WinSock (alias Tcpman) tries your first communications port (COM1) to see if your modem might be attached to it. If it's not, you need to tell Tcpman where your modem is.

1. **Double-click the Tcpman icon to start the Trumpet WinSock program.**

   You see a message explaining that you are going to have to register the program if you want to use it for more than 30 days. Fair enough — this is shareware, after all, not freeware.

2. **Assuming that it's okay with you to pay a modest sum to use all this neat software (Trumpet WinSock and its Ping program), click Accept.**

   You should see a window like the one shown in Figure 7-2. If you do, skip down to the next section, "Telling Trumpet WinSock about Your Internet Provider." If you see a message saying `Unable to load TCP` you need to tell Trumpet where your modem is.

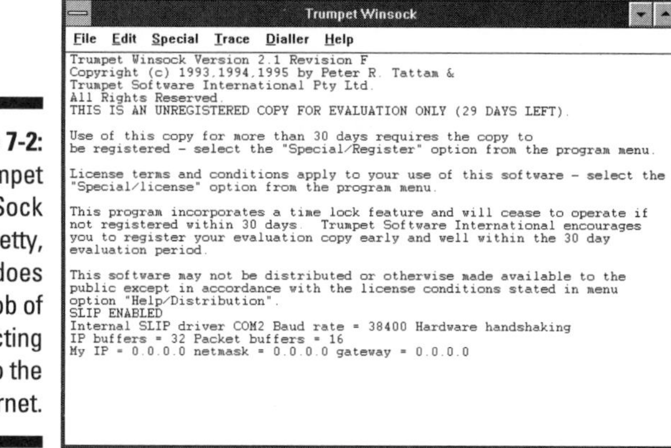

Figure 7-2: Trumpet WinSock isn't pretty, but it does the job of connecting you to the Internet.

3. **Click OK to make the message go away.**

   You see a window containing a whole bunch of text, ending with a message that says `Unable to open COM1 — Hardware is not available`; your modem is not attached to COM1, the first communications port on your computer.

4. **Choose File⇨Setup from the Trumpet menu.**

   You see the Trumpet WinSock Setup dialog box, shown in Figure 7-3. It's a scary-looking box, but stay calm.

5. **Change the SLIP port setting from 1 (that is, the COM1 port) to the number of the communications port your modem is attached to.**

   For example, if your modem is attached to your COM2 port, change the SLIP port setting to 2. Refer to the entry for your communications port that you made in Table 6-1.

Figure 7-3: Tell Trumpet WinSock how your modem is attached to your computer and how to connect to your Internet provider.

6. **Click Ok twice, once on the dialog box and once on the message box that appears.**

   Trumpet WinSock advises you that you need to restart the program for this change to take effect.

7. **Taking Trumpet WinSock's advice, exit from the program by choosing File⇨Exit and then restart the program by double-clicking its icon.**

Telling Trumpet WinSock about Your Internet Provider

Now you can fill in the fields in the Trumpet WinSock Setup dialog box based on information from your SLIP provider, referring to the notes you made in Table 6-1. Here's how to tell Trumpet WinSock about your particular Internet SLIP provider and who you are.

1. **If you're not already running Trumpet WinSock, double-click the Trumpet icon to start the program.**

2. **Choose File⇨Setup from the Trumpet menu.**

   You see the Trumpet WinSock Setup dialog box, shown in Figure 7-3.

3. **Click the box called Internal SLIP or Internal PPP, depending on whether you have a SLIP or PPP account.**

   Refer back to Table 6-1, where you wrote down the interface type. If you have a CSLIP account, also click the Van Jacobson CSLIP compression box.

4. **Enter your IP address.**

   That is, enter your computer's numeric Internet address. If your system uses "floating" addresses assigned each time you connect, leave this setting as zeros. The IP address is always in the form of four numbers (each between 0 and 255) separated by dots.

5. **Enter your Name server.**

   Enter the numeric Internet address of the provider's computer that handles decoding computer host names.

6. **Leave the Time server box blank.**

   It doesn't do anything useful.

7. **Enter your Domain suffix.**

   Type the domain name in which your computer will live, which is your computer's name omitting the first part. For example, because one of our computer's names is `chico.iecc.com`, its domain suffix is `iecc.com`. (Take a look at the note you made next to the "Your domain name" entry in Table 6-1.)

8. **Enter your MTU.**

   Enter the maximum data packet size that your provider can handle efficiently. If your provider doesn't give you an MTU, use the MSS (described in step 10, coming right up) plus 40, so if the MSS is 512, the MTU is 552, and if the MSS is 255, the MTU is 295.

   MTUs are used only with the SLIP and CSLIP accounts, so forget it if you have a PPP account.

9. **Enter your TCP RWIN, whatever that is.**

   Yes, it's another magic parameter. Leave it as 4096 unless your provider gives you a different value.

10. **Enter your TCP MSS.**

    This is a third magic parameter. Unless your provider gives you a different value, leave it as 512 if you have a SLIP connection and 255 for CSLIP connections.

11. **Leave the Demand load timeout (secs) as 5 seconds.**

12. **Enter a Baud rate.**

    Enter 38400 if you have a 486 or Pentium, or 19200 if you have a 386.

13. **Leave the Hardware handshaking box checked, unless you have a really cruddy old modem that doesn't properly signal the computer when the remote end connects.**

    If you run into trouble disconnecting from your Internet provider and you have an old modem, try clearing the Hardware handshaking box.

14. **Select your Online status detection method.**

    Select DCD (RLSD) unless you have a cruddy old modem, in which case leave it at None. This selection tells Trumpet how to know when you are connected to your Internet provider.

15. **Recheck all those settings to be sure they're right and then click Ok.**

    A box appears, warning you that you have to restart Trumpet WinSock for your changes to take effect. (Just Trumpet WinSock, not all of Windows.)

16. **Click OK.**

    (How come this button is named "OK" when the one on the dialog box was named "Ok"? This kind of thing drives our editors crazy!) The regular Trumpet WinSock window appears.

17. **Choose File⇨Exit to leave Trumpet WinSock and then double-click its icon in Program Manager to restart it (cognizant of all of the swell things you've told it).**

If you have to go back and change anything, you can get back to this dialog box by choosing File⇨Setup from the Trumpet WinSock menu.

Actually Making an Actual SLIP or PPP Connection

Thought this moment would never come, eh? Well, it's about time. You can tell Trumpet WinSock to dial and make a connection in two ways (one way would be too simple — computers are involved here): the manual way and the automatic way. The manual way is extremely manual: You type commands directly to your modem to make the connection and start the SLIP, CSLIP, or PPP session and then tell Trumpet WinSock to go ahead. The automatic way involves a script that tells Trumpet WinSock what to send to the modem, what to expect from the remote system, what to type next, and so on until the connection is made. The manual way works perfectly well if you don't mind doing the typing every time, although we find that setting up the automatic way is worth the effort.

Dial Ho!

"All right, already," you're doubtless saying. "Let's cut to the chase." Okay. Your Trumpet WinSock program should be configured to know about your Internet provider if you followed the steps in the last section.

The baud rate, handshaking, compression, and IP numbers in the Trumpet WinSock window reflect what you told Trumpet WinSock when you typed the zillion setup numbers.

1. **Choose Dialler⇨Manual login.**

   (Dialler's not misspelled — the author's from Australia.) Trumpet WinSock should say

   ```
   AFTER LOGGING IN, TYPE THE <ESC> KEY TO RETURN TO NORMAL
         SLIP PROCESSING.
   SLIP (or PPP) DISABLED
   ```

   Not being clairvoyant, you may not be able to guess that this message is Trumpet WinSock's way of telling you to begin typing.

2. **Type whatever command your modem needs to get it ready to dial the phone.**

   For our modem, we get its attention by typing **AT** and then a command that tells it always to use the port connection speed (&B1) that we programmed in regardless of the connection speed at the other end and to use hardware modem flow control (&H1).

   Sorry to say, modem command settings are among the least well standardized features of the PC biz. You can probably get by with whatever settings your modem comes with. Failing that, try the ones we use (AT&B1&H1) or, gasp, see if the modem manual makes any suggestions. For example, type **AT&B1&H1** and press Enter. The modem says *OK*.

   If you're not sure what commands get your modem in the mood, skip this step.

   Trumpet WinSock doesn't show what you're typing, so type carefully!

3. **Tell the modem Ahoy There, Dial the Telephone! and give it your provider's phone number.**

   For example, type **ATDT555-2368**.

   You can't see what you type, so type carefully. Your modem dials the phone, and when it makes the connection, it says

   ```
   CONNECT 14400/ARQ
   ```

   Holy Digital Data Stream, Batperson! You're connected. Now your provider greets you, and you can type your login name and password. (No, we're not going to tell you our password. We're not totally stupid. Almost, but not totally.)

4. **Type in your login name and password.**

Your Internet provider displays a message, similar to

```
Welcome to the Internet Access Co. Type 'new' at login and
       'new' for password to register for a new UNIX
       shell account. login: dummies
Password: ********
SL/IP session from (199.0.65.12) to 199.0.65.90 beginning....
```

Hey, how about that? SLIP started. (Or CSLIP or PPP, depending on what kind of account you have.)

5. **Now tell Trumpet WinSock that the connection has started by pressing** ESC.

   You see a message like

```
SLIP ENABLED
```

That's it — you're connected. That you are now on the Internet is not obvious. The best way to check is by using the Trumpet Ping program, described in the next section.

Testing Your Connection by Pinging

Later in this chapter, we show you a few more details of making a connection, but first you may want to make sure that the connection works. You can use a program called Trumpet Ping, a little program that "pings" remote hosts to make sure that you can in fact reach them. When you downloaded and installed Trumpet WinSock (in Chapter 6 and earlier in this chapter), Trumpet Ping came along for the ride.

1. **Go back to the Program Manager and double-click the icon for Trumpet Ping, a.k.a. Trumping.**

   You see the Trumpet Ping window, shown in Figure 7-4.

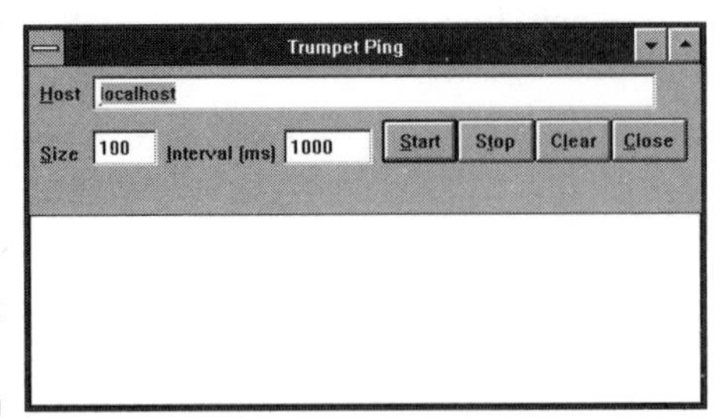

Figure 7-4: Trumpet is ready to ping, that is, to test your Internet connection.

2. **In the Host box, type either the name of your provider's server computer or a well-known system like** `rs.internic.net`.

3. **Click the Start button.**

   Trumpet Ping starts sending series of "ping" messages to the other computer. If it works, you should see responses like

   ```
   205.238.207.65 id = 56 rtt = 394ms
   ```

   The `rtt` number is the Round Trip Time for the ping to travel from your host to the other one and back (we bet that you expected this number to be more obscure). The round-trip time is reported in milliseconds ($^1/_{1000}$ second), so a round-trip time of 219 is $^{219}/_{1000}$ seconds, or about $^1/_5$ of a second. This amount is a reasonable round-trip time for a SLIP message; if the time is consistently more than 350, you probably have a setup problem. (In particular, make sure that your setup has MTU and MTS set to 512 or less, not the default 1500.)

4. **Click the Stop button to stop pinging.**

   Ping displays some statistics about all that pinging.

5. **Exit from Trumpet Ping when you are done.**

Now you know that you are on the Internet.

Hanging Up

One last important detail: How do you hang up? Fortunately, it's pretty easy:

1. **In Trumpet WinSock, choose Dialler⇨Bye to hang up the phone.**

   You don't have to exit from the WinSock programs, such as Eudora or Netscape, that you are using.

2. **If you don't plan to connect to the Internet again for a while, choose File⇨Exit to exit.**

Don't just tell Trumpet WinSock to exit, because it will, but without hanging up the phone. Be sure to hang up explicitly before you leave Trumpet WinSock.

Don't forget to register

Trumpet WinSock is shareware, and pretty darned good shareware at that. If you use Trumpet WinSock regularly, please choose Special⇨Register, which includes the registration instructions and the address (in Australia) to which to send the form and check. You can even register right over the Internet. Registration is not expensive ($25 as of this writing), and you feel great.

Later, after you've got your Web browser working, look at the Trumpet WinSock home page at this URL:

```
http://www.trumpet.com.au/wsk/
   winsock.htm
```

Some other programs that you downloaded are shareware, too. If the programs are worth using, they are worth registering.

More about Connections

If you're satisfied with manual dialing, you can skip the rest of this chapter and go on to Chapter 10, in which we tell you how to set up a bunch of other useful Internet software. Or you can skip the rest of this chapter for now and come back when you get tired of typing the commands all the time.

You can tell Trumpet WinSock how to call up and log in to your Internet provider so that you don't have to type the dialing command, your login name, and your password. This section describes how to create a login script that tells Trumpet WinSock what to do.

For our example, here's a slightly more complex login setup at another regional provider, ClarkNet (what we typed is in boldface):

```
atz
OK
at&c1&b1
OK
ATDT5551212
CONNECT 14400/ARQ Annex Command Line Interpreter * Copyright
            1991 Xylogics, Inc. Checking authorization,
            Please wait...
Connecting to port 37 using AT&T Paradyne V.32bis/V.42bis
            modem
Welcome to ClarkNet! Log in as "guest" for ClarkNet info and
            registration.
ClarkNet Username: dummies
ClarkNet Password: *******
Permission granted
```

```
      ClarkNet's Menu
    Now using Class B network address.
    1) Enter clarknet host (UUCP users only)
    2) Enter explorer host (All users and guest)
    3) SLIP (SLIP users only)
    4) PPP (PPP users only)
    5) Hosts? (All users)
    6) Who? (All users)
    7) Telnet (IP users only)
    8) Exit (All users)
Enter Number (1-8): 3
Switching to SLIP.
Annex address is 168.143.0.4. Your address is 168.143.1.87.
```

It's all in the script

Trumpet WinSock supports *scripts,* which are not altogether unlike the script for a play. The script describes what you (or the computer, on your behalf) type, what the modem or remote computer responds, what your computer types next, what the next response should be, and so on. In the preceding example, the computer types a couple of modem commands, and the modem replies `OK` after each one. Then the computer dials the phone, and the modem says `CONNECTED` and some other junk. The remote system prompts you with `Username`, the computer types the login name, the remote system prompts you with `Password`, and the computer types the password. Next is a long menu from the remote that ends with a request to enter the number to choose, and the computer types **3**. The script has to automate all that typing.

Trumpet WinSock uses two scripts that are stored in files: LOGIN.CMD, which logs you in, and BYE.CMD, which hangs up the modem. Trumpet comes with sample versions of both. Fortunately, the way you hang up a modem is now standardized well enough that the bye script always works, so we concentrate on the login script. Choose Dialler⇨Edit Scripts and then double-click `login.cmd` to start the Windows Notepad working on that script.

Here's the script for ClarkNet login (we go through it bit by bit afterward):

```
#
# initialize modem
#
output atz\r
input 10 OK\n
#
# set modem to indicate DCD
#
output at&c1&b1\r
input 10 OK\n
#
```

(continued)

(continued)

```
# send phone number
#
output atdt5552368\r
#
# now we are connected.
#
input 30 CONNECT
#
# wait till it's safe to send because some modems hang up
# if you transmit during the connection phase
#
wait 30 dcd
#
# wait for the username prompt
#

input 30 name:
output dummies\r
#
# and the password
#
input 30 word:
output hahaha\r
#
# we are now logged in
# so start SLIP
input 30 (1-8):
output 3\r display \n
display Connected. \n
#
#
# now we are finished.
#
online
```

In case it's not obvious, script lines that start with a pound sign (#) are comments. The computer disregards these lines because they're present for the benefit of humans who have to read the script.

This script starts by sending initialization commands to the modem. In the script, an `output` line is something to the remote system. (The `\r` is the Enter key, which used to be known as Carriage Return.) An `input` line is followed by a maximum number of seconds to wait and the message to wait for the modem or remote system to send.

```
#
# initialize modem
#
output atz\r
input 10 OK\n
```

```
#
# set modem to indicate DCD
#
output at&c1&b1\r
input 10 OK\n
```

To continue the example, we tell the modem to dial the phone and then wait up to 30 seconds for a `CONNECT` message. A `wait` command says to wait up to 30 seconds for the modem to turn on the DCD signal, which means that the modem is indeed connected to the remote system.

```
#
# send phone number
#
output atdt5552368\r
#
# now we are connected.
#
input 30 CONNECT
#
# wait till it's safe to send because some modems hang up
# if you transmit during the connection phase
#
wait 30 dcd
```

After the modem's connected, the remote host eventually prompts to enter a username. (The input line doesn't have to give everything the remote will send — just enough of it for the computer to figure out when it's time to send the next message.)

```
#
# wait for the username prompt
#
input 30 name:
output dummies\r
```

More waiting is required for the `Password` prompt (notice that, as lazy typists, we waited for only the tail end of it) before sending the password. No, that's still not our real password.

```
#
# and the password
#
input 30 word:
output hahaha\r
```

As in the login example earlier in this section, ClarkNet displays a long menu, ending with a prompt that ends with `(1-8):`. So after yet more waiting for that prompt, we were ready to select the entry we wanted, in this case by pressing **3**.

```
#
# we are now logged in
# so start SLIP
input 30 (1-8):
output 3\r
```

A `display` line displays a message merely for the benefit of the user sitting and watching Trumpet WinSock (that is, you). A final `online` line tells Trumpet WinSock that the connection is made, and the script is finished.

```
display Connected. \n
#
#
# now we are finished.
#
online
```

Your `login.cmd` script is a variation of this script. Make notes of what the remote says and what your computer has to type, and write alternating input and output lines. The modem-dialing lines (other than the phone number) and the display and output at the end should work as is (as are?).

Using your login script

After you've made a stab at creating a login script, save it, leave Notepad, and try running the script by choosing Dialler⇨Login from the Trumpet WinSock menu. If it works, your script should dial the phone, log you in, display `Connected`, and end with Trumpet WinSock saying `SLIP ENABLED`. But unless you're incredibly lucky, your script doesn't work on the first try. Look to see where the script messed up. Then go back into Notepad by way of Dialler⇨Edit Scripts and fix the lines starting at the place the script messed up. For all but the most horrible dialing situations, you should be able to get the script to work on the second or third try. For more hints about dialing scripts, see the INSTALL.TXT file that comes with Trumpet WinSock.

After your script works to your satisfaction, choose Dialler⇨Options and select Automatic login on start up only and then click Ok. This step says that in the future, whenever you start up Trumpet WinSock from the Program Manager, run the login script immediately so that you get connected right away.

What Next?

We haven't told you how to run WS_FTP to download files — a major omission. Not to worry — Chapter 9 covers this in explicit detail!

Chapter 8

Connecting to the Internet with Windows 95

In This Chapter

- Telling Windows 95 that you've got a modem
- Telling Windows 95 that you want to connect to the Internet
- Telling Windows 95 about your Internet provider
- Installing the extra stuff you need if you have a SLIP or CSLIP account (not a PPP account)

Suppose you've got a zoomy SLIP or PPP Internet account so that you can run Netscape and those other slick Internet programs. You've just upgraded to Windows 95, and you've heard that it comes with Internet software. "Great!" you think. "I'll just dial in and start surfing!"

Think again. Everyone expected Windows 95 to make connecting your computer to the Internet easy. As it turns out, Microsoft did sort of a good job — all the pieces you need to get on the Internet can be found in and around Windows 95. But it did a lousy job of putting those pieces in one place, and it did an even worse job of documenting where the pieces are. In this chapter, you get to put the jigsaw puzzle together.

To give you the general idea, here are the steps you have to follow:

1. Figure out whether you're already connected to the Internet.
2. Tell Windows 95 that you have a modem, if it didn't already find one.
3. Figure out whether you really want to be connected directly to the Internet anyway.
4. Tell Windows 95 that you'd like to dial in to a network, if it didn't already figure that out.
5. Tell Windows 95 who your Internet provider is.

6. Connect to your Internet provider.
7. Do some nitty-gritty stuff that you should ignore if at all possible.
8. Get software so that you can actually get useful work done.

This chapter describes each step in detail. Chapter 6 describes how to find an Internet provider, if you don't already have an account. Be sure to read the section entitled "What Are SLIP and PPP Again?" so that you know what kind of account to get.

It's much easier to get Windows 95 to connect to a PPP account than to a SLIP or CSLIP account. When you open your Internet account, ask for a PPP account to save yourself some trouble.

Maybe You're Already Connected to the Internet

Start with the easy way out: You may already be connected to the Internet. That's a likely scenario if you are using your computer at work or school and are connected to a local area network, or *LAN*. That LAN may be connected to the Internet directly. A direct connection has several advantages: It's usually fast, and it's usually free to you. It does, however, have the disadvantage that if you're at work, your supervisors probably expect you to get some work done. (Some companies actually have fairly strict policies about what you're allowed to do on their computers and on their time, so before you go surfing the Internet from work, you might want to make some discreet inquiries.) Of course, if you're a student, these constraints don't apply.

Another advantage of being connected to the Internet from work is that you usually don't have to set it up on your computer — the higher-ups pay network wizards to do that for you. If you're connected to a LAN at work and you think it's prudent to surf the Net from there, you'll still need some software to actually see what's going on out there in Netland. See the section "Getting a good FTP program" later in this chapter for information on using Windows 95's FTP program to download software and Chapter 10 for software that you may want to download and use.

Hey, Windows 95 — I Have a Modem!

Okay, your computer isn't on the Internet already, so you have to do it yourself. To access the Internet, whether you do it via an Internet provider or the Microsoft Network (MSN), you have to tell Windows 95 that you have a modem. (You do have a modem, right? If you've gotten this far and you're not sure, you haven't been paying attention!)

You probably never had this problem before — DOS and Windows 3.1 didn't know and didn't care whether you had a modem. Well, Windows 95 wants to be in charge of everything, so it really wants to know. Fortunately, Windows 95 will tell you all about what it thinks is inside your computer. Here's how to see what it thinks:

1. **Click Start on the Taskbar and choose Settings⇨Control Panel.**

   You see one of the folders that should be familiar to you now that you're working in Windows 95. The last (or almost last) entry in this folder is labeled System.

2. **Double-click the System folder.**

   Windows 95 displays your System Properties. This dialog box has four tabs on it, one of which is the Device Manager.

3. **Click the Device Manager tab.**

   You see a Modem entry on your list of devices.

4. **Click the + (plus sign) beside the modem entry.**

   Your modem should be listed on the System Properties window, which looks like Figure 8-1.

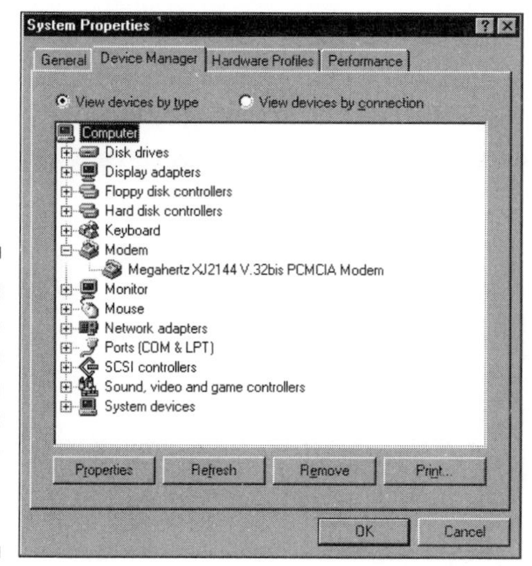

Figure 8-1: The Device Manager in System Properties on the Control Panel.

5. **If your modem is listed, you're done. Skip the rest of these steps.**

   If you see your modem listed, you may congratulate Windows 95 — it found your modem (and you were luckier than we were). If Windows 95 didn't find your modem, you can tell Windows 95 about your modem specifically. In fact, Windows 95 has a cute little Wizard that guides you through the modem-installation process. Continue to the next step to find this Wizard.

6. **Click the Cancel button to close the System Properties dialog box, and double-click Add New Hardware, which should be one of the first items listed in the Control Panel.**

   After it introduces itself, the first question this Wizard asks you is whether it should look for the hardware itself or let you tell it about your new hardware. If Windows 95 hasn't already figured out that you have a modem, you're going to have to tell it.

7. **Click No and save some time, especially if you know the make and model of your modem, and skip to step 9.**

   If you choose to let Windows 95 look for your modem, you see a dialog box telling you whether it found anything.

8. **Click Details to see exactly what it found.**

   You should see a modem mentioned on this list. If you see other things as well, don't worry about them; you'll have the opportunity to cancel out of the various Wizard programs before they wreak any mayhem on your system. Just keep clicking the Cancel button until the Install New Modem Wizard appears.

   If you choose to tell Windows 95 about your modem specifically, you see a listing of hardware components similar to the one you looked at earlier.

9. **Double-click Modem.**

   No matter how you got here, you're looking at the Windows 95 Install New Modem Wizard. Its first question is whether you'd like it to look for the modem for you.

10. **Answer Yes to this question because this process gives Windows 95 a chance to see whether it can talk to your modem.**

    You see the Verify Modem dialog box shown in Figure 8-2.

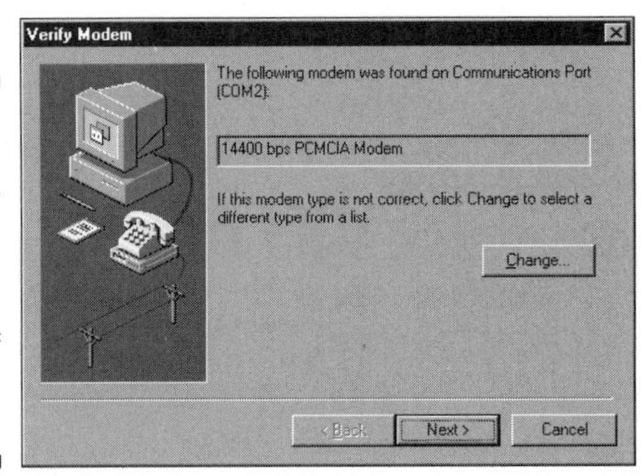

Figure 8-2: The Install New Modem Wizard guesses what kind of modem you have.

11. Click the Change button in this dialog box so that you can tell Windows 95 specifically about your modem.

12. Select your modem manufacturer from the list on the left and the specific model of your modem from the list on the right.

If your modem isn't on the list, choose something that you know works — the Standard Modems at the top of the list is a good choice if nothing else looks right. If a Windows 95 install disk came with your modem, you can try inserting the diskette in your diskette drive, clicking the Have Disk button, and seeing whether Windows 95 can find the installation information on the diskette.

13. Either way, you're ready to let Windows 95 go at the modem; click OK and move on to complete the installation.

There's one more thing you need to do to get your modem ready to dial: Windows 95, in its ceaseless quest to tailor itself to how you work, wants to know where you're dialing from and how you place your telephone calls. Actually, it has a good reason for this — well, sort of a good reason. What you dial to make a phone call depends on where you are. So if Windows 95 knows where you are, it knows whether to dial 9 for an outside line, whether your Internet Service Provider is in one area code and you're in another, and the like. If you have a desktop computer, you won't need to think about this much — just set it up once, and you're done. But if you have a portable computer that you take from place to place (say, home and office, and perhaps home and office are in different area codes), setting up two locations (call them *Home* and *Office*) and switching between them is a handy option.

The way you set up a location initially and later switch to a different location is through the Modems icon in the Control Panel. If you didn't have a Modems icon before, you've got one now — it appears when you tell Add New Hardware that you have a modem.

14. Double-click Modems.

You see a dialog box with a button labeled Dialing Properties. This dialog box is where you tell Windows 95 about where you are. (Microsoft could have called the button *Locations,* but that would have been too obvious.)

15. Click Dialing Properties.

You see the Dialing Properties dialog box, like the one in Figure 8-3.

The Dialing Properties dialog box contains everything Windows 95 wants to know about where you are. Because you've got to be somewhere, Windows 95 decides that you're at your Default Location.

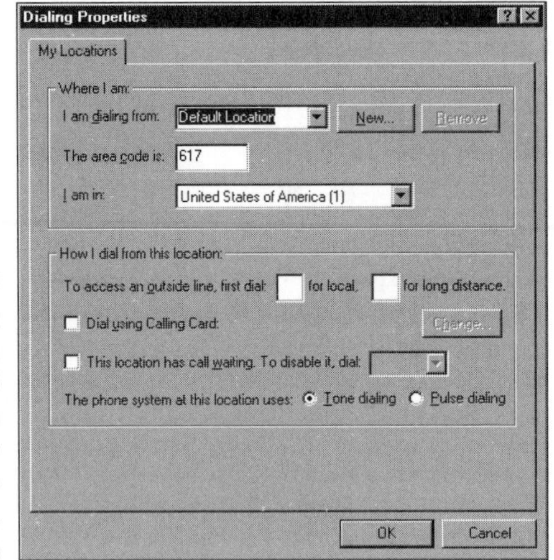

Figure 8-3: Telling Windows 95 where you are and how to dial the phone.

16. **If this is the only place that you expect to be using this computer, just change the settings appropriately.**

    If you expect to be using your computer in a number of places (places with different phone numbers, that is), you may want to use the New button to create a location for each of those places. Then whenever you're in a new place, you tell Windows 95, and Windows 95 knows whether it needs to dial any extra codes before a phone number. For example, if you're in a different country, Windows 95 may need to dial the area code and country code. If you're dialing from inside an office, you may need to dial 9 for an outside line, or perhaps something else like 98 for a long-distance outside line. You can enter this stuff in the How I dial from this location area of the dialog box.

    Use the New button and define as many locations as you think you're likely to need. When the time comes to dial the phone, Windows 95 gives you a chance to choose which location you are at.

17. **When you're done, click OK.**

Congratulations: It's a modem. If you want to check that it's actually working and communicating with Windows 95, click the Diagnostics tab on the Modem Properties dialog box (the one you were just looking at to define your locations) and select your modem from the list that appears. Click the More info button to encourage Windows 95 to try to communicate with your modem. If it succeeds, you see a dialog box full of incomprehensible and irrelevant stuff. If it doesn't succeed, you see a message like `Unable to communicate with Modem` — in which case, you should go find an expert. Click the OK buttons until the Modem Properties dialog box goes away and close the Control Panel. Job well done!

Using a telephone calling card

Getting Windows 95 to dial a telephone calling card number for you is possible but not easy. If you use a calling card for long-distance calls, you can enter the calling card number as well. In the Dialing Properties dialog box (which you display by double-clicking the Modems icon on the Control Panel), click the Dial using Calling Card check box, and you see the Change Calling Card window. Windows 95 has thoughtfully provided a number of predefined calling card formats for you to use, but you can't use them quite the way you might expect. You'd like to be able to type your calling card number into that little gray box labeled Calling Card Number, but you can't. What you can do is use Windows 95's list of calling cards to create your own personalized calling cards.

To use a telephone calling card with Windows 95, click the New button to create a new personalized card, and enter the name for that card. Note that you still can't enter the thing you want to enter — your calling card number. Click the Advanced button to see the Dialing Rules dialog box. Click the Copy From button to choose the long-distance calling card you use — with luck, your type of calling card appears on the list. Click OK to select the type of calling card you use and click Close to close the Dialing Rules dialog box. Presto! — you can type your credit card number.

Now if you want to go back and try to understand or change the dialing formula, click Advanced again. Click the ? on the title bar and point to one of the dialing formulas. You get some hint about what these things mean.

Do You Really Want to Be Connected Directly to the Internet?

So you've got a modem. If you're reading this, you clearly want to be connected to *somebody* out there. The question is, "Do you want to be connected directly to the Internet?"

You do have an alternative. You may already have discovered that Windows 95 comes complete with software for using Microsoft's own network, called the *Microsoft Network,* or MSN for short. (The U.S. Department of Justice has noticed this as well, but that's another story.) That's what the MSN icon is doing on your Windows 95 desktop. If you're not already connected to the Internet, you may want to use MSN as your gateway to the Internet. Microsoft would certainly like you to.

If you'd like to try MSN, take a look at Chapter 14 in *The Internet For Dummies,* 3rd Edition. It talks all about using the Internet via the Microsoft Network. And if you decide that that's definitely what you want to do, try *The Microsoft Network For Dummies* by Doug Lowe (IDG Books Worldwide, Inc.).

Microsoft is spending a great deal of time and money nowadays hyping the fact that it intends to make MSN look more like an Internet access provider and less like a CompuServe/AOL/Prodigy wannabe. As of this writing, you can do all the major things that people seem to want to do on the Internet from MSN: send and receive mail, look at newsgroups, and surf the World Wide Web. The main things you can't do are use Internet Relay Chat (IRC, see Chapter 18) and make your own Web pages (see Chapter 14).

So you've decided not to use MSN? That's okay — Microsoft graciously permits you to access your Internet provider from Windows 95 anyway.

Gimme a Real Network

To use a real Internet account, you have to tell Windows 95 that you'd like to dial in to a network and then (of course) tell it all kinds of gory technical details about it. Yes, we know that Windows 95 was supposed to let you skip that kind of thing, but think again!

Stop! Maybe Professor Marvel will do all this for you!

You have probably noticed that Microsoft is big into *Wizards* nowadays. Microsoft's idea is to take all the steps, such as the ones we've outlined in this section for connecting to the Internet, and program them into your computer. The Wizard asks questions when it needs to make a choice about what you want to do.

If you don't have the Wizard, or you're too macho to ask for the Wizard's help, skip to "It's a beautiful day in the neighborhood," later in this chapter.

Such a Wizard exists for connecting your computer running Windows 95 to the Internet. Why, you ask, don't we just tell you about the Wizard, and let her explain it all? Because, like all Wizards, she's not particularly predictable, especially about when she shows up and where you're likely to find her.

We know that you can get the Wizard by purchasing Microsoft PLUS!, a product containing features that many of us think should have been included in Windows 95 in the first place. Instead, after almost giving away Windows 95, Microsoft is charging $45 or more for the "rest" of the operating system. Buy and install PLUS! if money isn't an issue. You definitely get the Wizard that way.

If you know someone who's already connected to the Internet, ask your friend to download a copy of the Microsoft Internet Explorer (the Web browser we talk about in Chapter 14 of *The Internet For Dummies,* 3rd Edition). Sometimes, when you install Internet Explorer, the Wizard comes along for the ride! Or else you can look around on your computer and see if you have a file named INETWIZ.EXE on your computer. (You can check this by opening the Windows Explorer and choosing Tools⇨Find⇨Files or Folders. Look in My Computer for a file named INETWIZ.EXE.) If you find INETWIZ.EXE, that's the Wizard — drag it onto the desktop for easy access. You may also find that you have an icon that looks like the one in Figure 8-4 on your desktop. That's the Wizard you want!

Figure 8-4: The Internet Wizard icon.

What good is the Internet Wizard? It takes you through the following steps (click on the Next button to proceed from step to step):

1. **Double-click the Internet Wizard icon.**

   After the obligatory welcome, the Wizard asks whether you want to access the Internet via the Microsoft Network or via an Internet service provider. Because Microsoft Network can be installed and configured with Windows 95, that option is an easier way of installing it. If that's what you want to do, don't bother with Ms. Wizard here.

2. **Tell the Wizard that you have an account with a different provider.**

   You do, right?

3. **Choose whether to install Microsoft Exchange.**

   Next, the Internet Wizard asks about Internet Mail and Microsoft Exchange. Reasonable people seem to differ about the value of Microsoft Exchange — some people see Exchange as lacking necessary features, such as signature lines and message sorting. On the other hand, if you are already getting mail from a number of sources, or if you decided to install the Microsoft Network, you've got it anyway, so you may want to give it a try.

   The Wizard asks if you're ready for Ms. Wizard to install some files.

4. **Choose Next to continue with the installation.**

   Make sure that you have your Windows 95 distribution media handy — the CD-ROM that it came on, your 13 diskettes, or the diskettes you created when you got Windows 95 preloaded on your system.

   After much whirring and clicking and installing of diskettes (if you went that route), you are asked for the name of your Internet provider. The Wizard needs this information to create a dial-up connection named after your provider.

5. **Type the name of your Internet provider.**

   Then you are asked for the telephone number you dial to contact the Internet.

6. **Type the access phone number for your Internet account.**

   Including the area code is important because Windows 95 uses the area code when figuring out how to dial the phone (whether to dial an area code or not).

   Next, Ms. Wizard needs your username and password so that it can try to sign on.

7. **Type the user name and password for your account on your Internet provider.**

   Here we get to the really geeky stuff. Your Internet provider may have given you an address for your computer. These addresses are called IP (for Internet Protocol) and are numbers in the form 123.456.789.912 (though you may not have three digits between each set of periods). Look at the section "Some Nitty-Gritty Stuff That You Should Ignore If at All Possible" later in this chapter for more information.

8. **If you were issued an IP address, check the Always use the following button and enter your IP address and your subnet mask (a number like 255.255.255.0).**

   The next step is more geeky stuff, also explained in the "Nitty-Gritty" section. If you know these numbers, type them in. If you don't, try leaving them blank.

9. **Type the other IP addresses that the Internet Wizard asks for, if you know them.**

   Ever nosy, Ms. Wizard wants to know your e-mail address and your mail server (where it should send your mail) if you told it you want to use Microsoft Exchange for your Internet mail.

10. **Type your e-mail address and the name of your mail server.**

    Your mail server is the name of the computer where you send and receive mail. Usually this is a computer at your Internet service provider, something like `postoffice.oz.net`. Your e-mail address is something like `dorothy@oz.net`.

You're done! Click the Finish button (as if you had any choice!).

Windows 95 may take this moment to restart your computer. Let it; you won't be able to get onto the Internet if you don't. When you come back, you have, we hope, an icon like the one in Figure 8-5 on your desktop.

Figure 8-5: The Internet icon on your desktop.

Double-click that icon and see what happens. With any luck, you see the Microsoft Internet Explorer. As soon as you type the URL of a Web page you'd like to see, you may actually be online!

Using the Internet Wizard lets you skip lots of unpleasant dialog boxes and menus. In fact, you can skip all the way down to the section "You Wanted to Get Some Useful Work Done on the Internet?" near the end of this chapter to see about getting some real software. But you may want to take a look at the step-by-step portions of this chapter anyway in case Ms. Wizard didn't get everything exactly right or in case something changes in your setup.

It's a beautiful day in the neighborhood

The first thing you need to do is tell Windows 95 that you want to talk on the phone. If you have any kind of network installed on your computer, a Network Neighborhood icon appears on your Windows 95 desktop. It also appears if you told Windows 95 during installation that you want to talk on the phone or if (for reasons known only to itself) the Windows 95 install program just decided to put it there. If you don't have a Network Neighborhood, don't panic (yet) — we'll get you into the neighborhood anyway. You need that Network Neighborhood icon to set up your Internet connection.

I've got the icon!

If you *do* have a Network Neighborhood icon, you're not out of the woods yet. *Right*-click (that is, click using the right mouse button) the Network Neighborhood icon to see what happens. You get a pop-up menu including a selection labeled Properties. Choose Properties, and you see a dialog box showing you what Windows 95 thinks you use to connect to another computer. Figure 8-6 shows you a sample network configuration that appears on the Configuration tab in the Network window.

Does your Network Neighborhood contain entries for Dial-Up Adapter? It should contain *at least* the following entries:

- Dial-Up Adapter
- TCP/IP -> Dial-Up Adapter

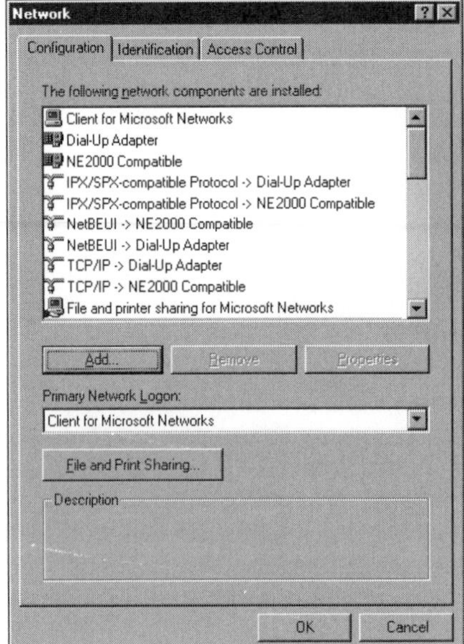

Figure 8-6: Here's what Windows 95 thinks about our Network Neighbor-hood.

In the sample in Figure 8-6, *lots* of things connect this computer to other computers. If everything's been working so far, don't worry about any stuff in there that you don't understand. As long as you have the two Dial-Up Adapter entries, you can connect to the Internet. Skip down to the section "Welcome to the neighborhood" later in this chapter.

Moving into the neighborhood

If you do *not* have a Network Neighborhood icon, here's what to do:

1. **Go to the Taskbar and choose Start⇨Settings⇨Control Panel to start messing with Windows 95's guts.**

   You still have one more chance to get lucky. In the Control Panel window, you *may* see an icon labeled Network. If you do, you can double-click it. If you see the Dial-Up Adapter and TCP/IP -> Dial-Up Adapter, you're all set. Skip the rest of this section.

   Otherwise, you'd better see an icon labeled Add/Remove Programs, usually in the upper left. If you don't, you're in deeper than you want to be — call your local guru for help.

2. **Double-click the Add/Remove Programs icon.**

   You see a dialog box with three tabs at the top. The middle tab is labeled Windows Setup.

3. **Click the Windows Setup tab.**

   You see the Add/Remove Programs Properties window, like in Figure 8-7.

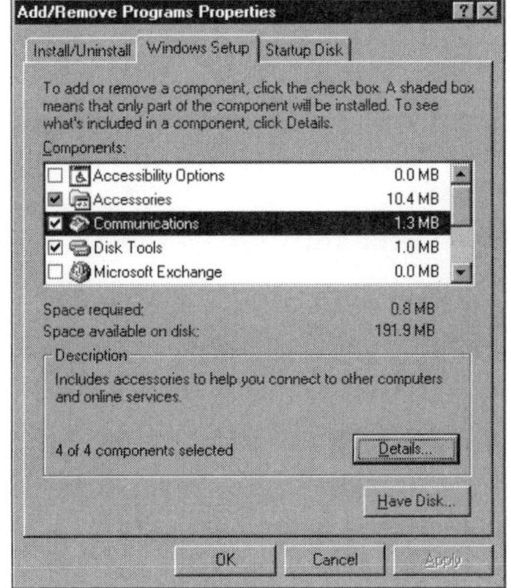

Figure 8-7: The Windows Setup tab of the Add/Remove Programs Properties dialog box in the Control Panel.

4. **Make sure that the Communications option is checked.**

   Do not uncheck anything that is already checked — otherwise, you'd be telling Windows 95 to remove parts of itself from your computer! Checking the Communications option tells Windows 95 to add four items in your configuration: Dial-Up Networking (which is what you're after here), Direct Cable Connection (useful for connecting together computers that are physically near each other), HyperTerminal (a simple communications program), and Phone Dialer (which might be useful to see whether you've got everything else set up correctly).

5. **Click OK.**

   Windows 95 asks where it can find the CD or diskettes that you bought Windows 95 on. It also asks to reboot your computer. After it does, you see a Network Neighborhood icon on your desktop.

Welcome to the neighborhood

Great! You've got a Network Neighborhood icon that you can use to configure your connection to an Internet account. Now all you have to do is make sure that Windows 95 knows that your PC should be talking on the telephone.

1. ***Right*-click (that is, click using the right mouse button) the Network Neighborhood icon.**

   You see a pop-up menu that includes Properties.

2. **Choose Properties.**

   You see the Network dialog box showing you what Windows 95 thinks you use to connect to another computer. Refer back to Figure 8-6 to see a sample network configuration. If your configuration contains the Dial-Up Adapter and TCP/IP -> Dial-Up Adapter, you're all set — skip the rest of these steps.

3. **If you don't have a Dial-Up Adapter and TCP/IP -> Dial-Up Adapter, click the Add button.**

   You see the Select Network Components dialog box.

4. **Select Adapter and click the new Add button.**

   You see the Select Network adapters dialog box.

5. **Scroll down the list of manufacturers to Microsoft and click Microsoft. In the right-hand box, click Dial-Up Adapter.**

   (We know — Microsoft didn't make your modem, but the folks there did write the software that's going to let your modem talk on the phone.) Figure 8-8 illustrates this series of steps.

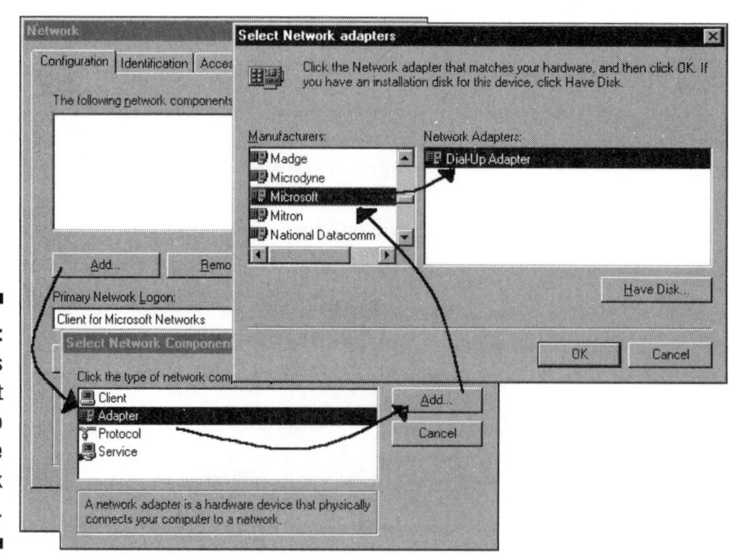

Figure 8-8: The series of steps that you follow to add some network hardware.

6. **Click OK to finish.**
7. **Now repeat steps 3 through 6 to add the TCP/IP protocol that the Internet uses: Click the Add button, select Protocol, and click the new Add button. Scroll down the list of manufacturers to Microsoft again and click Microsoft. In the right-hand box, click TCP/IP. Click OK to finish.**
8. **Click OK to close the Network dialog box.**

   Windows 95 may ask you to restart your computer (again).

Closer and closer, nearer and nearer — but not there yet.

Meet My Internet Provider

You may have noticed that Windows 95 does not yet know a couple of things about you and your Internet provider (hard to believe, but true). These facts include the telephone number that you use to dial your Internet provider, your username, and your password. Some of the less obvious stuff includes your Domain Name Servers and the like. Here's what you'll need to have handy:

- Your Internet service provider's telephone number
- Your username
- Your password

Making the connection

To type the phone number that you're going to dial:

1. **Choose Start⇨Programs⇨Accessories⇨Dial-Up Networking from the Taskbar.**

   You see the Dial-Up Networking window like that shown in Figure 8-9, with a line that says Make New Connection.

Figure 8-9: The Dial-Up Networking window.

2. **Double-click the Make New Connection line.**

   You see another of Windows 95's cute Wizards. This one asks you three questions to learn about your connection.

3. **What's it called?**

   Give your connection a name. Because our Internet service provider is named The Internet Access Company, we call ours *TIAC* — pretty creative, huh?

4. **What modem are you going to use?**

   You see the description of your modem in a choice box. If you have only one modem, you're all set with this step. Otherwise, choose the modem that you want this connection to use.

5. **Click Next to proceed to the next step in the Wizard.**

6. **What's the phone number?**

   Enter the telephone number of your Internet provider. Notice the choice boxes for your area code and for your country. Windows 95 wants to know where your Internet provider is so that it can figure out what to do with those dialing rules that we discuss in the "Hey, Windows 95 — I Have a Modem!" section.

7. **Click Next to proceed to the next step in the Wizard.**

8. **Click Finish.**

   Your connection is added to the list of available connections, and you're done.

Well, sort of. Accounts at Internet providers come in a couple of flavors. Vanilla is a PPP account with a dynamic IP address. (Impress your friends — when they ask you if you use the Internet, don't just say, "Yes," say, "I like my PPP account even though it has a dynamic IP address.") If you have a PPP account, you're all set — skip down to the "At Last — Connecting To Your Internet Provider" section later in this chapter. If you have a SLIP account, you'd better read on.

SLIP-sliding away

Windows 95 really wants to use a PPP account to talk to other computers on the Internet. If you're willing to work for it, Windows 95 will condescend to using the older SLIP and SLIP's cousin CSLIP. For it to do so, you must have bought Windows 95 on a CD-ROM — see the sidebar "I bought WHAT?"

If you have a SLIP or CSLIP account, call your Internet provider. You may be able to turn it into a PPP account with a single phone call (we did, with TIAC) and save yourself from following a whole bunch of boring steps in getting SLIP or CSLIP set up on your computer.

I bought WHAT?

You probably got Windows 95 in one of three ways: You bought it on CD-ROM, you bought it on diskettes, or it came preloaded on your computer. If you bought it on diskettes, you may be surprised to know that you got something different than your office mate who bought it on CD-ROM. Specifically, you got 13 diskettes (worth at least $7 right there) and not as much software. You are missing about 40 files, including a collection called DSCRIPT. That collection contains two things: support for SLIP connections and a scripting utility that allows you to sign on without having to type your name and password each time.

If you have access to the Internet, you can get these files easily. They are available on the Microsoft Web site, for example, at `http://www.microsoft.com`, or, at this writing, more specifically:

```
http://www.microsoft.com/kb/
   softlib/cdextras.htm
```

Of course, if you could get on to the Internet, you wouldn't have these problems at all. Another approach is to get these files off CompuServe. This approach has a couple of advantages: 1) You don't already have to be on the Internet to do it, and 2) you may already have gotten a disk from CompuServe that allows you to sign on and try out its service. If you haven't gotten such a disk, you can call CompuServe at 800-487-0453 — the folks there will be glad to send you one. The disk signs you up for the CompuServe service. With the disk, you usually get one free month and ten free hours, so you don't *have* to spend any money if you don't want to.

When you're on CompuServe, from the WinCim program menu, choose Services⇨Go and enter **WUGNET**. After you've joined and all, choose Library⇨Search and enter **DSCRPT.EXE** as the filename to search for. Download that file, put it in an empty folder on your system, find it by using the Explorer, and double-click it to decompress it. Now you're ready to join those lucky folks who bought Windows 95 on a CD-ROM and install your SLIP connection.

To get set up for SLIP or CSLIP, you revisit some of the procedures from earlier in this chapter.

1. **Go back to Control Panel and double-click the Add/Remove Programs icon.**

   This is the same thing that you do in the "Moving into the neighborhood" section.

2. **Click the Windows Setup tab in the Add/Remove Programs Properties dialog box (refer to Figure 8-7).**

   This is the same choice that you make in the "Moving into the neighborhood" section.

3. **This time, click the Have Disk button because Windows 95 is convinced that you're installing somebody else's software.**

   The Install From Disk dialog box asks where to copy the manufacturer's files from.

4. **If you have the Windows 95 CD, type** D:\ADMIN\APPTOOLS\DSCRIPT **(but substitute the letter of your CD-ROM drive for the D in that path name if your CD-ROM drive is different).**
5. **If you just downloaded the files from CompuServe, enter** C:\COMPUSRV\DOWNLOAD **(or whatever folder you downloaded the file into).**

   If you've managed this correctly, you see the Have Disk dialog box shown in Figure 8-10.

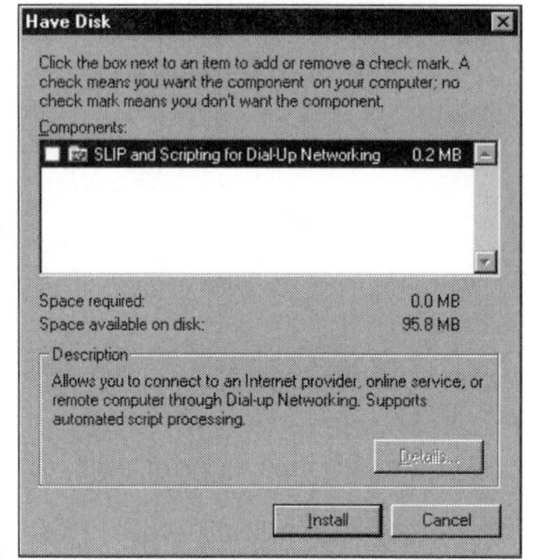

Figure 8-10: The Have Disk installation dialog box for SLIP support.

6. **Check the SLIP and Scripting for Dial-Up Networking box and click the Install button.**

   After the appropriate whirring and clicking and flashing of message boxes, you see the Windows Setup tab of the Add/Remove Programs Properties again.
7. **Click OK.**

   Now you need to create a new connection or change the connection you already have to make it use the SLIP driver you just loaded.
8. **Get back to your Dial-Up Properties window by choosing Start⇨Programs⇨Accessories⇨Dial-Up Networking from the Taskbar.**

   You see the Dial-Up Networking window, like that shown back in Figure 8-9.
9. **If you don't have a connection to modify, follow the steps described in "Making the connection" earlier in this chapter.**
10. ***Right*-click the connection that you want to turn into a SLIP connection, and choose Properties from the pop-up menu.**

    You see the Server Types dialog box shown in Figure 8-11.

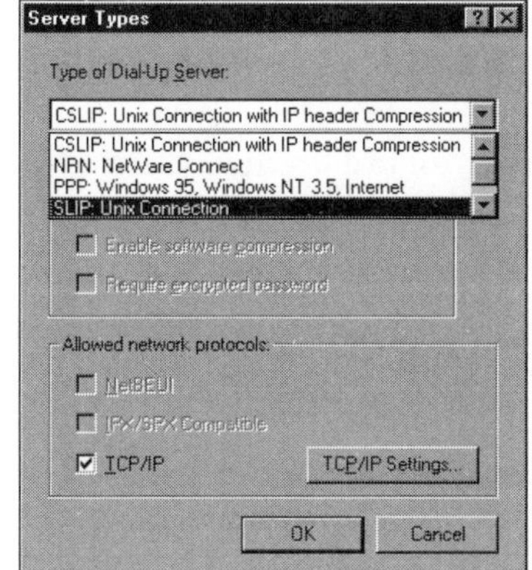

Figure 8-11: The Server Types dialog box.

11. **Select SLIP or CSLIP, depending on the type of account you have with your Internet provider.**

    If you're not sure, select SLIP.

12. **Click OK to accept the changes to this connection.**

    You're ready to test the connection. Read on!

There are reasons why people don't like to use SLIP accounts anymore, and you're about to find out two of them. The first is that SLIP has no way of logging on automatically. Another is that SLIP has no way of determining what your IP address is. If you're lucky, your Internet provider assigned you a permanent IP number with your SLIP account (this permanent number is more important for SLIP accounts than for PPP accounts). If you're not so lucky, every time you sign on, you'll have to figure out what IP address your Internet provider gave you today and enter it. You see how to do that when you actually dial in to the Internet.

Windows 95 *may* be able to help you with typing your username and password and with figuring out your IP address — see the sidebar "Is anybody reading from the script?" later in this chapter.

At Last — Connecting to Your Internet Provider

After only hours of agony, you're ready to call up your Internet account.

1. **If you've closed the Dial-Up Networking dialog box, you'll have to open it again by choosing Start⇨Programs⇨Accessories⇨Dial-Up Networking from the Taskbar.**
2. **Double-click the connection name you just created (in the "Making the Connection" section).**

   Windows 95 suggested *My Connection* for the name.

   You see a Connect To dialog box like that shown in Figure 8-12. Windows 95 may or may not suggest a username, depending on whether you have other networking set up. Make sure that the right username is in the box, and remember, cApiTaliZaTioN matters!

Figure 8-12: Windows 95's Connect To dialog box dials the phone and makes the connection.

3. **Enter your password in the Password box.**
4. **Decide whether to check the Save password check box so you don't have to enter your password again.**

   Advantage: You don't have to type your password every time you want to call the Internet. Disadvantage: Anyone can walk up to your PC and sign on to the Internet as you.
5. **Fill in the Phone number and Dialing from boxes.**

   The phone number should be familiar from the "Make a new connection" Wizard. You can type a new telephone number here, although you probably don't want to — you'd be better off modifying the telephone number permanently (see "Some Nitty-Gritty Stuff That You Should Ignore If at All Possible," just ahead in this chapter) or creating a new connection.

   The Dialing from box contains the name of the location where Windows 95 thinks you are right now. This box should be familiar from the "Hey, Windows 95 — I Have a Modem!" section way back at the beginning of this chapter. See how all the pieces are beginning to fit together?
6. **Click the Connect button.**

   If you're using a PPP account, you see a series of messages starting with `Initializing` and ending with `Connected`. Skip to step 8.

If you're using SLIP, you see `Initializing`, `Dialing`, and then a terminal window.

7. **If you use SLIP, sign on to your Internet provider and do whatever you have to do to get your IP address.**

   (Ask your Internet provider if you don't know.) In many cases, your provider issues you an IP address after you type your password.

8. **Then click Continue on the terminal screen.**

   Windows 95 asks you for your SLIP Connection IP address.

9. **Type the address you read off the screen and click OK.**

   You see the Connected box.

10. **Celebrate, because you are finally connected to the Internet!**

    The Connected box stays on your desktop until you disconnect. You may want to minimize it so that it just appears on the Taskbar — we usually do.

11. **When you're ready to disconnect, click the Disconnect button.**

    The dialog box automatically goes away.

Congratulations: You're on the Internet!

Is anybody reading from the script?

Microsoft has included an undocumented scripting utility that allows Dial-Up Networking to automatically log on and in many cases determine what your IP address is and tell Dial-Up Networking about it automatically. When you install the SLIP files, a couple of other things are also copied to your hard disk (don't you hate it when they do that?). Use Windows Explorer and look in the PROGRAM FILES\APPLICATIONS folder. See those files labeled (in the Type column) Dial-Up Networking Script? You have a program that reads scripts and has conversations with computers that Dial-Up Networking is trying to connect with.

On the Taskbar, choose Start⇨Programs⇨Accessories⇨Dial-Up Scripting Tool. The Help button on this screen is very useful — it's the only documentation on the scripting language. Fortunately, it's pretty simple. A couple of example files are in the PROGRAM FILES\APPLICATIONS folder. You should be able to load one of them into Windows Notepad and change it so that the script logs you on automagically, responding to your Internet provider's prompts.

When you've got a script file that you think will work with your account, associate it with a dial-up connection, using the Dial-Up Scripting Tool. You may want to leave the Step through script box checked and the Start terminal screen minimized button unchecked.

When you dial your connection, you see the same terminal window that you saw before you tried to use the script. If you check Step through script, you also see a script box in which you see your script go by. Every time Dial-Up Networking gets to script command, it stops until you push the Step button. This option lets you see what your Internet provider's computer typed and how your script responded.

Some Nitty-Gritty Stuff That You Should Ignore If at All Possible

When you call your Internet provider, you are connecting your computer to the Internet. Think about what this means for a second — hundreds of thousands of computers worldwide need to be able to find your computer and talk to it. Furthermore, they want to be able to talk to your computer more or less instantaneously. Therefore, that somebody out there needs to know something about your computer should come as no surprise.

To allow the rest of the computers on the Internet to find your own computer, you need to enter some additional information. You may also have received one or more of the following pieces of information from your Internet provider:

- **A permanent IP address:** This number, which is in the form 123.45.67.89, is your real address on the Internet. If you didn't get one, your Internet service provider invents one for you every time you call up.
- **One Domain Name Server (DNS) address or more:** These addresses, which use the same kind of numbers as your IP address, are for the computers that your computer can ask for directions to find other computers.
- **A domain name:** This name indicates the family of computers that your computer is a member of. It's usually a name related to your Internet service provider. One of our Internet providers is TIAC, so one of our domain names is `tiac.net`.
- **A host name:** This is the name by which your computer will be known on the Net. You won't use the host name unless you're going to do some really geeky stuff.

You can tell Windows 95 about this stuff, like this:

1. **From the Dial-Up Networking browser (refer to Figure 8-9), *right*-click your connection name.**

   You see a pop-up menu that includes Properties.

2. **Choose Properties.**

   You see general information about this connection.

3. **Click the Server Type button.**

   You see the Server Types dialog box shown back in Figure 8-11.

4. **Click the TCP/IP Settings button.**

   You see the TCP/IP Settings dialog box shown in Figure 8-13.

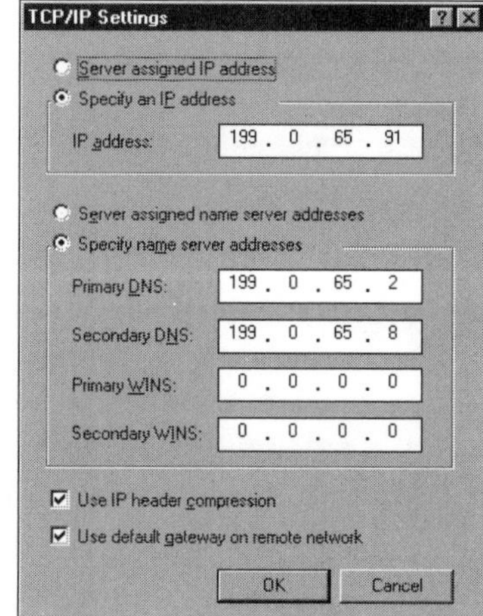

Figure 8-13: Windows 95's Dial-Up Networking TCP/IP Settings dialog box.

This dialog box is the place to type your permanent IP address and your Domain Name Server IP addresses, if you know them. In many cases, neither Windows 95 nor your Internet service provider cares if you don't bother.

5. **If your Internet provider gave you this information, type it in. If your Internet provider didn't tell you an permanent address, click Server Assigned IP address.**
6. **Click OK until you're back at the Dial-Up Networking window.**

When you're looking at the properties for a connection, you can click the Server Type button. Notice that the Server Types dialog box, shown back in Figure 8-11, has check boxes for NetBEUI and IPX/SPX Compatible. You can clear these check boxes and speed up your network communications a little bit.

You Wanted to Get Some Useful Work Done on the Internet?

Windows 95 includes some basic utilities that you need in order to get on the Internet and download programs from the Internet. These utilities are just enough to let you download some of the really good stuff that's out there. You need an FTP program for transferring files (programs and data) from the Internet to your PC (as discussed in Chapters 9 and 10). *FTP* stands for *File Transfer Protocol,* and it's the way most files on the Internet get from one computer to another. You also need a program to unzip files from the Internet. *Zipping* is a popular form of compressing the information in a file so that it takes less time for FTP to get it from there (wherever in the world, literally, *there* might be) to your computer. And you need a place to put all that stuff.

Park programs here

Start with the last item that you need to figure out: a place to put all the stuff you pick up. Using the Windows 95 Explorer, create a folder under the Program Files folder called Internet Utilities.

Getting a good FTP program

Now, to download programs and other files, you need a good FTP program. Windows 95 comes with an old-fashioned FTP program. It's a pain to use, but you can use it to get a better FTP program called WS_FTP. WS_FTP is one of the most popular Windows-based FTP programs around. Here's how to get it:

1. **Before you run the FTP program that comes with Windows 95, connect to your Internet provider so that you're on the Net.**
2. **To run the FTP program, choose Start⇨Run from the Taskbar and type** FTP **as the name of the program that you want to run.**

   You see a black window with the prompt `ftp>` in it. This program is a throwback to the old command-line days, so warm up those fingers. First of all, you need to connect to the computer where WS_FTP is.
3. **Type**

   ```
   open ftp.csra.net
   ```

   Either you'll be asked for a username and a password, or you'll get some message about how your connection was refused. In either case, don't panic. If you get `Connection refused`, the server is busy, so see the sidebar "Other places to get stuff." If you're lucky and FTP is asking you for a username and a password, you'll be glad to know that the folks who run the Central Savannah River Area Internet establishment allow you to get files from their computer without requiring that you have an account with them. Many FTP systems allow people to sign on this way as a courtesy and as a way to make their files generally available to the Internet community.
4. **To get in, type** anonymous **as a username and type your e-mail address as a password, like** `somebody@provider.com`**.**

   Now that you're in, tell FTP that you're going to be downloading a program.
5. **Type**

   ```
   binary
   ```

FTP responds with the message `200 Type set to I.`

Now get the program into the directory that you created.

6. **Type**

```
get /pub/win32/ws_ftp32.zip "\Program Files\Internet
      Utilities\ws_ftp32.zip"
```

You're probably talking to a UNIX system at the other end of your FTP connection. If you're planning to do this a lot, you'll probably want to get a copy of *UNIX For Dummies* (by Levine & Young, IDG Books Worldwide) because UNIX systems are *very picky* about capitalization, spaces, and quotes. So make sure that you've typed your command *exactly* as it appears here — capitals on *P* in *Program, F* in *Files, I* in *Internet,* and *U* in *Utilities* only; quotes before the first \ and at the end; \ (backslashes) where you see backslashes; and / (forward slashes) where you see forward slashes.

In response to this `get` command, FTP copies the file from the FTP server at CSRA to your computer, using the filename you typed.

After FTP has finished transferring the file, you get a message that includes the words `Transfer complete`. Your FTP session should look like the one in Figure 8-14.

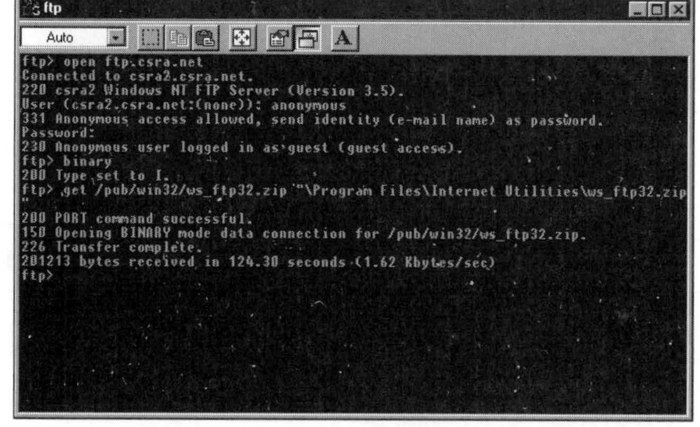

Figure 8-14: Here's the transcript of your conversation with an FTP server.

7. **Type** disconnect **to tell the folks at CSRA that you're done.**

Now you've got the file WS_FTP32.ZIP on your hard disk.

Getting a good unzipping program

After you've downloaded the FTP file, you can do exactly nothing with it because it's compressed in ZIP format (that's what the .ZIP stands for on the end). Fortunately, Connecticut shareware author Nico Mak has written a program called WinZip that decompresses those files, and he's willing to let you try it out for free.

You should still be running the FTP program that comes with Windows 95, as described in the preceding section. Follow these steps to get the WinZip program:

1. **From the** `ftp>` **prompt, type**

   ```
   open ftp.winzip.com
   ```

2. **As before, sign on as** anonymous **and enter your e-mail address as your password.**
3. **Type** binary **to tell FTP that you're interested in a program and type**

   ```
   get /winzip/winzip95.exe "\Program Files\Internet
         Utilities\winzip95.exe"
   ```

   Once again, if you've minded your *P*s and *Q*s (well, your quotes and slashes), you see the `Transfer complete` message after the file gets to you.

4. **Type** disconnect **to tell the folks at WinZip that you're done and type** quit **to exit the FTP program.**

With any luck, you'll never have to use that cruddy old FTP program again! You've got WinZip and WS_FTP, ready to install.

Now would be a good time to disconnect from your Internet provider, especially if it charges by the hour. If you don't disconnect yourself, it may hang up on you, in which case you'll see a dialog box like that shown in Figure 8-15. If you're done, click the Cancel button to tell Dial-Up Networking not to bother you.

If you want to hang up yourself (and possibly save yourself some money), go to the Taskbar and find your dial-up connection there. Restore it on-screen if it's minimized and click the Disconnect button. Dial-Up Networking goes away, and you're no longer on the Internet.

Installing WinZip

You're almost there: All you have to do is install WinZip and then unzip WS_FTP, and you're ready to download all the software that you can get your hands on.

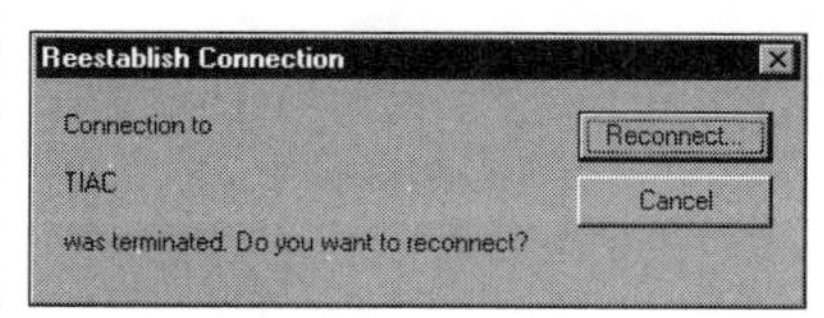

Figure 8-15: Dial-Up Networking asks what you'd like to do when your Internet provider hangs up on you.

Installing WinZip is a two-step process. First, you decompress the installation files, and then you use WinZip's setup program to install them. After you're done with the install, those decompressed installation files are pretty useless, so you may as well put them someplace where you can delete them to save some space on your disk. That's why we put them in our Temp directory — we know that we can delete everything in there whenever we want.

To install WinZip

1. **Choose Start on the Taskbar to run the program in the file \Program Files\Internet Utilities\winzip95.exe.**

   You can either type all that or use the Browse button to point to it. You see the WinZip Self-Extractor dialog box.

2. **Click OK.**

   WinZip automatically installs itself. You may have to click OK a couple of times to confirm WinZip's suggestions — they're all reasonable ones. After you're all finished, you see the WinZip screen, like that shown in Figure 8-16.

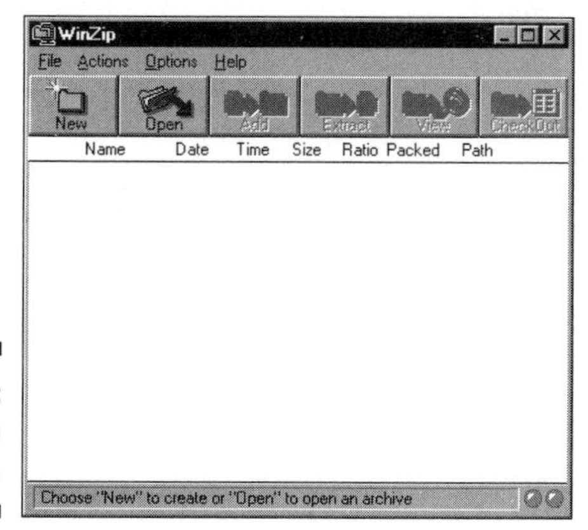

Figure 8-16: The WinZip window.

Other places to get stuff

Like traffic anywhere, traffic on the Information Superhighway can get kind of congested. If you're running into a traffic jam and can't get into `ftp.csra.net` or `ftp.winzip.com` (the latter is particularly hard to get into), you may be able to find the same software somewhere else. Here are some sites to try for WS_FTP:

What to Open	*What to Get*
`ftp.csra.net`	/pub/win32/ws_ftp32.zip
`ftp.coast.net`	/pub/systems/pc/simtel/win95/winsock/ ws_ftp32.zip

Here are some sites where you can get WinZip:

What to Open	*What to Get*
`ftp.winzip.com`	/winzip/winzip95.exe
`ftp.winsite.com`	/pub/pc.win95/miscutil/winzip95.exe
`ftp.csusm.edu`	/pub/winworld/win95/winzip95.exe

In the future, if you want to run WinZip, choose Start⇨Programs⇨WinZip⇨WinZip 6.0 32 bit from the Taskbar.

Installing WS_FTP

To install WS_FTP — remember, that's what you were trying to do originally — follow these steps:

1. **Open the WS_FTP.ZIP file that you downloaded earlier.**

   That is, click the Open button and find WS_FTP.ZIP (it should be in \Program Files\Internet Utilities unless you chose another place for it when you got it).

2. **Click the Extract button and specify the Extract To folder as c:\Program Files\Internet Utilities.**

   You can use the Directories/Drives box to point to this folder if you don't want to type that all yourself. Figure 8-17 illustrates the Extract dialog box.

3. **Click the Extract button.**

   After WinZip finishes extracting the WS_FTP program files from the ZIP file, you can close WinZip.

4. **Choose File⇨Exit from the WinZip menu.**

   You're all done with it for now.

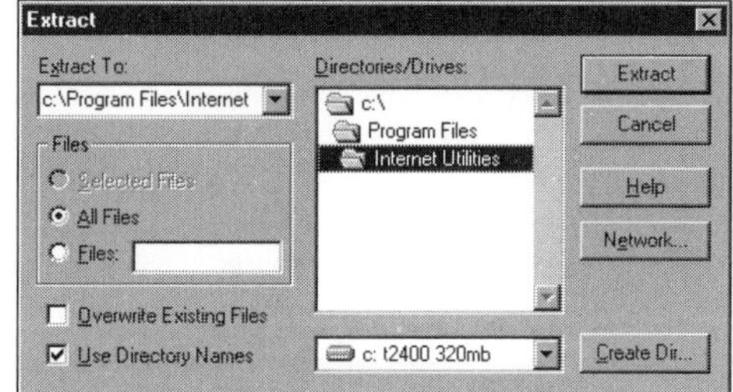

Figure 8-17: Extracting WS_FTP to c:\Program Files\Internet Utilities.

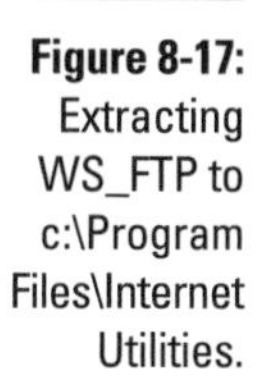

Making WS_FTP easy to start

The last thing that you may want to do is put WS_FTP on your Start menu so that you can get to it quickly from the Taskbar:

1. **Choose Start⇨Settings⇨Taskbar from the Taskbar.**
2. **On the Start Menu Programs tab, click the Add button to start the Customize Wizard.**
3. **Click the Browse button on the Create Shortcut window to find C:\Program Files\Internet Utilities\WS_FTP.EXE or type that name in the Command line box.**
4. **Click Next to tell Windows 95 where to put the shortcut and click Next again to tell it that Programs is fine.**
5. **Finally, click Finish to finish putting WS_FTP on the menu.**

Now when you click the Start button on the Taskbar, you see WS_FTP at the bottom of your Programs list.

What's Next?

Congratulations — you're on the Internet, and you're ready to download all sorts of interesting software.

Chapter 9 tells you the general procedures for downloading and installing software from the Internet, and Chapter 10 lists programs that are worth downloading.

Chapter 9

Grabbing Software over the Net

In This Chapter

- Getting files using an FTP program
- Decompressing compressed files with WinZip
- Checking software for viruses
- Installing software in Windows Program Manager or the Windows 95 desktop
- Using FTP to copy programs to your computer

After you have installed Trumpet WinSock or something similar (if you use Windows 3.1) or you have gotten Windows 95's TCP/IP program to work, you have an FTP program and you are ready to grab software right off the Internet. All the programs described in Chapter 10, in fact, are available as freeware or shareware by FTP.

Luckily, if you followed the instructions in Chapter 6, you already have a nice FTP program called WS_FTP, which is just what you need. You also can use a Web browser (like Netscape or Mosaic) for downloading files.

You need to know a few things, however, about downloading and running software from the Net, and this chapter tells you about them. You need a few well-chosen software tools, including a program to decompress compressed files. These useful little programs are usually called *utilities* in the jargon.

Instructions in this part of the book assume that you are using a PC running DOS and Windows 3.1 or Windows 95. If you are using a Macintosh, you use different unzipping software and a different FTP program. The concepts, however, are the same.

Using WS_FTP to Download Files

WS_FTP is good enough that even when we're using commercial WinSock packages that come with their own FTP programs, we still use WS_FTP because we like this program the best. To use WS_FTP to copy files from FTP servers on the Internet to your own computer, you do the following things (we give you more exact instructions in a minute):

1. **Connect your computer to the Internet.**

   That is, log in to your Internet account.

2. **Connect to the FTP server.**

3. **Tell the FTP program what file you want from the FTP server, where you want to put that file on your hard disk, and whether the file is ASCII (plain, unformatted text) or binary (anything else).**

4. **Start the transfer.**

   You may want to step out for coffee at this point, if the file is large.

5. **Disconnect from the FTP server.**

6. **Log out of your Internet account (assuming that you are done using the Internet).**

While you are connected to the FTP server, you can transfer more than one file. You can even transfer a file *from* your computer *to* the FTP server, but you'd better be sure that you have permission to put it there!

Dialing for files

Here's how to use the WS_FTP program to transfer a file from an FTP server to your computer:

1. **Run the WS_FTP program by double-clicking its icon.**

   You see the FTP Client Connect to dialog box, shown in Figure 9-1. This dialog box lets you enter information about the FTP server you want to connect to. WS_FTP saves information you enter so that you can easily connect to the FTP server again.

2. **In the Config name box, enter the name you want to use for this FTP server.**

   If you want to FTP to `rtfm.mit.edu`, for example, which contains FAQs for all Usenet newsgroups, you might enter **USENET FAQ Central**.

3. **In the Host name box, enter the name of the FTP server.**

   This name can be a regular Internet name, such as `oak.oakland.edu`, another useful FTP server, or a numeric address.

4. **Set the Host type box to *auto detect,* unless you know what kind of computer it is.**

   This step tells WS_FTP to guess which operating system the FTP server is using.

5. **If you actually have a username on the FTP server, enter your username and password in the User ID and Password boxes. Otherwise, click the Anonymous Login box and type your e-mail address when WS_FTP asks.**

FTPing with your Web browser

You can use a Web browser, such as Netscape or Mosaic, as an FTP program. Instead of giving your browser a Web page's *URL* (address), you type the file's URL on an FTP server. Type **ftp://**, followed by the name of the FTP server and the file pathname. For example, to get a file named WINZIP95.TXT from the WINZIP directory on the `ftp.winzip.com` server, you type

```
ftp://ftp.winzip.com/winzip/
winzip95.txt
```

Your browser downloads the file. If the file is not a text file or Web page, your browser asks you what to do with the file — tell your browser to save the file on your hard disk.

If you choose to use anonymous FTP, WS_FTP asks for your e-mail address, which it uses as your password — the usual thing to do when you FTP anonymously.

If you want WS_FTP to store the password in the Password box rather than ask for it every time to connect to the FTP server, click the Save Password box. An X shows that a box is selected.

Leave the Account box blank, unless you have your own username on the FTP server and you know which account to enter.

6. **In the Remote Dir box, enter the directory you want to look in on the FTP server.**

   Alternatively, you can leave this box blank and look around yourself.

7. **In the Local Dir box, enter the directory on your own PC in which you want to store downloaded files.**

8. **Click the Save Config button to save this information.**

9. **Click OK.**

   WS_FTP tries to connect to the FTP server.

Figure 9-1: Which FTP server do you want to talk to?

Do you copy?

After you connect to the FTP server, you see the WS_FTP window, shown in Figure 9-2. WS_FTP displays information about your computer files in the left side of the window (entitled *Local PC info*) and the FTP server's directories and files on the right side (entitled *Remote host info*). On each side are buttons to change directories (ChgDir), make directories (MkDir), delete directories (RmDir), view files, and so on. Naturally, you don't have permission to delete or change anything on most FTP servers, so don't even try.

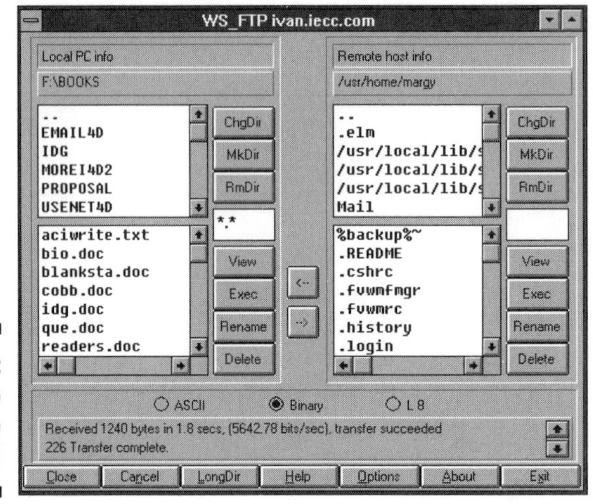

Figure 9-2: Prepare to receive some files!

To move from directory to directory on the FTP server, choose directory names from the list box. Or you can click the ChgDir button and enter the directory's full pathname.

Here's how to copy a file:

1. **Click the ASCII or Binary radio buttons near the bottom of the window.**

   For files that consist entirely of text, choose ASCII. For anything else, choose Binary.

2. **Choose the file you want on the FTP server.**
3. **Choose the directory to put the file in on your own computer.**
4. **Click the left-pointing arrow button in the middle of the window.**

   WS_FTP downloads the file. For large files, this step can take time, and WS_FTP displays your progress as a percentage completed.

FTP won't speak to me!

If you have a problem connecting to the FTP server, messages appear in the two-line box at the bottom of the WS_FTP window. You can scroll this little box up and down to see what happened. For example, `rtfm.mit.edu` is frequently overloaded and doesn't let you log on. But the FTP server sends helpful messages about other FTP sites that may have the information you want. You can see these messages in the two-line box.

Double-click the messages the FTP server sends, if you really want to see them. WS_FTP opens a big window so that you can see the messages better. To close the window, click Close.

Hang up!

To disconnect from the FTP server after you are finished, click the Close button at the bottom of the WS_FTP window. If you want to exit from the program, click the Exit button, which hangs up and exits.

Connecting again

To call someone else, click the Connect button on the WS_FTP window. You see the FTP Client Connect to window again. Fill in the information and click OK to make the connection.

To call an FTP server you've called before, click Connect. In the FTP Client Connect to window, click the arrow button to the right of the Config name box. You see a list of the configurations you entered before — choose one and then click OK.

Ready to Decompress with WinZip

You need an unzipping program to deal with compressed files, specifically those files with the file extension *.ZIP* (these files are called, amazingly, *ZIP files*). Programs with names like PKZIP, PKUNZIP, and UNZIP have been around for years. These programs are especially useful on the Internet, because compressed files take up less space on FTP servers and take less time to download.

PKUNZIP, UNZIP, and their brethren work fine, but they are DOS programs and not real convenient to use from Windows. Using the MS-DOS icon every time you want to run one is annoying. Luckily, a Connecticut programmer named Nico Mak wrote a nice little Windows program called WinZip that can both unzip and zip things for you, right from Windows.

Grabbing WinZip

To install WinZip, you take three major steps: get the file, unzip the file, and create an icon for WinZip. In the following steps, we use the WS_FTP program to do the transferring, but you can use any FTP program. Here we go.

If you already have WinZip (which is also available through mail or from various shareware outlets), skip this entire section. If you have and love PKZIP and PKUNZIP or UNZIP and don't mind running these programs from DOS, you can skip this section, too.

Here's how to get WinZip by FTP:

1. **Connect to the Internet.**

   That is, run the Trumpet WinSock program, or whatever program you use to get connected, and choose Connect from the menu bar.

2. **When you are connected, run the WS_FTP program or another FTP program.**

   If you use WS_FTP, you see the window shown in Figure 9-1. The program wants to know what FTP server to connect to.

3. **In the Host name box, enter** `ftp.winzip.com`**.**

4. **Click the anonymous Login box.**

   The word *anonymous* appears in the User ID box, and asterisks representing your e-mail address appear in the Password box. If the asterisks don't appear, type **anonymous** in the User ID box and your e-mail address in the Password box.

5. **Type** winzip **in the Remote Dir box to tell WS_FTP to look in the WINZIP directory for the file.**

6. **Type** c:\util **(or the name of the directory you want to put the WinZip program files in) in the Local Dir box.**

   Doing so tells WS_FTP where to store the file you download.

7. **Click OK.**

   WS_FTP connects to the WinZip FTP server. This server is often busy — if you can't get through, try again in a few minutes or late at night.

   When you are connected, WS_FTP lists your Local Dir files on the left side of the window and the WINZIP directory files on the right side of the window.

8. **If you use Windows 3.1, click wz60wn16.exe in the right-hand list.**

   Doing so selects WinZip 6.0 for Windows. If you use Windows 95, click WINZIP95.EXE.

These version numbers may change because Nico Mak upgrades WinZip frequently. If you are not sure which file to download, click a TXT file (one with the extension `txt`) and then read that file by clicking the View button.

9. **Click Binary to tell WS_FTP that you are downloading a binary file, not a text file.**

10. **Click the left-pointing arrow between the two lists of files.**

    Doing so tells WS_FTP to copy the file from the right-hand list (on the FTP server) to the left-hand list (your PC).

    You see a Transfer Status window, which disappears when the transfer is done.

11. **Click the Exit button to disconnect from the WinZip FTP server and exit from the WS_FTP program.**

If you have a Web browser, look at this Web page instead:

```
http://www.winzip.com/
```

The WinZip FTP site is really busy, so you may need to try to connect at several different times of day.

Decompressing WinZip

Now you can install WinZip from the file you downloaded. To decompress and install WinZip

1. **In Windows File Manager or My Computer, double-click the name of the file you just downloaded.**

   A dialog box asks whether you want to go ahead and set up WinZip.

2. **Click the Setup button.**

   The setup program asks what directory you want to put the program into. The program suggests C:\WINZIP, but you can change the directory if you want to put the file somewhere else.

3. **Click OK.**

   Follow the directions on-screen. WinZip displays information about the program and then asks what kind of installation you want to do.

4. **Leave Express Setup selected and click OK.**

   WinZip asks you to agree to its license agreement.

5. **Click Yes, assuming you agree.**

   Now WinZip is installed, and it runs. You see the WinZip window, shown in Figure 9-3.

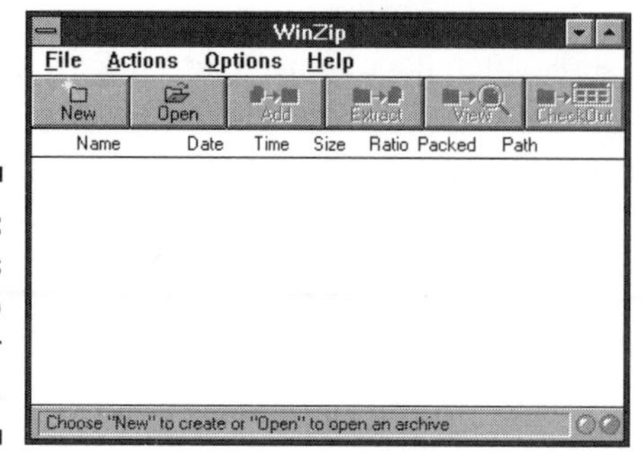

Figure 9-3: WinZip is ready to unzip your files.

Now you have the WinZip program. No more DOS commands for you! You are ready to unzip programs you download from the Internet. A WinZip icon appears in Windows Program Manager (if you use Windows 3.1) or WinZip in your Programs menu (if you use Windows 95).

Running WinZip

Give it a try! Double-click that icon, if WinZip isn't already running.

WinZip may display a bunch of helpful messages, including a question about your intention to register your copy, the first time you run the program. (We talk about this subject at the end of Chapter 10.)

WinZip's window

After WinZip is finished with its configuration questions, a window similar to Figure 9-3 appears.

To open a ZIP file (which the WinZip folks call an *archive*), click the Open button and choose the directory and filename for the ZIP file. Poof! WinZip displays a list of the files in the archive, with their dates and sizes.

WinZip remembers the last four ZIP files you opened and lists them at the bottom of the File menu. Thanks to this feature, reopening a ZIP file you used recently is easy.

Unzip it!

Sounds suggestive, we know, but it's not as much fun as it sounds. If you want to use a file from a ZIP file, you need to *extract* that file after you have opened the ZIP file — that is, you ask WinZip to decompress the file you want to use and to store it in a new file, not as part of the ZIP file.

To extract a file

1. **Choose the file you want to extract from the list of files.**

   You can choose files listed together by clicking the first file and then Shift+clicking the last one. To select an additional file, Ctrl+click it.

2. **Click the Extract button.**

   A dialog box asks which directory you want to put the file in and whether you want to extract all files in the archive or simply the file you selected.

3. **Select the directory in which to store the unzipped files.**

4. **Click OK.**

   WinZip unzips the file. The ZIP file is unchanged, but now you have the decompressed file (or files), also.

Zip it!

To add a file to a ZIP file

1. **Open the ZIP file by using the Open button.**

2. **Click the Add button.**

   You see the Add dialog box, shown in Figure 9-4.

3. **Use the Directories/Drives box to select the directory that contains the file (or files) you want to add.**

   Select the files you want from the Select Files list.

4. **Choose a setting for the Action box.**

   Decide whether you want WinZip to compress the files into the ZIP file, leaving the original files untouched (Add), or whether you want WinZip to delete the original files after they have been added (Move).

5. **Click the Add (or Move) button to do the deed.**

When you choose files, you can select a group of files that is listed together by clicking the first one and then Shift+clicking the last one. To select an additional file, Ctrl+click it.

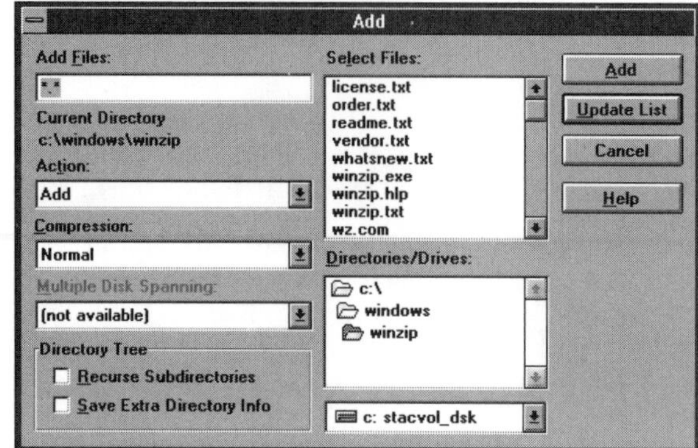

Figure 9-4: Adding a file to a ZIP file.

Making your own ZIP file

To make a new ZIP file

1. **Click the New button in the WinZip window.**
2. **Choose the directory in which you want to store the new ZIP file and enter a name for the file.**

   Make sure that the file extension is *.ZIP* (or omit the file extension, and WinZip adds *ZIP* itself).
3. **Click OK.**
4. **Add files to your new ZIP file, as explained in the preceding section.**

Zipped out?

When you're all finished zipping and unzipping, quit WinZip by choosing File⇨Exit.

WinZip is close friends with Windows File Manager. If you drag a ZIP file from File Manager to the WinZip window, WinZip automatically opens the file. If you drag another kind of file, or a group of files, to WinZip, it's added to the current archive. (If a current archive doesn't exist, it starts a new one and asks you what to call it.)

Now that you know how to unzip software you get from the Internet, you're ready for the next topic: safe software.

Scanning for Viruses

We all know that you practice safe software. That is, you check every new program to make sure that no hidden software viruses, which might display obnoxious messages or trash your hard disk, are lurking around. If doing so is true of you, you can skip this section.

For the rest of you, using a virus-scanning program is a good idea. Otherwise, you never know what naughty piece of code you might unwittingly FTP to your defenseless computer.

If you use MS-DOS 6.2 (or later)

DOS 6.2 and Windows 3.1 come with a virus checker built right into the Windows File Manager. Here's how to use the virus checker:

1. **Run File Manager.**
2. **Choose Tools⇨Antivirus.**

   You see the Microsoft Anti-Virus window, shown in Figure 9-5.
3. **Choose a disk drive, by clicking it in the Drives box.**
4. **Click the Detect and Clean button.**

   If you are scanning a large hard disk for viruses, this step can take several minutes.

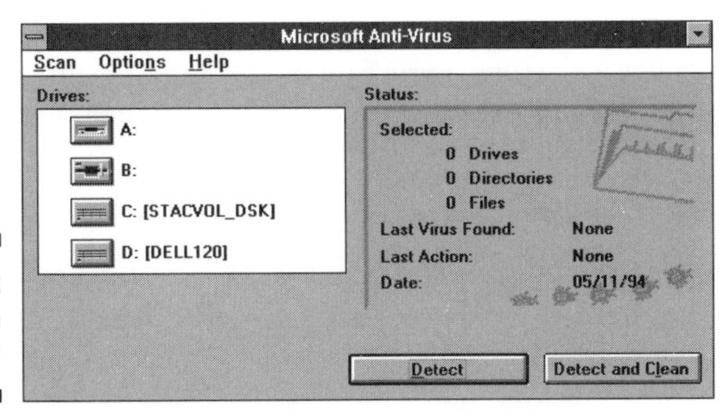

Figure 9-5: Evict those viruses!

Running Anti-Virus after obtaining new software is a good idea. The FTP servers on the Internet make every effort to keep their software archives virus-free, but nobody is perfect. Don't get caught by some prankster's idea of a joke!

If you use an earlier version of MS-DOS

Upgrading from DOS 6.0 or 6.1 to 6.2 costs about $10, so we suggest that you do so. DOS 6.2 has lots of nice little features and installs easily and quickly. If you don't want to upgrade, many virus checkers are available on the Net. Use your FTP program to connect to `oak.oakland.edu` and go to the `/pub/msdos/virus` directory. Follow the instructions in the section "Netting a Program" later in this chapter.

If you use PC-DOS

PC-DOS comes with IBM's own antivirus program, which you can run from the DOS command line as IBMAVD or from Windows by clicking the IBM AntiVirus icon in the PCDOS 7.0 Tools window in the Program Manager.

If you use Windows 95

Strangely, Windows 95 doesn't come with virus-checking software. You may want to download one from the Net. Take a look at the Consummate WinSock Apps List on the World Wide Web, described in Chapter 10, to find one.

Netting a Program

Now you are ready to grab software from the Net, unzip it as necessary, make little icons for the software, and check it all over for diseases. This section gives you general instructions for getting a program off the Internet and installing it on your PC. We are assuming that you know which program you want and that you know which FTP server has the program.

Luckily, in Chapter 10, when we mention a program you can download, we tell you which FTP servers you can find it on. Programs you can download include mail readers, newsreaders, and programs for accessing the World Wide Web.

Getting hold of the program

To copy the file from the FTP server to your own computer

1. **If you want to make a separate directory for the program, do so.**

   Otherwise, you can store the program in your \INTERNET directory.

2. **Connect to the Internet.**

3. **Run your FTP program (WS_FTP or whatever).**
4. **Connect to the FTP server that has the program you want.**

   Most FTP servers with software archives accept anonymous connections.
5. **Choose the directory on the FTP server that contains the file you want and choose the directory on your computer in which to put that file.**
6. **Tell your FTP program to download the file in Binary mode.**

   In WS_FTP, click the Binary option.
7. **Choose the file to download.**
8. **Start the download (in WS_FTP, click the left-pointing arrow button in the middle of the window).**

   Repeat steps 5 through 7 for each file you need.
9. **Disconnect from the FTP server and exit from the FTP program (in WS_FTP, click the Exit button).**
10. **Disconnect from the Internet to save connect charges.**

Unzipping the program files

Most programs are stored on FTP servers in ZIP files, both to save disk space on the FTP server and to save transfer time while FTPing the file. If the program isn't in a ZIP file, skip this section.

1. **In Windows File Manager or Explorer, double-click the ZIP file.**

   This step runs WinZip and opens the ZIP file. WinZip shows you the files the ZIP file contains.
2. **Click the Extract button.**

   You see the Extract dialog box, shown in Figure 9-6.

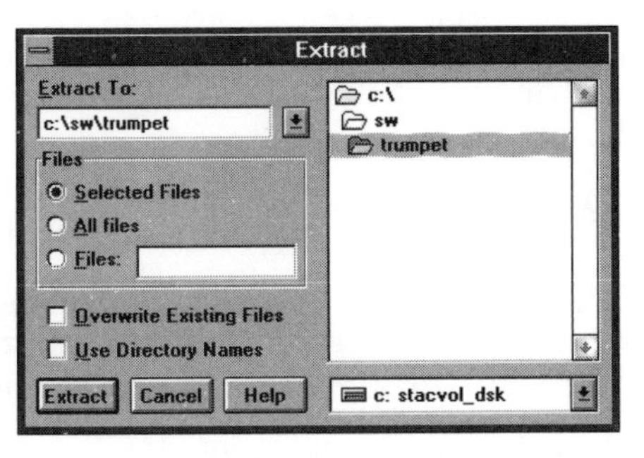

Figure 9-6: To get the compressed files from a ZIP file, just add water!

3. **In the Extract To box, type the full pathname of the directory in which you want the files to be stored.**

   Alternatively, you can use the directory box to its right to choose the directory.

4. **Choose All files so that you extract all the files in the ZIP file.**

5. **Click Extract.**

   WinZip begins copying and decompressing the files from the ZIP file into their new home. As long as WinZip is decompressing files, the little light in the lower-right corner of the WinZip window remains red. When WinZip finishes copying files, the light turns green. Is this cute, or what?

6. **To leave WinZip, choose File⇨Exit.**

7. **Now that you have decompressed the files that are in the ZIP file, you can delete the ZIP file if you need the space on your disk.**

   Another good idea is to copy the ZIP file to a diskette to add to your software archive. This diskette is invaluable if you need to reinstall the program later, install the program on another computer, or give the program to a friend.

If the ZIP file contains any files named READ.ME or README.TXT or anything else with a *.txt* or *.doc* extension, read those files by using Windows Notepad or your word-processing program. These files may contain instructions for installing and configuring the program that are more accurate than what we are about to tell you.

Installing the program

Now the program is ready to run, but there is no icon for it. A few housekeeping tasks remain.

If the program comes with a file named SETUP.EXE or INSTALL.EXE, run it by double-clicking the filename in File Manager.

To make an icon for the program in Windows 95, simply drag the filename of the program onto the desktop or onto an open folder on the desktop. Windows 95 creates a shortcut icon for the program.

To make an icon for the program in Windows 3.1

1. **Open both the Program Manager and File Manager and arrange the screen so that you can see the program group you want to put the icon in (in Program Manager) and the program name (in File Manager).**

2. **Drag the program name from the File Manager into the Program Manager and place it in the program group where you want it.**

   You see a new icon in your new program group.

Associating the program with data files

If the program uses files as input, associate those files with the appropriate file extension. These programs include editors, word processors, draw programs, and other programs that store their data in files. For programs that don't work on input files, skip these steps.

Here's what to do in Windows 3.1:

1. **In Windows File Manager, choose File⇨Associate.**

   You see the Associate dialog box.

2. **In the Files with Extension box, type the filename extension of the files that your new program works with.**

   For example, if you just installed a graphics program that displays GIF files, type **GIF**. The Associate With box shows the program that is associated with that type of file. If you see *(None)*, no program is currently assigned to that type of file.

3. **Click the Browse button, select the filename of the program you just installed, and click OK.**

4. **Click OK to make the Associate dialog box go away.**

Now File Manager knows what program to run when you double-click files with that extension. For example, WinZip automatically associates itself with the ZIP extension so that when you double-click a ZIP file in File Manager, WinZip runs to display the contents of the ZIP file.

In Windows 95, do the following:

1. **In Windows Explorer, choose View⇨Options.**

   You see the Options window.

2. **Select the File Types tab.**

   You see a list of registered file types, that is, types of files for which Windows 95 knows what program to run. As you select each file type on the list, you see details about the file type, including the filename extension and the program that is associated with it.

3. **Click the New Type button.**

   You see the Add New File Type dialog box.

4. **Type the description of the file type and the filename extension into the first two boxes.**

5. **Click the New button.**

   If a program is already associated with that filename extension, Windows tells you about it. If not, you see the New Action window.

6. **In the Action box, make up a description of what double-clicking a file of this type will do.**

   For example, if double-clicking a graphic will display the file, type something like **Display the graphics file**.

7. **Click the Browse button, select the program you just installed, and click Open.**

8. **Click OK in the New Action dialog box.**

   You return to the Add New File Type window. (Windows 95 sure has enough windows — far more than 95!)

9. **Click the Close button.**

   You return to the Options window, and the new file type appears on the list of registered file types.

10. **Click the Close button.**

Now Windows 95 understands your new program. Double-clicking files of the type you specified will now run your new program automagically.

Configuring the program

Now you can run the program by double-clicking its icon. Hooray! You may have to tell the program, however, about your Internet address or your computer or who knows what before it can do its job. Refer to the text files, if any, that came with the program or choose Help from the program's menu bar to get more information about how to configure and run your new program.

So Where Are All the Programs?

You are raring to download and install a program — you know all the moves! Chapter 10 has scads of WinSock programs you can download and run.

Chapter 10

Cool WinSock Software

In This Chapter

- How to find WinSock software on the Internet for use with Windows 3.1 or Windows 95
- Elegant e-mail programs
- Beautiful Web browsers
- Fabulous FTP programs
- Nifty newsreaders
- And more!

If you have read Chapter 9, you know how to use an FTP program to download a program from an FTP server on the Internet, install the program using Windows 3.1 or Windows 95, and run it. So what programs might you want to download and install? This chapter tells all.

If you are looking for IRC, telnet, or Gopher programs, see Chapters 18, 19, and 20, which describe these three Internet services.

Before you can use any program described in this chapter, you must be up and running with an Internet SLIP provider, as described in Chapters 6, 7, and 8. You also need some blank space on your disk, usually no more than 1MB per program (sometimes much less).

Super Sources of Software

Several Internauts have created Web pages that list (and rate) hundreds of useful WinSock programs, including what they do, how well they work, and where you can find them.

The Consummate WinSock Apps List

By far the best Web page about WinSock programs is the Consummate WinSock Apps List, created by Texas undergraduate Forrest Stroud.

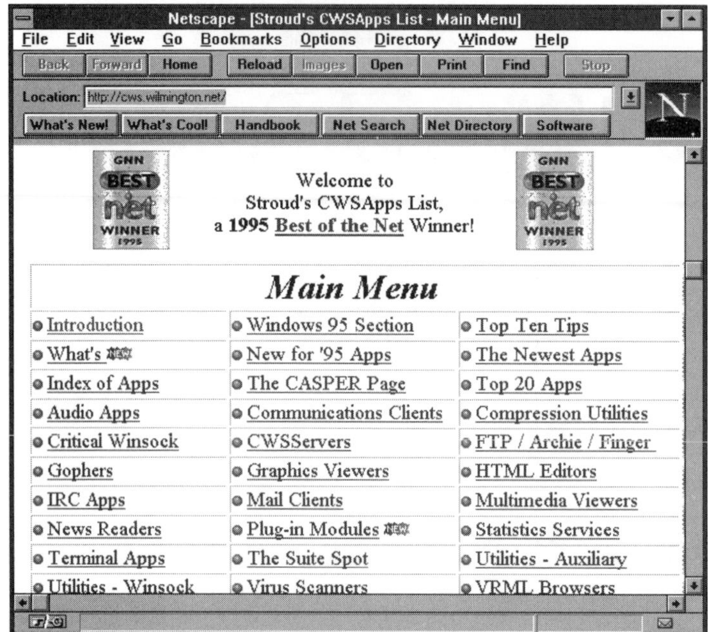

Figure 10-1: The Consummate WinSock Apps List is the easiest way to find all kinds of WinSock programs.

The Consummate WinSock Apps List is at a bunch of sites, including these:

```
http://cwsapps.texas.net/
http://cws.wilmington.net/
```

To use the Consummate WinSock Apps List, find the listing of the types of programs (shown in Figure 10-1) and click the type of program you want. You get a Web page listing programs of that type. Figure 10-2 shows part of the listing of mail clients (that is, e-mail programs).

Many entries in the Consummate WinSock Apps List contain links to a home page for the program so that you can get full details about the program. Entries also contain a link to an FTP server from which the program can be downloaded. To download the program, click the Location link and tell your Web browser where to save the program file. (Then see Chapter 9 for more information about installing software.)

Forrest updates the list constantly, adding new programs and changing the listing to refer to new program versions. Browsing the pages from time to time to see what's new (or clicking the Newest Apps link on the main page) is well worth the effort.

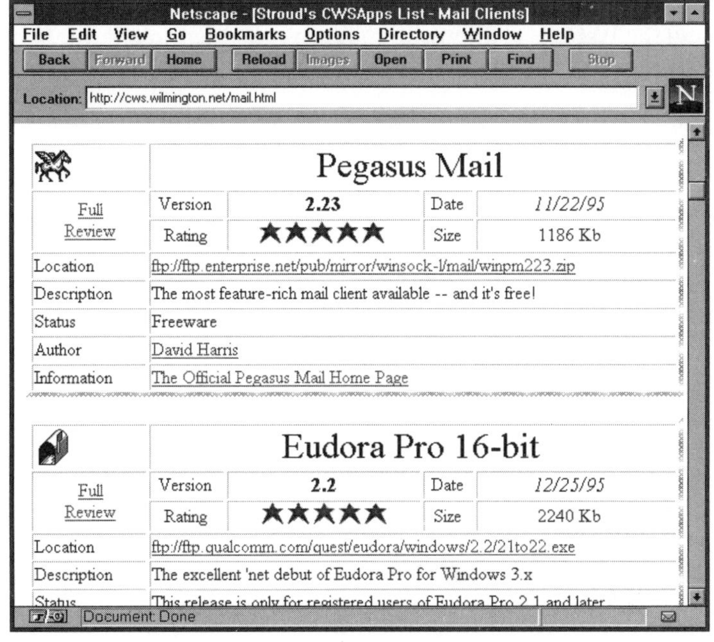

Figure 10-2: Here is information about two excellent mail programs.

Everything You Need to Surf the Net — For Free!

That's the actual name of the page at

```
http://www.primenet.com/~tcp/
```

Like the Consummate WinSock Apps List, E.Y.N.T.S.T.N.F.F. lists programs by type, with links to FTP servers from which you can download them. This page doesn't list as many programs, though, nor does it contain as many details about each program.

Windows95.Com

Can you *believe* Microsoft didn't register the domain name `windows95.com`? Apparently, Steve Jenkins, an M.B.A. student in Utah, did first, and he's using the domain name to host a site that contains information about lots of Windows 95-compatible shareware, including Internet programs. The URL is

```
http://www.windows95.com/
```

As Mr. Jenkins points out, his page is in no way connected with Microsoft. If you can't find the Web page, Microsoft may have decided to put Mr. Jenkins out of business, because it owns the trademark to the name Windows 95. Stay tuned!

WinSite

WinSite is a huge repository of freeware and shareware programs for Windows and Windows 95, including WinSock programs.

```
http://www.winsite.com/
```

WinSite is partially supported by America Online, which is making an effort to give back to the Internet in return for all the free stuff that AOL users get from the Net. You can use your FTP program to get files from WinSite by connecting to `ftp.winsite.com` and going to its `pub/pc/win3/winsock` directory.

The Papa FTP Server

If you don't have access to the World Wide Web, you can download WinSock programs from many FTP servers, including the one at `papa.indstate.edu`. Go to the `winsock-l` directory and look around. This site coordinates with the Consummate WinSock Apps page and has much of the same software.

Yahoo!

Unless Yahoo! has reorganized since this book went to press, here's how to get to its list of pages with information about WinSock programs. Start at the Yahoo! page (`http://www.yahoo.com/`), click Computers and Internet, click Software, click Protocols, and click WinSock.

Elegant E-Mail

A good e-mail program makes sending, reading, forwarding, replying to, and saving mail messages easy. Ideally, the program should be able to sort incoming messages into folders based on what's in the headers. Luckily, several excellent e-mail programs are available as shareware or freeware.

If you use Windows 95, you may want to use Microsoft Exchange, which comes with Windows 95. See Chapter 8.

Your online service can do it, too

What if you have an account with an online service? Can you use all this cool WinSock software? The answer depends on the service.

- America Online lets you use all WinSock software except for e-mail programs. Go to the AOL keyword *winsock* to get information about the AOL WinSock program.
- CompuServe lets you use WinSock software if you use its NetLauncher package. NetLauncher comes with Spry Mosaic (a WinSock Web browser), but you can use other WinSock programs, too.
- Prodigy doesn't support WinSock programs.
- The Microsoft Network (MSN) can act like a SLIP or PPP account, so you can use WinSock software with it.
- NetCruiser lets you use WinSock programs — see Chapter 12.
- GNN can, too — see Chapter 13.

Eudora

Our favorite e-mail program is Eudora, by Qualcomm. A shareware version of Eudora is available via FTP. If you find that you like Eudora, send Qualcomm a check for the cost of the program (about $70) to get the commercial version, which is even better than the shareware one. If you have questions about the commercial version, you can send e-mail to `eudora-sales@qualcomm.com` or call 800-2EUDORA. (Hmm. If you could send e-mail, you probably wouldn't have to ask the question.)

Getting Eudora

The shareware version of Eudora is available from

```
ftp://ftp.qualcomm.com/quest/windows/eudora/
```

It's also on lots of other FTP servers. Look for a file with a filename starting with EUDOR. Eudora is also included on disks in several books about e-mail, including our *Internet E-Mail For Dummies* (IDG Books Worldwide, Inc.).

The file is probably a self-extracting ZIP file. To run the file, simply double-click its name in File Manager. Several files pop out. If one has a name like `readme.txt`, read it in Windows Notepad or any word processor — this file contains late-breaking news about Eudora.

Installing Eudora

To make Eudora convenient to run, make an icon for it in Windows 3.1 Program Manager. Run the Windows File Manager. Arrange the windows so that you can see the WEUDORA.EXE file (which is the actual program file) in File Manager and the Program Manager program group you want the icon to be in. Drag the file WEUDORA.EXE from the File Manager to the Program Manager program group you want the icon in. A nice little picture of a stamped letter appears in Program Manager. There's your Eudora icon!

In Windows 95, run My Computer or Explorer and file the WEUDORA.EXE file in the Eudora program directory. Then drag the file onto the desktop. Windows 95 creates an icon, which is a shortcut to the program.

Before you can use Eudora, you have to tell it about yourself:

1. **Double-click the Eudora icon (the little picture of a stamped letter).**

   You see the PC Eudora window. We don't include a picture of it here because it is blank except for the menu bar at the top.

2. **Choose Special➪Configuration.**

   You see the Configuration dialog box, shown in Figure 10-3.

Configuration

Network Configuration
POP Account:
Real Name:
SMTP Server:
Return Address:
Check For Mail Every 0 Minute(s)
Ph Server:

Message Configuration
Message Width: 80 Message Lines: 20 Tab Stop: 8
Screen Font: Courier New Size: 10
Printer Font: Courier New Size: 12
Auto Receive Attachment Directory:
Cancel OK

Figure 10-3: Telling Eudora your life's story.

3. **In the POP Account box, enter your e-mail address.**

   This entry doesn't have to be an address on your Internet provider's computer — it's wherever your mail comes.

4. **In the Real Name box, enter your real name as you want it to appear in parentheses after your e-mail address.**

5. **Leave the SMTP Server box blank to indicate that the same computer on which you receive your mail will handle sending mail, too.**

   Also, leave the Return Address box blank, which means that you want the return address on your e-mail to be the same e-mail address you entered in step 3.

6. **In the Check For Mail Every box, enter** 30 **so that while you are connected to the Internet, Eudora automagically checks your mailbox for mail every 30 minutes.**

   Enter a larger number to check less often. Don't enter a number smaller than 15 because doing so ties up both your own Internet connection and your Internet provider's mail server.

7. **Leave everything else as it is (for now).**

   You may want to change some settings later, but these settings should do for now.

8. **Click OK to save these settings.**

Eusing Eudora

Here is a quick list of things you can do in Eudora (Eudora Pro, the program's commercial version, is shown in Figure 10-4):

- To create a new message, choose Message⇨New, press Ctrl+N, or click the New Message button on the toolbar.
- To see the messages in your Inbox, choose Mailbox⇨In or press Ctrl+I.
- To read a message, double-click the message in your Inbox or other folder.
- To delete a message after you've read it, choose Message⇨Delete, press Ctrl+D, or click the Delete (trash can) button on the toolbar.
- To get your incoming messages from your Internet provider, choose File⇨Check Mail, click the Check Mail button on the toolbar, or press Ctrl+M.
- To send your outgoing messages to the Internet, choose File⇨Send Queued Messages or press Ctrl+T.

See Chapters 6 and 7 of *The Internet For Dummies,* 3rd Edition, for a complete description of how to use Eudora.

Pegasus

Pegasus is an excellent freeware e-mail program. Its author, David Harris, lives in New Zealand and doesn't sell a commercial version of the program. He just gives it away over the Internet and supports the project by selling the manuals.

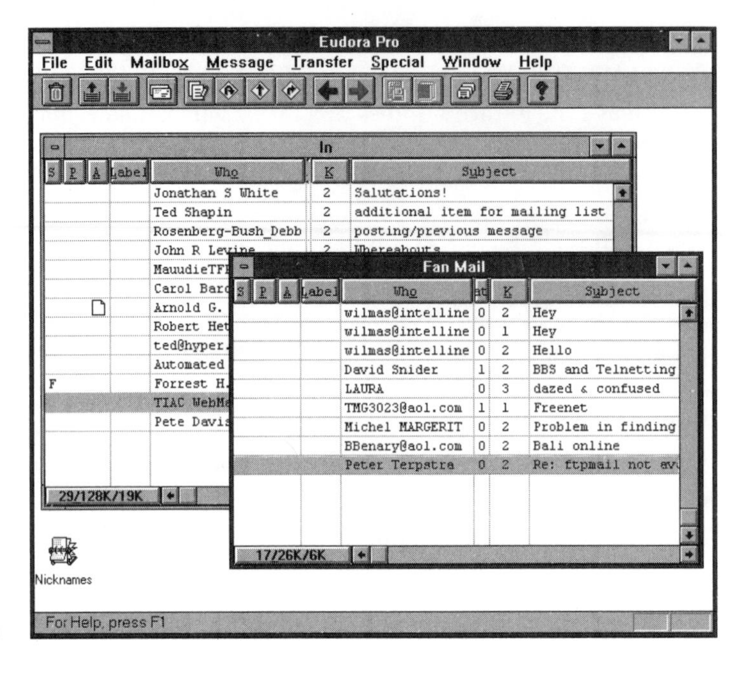

Figure 10-4: Eudora lets you sort your mail into many different folders so that you don't have to leave all your mail in your Inbox.

Don't think that because it's free, it's not good — Pegasus rivals the good commercial programs! If you feel like supporting Mr. Harris's Pegasus project, or if you plan on using Pegasus extensively, you can order a set of Pegasus manuals from him.

Pegasus is also available for DOS, the Mac, and a few other systems. It handles both Internet mail and Novell network mail and is available in over a dozen languages (actual human languages, like French and German). Amazing for a free program!

Getting Pegasus

You can find information about Pegasus, as well as downloading the latest version or ordering a set of manuals, at

```
http://www.cuslm.ca/pegasus/
```

So who is Eudora, anyway?

According to the Eudora manual, the program's author was reading Eudora Welty's short story, *Why I Live at the P.O.*, and he got inspired. It's nice to know that even nerds read some real books from time to time.

Installing Pegasus

Pegasus arrives in a ZIP file with a name like WINPM223.ZIP. Here's how to install it:

1. **Make a directory for the Pegasus program files using File Manager or Explorer.**

   Mr. Harris recommends calling the directory PMAIL.

2. **Run WinZIP (or another ZIP program) to unzip the file you downloaded.**

   The file contains (at least for version 2.23)

   - INSTALL.TXT, a text file with installation instructions
   - WGUIDE.EXE, the online documentation
   - WINMAIL.ZIP, a ZIP file that contains the actual program

3. **Make an icon for the online documentation, by dragging the filename WGUIDE.EXE to the Program Manager (in Windows 3.1).**

   In Windows 95, drag the filename from My Computer or Explorer to the desktop. It's an ugly MS-DOS icon, but it works.

4. **Double-click the icon to run the program that displays the documentation.**

   The documentation appears with instructions about how to read it. When you are done, keep pressing the Esc key until the program ends.

5. **To unpack the program itself, use WinZIP to unzip it into the directory you created.**

   Dozens of files appear, most of them of no interest to you.

6. **Make an icon for the Pegasus program by dragging the WINPMAIL.EXE filename to the Program Manager.**

   In Windows 95, drag the filename from My Computer or Explorer to the desktop. A lovely little flying horse appears.

7. **Double-click the Winpmail icon (that is, Windows Pegasus Mail) to run Pegasus (at last!).**

   You see the Setting up mailboxes dialog box, shown in Figure 10-5.

8. **Click the choice appropriate for you.**

   If it's just l'il ol' you using your computer, and you have just one l'il ol' Internet account, take the first choice. Pegasus asks you where you want your e-mail directory to be, suggesting C:\PMAIL\MAIL. You can change the location if you want your e-mail messages stored elsewhere.

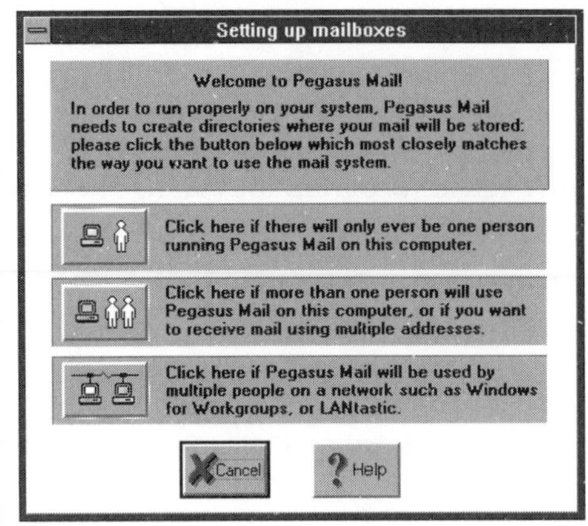

Figure 10-5: Pegasus wants to know how many people plan to use this installation.

9. **Click OK to tell Pegasus to make you a mail directory.**

   Pegasus searches your computer for a file named WINSOCK.DLL, which is part of Trumpet WinSock (or whatever software you use to connect to the Internet). When Pegasus finds the file, it asks whether it should use the file to connect to the Internet. (Well, what else would you use WINSOCK.DLL for? A virtual paperweight?)

10. **Click Yes.**

    You see the big, scary TCP/IP Network Configuration dialog box, shown in Figure 10-6. The left half of the dialog box is where you tell Pegasus how to send outgoing mail, and the right half lets you tell Pegasus how to get your incoming mail.

TCP/IP Network Configuration

WinSock information/settings
(Not loaded)
TCP/IP socket timeout 30

Outgoing (SMTP) mail
Relay host:
From field:
Send mail at once (don't queue)
Prefer for outgoing Internet mail
Use for all outgoing mail
Send queue during idle checks
Note: outgoing mail will only be sent if you have entered a valid username and password in the POP3 section.

Incoming (POP3) mail
Host:
Port: 110
Username:
Password:
Leave mail larger than 0 KB
Poll new mail after 0 secs idle
Message count only on idle poll
Allow checks when minimized
Delete retrieved mail on host
Check when opening new mail
Download only unread mail

OK Help Cancel

Figure 10-6: You have to tell Pegasus about your Internet account before it can get your e-mail.

11. **For the Relay host, enter the name of your mail gateway (your Internet provider's host computer that accepts your outgoing mail and sends it along to the Internet).**

    If you don't know the name, call your Internet provider and ask.

12. **For the Host, enter the name of your mail server (your Internet provider's host computer that stores your incoming mail until you are ready to pick it up).**

    The host may be the same computer as the Relay host. The host is usually the same as the part of your e-mail address after the at sign. For example, if your e-mail address is `elvis@presley.com`, you should probably enter `presley.com`. Again, your Internet provider will tell you the name to use.

13. **For the Username, enter your username.**

    Your username is the part of your e-mail address that comes before the at sign.

14. **Type your password in the Password box.**

    On-screen, you see asterisks.

15. **Click OK.**

    You see the Pegasus Mail window (shown in Figure 10-7), and Pegasus tries to get your mail (which won't work if you're not online with your Internet provider).

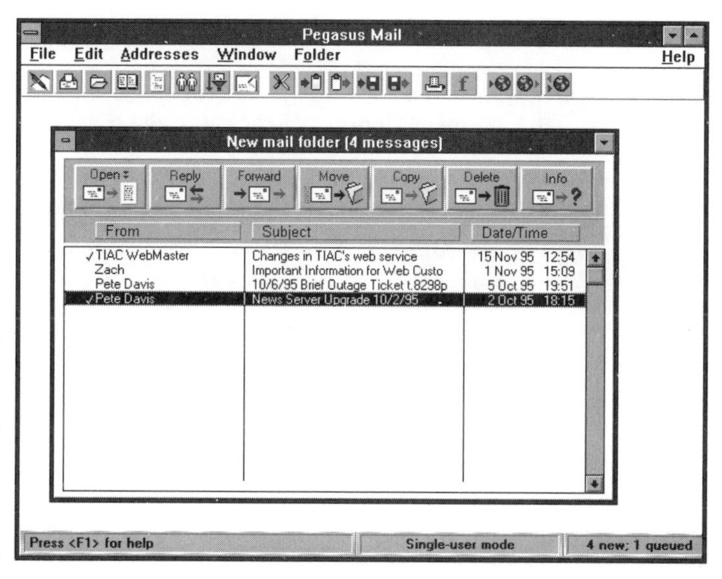

Figure 10-7: Pegasus Mail is easy to use, and the price is right.

After you see the Pegasus Mail window, you are up and running.

Using Pegasus

Here are some things you can do with Pegasus:

- To create a new message, choose File⇨New Message, press Ctrl+N, or click the Compose a new message button on the toolbar (the leftmost button).
- To see your new messages, choose File⇨Read New Mail, press Ctrl+W, or click the Read new mail button on the toolbar (the second button from the left on the toolbar).
- To read a message, double-click the message in your New mail folder or other folder.
- To delete a message after you've read it, click the Delete (trash can) button on the toolbar.
- To get your incoming messages from your Internet provider and send outgoing messages you composed, choose File⇨Check and Send Mail.

Other programs

Other e-mail programs include

- E-Mail Connection, another excellent freeware program. It's supposed to be as good as Pegasus and Eudora, which is darned good. Its home page is

  ```
  http://www.connectsoft.com/products/free_emc25.shtml
  ```

- Netscape Navigator, which is described in the next section. If you have Version 2.0 or later, choose Window⇨Netscape Mail (see Figure 10-8).

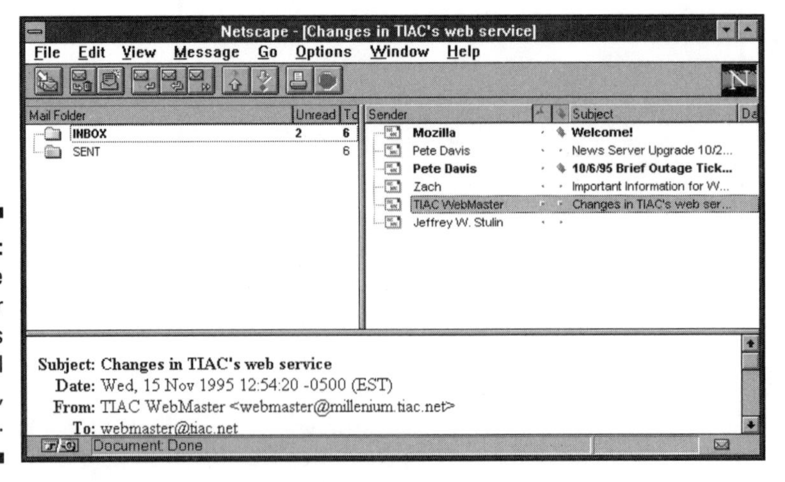

Figure 10-8: Netscape Navigator 2.0 includes an e-mail program, too.

- Microsoft Exchange, which comes with Windows 95, can handle mail from Microsoft Network or your SLIP or PPP Internet account. See Chapter 8.

Many Usenet newsreaders can send e-mail messages; to post an article to a moderated group, they have to e-mail it, so they usually also let you send mail to anyone else.

Beautiful Browsers

A good Web browser can handle lots of different types of information, like graphics, sound, and movies. It should have a good hot list or other method of saving the URLs of pages that you use often. And it should display all kinds of Web pages, including those designed to work with Netscape and to use HTML 2.0 (a version of the language in which Web pages are written).

Netscape Navigator

The star of Web browsers is, of course, Netscape Navigator. Netscape Communications, the company that makes Netscape Navigator, went public in 1995, and its stock went through the roof. Of course, most people who use Netscape download it for free from the Net, so it remains to be seen how profitable the company will turn out to be. Netscape is letting people download and use beta test versions of the program and asking folks to pay for the final versions — the registration fee is less than $50.

Getting Netscape Navigator

Netscape Navigator (or just Netscape, for short), is available from

```
http://home.netscape.com/
```

The file is large (2MB), so it takes a while to arrive, even with a fast modem. Be sure to save the file to a temporary directory, like C:\TEMP, not to the Netscape program directory.

If you use Windows 3.1, download the 16-bit version, even if you've installed the Win32s package that supports some 32-bit programs. Windows 95 users should download the 32-bit version. Versions for Macs and several flavors of UNIX are also available.

Installing Netscape Navigator

When you download Netscape Navigator, you get a self-extracting ZIP file with a name like N16E20B5.EXE — an unpronounceable bunch of characters, the name means that it's a Netscape Navigator 16-bit version (for Windows 3.1, not Windows 95), Version 2.0, beta test release 5. To install it:

1. **Create a temporary directory and move the file you downloaded into the new directory.**

   Don't put the file you downloaded into the directory that you want the Netscape program to end up in.

2. **Run the file by double-clicking its filename in File Manager or Explorer.**

   The file expands into a whole bunch of files.

3. **Double-click the filename SETUP.EXE in File Manager or Explorer.**

   The Netscape Setup program runs. During the setup, it asks what directory you want to install the program in.

If you have a previous version of Netscape installed, you can install the new version in the same directory.

Using Netscape Navigator

To run Netscape Navigator, double-click its icon. The first time it starts, Netscape shows you a page of legal boilerplate. Click Accept, if you can deal with the conditions. You then see the Netscape window, shown in Figure 10-9 (showing the home page for Egg Farm Dairy, makers of quality artisan cheeses). Like any Web browser, to follow a hyperlink (text that appears underlined in blue, or pictures with blue borders), just click one. To go to a particular URL (Web page), type the URL into the Location box near the top of the Netscape Navigator window. Use the Back button on the toolbar to return to the previous page or choose Go from the menu to see a list of the pages you've visited recently.

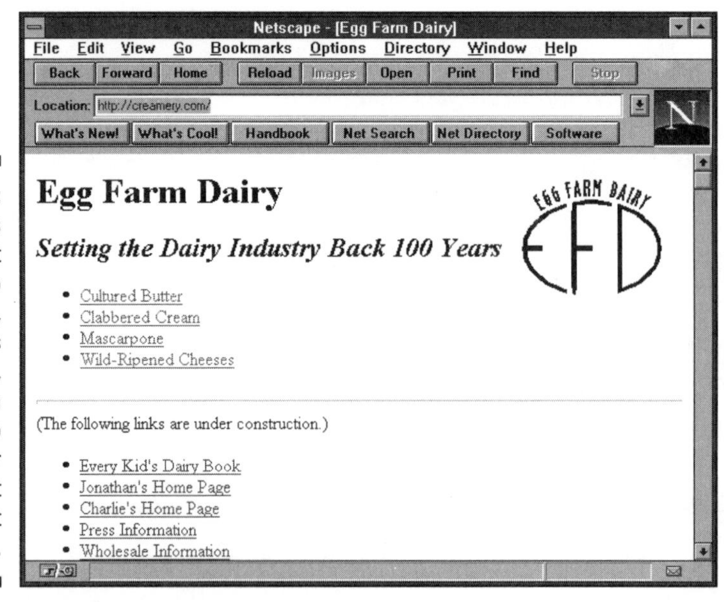

Figure 10-9: Netscape is the most famous Web browser, and it works pretty well, too. You can use it to order excellent goat cheese.

Netscape Navigator 2.0 includes an e-mail program: Choose Window⇨Netscape Mail to see the Main window. Netscape also includes a Usenet newsreader, which you can use by choosing Window⇨Netscape News.

WebSurfer

WebSurfer comes from NetManage, the folks who created Internet Chameleon, a suite of Internet programs. We like Internet Chameleon — in fact, we chose it for our book, *The Internet For Windows For Dummies Starter Kit* (IDG Books Worldwide, Inc.). NetManage has put WebSurfer 4.6 (and may put future versions) on the Net for free, and you can download and use it whether you use Internet Chameleon or not. WebSurfer really is free — no shareware fees or time limits.

Getting WebSurfer

To get your copy of WebSurfer, go to this URL:

```
http://www.netmanage.com/netmanage/download.html
```

Follow the instructions on the page to download the program.

Installing WebSurfer

WebSurfer arrives in the form of a self-extracting ZIP file with a name like WEB16.EXE. To install it:

1. **Create a temporary directory (or use C:\TEMP, if it exists) and move the file you downloaded into the new directory.**

   Don't put the file you downloaded into the directory that you want the WebSurfer program to end up in.

2. **Run the file by double-clicking its filename in File Manager or Explorer.**

   The file expands into a whole bunch of files.

3. **Double-click the filename SETUP.EXE in File Manager or Explorer.**

   The WebSurfer Setup program runs. During the setup, the program asks what directory you want to install the program in. If you use NetManage software already, you can install the new WebSurfer in the same directory as the other NetManage programs.

   If you use a product other than NetManage's Internet Chameleon to connect with the Internet (like Trumpet WinSock, for example), the setup program asks if you want to keep your existing WinSock DLL or replace it with NetManage's. If your Internet connection works fine, leave things alone and click Yes to keep your existing connection.

When it is done, the setup program creates a Program Manager group and icon for WebSurfer.

This page is Netscape enhanced

Lots of pages on the Web are "Netscape enhanced," which means that they use Netscape features that not all other Web browsers can handle. For example, Netscape added ways to center text, let text flow around pictures, break the page up into frames, and other nice formatting touches. The commands required aren't standard, so some other Web browsers ignore them.

Most Netscape-enhanced pages, in fact, look fine in other up-to-date browsers, such as NetManage's WebSurfer, Microsoft's Internet Explorer, and NCSA Mosaic 2.0.

Using WebSurfer

WebSurfer can handle most Netscape extensions, as well as the fancy formatting to be added to the newest Web standard, HTML 3.0. Figure 10-10 shows WebSurfer displaying a page with wallpaper and a right-aligned graphic, two types of advanced formatting.

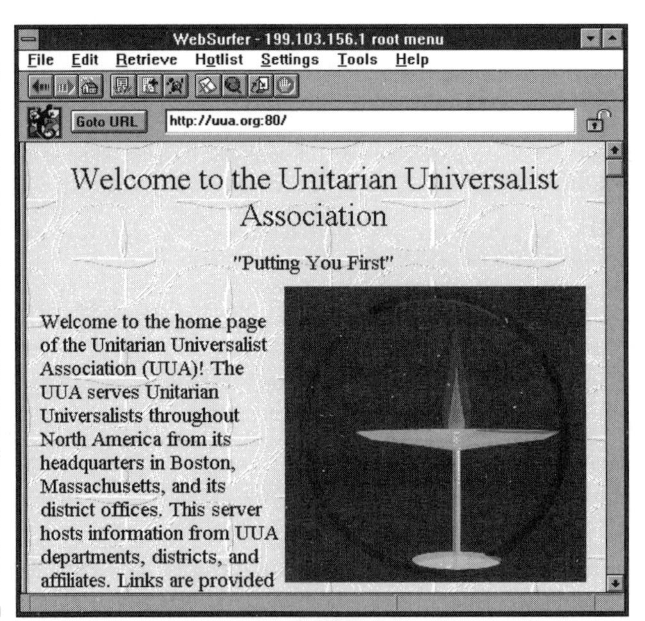

Figure 10-10: WebSurfer gives Netscape a run for its money. (Thanks to the Unitarian Universalist Association for this nice example of wallpaper, and to David C. Kay, who created it.)

WebSurfer can also import the hot list or bookmark files from other Web browsers, so you don't have to create your hot list from scratch when you switch to WebSurfer.

Other browsers

Other good browsers include

- Internet Explorer, from Microsoft, works only under Windows 95. You can get it for free from

  ```
  http://www.microsoft.com/
  ```

- NCSA Mosaic is the original graphic Web browser, the one that made the World Wide Web famous. Although Netscape has gotten a lot more press, recent versions of NCSA Mosaic are excellent, rivaling Netscape. You can find it at

  ```
  http://www.ncsa.uiuc.edu/SDG/Software/WinMosaic/
  ```

- I-Comm is a Web browser that doesn't require a SLIP or PPP connection. Instead, the browser works with a UNIX shell account. (It therefore doesn't really belong in this chapter, but I-Comm is too interesting a program to omit.) For more information, see

  ```
  http://www.talentcom.com/icomm.htm
  ```

Fabulous FTP

A good FTP program lets you store the host names of FTP servers you use often, including the name of the directory you usually want to download from. It also lets you see the messages that the FTP server sends you (these messages sometimes tell you what other servers have files of interest, or that the FTP server is moving, or when the server will be down).

WS_FTP is the FTP program we told you to download back in Chapters 6 and 7. It's still our favorite. But if you want to try another one, check out CuteFTP, a shareware FTP program written by Alex Kunadze. Some people like CuteFTP as well as WS_FTP, although we've found it's more likely to crash. CuteFTP is available at

```
http://papa.indstate.edu:8888/CuteFTP/
```

Or use your Web browser for downloading files, as described in the sidebar "FTPing with your Web browser" in Chapter 9.

Nifty Newsreaders

A Usenet newsgroup is a public bulletin board in which Internet users can discuss, complain, or exchange useful information (occasionally) on a particular topic. Over 10,000 newsgroups cover an amazing array of topics. Chapter 9 in *The Internet For Dummies,* 3rd Edition, tells you all about how to read Usenet newsgroups and even post your own articles.

Free Agent

Our favorite WinSock newsreader is Free Agent, the freeware version of a commercial product called Agent. If you use Free Agent a lot, you may want to upgrade to Agent — it's not expensive and lets you read your mail and your news with the same program. You can find out about Free Agent at this Web page:

```
http://www.forteinc.com/forte/agent/freagent.htm
```

Getting Free Agent

You can download Free Agent (which is about 800K) from these sites:

```
ftp://ftp.forteinc.com/pub/free_agent/fagent10.zip
ftp://papa.indstate.edu/winsock-l/news/fagent10.zip
```

Installing Free Agent

To install Free Agent:

1. **Create a new directory for the program and put the ZIP file you downloaded in it.**
2. **Unzip the zip file, using WinZIP.**

   A bunch of files appears.
3. **Read the README.TXT file by double-clicking its filename in File Manager or Explorer.**

   README.TXT contains late-breaking news about the program.
4. **Make an icon for Free Agent by dragging the filename AGENT.EXE from File Manager to Program Manager (in Windows 3.1).**

   In Windows 95, drag the filename from My Computer or Explorer onto the desktop.

Running Free Agent

The first time you run the program, Free Agent asks you for configuration information. Intelligently, if you have been using another newsreader, it extracts most of this information from that newsreader's configuration files. (How nice!)

The second time you run the program, it asks you for permission to register you as a user. Go ahead — this step doesn't cost you anything. Registering is good because it lets Forte, Inc., notify you about new releases.

You can customize Free Agent seven ways from Sunday. It usually looks something like Figure 10-11.

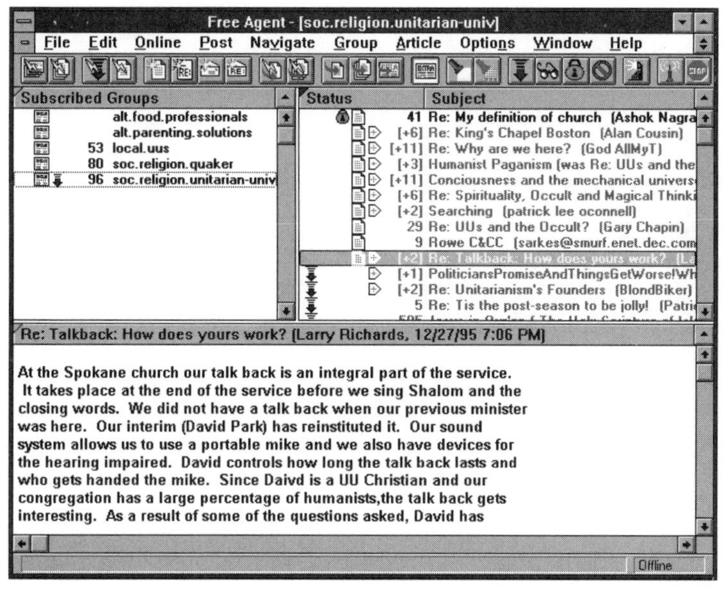

Figure 10-11: Free Agent lists the newsgroups you subscribe to, the articles in the selected newsgroup, and the text of the selected article.

Other newsreaders

Other newsreaders you may want to try include

- Netscape Navigator 2.0, a Web browser that comes with a built-in newsreader. Choose Window⇨Netscape News to see it.
- News Xpress, a freeware newsreader from Hong Kong. You can download it from this site (it's in a ZIP file whose name starts with NX):

  ```
  ftp://ftp.hk.super.net/pub/windows/Winsock-Utilities/
  ```

  The News Xpress FAQ is at

  ```
  http://www.malch.com/nxfaq.html
  ```

- WinVN is another well-regarded newsreader, with a home page at

  ```
  http://www.ksc.nasa.gov/software/winvn/winvn.html
  ```

  You can download either the 16-bit (Windows 3.1) or 32-bit (Windows 95) version from this site (it's in a ZIP file whose name starts with WV):

  ```
  ftp://ftp.ksc.nasa.gov/pub/winvn/win3/
  ```

Other Programs

For information on IRC (Internet Relay Chat) programs, see Chapter 18, which tells you all about IRC. Telnet programs are described in Chapter 19 and Gopher programs in Chapter 20.

Searching FTP archives with Archie

If you are looking for a file that you know is available by anonymous FTP and you know the approximate or exact filename, you can use a system called Archie to find out which FTP servers the file is stored on. Get WSArchie, a freeware Archie program from this Web page:

```
http://dspace.dial.pipex.com/town/square/cc83/
```

Or look in the Consummate WinSock Apps List (described at the beginning of this chapter) for the location.

Video viewers

If you want to see the video clips that occasionally show up on Web pages, you need a video viewer. The best one we know of is Net Toob, from Duplexx Software. Its home page is at

```
http://www.duplexx.com/
```

The viewer is big (a bit less than 1MB), so it takes a while to arrive. The wait is worth it, though — Net Toob can show video clips in lots of standard formats, including MPEG and Quick Time. The cost to register is only $15.

Doing Your Part

After you've used a new program for a few weeks, you should begin to feel guilty. Someone has gone to enormous effort to make this wonderful piece of software, and you haven't even said thank you. It's time to Do Your Part.

Free versus not-quite-free

Software that comes from the Internet falls into three broad categories:

- **Freeware:** Given away for free. Restrictions may limit what you can do with the software — most freeware owners don't let you resell their programs, for example. The UNZIP program is freeware, as are Pegasus and WS_FTP.
- **Shareware:** Given away for a limited trial period. If you plan to continue to use the program, you are honor-bound to pay for it. WinZip and Trumpet WinSock are shareware programs. Usually, when you register your shareware, you get a printed manual and a key that turns off any "please register me" screens.
- **Beta test versions:** Test versions given away for a limited trial period. The idea is that when the final version is available, you will buy it. By definition, beta test versions are full of bugs, because the programming team isn't done getting the bugs out. Beta test versions of Netscape Navigator are available via FTP, bugs and all.

To find out which category your new program falls into, choose Help⇨About or look for other menu choices that offer information about registering. For example, WinZip has a command called Help Ordering Information.

If you are using a shareware program and you find it to be valuable, go ahead and pay up. It's never a great deal of money, and you become a registered user, entitled to receive information about updates and related programs. Besides, you feel great about what a wonderful, generous person you are, and you make it more likely that people will continue to write useful shareware. (***Note:*** Neither of the authors of this book distributes any shareware programs, so we have no vested interest!)

Registering WinZip

To pay by check, send $29 to Nico Mak, P.O. Box 919, Bristol, CT 06011-0919. To pay by credit card, call the Public (software) Library at 800-2424-PsL or 713-524-6394, or fax 713-524-6398. You can also mail credit-card orders to PsL at P.O. Box 35705, Houston, TX 77235-5705. To congratulate Mr. Mak on a job well done, you can e-mail him at `info@winzip.com`.

For the latest information about paying for WinZip, choose Help⇨Ordering Information from the WinZip menu. This command also allows you to print an order form to submit to your company for payment — after you see the help topic, choose File⇨Print Topic.

What about PKZIP and PKUNZIP?

If you've been zipping and unzipping files for a while, you probably have and use the PKZIP and PKUNZIP programs. These programs have been around much longer than WinZip has, and they run under DOS. WinZip, in fact, still can run PKZIP and PKUNZIP behind the scenes to do some obscure zipological tasks.

PKWare, who wrote PKZIP and PKUNZIP, says that it's coming out with a Windows version to rival WinZip any day now. To check on its status, take a look at PKWare's Web site at `http://www.pkware.com/`.

If you are an old-fashioned kind of person and want PKZIP and PKUNZIP, they are available from PKWare's Web site or by FTP. The FTP site `oak.oakland.edu` has the programs in the directory named `/pub/msdos/zip`, in a file named PKZ204G.EXE.

PKZIP and PKUNZIP are shareware. To register your copies, send $47 to PKWare, Inc., 7545 N. Port Washington Road, Glendale, WI 53217-3422. You can also register online with a credit card on the PKWare Support Bulletin Board System at 414-352-7176.

Part III

Three More Entrance Ramps

"IT HAPPENED AROUND THE TIME WE SUBSCRIBED TO AN ONLINE SERVICE."

In this part . . .

In *The Internet For Dummies,* 3rd Edition, we describe three of the most popular online services that give you access to Internet services: CompuServe, America Online, and Microsoft Network. We also tell you how to use that old standby among Internet accounts, the UNIX shell account.

In this part of *this* book, we describe yet more online services: Prodigy, Netcom, and GNN. All three make it easy to sign up for an account, send and receive e-mail, surf the Web, and read Usenet newsgroups. Read these three chapters for how to use these on-ramps for the Information Supersoaker, er, highway.

Chapter 11

Connecting to the Internet via Prodigy

In This Chapter

- Installing the Prodigy software
- Signing up for a Prodigy account
- Jumping online
- Hanging up
- Telling Prodigy where to jump
- Sending and reading e-mail
- Jumping on the Web
- Jumping into Usenet newsgroups
- Finding out more about Prodigy

Prodigy is perceived by many people as the weak sister of the Big Four commercial online services — America Online (AOL), CompuServe, Microsoft Network (MSN), and Prodigy. Because Prodigy carries advertisements and because of its large print and old-fashioned look, many users have moved to other services. Prodigy was the first of the big commercial online services to offer a World Wide Web browser, and in 1994, people signed up for Prodigy accounts in droves. When the other online services added Web browsers, Prodigy lost its advantage.

Prodigy comes with its own access software that runs on DOS and Windows machines and Macs. This chapter describes Prodigy's Internet-related capabilities, including e-mail, Usenet newsgroups, and the World Wide Web. The instructions apply to Prodigy's Windows software, using Version 1.1. Your software version may not look exactly the same — Prodigy updates its software all the time.

Since 1994, Prodigy has added lots of Internet services and completely rejuvenated its outdated software. Now using the World Wide Web, Usenet newsgroups, FTP, and Gopher from Prodigy is easy. It looks better than it used to but is still clunkier to use and has less Prodigy-specific content than some of its competitors.

The pros and cons of Prodigy

Prodigy has some excellent services, such as its Homework Helper for kids and its news clipping service. You can use the World Wide Web, Usenet newsgroups, FTP, and Gopher from Prodigy, too. And you can set up additional IDs for other family members so that each person has a mailbox. Prodigy also lets you block your family's user IDs so that kids can't use "adult" services.

On the other hand, Prodigy carries advertisements on many of its screens, which annoys users. Also, its Web browser and updated e-mail program are not well integrated with the rest of the software; jumping back and forth between programs can be confusing. Finally, you can't use WinSock programs with your Prodigy account (as you can with AOL and CompuServe).

For the complete scoop about Prodigy, run right out and buy *Prodigy For Dummies* (IDG Books Worldwide, Inc.) by Gus Venditto.

Signing Up for Prodigy

To sign up for a Prodigy account, get hold of a Prodigy Membership Kit, including a program disk and a booklet with your user ID and your temporary password. If you don't have a Prodigy Membership Kit lying around under your pile of computer magazines (or gardening magazines or whatever), call Prodigy at 800-PRODIGY (that's 800-776-3449). Install the software and then use the software to call Prodigy and set up your account.

Using Windows 95

Here's how to install the Prodigy software:

1. **Click the Start button and choose Settings⇨Control Panel.**
2. **Double-click the Add/Remove Programs icon.**

   You see the Add/Remove Programs Properties dialog box.
3. **Click the Install button.**

   Windows asks you to put the program disk in your disk drive.
4. **Stick the Prodigy Installation disk in the drive and click Next.**

   Windows finds the setup program — INSTALL.EXE — on the Prodigy Installation disk.
5. **Click Finish.**

"Finish?" You're Latvian! But click it anyway. The installation program starts up, and you see the encouraging window shown in Figure 11-1. Prodigy suggests that its software go in the directory C:\PRODIGY.

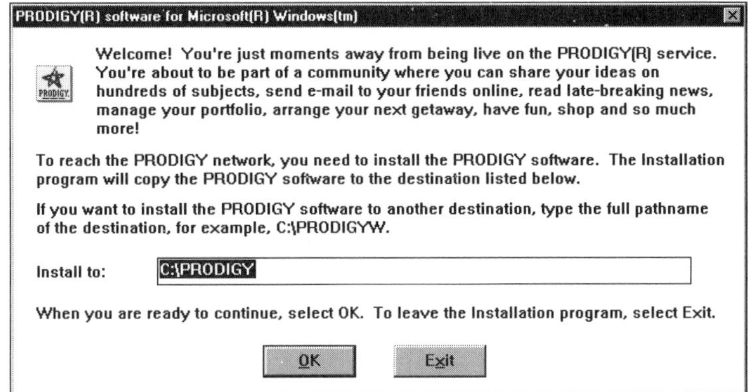

Figure 11-1: Prodigy is ready to install its software.

6. **If you want to install the program files in a different directory, type over the directory name.**
7. **Click OK.**

   Next, the installation program needs to know your modem's location. Thoughtfully, the program offers to look around for your modem (see Figure 11-2). If you are currently on the phone and using your modem, switch to the program that's using the modem and hang up.

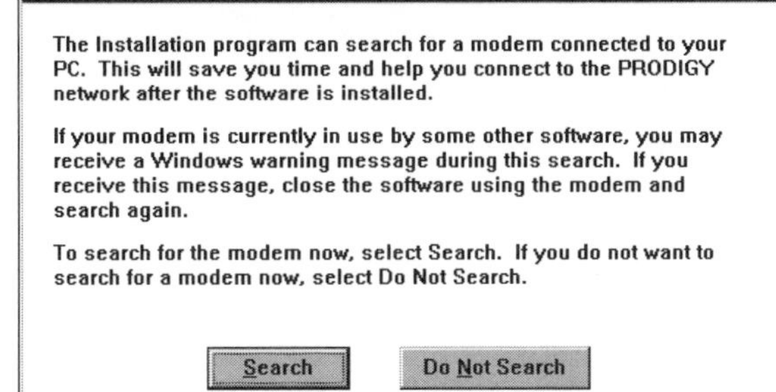

Figure 11-2: Where's your modem, anyway?

8. **Click Search.**

   Prodigy looks around at the likely places a modem might be installed. You see a message like `Modem found on Port: Com2.`

9. **Click OK to thank Prodigy for finding your modem.**

   Now the installation program copies lots of files to your hard disk. When the program finishes, you see a congratulatory message.

10. **Click OK.**

    The installation program ends, leaving you with a new Prodigy folder, shown in Figure 11-3. You have a new entry on your Start⇨Programs menu, too: PRODIGY_R_ software. (The _R_ is supposed to be a registered trademark symbol, we guess.)

Figure 11-3: These programs come with Prodigy.

If you have trouble installing the Prodigy software, call Prodigy Member Services at 800-PRODIGY (800-776-3449).

Using Windows 3.1

Here's how to install the Prodigy software:

1. **Put the Prodigy Installation disk in the disk drive.**
2. **Choose File⇨Run from the menu in Windows Program Manager.**

   The Run dialog box appears.

3. **Type** a:install **in the Command Line box and click OK.**

   If your disk drive is B:, type **b:install** instead.

4. **Complete steps 6 to 10 in the preceding section, "Using Windows 95."**

Using a Mac

To install the software on your Mac, follow the instructions that come with your Prodigy Installation disk. (Don't worry — the steps are easy.)

This chapter describes how to use Prodigy's Windows-based software. The figures show the way the program looks under Windows 95, but the Windows 3.1, Mac, and DOS versions look similar so that you can follow right along.

Setting up your account

Before you can use Prodigy, you have to set up your account. Your Prodigy Membership Kit should have a booklet with your user ID and your temporary password, which you need to sign up. Follow these steps:

1. **For Windows 95 users, click the Prodigy icon in the Prodigy folder on your desktop or click Start⇨Programs⇨Prodigy⇨Prodigy_R_.**

   For Windows 3.1 users, double-click the Prodigy icon in the Prodigy program group in Program Manager. Either way, you see the Prodigy Sign-On window, shown in Figure 11-4.

Figure 11-4: Prodigy's Sign-On window waits for you to enter your user ID and password.

2. **Type your user ID in the User ID box (copy the number from the cover of your Prodigy Membership Kit) and press Enter.**
3. **Type your temporary password in the Password box and press Enter.**

   Don't worry — you can change your password. Unfortunately, you can't change your user ID.
4. **Follow the instructions to choose a phone number near you.**

   With luck, Prodigy has a phone number that is a local call for you.
5. **Follow the directions to enter your credit-card number and other information.**

When the setup process is finished, you see the Prodigy Sign-On window again. Now your Prodigy account is ready to use.

When good connections go bad

What do you do if you can't connect to your Prodigy account? Prodigy comes with a nifty program called ASSIST that troubleshoots your Prodigy software and modem to find out what's the matter. Double-click the ASSIST icon in the Prodigy folder (or Program Manager group) and follow the instructions. ASSIST knows the last error you ran into with Prodigy and takes the appropriate action. You can usually avoid calling Prodigy's technical-support number (800-PRODIGY).

Progressing with Prodigy

Now that you have the software you need to use your Prodigy account, all you have to do is fire up the software. To connect your computer to Prodigy

1. **For Windows 95 users, click the Prodigy icon in the Prodigy folder on your desktop or click Start⇨Programs⇨Prodigy⇨Prodigy_R_.**

   For Windows 3.1 users, double-click the Prodigy icon in the Prodigy program group in Program Manager. You see the Prodigy Sign-On window, shown in Figure 11-4.

2. **Enter your ID and password and press Enter.**

3. **Choose one of the four options in the list of destinations or enter a Jumpword or URL in the Go to a Jumpword or Internet URL box.**

   You'll find out about Jumpwords in the section "The Joint Is Jumping," later in this chapter. This list shows the four destinations:

   - Choose Highlights to see the news of the day.
   - Choose Web Browser to use the World Wide Web (described in the section "Jumping on the Web," later in this chapter). Alternatively, enter the URL of the Web page you want to see in the Go to a Jumpword or Internet URL box.
   - Choose Hot List to see your list of favorite Prodigy services.
   - Choose Member Help Center to get help with Prodigy or to find out about your account's status.

   For now, choose Highlights.

4. **Click Connect.**

   Prodigy dials the phone, makes the connection, logs you in, and displays the requested information. Figure 11-5 shows the Prodigy Highlights window. You're ready to roll!

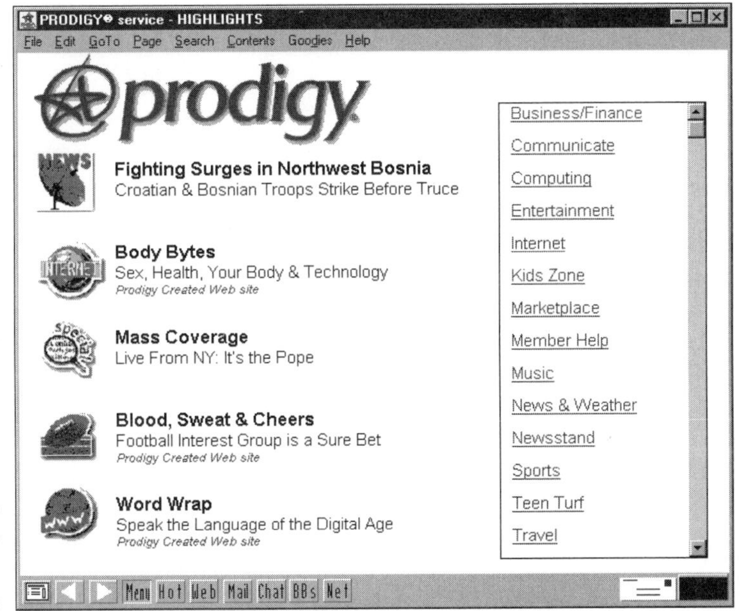

Figure 11-5: The Highlights window is Mission Control for Prodigy services.

If you decide not to sign on after all, you can click the Cancel button in the Connecting to Prodigy dialog box, which appears while Prodigy dials and signs on.

Highlights of Prodigy

The left side of the Highlights window displays buttons for interesting things to do (see Figure 11-5). The right side contains a list of the major topics.

To get back to the Highlights window whenever you are connected to Prodigy, click the Highlights icon on the left end of the toolbar at the bottom of the Prodigy window, choose GoTo⇨Highlights, or press F5. Whichever way you use, the Highlights window makes a good place to return to when you finish with one Prodigy service and before you decide what to do next.

Hello, here's your new software

From time to time, the Prodigy folks release a new software version. Rather than mail you a disk to install, Prodigy sends the software update to your computer right over the phone. When you least expect an interruption, while you're connected to Prodigy, you see a dialog box telling you that a software update is available. Prodigy always gives you the option of skipping the update and downloading the new version another time, in case you're in a hurry, because downloading can take anywhere from three minutes to more than a half hour. You usually don't have to pay for connect time while the software is downloading. The message tells you how long the downloading and installation take and whether you'll be charged.

Is technology a brave new world or what? Software that installs itself!

By the way, if you would rather not receive your software updates over the phone (for example, calling Prodigy is a toll call for you), you can frequently get new software on disk. Press Ctrl+J and type **help** to find out how to upgrade your software.

Hang me up!

When you finish using Prodigy, be sure to disconnect. You pay by the minute, so the less time you're on, the better (from your point of view, anyway). To hang up, choose File⇨Exit, click the Close button in the window's upper-right corner, or press Alt+F4. You see the screen shown in Figure 11-6. Press Enter or click the End This Session button to leave Prodigy.

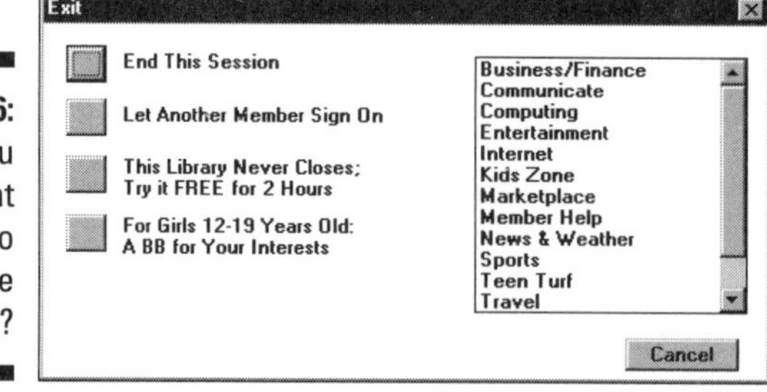

Figure 11-6: Are you sure that you want to leave Prodigy?

The Joint Is Jumping

Prodigy has hundreds of online services, each identified by a *Jumpword.* To get to the service, you *jump* to that service (sounds exhausting). Whenever you want to jump to a different service, you can press Ctrl+J or choose GoTo⇨Jump To. The Go To dialog box asks for the Jumpword to go to, as shown in Figure 11-7.

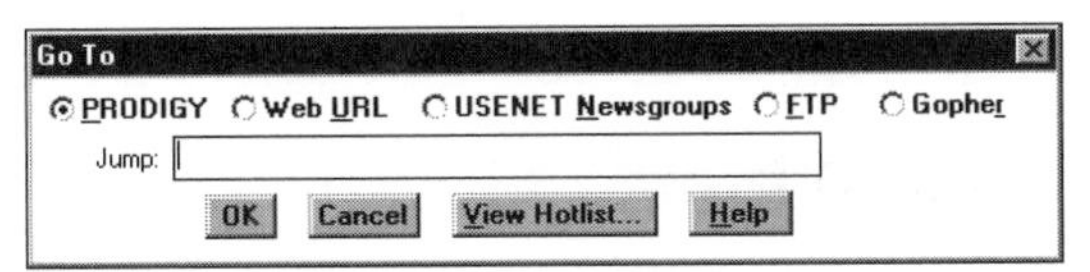

Figure 11-7: Where do you want to go?

You can enter five different types of information in the Go To dialog box:

- A Prodigy service's Jumpword (HELP, for example): Click PRODIGY, if necessary, and then enter the Jumpword in the Jump box. If you're unsure about a Jumpword, you can guess at Jumpwords, you may see them listed on Prodigy pages, or you can choose GoTo⇨A-Z Index for a listing of Jumpwords.
- A World Wide Web page's URL (for example, `http://www.yahoo.com/`): Click Web URL and then enter the URL in the box (but omit the `http://` part, which already appears to the left of the box). See the section "Jumping on the Web," later in this chapter.
- A Usenet newsgroup's name (for example, `rec.humor.funny`): Click USENET Newsgroups and then enter the newsgroup name in the box. See the section "Jumping into Newsgroups," later in this chapter.
- An FTP server's Internet host name (for example, `ftp.microsoft.com`): Click FTP and then enter the host name. The Prodigy Web Browser lets you download files from FTP archives. See the section "Jumping into FTP archives," later in this chapter.
- A Gopher menu's URL (for example, `gopher://wx.atmos.uiuc.edu/11/States`, which displays weather data): Click Gopher and then enter the URL in the box (but omit the `gopher://` part, which already appears to the left of the box). You use the Prodigy Web Browser to see Gopher menus, so see the section "Jumping into Gopher menus," later in this chapter.

When you've specified where you want to go, click OK. To go to the Member Help Center, for example, click PRODIGY, if necessary, type **HELP** in the Jump box, and click OK.

Finding where to jump

You can also see a complete list of Prodigy's Jumpwords by choosing GoTo⇨A-Z Index or by pressing F7.

Services you'll want to jump to

Here are some Prodigy services you may need:

- In the Member Help Center (the Jumpword is **HELP**), you can find out about your account and how to use Prodigy. You can choose the Member Help Center from the Prodigy Sign-On window.
- To see how much time you've been connected this month (and what your bill looks like), use the Jumpword **ACCOUNT**.
- To find out which pricing plan you're using and change to a different plan, if you prefer, use the Jumpword **FEES**.
- To read the Prodigy member agreement, use the Jumpword **AGREEMENT**. You may as well find out what you've agreed to by using the Prodigy service.

Other tips

Here are other tips for using Prodigy:

- To see the Highlights window, click the button in the lower-left corner of the Prodigy window (the leftmost button on the toolbar, which Prodigy puts along the bottom of its window).
- If more than one screenful of information for a topic is available, use the toolbar's Forward and Back buttons — the right- and left-pointing triangle buttons near the left end of the toolbar.
- You can use cut-and-paste commands to move information between the Windows version of the Prodigy software and other Windows programs. Sometimes you can select text — press Ctrl+C to copy text to the Windows Clipboard. In other cases, you can choose Edit⇨Snapshot or press Ctrl+A. Prodigy offers to capture an area of the Prodigy window (or the entire Prodigy window) as a graphics image on the Clipboard.

Jumping on the Internet

One way to use Prodigy's Internet services is to click Internet in the Highlights window or press Ctrl+J and type **internet** as the Jumpword. Either way, you see the Internet window, shown in Figure 11-8.

Figure 11-8: Here's information about Prodigy's Internet-related services.

The Internet window lets you go to Prodigy's Web Browser and read Usenet newsgroups, but, strangely, the window doesn't contain links to e-mail, FTP, or Gopher. Luckily, finding these other Internet services is not difficult — the rest of this chapter explains how to use these services.

Take a Letter

Prodigy lets you send and receive e-mail from other Prodigy users and anyone with an Internet address. Prodigy comes with a separate e-mail program, called Prodigy Mail (another creative name). To send and receive e-mail, you run the Prodigy Mail program. While the Prodigy Mail program is running, you can't do anything else with Prodigy, and the regular Prodigy window is inert and unresponsive.

To use Prodigy's e-mail program, click the Mail button on the toolbar at the bottom of the Prodigy window. If you have new mail waiting, an envelope icon appears near the right end of the toolbar — click this icon. You see the Prodigy Mail window, shown in Figure 11-9. Any received e-mail messages appear in the upper half of the Mail window.

When you finish reading and sending messages and you want to do something else with Prodigy, choose File⇨Exit or press Alt+F4 to exit from the Prodigy Mail program. You return to the Prodigy window, which displays a message suggest-

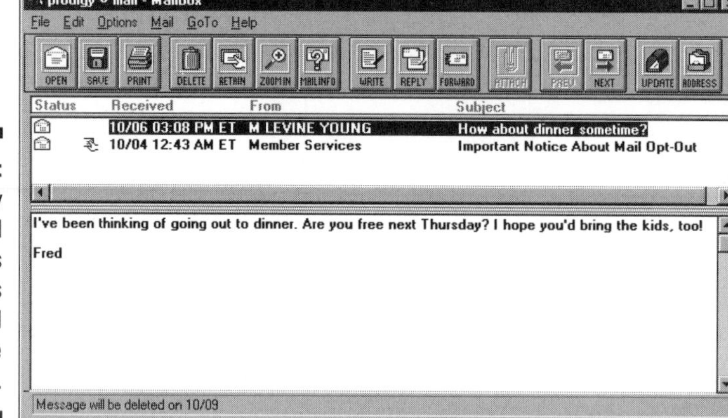

Figure 11-9: The Prodigy Mail program lets you (guess what?) send and receive e-mail.

ing that you use "your favorite navigation techniques" to see more information from Prodigy. For example, press F5 or click the Menu button on the toolbar to return to the Highlights window.

Addressing your mail

To send a message to another Prodigy user, address the message to his user ID (ABC123A, for example). To send a message to someone on the Internet, use his Internet address. Your own Internet e-mail address is your user ID followed by `@prodigy.com`. If your user ID is ABC123A, for example, your e-mail address is `ABC123A@prodigy.com`.

Reading your mail

Each received message appears in the top half of the Prodigy Mail window, with the date received and subject line. Double-click a message you want to read or select the message and click the Open icon on the Prodigy Mail window's toolbar. (This toolbar is displayed in the usual Windows location, just below the menu bar, rather than at the bottom of the window.)

Peculiarly, messages appear in the lower half of the Mail window, and certain messages make the entire Prodigy Mail window shrink to an icon, revealing the Prodigy window, which displays the mail message. Why? We're not sure. This occurrence looks alarming, but stay calm. A Return to Mail button appears in the lower-right corner of the window: Click this button, and the Prodigy Mail window reappears, looking none the worse for wear.

Hello, MNZF79B?

Prodigy uses ugly, hard-to-remember usernames, such as MNZF79B. Prodigy now allows you to choose a *NetName,* that is, a name you can use instead of those ugly usernames. To choose a NetName, use the Jumpword **NET NAME** and follow the instructions.

Except for the bizarre messages that Prodigy Mail doesn't display, when you double-click an e-mail message, the text appears in the lower half of the Prodigy Mail window.

When you're reading a message, here are things you may want to do:

- To reply to the message, click the Reply icon on the Prodigy Mail toolbar or press Ctrl+R. See the section "Writing a message," later in this chapter, to find out how to compose and send the message.
- To forward the message to someone else, click the Forward button on the Prodigy Mail toolbar or press Ctrl+F. See the section "Writing a message," later in this chapter, to find out how to compose and send the message.
- You may want to save a particularly juicy message on your hard disk. After opening the message, choose File⇨Save Message from the Prodigy Mail menu and tell Prodigy where to put the file.
- You can print the message by choosing File⇨Print from the Prodigy Mail menu or by pressing Ctrl+P.
- Delete a boring message by pressing Ctrl+D or clicking the Delete icon on the toolbar. The message doesn't actually go away until you exit from the Prodigy Mail program: Instead, the message hides in the trash can icon, which appears next to the message in the list of messages.
- Prodigy normally deletes your mail after about two weeks. If you want to keep mail in your Inbox longer, click the Retain icon on the Prodigy Mail toolbar or press Ctrl+E. Prodigy then keeps the message hanging around for an extra ten days.
- To see the next message on your list, press Ctrl+PgDn. To return to the preceding message, press Ctrl+PgUp.

If mail arrives while you're using Prodigy Mail, the Update icon near the right end of the toolbar turns into a NewMail icon. Click this icon to retrieve the new messages, which appear in your list of messages.

Writing a message

To compose a brand-new message, click the Write button on the toolbar or press Ctrl+W. You see the Prodigy Mail Write window, shown in Figure 11-10.

Two other ways to see the Mail Write window are to reply to a message you're reading (by clicking the Reply icon or pressing Ctrl+R) or to forward a message (by clicking the Forward icon or pressing Ctrl+F).

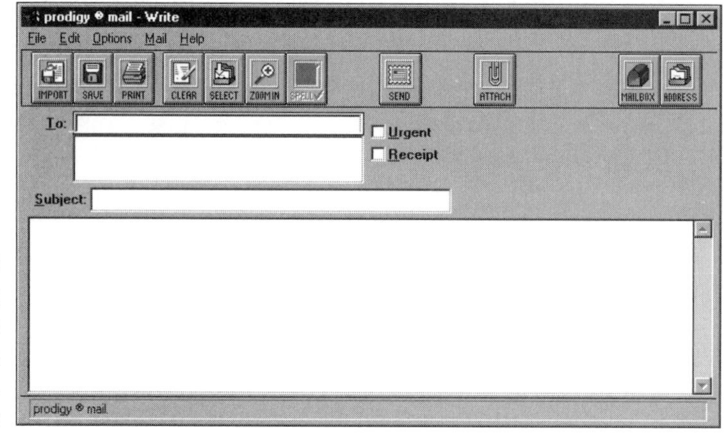

Figure 11-10: You're ready to write a message.

Here's how to compose your message:

1. **In the To box, enter the user ID of another Prodigy user (or your own, if you like to talk to yourself) or an Internet address, and press Enter.**

   When you press Enter, the address appears in the list below the To box. You can keep typing addresses and pressing Enter if you want to send your missive to other people.

   If you're replying to a message, your message is already addressed to the person who sent that message.

2. **In the Subject box, type a subject line for the message.**

   Remember to make the subject line specific. If you are replying to or forwarding a message, the original message's subject appears in the Subject box.

3. **In the large box, type the message's text.**

   If you are using Windows, you can use the cut-and-paste commands to copy information to the message's text. For example, you can copy information from a word-processing document to the Windows Clipboard (using Edit⇨Copy or Ctrl+C) and paste the information in your e-mail message by pressing Ctrl+V.

4. **Check the spelling of your e-mail message by clicking the Spell button on the Prodigy Mail toolbar.**

   Sending e-mail with typos is tacky. And including a built-in spell checker is such a nice Prodigy Mail feature.

5. **If you want to attach a file to the message, click the Attach button on the Prodigy Mail toolbar or choose File⇨Attach.**

   Choose the file you want to attach and click OK. You can attach as many as three files to each e-mail message.

   Attachments can be sent only to other Prodigy users, not to folks on the Internet or other online services.

6. **To send the message, click the Send button on the Prodigy Mail toolbar or press Ctrl+S.**

   Prodigy Mail sends the message while continuing to display the message in your window. To compose another message, click the Clear icon to clear away the entries for the last message.

7. **To return to the Prodigy Mail Inbox, press Ctrl+M or click the Mailbox icon.**

   Prodigy asks whether you want to discard your unsent message. Yes, Prodigy sent your message when you clicked the Send button. Prodigy is wondering about that *next* message you *may* have been thinking about writing.

If you want to test your ability to send an e-mail message, send one to this address:

```
moreint2@dummies.com
```

You'll get a personalized response from our mail robot.

Other mail tricks

This section lists a few other things you may want to know about using the Prodigy Mail program:

- You can include in a mail message a text file from your hard disk. For example, you can send a text file with a list of things you want for your birthday to your mother without retyping the list. Click the Import button on the Prodigy Mail toolbar or choose File⇨Import when you are composing the message.
- Prodigy keeps addresses you plan to use frequently in an address book. To see your address book, click the address button on the Prodigy Mail toolbar. You can store both Prodigy user IDs and Internet addresses, and you can assign a *nickname* to each address, which makes typing easier. If your best friend has a CompuServe account, for example, remembering the string of numbers that makes up her account number is tough. Assign

her a nickname in the address book so that you can type the nickname, not her Internet address. You also can create a list of addresses, if you frequently send messages to the same group of people.

- You can change some things about the way the Prodigy Mail program works. Choose Options⇨Preferences to see your options.

You can't use any other Prodigy services while Prodigy Mail is running. To leave the Prodigy Mail program, choose File⇨Exit or press Alt+F4.

Jumping on the Web

Prodigy comes with a separate Web browser program, called, not surprisingly, Prodigy Web Browser. Prodigy Web Browser looks a great deal like Mosaic or Netscape. To load the Web browser, click the Web button on the toolbar at the bottom of the Prodigy window. You see the Prodigy Internet Forum window (not the Web browser yet), shown in Figure 11-11.

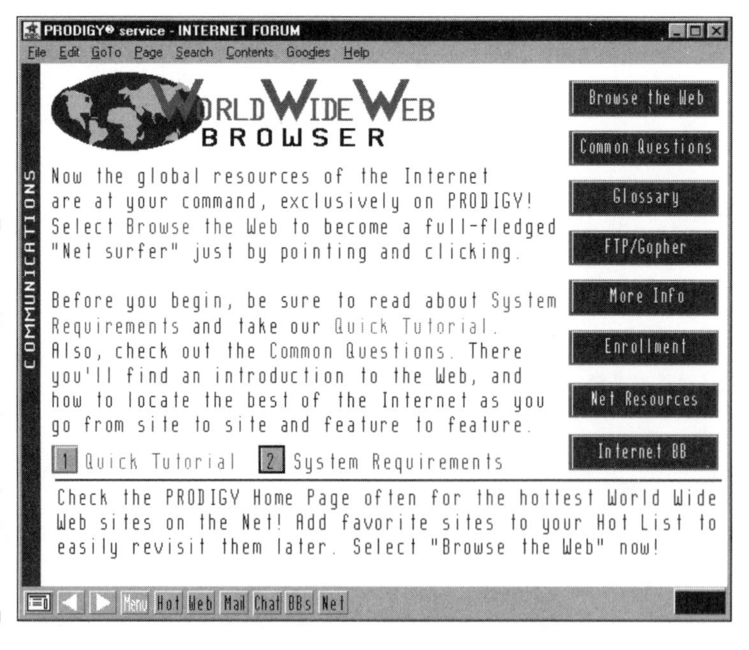

Figure 11-11: In the Internet information window, take a look at the information Prodigy provides about the Internet.

To load the Prodigy Web Browser program, shown in Figure 11-12, click the Browse the Web button. (If you choose Web Browser in the Sign-On window when you connect to Prodigy, you see the Prodigy Web Browser, too — doing so is a quick way to connect directly to the Web.)

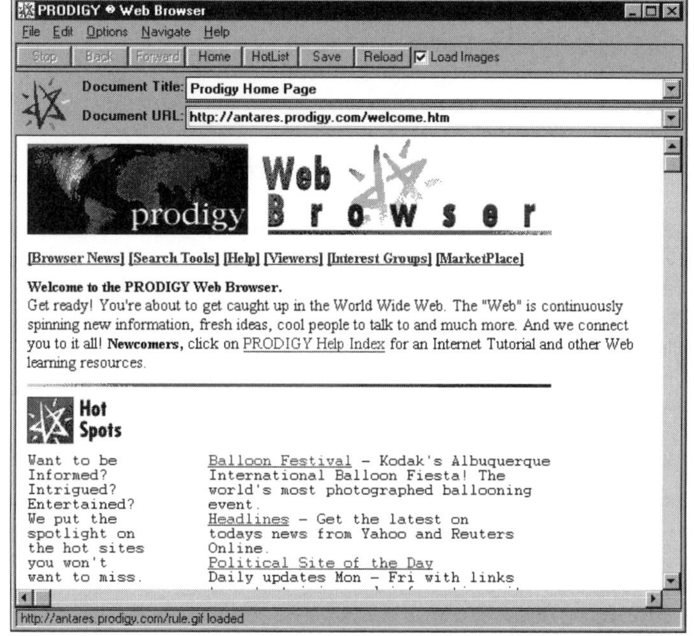

Figure 11-12: The Prodigy Web Browser displays Prodigy's own home page.

If you know the URL of the Web page you want to see and the Prodigy Web Browser isn't running, choose GoTo➪Jump To, click Web URL, and type the Web page's URL. If the Web browser is already running, type the URL in the Document URL box.

To use the Prodigy Web Browser, click highlighted (blue-underlined) words and phrases. This Web-browsing program is similar to Mosaic.

When you finish using the Web browser, choose File➪Exit. You stay online with Prodigy, though — the regular Prodigy window reappears.

Making your own Web page

A great feature of Prodigy is that you can create your own Web home page for all Internet users to see. Go to the Prodigy home page (by choosing Navigate➪Home Page on the Prodigy Web Browser menu bar) and scroll down to the blue Personal Web Pages link. If you can't find the Personal Web Pages link, you can type its URL in the Document URL box instead and press Enter.

```
http://pages.prodigy.com/
```

Follow the directory on the Prodigy Personal Web Pages page to create your own page. You don't have to know the technical ins and outs of Web page creation — you simply fill in the blanks.

Jumping into Gopher menus

Like many Web browsers, the Prodigy Web Browser can display Gopher menus. To see a Gopher menu, you have to know its URL. (See Chapter 5 for an explanation of URLs and Gopher.) Simply type a Gopher menu's URL anywhere you can type a Web-page URL.

Jumping into FTP archives

The Prodigy Web Browser can get files from FTP archives, too. You can't *upload* files (copy files from your computer to the FTP server), and you can't use your own account on an FTP server. But what you *can* do is what most people want to do: Connect to publicly available FTP servers (using anonymous FTP) and download files to your PC.

To connect to an FTP server, enter the FTP server's URL anywhere Prodigy lets you type a URL. An FTP server's URL looks like

```
ftp://ftpservername/
```

For example, the Microsoft FTP server's URL (at `ftp.microsoft.com`) is

```
ftp://ftp.microsoft.com/
```

Jumping into Newsgroups

Prodigy has its own bulletin boards (BBS, in Prodigy parlance), but you may also want to read and participate in the more unruly Usenet newsgroups. Usenet newsgroups are accessible by almost all Internet users and by people on most commercial online services. On a newsgroup, almost every conceivable topic is available (although we haven't been able to find one about keeping chickens in your backyard). For general information about Usenet newsgroups, see Chapter 9 of *The Internet For Dummies,* 3rd Edition.

Jumping the first time

To read Usenet newsgroups for the first time, Prodigy makes you go through extra steps:

1. **Click the Net button on the toolbar at the bottom of the Prodigy window. Or press Ctrl+J and type the Jumpword** usenet.

   You see the USENET Newsgroups window.

2. **Click the Access Control button.**

   The first time you try to read a Usenet newsgroup, you see the Access Control dialog box. Prodigy requires you to choose which of the names attached to your account can have access to newsgroups. (Some wild, woolly, and downright dirty and offensive stuff is available.)

   Remember that you can have as many as six people using your account. The person who signed up for Prodigy gets the user ID that ends with *A*, and the other users get the letters *B* through *F.* The *A* user is the owner and controls access for everyone else.

   If you're not reading Usenet newsgroups for the first time, skip to the next section.

3. **If you haven't already chosen which users have access to Usenet newsgroups, click the Select Names button.**

   The Select Names dialog box appears.

4. **Click a user who should be allowed to read newsgroups and then click OK.**

   That is, would you mind looking over this person's shoulder only to find that he is reading one of the `alt.sex` newsgroups or a group about Nazi sympathizers?

   When you click OK, Prodigy asks you to click the Accept button to promise that you understand the grave moral danger in which you may be placing your family.

5. **Click Accept if you want to take that chance.**

You're ready to experience the complete Usenet newsgroup adventure! Read on to see what happens next. If you aren't familiar with Usenet, you may want to click topics in the Usenet Newsgroups window; these topics explain how Usenet newsgroups work.

Reading a newsgroup

To read newsgroups, you can either begin at the USENET Newsgroups window or jump directly into the newsgroup you want. To go directly to a newsgroup, you must know its exact name.

These steps show you how to begin reading newsgroups, after you've taken care of the question of who should be allowed to read them:

1. **To start at the USENET Newsgroups window, click the Net button on the toolbar at the bottom of the Prodigy window or press Ctrl+J and type the Jumpword** usenet.

   You see the USENET Newsgroups window, shown in Figure 11-13.

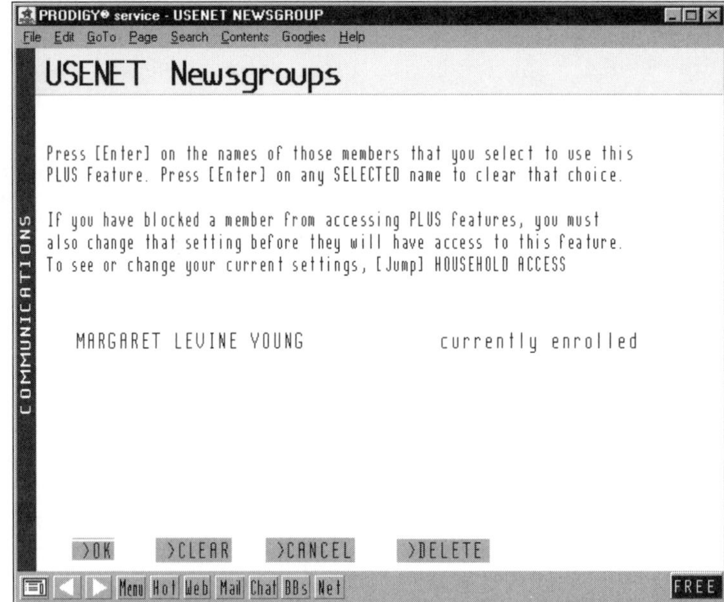

Figure 11-13: The USENET Newsgroups window shows which users of your Prodigy account are allowed to read newsgroups.

2. **Click Explore Newsgroups.**

   You see Your USENET Newsgroup List, shown in Figure 11-14.

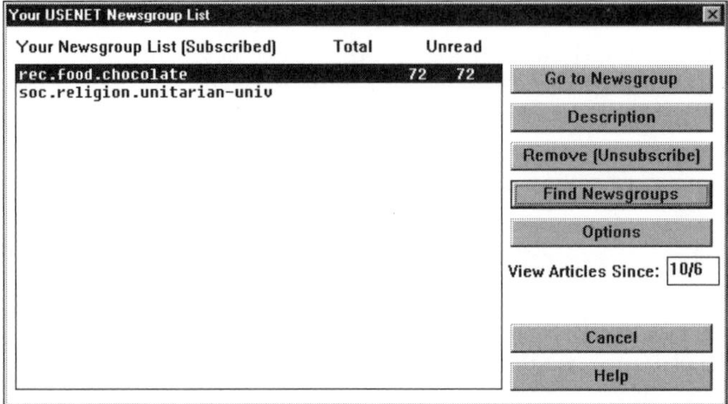

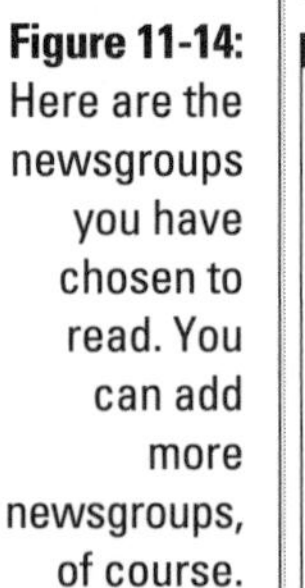

Figure 11-14: Here are the newsgroups you have chosen to read. You can add more newsgroups, of course.

If the newsgroup you want to read doesn't appear on the list, see the section "Finding a newsgroup," later in this chapter.

3. **Click the newsgroup name you want to read and click Go to Newsgroup.**

   You see the list of newsgroup articles, as shown in Figure 11-15.

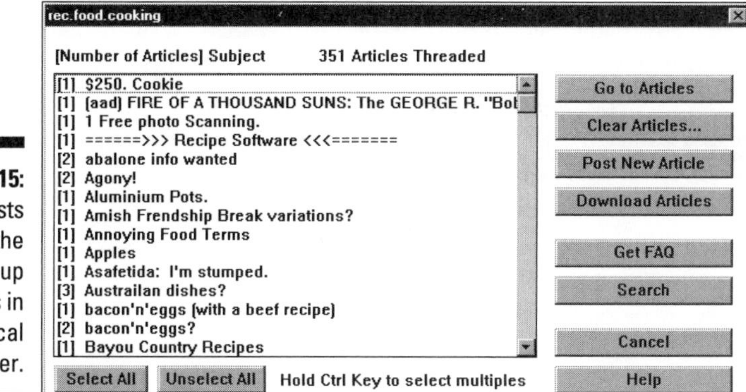

Figure 11-15: Prodigy lists the newsgroup articles in alphabetical order.

The section "Reading newsgroup articles," later in this chapter, tells you what to do next.

Jumping to a newsgroup you know

If you know the exact name of the newsgroup you want to read, follow these steps:

1. **Press Ctrl+J or choose GoTo⇨Jump To.**

   You see the Go To dialog box, shown in Figure 11-7.

2. **Click the USENET Newsgroups button, type the newsgroup name in the box, and click OK.**

   If you're reading a newsgroup you've never read, Prodigy asks whether you want to add the newsgroup to your hot list (to the newsgroups to which you subscribe).

3. **Click Yes, assuming that you expect to read the newsgroup regularly; otherwise click No.**

   You see a window that lists the newsgroup articles.

Reading newsgroup articles

After you tell Prodigy which newsgroup you want to read, you see the list of newsgroup articles you haven't read yet (refer to Figure 11-15). The articles are grouped together into *threads,* which is an article and all its responses. For each thread, you see the number of articles in the thread and the thread subject.

Double-click a thread to read the articles in the thread. Prodigy displays the first unread article in the thread (the first article *you* haven't read — see Figure 11-16).

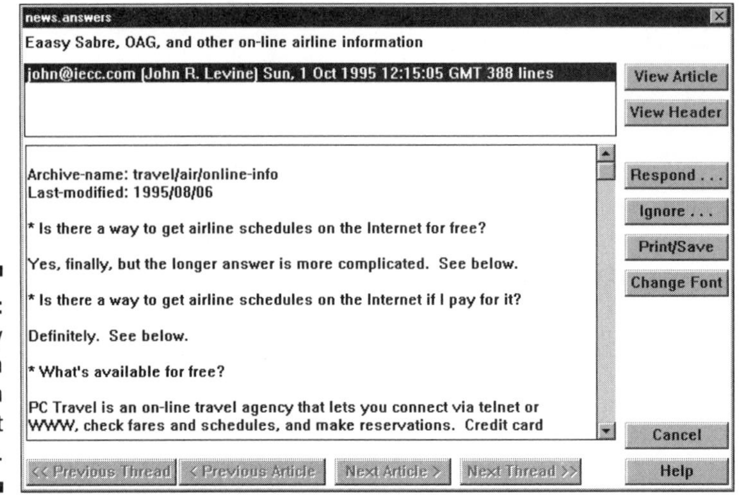

Figure 11-16: Prodigy displays an article from a Usenet newsgroup.

After you finish reading the article, you can click one of the following buttons:

- **Print/Save:** Prints the article. This button also lets you save the article in a file on your disk.
- **Ignore:** Tells Prodigy to ignore all subsequent articles by this author, by clicking the Ignore button. Clicking Ignore is an effective way to deal with people who are annoying you — far more effective than complaining to them or about them.
- **Next Article:** Looks at the next article in the thread.
- **Next Thread:** Looks at the first article in the next thread.
- **Cancel:** Returns to the list of threads in this newsgroup.

When you finish reading the articles in the newsgroup, click Cancel. You return to the list of newsgroups you subscribe to or to whatever you were doing before you began reading this newsgroup.

Before you leave the newsgroup, you may want to click the Clear button, to tell Prodigy that you don't want to see these articles the next time you run the newsreader. When you click Clear, Prodigy gives you two options: Clear the articles that appear in your list so that you don't see them the next time or clear all the articles in the newsgroup. Either way, Prodigy marks even the articles you didn't read as read so that you don't see them next time. Clearing the old articles makes picking out the new articles that appear easier.

Reading the FAQ (list of frequently asked questions and their answers) for any newsgroup you read is a good idea. Click the Get the FAQ button to the right of the list of articles.

Mouthing off

The best way to respond to an article is usually by sending e-mail to the person who wrote the article. While you're reading the article, click the Respond button. Prodigy asks whether you want to send a Public reply (by posting an article) or a Private reply (by sending e-mail to the person who wrote the article). Unless you're sure that the thousands of people who read the newsgroup are interested in what you have to say, choose Private (Reply Privately to Author only). When you click OK, you see the Send A Private Reply dialog box, preaddressed to the author. Fill in your message and click Send, OK, and then Close.

What? You want to *post* your reply so that everyone in the newsgroup can read it? Or you have a new subject to bring up? You can do that, we suppose. Click the Respond button, choose Post Public Reply, and then click OK. You see the Post A Public Follow Up dialog box, shown in Figure 11-17.

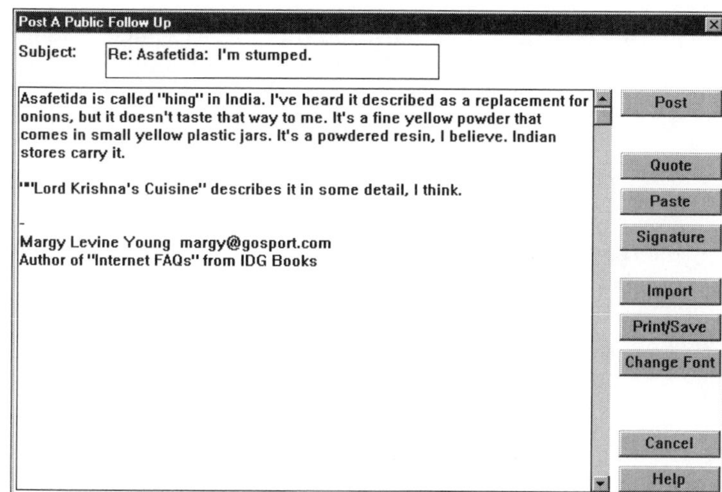

Figure 11-17: You can post articles to newsgroups, but be sure that you have something friendly, well-written, helpful, and accurate to say.

When you have composed and proofread your reply, click Post to send the message to the wide world of Usenet. Then press Close to leave the Post A Public Follow Up dialog box.

If you want to post a new article, but not in response to an existing article, you can also click the Post An Article button to the right of the list of articles in the newsgroup.

Prodigy appends a few lines of text, called your *signature,* to every article you post. To look at or change your signature, click the Signature button in the newsreader. Your default signature (the one Prodigy uses if you don't change your signature) consists of your name and e-mail address.

Finding a newsgroup

What if you don't know which newsgroups you want to read? You can search for a newsgroup about a topic, by clicking the Find Newsgroups button on Your USENET Newsgroup List (shown in Figure 11-14). To search for a newsgroup, click the Find Newsgroups button, enter a word, and click Find Now. Prodigy lists newsgroups that contain the word in the title or description. You can choose newsgroups from the list to look at or subscribe to.

To see a list of recently formed newsgroups, click the Find Newsgroups button on Your USENET Newsgroup List, click Latest Newsgroups Added, and click Find Now.

Doing Other Things

Prodigy doesn't provide a way to use Internet services such as telnet, Archie, or finger. Perhaps Prodigy will add these facilities in the future.

For More Information

Prodigy offers a great deal of other services that we haven't described because they don't relate to the Internet. Prodigy has great services for kids and lots of investment information. To get more information about Prodigy, read *Prodigy For Dummies,* choose Help, or go to the Jumpword HELP.

Chapter 12
Connecting to the Internet via Netcom

(contributed by Douglas J. Muder)

In This Chapter

- Installing the NetCruiser software
- Signing up for a Netcom account
- Getting online
- Hanging up
- Taking Netcom on the road
- Telling NetCruiser where to cruise
- Sending and reading e-mail
- Jumping onto the Web
- Cruising in and out of the Netcom Homeport
- Jumping into Usenet newsgroups
- Doing other Internet stuff
- Using WinSock programs with NetCruiser
- Using Netcom without NetCruiser
- Finding out more about Netcom and NetCruiser

Netcom is a large, fast-growing, national Internet access provider based in San Jose, California. Netcom offers a full range of Internet services at rates that are very reasonable for the frequent user. Netcom provides a free software package, NetCruiser, that allows you to browse the Web, send e-mail, read newsgroup articles, participate in Internet Relay Chat (IRC), and access other computers via Gopher, FTP, or telnet. NetCruiser is the only software that you need to use Netcom's services. You can even use NetCruiser 2.1 with popular WinSock applications like Netscape and Eudora. (See Chapter 10 for information about WinSock programs.)

This chapter describes NetCruiser 2.1. Netcom updates its software from time to time, so if you have a later version, it may behave slightly differently. If you have an earlier version, you can download the current version of NetCruiser for free from Netcom's home page at `http://www.netcom.com`.

You can use NetCruiser 2.1 (Netcom's software) with Windows 3.1 and Windows 95. This chapter concentrates on running NetCruiser under Windows 95, but we throw in a couple of comments regarding Windows 3.1 as well.

Getting Set Up for Netcom

Lately, Netcom has been trying the AOL trick of sending unsolicited disks in the mail. (If you're on as many mailing lists as we are, you've probably gotten at least one disk already, so you can add your Netcom diskette to your AOL coaster set.) Netcom hasn't gone so far as to offer free trial hours, but at least it is now waiving the $20 sign-up fee it used to charge. If you don't already have a disk lying around, you can call Netcom at 800-353-6600 or send it e-mail at `personal@netcom.com`. (This address may look like the place to send personal messages to Netcom people, but actually the "personal" is for personal sales as opposed to business sales.)

If you already have some kind of Web access, you can download the latest version of NetCruiser from Netcom's Web page:

```
http://www.netcom.com
```

Just click the Join Netcom link when you get to the home page. Netcom claims that it takes 20 minutes to download with a 14.4 Kbps modem.

If your Web connection is slow that day, downloading can take considerably longer. After you have downloaded the file CRUISER.EXE, put it in a directory by itself and run it. The file will give birth to four other files, which are the same ones that are on the disk that Netcom sends in the mail.

If you're using a Mac

At the moment, you're out of luck. But maybe not for long. Netcom just announced a Mac version of NetCruiser at the San Francisco MacWorld Expo in January 1996. Netcom expects the Mac version to be available "during the first quarter of 1996" (that is, "Real Soon Now").

A few hearty Mac users use Netcom without NetCruiser by using it as a regular SLIP or PPP account. They connect using MacTCP and third-party software. Contact Netcom for help (408-983-5950).

The pros and cons of Netcom

Netcom comes with a full-service, all-in-one software package — NetCruiser — that handles Web browsing, e-mail, reading and posting to Usenet newsgroups, Internet Relay Chat, telnet, FTP, and Gopher. NetCruiser is easy to set up and relatively simple to use, but if you absolutely must have WinSock applications like Netscape or Eudora, you can use those programs, too.

If you plan to be online a lot, Netcom is a good deal: $19.95 a month gets you 40 *peak* hours (officially defined as any time you are awake) and unlimited usage during *nonpeak* hours (when you are asleep — okay, weekends, too). Additional peak hours are $2 each. With more than 200 phone numbers nationwide, Netcom is probably a local call — not just from your home, but also from the home of any boring relative you might happen to visit.

Netcom is an expensive choice for the occasional user. If you just want an e-mail address and don't plan to spend much time online, you still pay $19.95 a month. Other services let you maintain an inactive account for as little as $5 a month.

Netcom's biggest problem is that it is growing too fast — more than 300 percent in 1995. You can almost always get a phone line, but whether you manage to log in to a computer that works is another question. During busy times, you may have to log in four or five times before you get a session established, and even then you may get cut off by some NetCruiser system error. (Once we had to turn off the power switch and start over.) Patience is required. If your typical Web session is to check the mail and get a quick weather forecast before running out the door, you probably want a different service.

Netcom's growth will have to level out soon (or else Netcom will sign up everyone on the planet five or six times), so we can hope that performance will improve. We can hope for the software to improve as well — NetCruiser 2.1 was the first version to work with Windows 95 and the first to provide a toolbar for installing and working with WinSock programs, so don't be surprised that occasional glitches exist.

Installing the NetCruiser software

You need to do two things before you get rolling: You have to install the NetCruiser software, and you have to register for a Netcom account. The Setup program on the installation disk guides you through both steps, in that order.

The instructions that follow are for installing NetCruiser 2.1. Later versions might be slightly different. In general, though, Netcom has done a pretty good job of automating the process and telling you what you need to know or do at each step. Most screens during installation have a Help button as well. Naturally, the instructions Netcom gives you are more up-to-date than ours. If you just follow the instructions on-screen, you should be okay.

In order to install and run NetCruiser, you need the following:

- A 386 processor or better
- Windows 95 or Windows 3.1 with DOS 5.0 or better
- Four or more megabytes of *RAM* (Random Access Memory) in your computer
- Four or more megabytes of free space on your hard drive
- A 9600 baud (or faster) modem

If you have all that

1. **Insert the NetCruiser disk into your disk drive.**

   Or if you downloaded the software from Netcom's Web page, as we described previously, remember where you put the software, run the Setup program, and skip to step 4.

2. **In Windows 95, click the Start button and choose Run. In Windows 3.1, choose File⇨Run from the Program Manager.**

3. **Type** a:setup **or** b:setup, **depending on whether you put the disk into drive A or B, and press Enter.**

   After a brief delay, you find yourself looking at the Netcom logo, and the Welcome to NetCruiser Setup window appears. This window wants to know what directory it should put the Netcom files into, and it offers the perfectly reasonable suggestion: C:\NETCOM.

   If, for some bizarre reason, you already have a directory named C:\NETCOM, you need to make a decision. You can either type another directory name into the window or (better yet) click the Exit Setup button, go off and change the name of the other directory, and start over again. If C:\NETCOM causes you no problems, then you don't have to type anything.

4. **Click the Continue button.**

   Setup copies a bunch of files into the newly created C:\NETCOM directory. Setup also creates icons and does other, more technical things. In the course of doing these technical things, Setup may decide that it needs to change your AUTOEXEC.BAT file. A lot of people are kind of touchy about their AUTOEXEC.BAT files, so Setup asks permission to make any changes. If you've never thought twice about your AUTOEXEC.BAT file, you don't need to start now — just click the Yes button. Setup stores a copy of your old AUTOEXEC.BAT file in case some guru needs to undo all this later.

If all goes according to plan, the Setup program announces that its mission is complete. You now have a choice: go straight into registering for your Netcom account by clicking Start Registration or click Exit and take a break for a while.

Setting up your account

After NetCruiser is installed, set up your Netcom account next. If you clicked the Start Registration button at the end of the NetCruiser installation, you're already under way. But if you decide that you've already had enough excitement for one sitting, you can restart the process by finding the Netcom folder. Setup put the Netcom folder in either the Program menu (Windows 95) or in the Netcom program group in the Program Manager (Windows 3.1). The NetCruiser Registration program is inside this folder or group.

Before you start registration, you need to have a few things:

- **NetCruiser.** If you haven't installed NetCruiser yet, go back to the section "Installing the NetCruiser software" earlier in this chapter.
- **A modem.** Registration happens online, so make sure that your computer is connected to a modem and (if the modem is external) that the modem is turned on.
- **A credit card.** Netcom wants to know what to bill your monthly account usage to.
- **A catchy username.** Pick a name that you won't be embarrassed by later on.
- **A password.** Pick a password that you have some chance of remembering.

With all that in hand

1. **Either click the Start Registration button at the end of the NetCruiser installation process or double-click the NetCruiser Registration icon in the Netcom folder in the Program menu (Windows 95) or the Netcom program group in Program Manager (Windows 3.1).**

   The registration program asks some yes/no questions about whether you are in the United States and whether you need to dial 9 (or something else) to get an outside line. Answer by clicking the check boxes. After you are done, click the Continue button on the screen. If you have second thoughts about the whole process, you can click the Cancel button. But you'll get plenty of chances to do that later.

2. **Fill out the User Information screen.**

   Give the address where you want a bill sent (assuming Netcom didn't succeed in charging your credit card), not the address where your computer is. Netcom insists on a home phone number, though the Work Phone and Company Name lines are optional. After you are done, click Continue.

3. **Choose a username.**

   Before you get clever and pick something like *LotsaLaffs,* remember that this is going to be the start of your e-mail address. People you've just met are going to be asking for it. (You only get eight characters, so *LotsaLaffs* wouldn't work anyway.)

4. **Choose a password.**

   Something that's easy for you to remember and hard for somebody else to guess. Your password can be six, seven, or eight characters long. What you type shows up on-screen as a series of asterisks. You have to type your password twice so that the program can tell if you make a typographical error.

   We suggest using your parents' wedding anniversary or some combination of a few letters of the street that you grew up on with some numbers from your dad's birthday.

5. **Tell them your mother's maiden name.**

   This is in case you call Netcom a week from now and say, "I forgot my password." Your mother's maiden name, of course, is a state secret. No one else could possibly know it.

6. **The registration program goes away for a minute or so and checks out your modem. Let it.**

   When the program comes back, you see the Registration Status screen. (You've gotten so far into the process that your registration is beginning to have a little status.) The Modem Configured line should be checked (if it isn't, click the Modem Setup and Diagnosis button), and a blue arrow points to an 800 number.

7. **Click Continue to dial the 800 number.**

   This step may take a while, or you may need to try again if the registration computer is too busy to deal with you. This step requires patience, but usually a delay does not mean that anything is going wrong. Just acknowledge any error messages and click the Stop button if everything is taking too long. Try again by clicking Continue.

8. **Choose an access number.**

   NetCruiser is going to call this number whenever you log in. If you are in a well-populated area, you might have a choice of two or more numbers. Or only one Netcom number may be in your area code. You can change your access number later if you move, go on vacation, or think you made a mistake. (See "Changing your access number," later in this chapter.) Netcom confirms your choice.

9. **You may need to choose another username.**

   What? You mean Netcom already has a "Butthead"? Go figure.

10. **Give Netcom a credit card number.**

    You knew it had to come to this. Visa, Mastercard, or American Express. If you are having second thoughts and don't really want to be charged $19.95 this month, bail out by clicking Cancel.

11. **Read the terms and conditions.**

    Yeah, right.

12. **Create your account.**

    Click OK and you're all set.

If you run into any problem that these instructions don't handle, call Netcom's technical support folks at 408-983-5970.

Calling Netcom from Your Computer

After you have everything set up, NetCruiser appears in a Netcom folder in your Program menu (Windows 95) or in the Netcom program group in Program Manager (Windows 3.1). Double-clicking the NetCruiser icon gives you a NetCruiser Login dialog box. Your username is already on the screen. Type your password into the password box and press the Enter key.

The blue bar at the top of the Login dialog box shows you the progress of your login request. Several things have to happen in between typing your password and doing anything useful or interesting: NetCruiser has to find your modem, dial the access number, and get an answer. Then Netcom's login computers have to check your username and password and find a host computer that has the time to deal with you. Any of these steps can fail. But if you just keep trying, you will get through.

Usually NetCruiser realizes when something has gone wrong with the login process, and it tries again automatically. But sometimes your login request seems to hang in space. If you're as impatient as we are, you may want to click the Stop Login button and start over. Unfortunately, NetCruiser 2.1 has the annoying habit of crashing about every fourth or fifth time we do this. Sometimes it crashes so badly that when we start NetCruiser again, it goes right back into the same error mode. If this happens to you, we have two suggestions: First, make sure that your modem was hung up properly when NetCruiser failed. If it wasn't, break the connection yourself. Second, restarting the computer will get NetCruiser out of even the most persistent error modes.

Hanging up

End your Netcom session by choosing File⇨Exit. NetCruiser responds like a jilted lover and asks if you are sure that you want to leave. Steel yourself and click Yes.

What if you're not calling from home?

The biggest advantage Netcom has over a local Internet access provider is that you can take it on the road with you and (usually) not have to pay long-distance charges. (Okay, that's not so unusual. But if you do it right, your *host* won't have to pay long-distance charges, either.)

If you are using someone else's computer and they have NetCruiser set up already, then you can just start NetCruiser, type your username in place of theirs, and log in normally.

If they don't have NetCruiser, you can install it if you have your installation disk. This doesn't cost your host anything or commit them to establishing a Netcom account, and you can just remove the Netcom folder from their hard drive when you leave. (Just be sure not to click the Start Registration button at the end of the NetCruiser installation process.)

If you have your computer with you, you will still need to tell NetCruiser to call the local Netcom phone number instead of the one it usually calls. See the section "Changing your access number," later in this chapter. ***Remember:*** Change the number back when you get home!

Changing your access number

Choosing the lowest-cost access number is important because you will be connected to it for many hours a month. (If you aren't going to be online that much, you should get a cheaper Internet account.) If you move, travel, change your local calling plan, or discover that Netcom has added new telephone numbers in your area, you may want to change your access number.

You don't need to be online to change your number. Just start NetCruiser. When the Login dialog box appears, do the following:

1. **Choose Settings⇨Phone Number.**
2. **Select Directory from the Phone Number dialog box.**

   Unless you happen to know the local Netcom number by heart, that is. (Where is Rain Man when you need him?) In that case, you can just type it into the Dial box.
3. **Scan through the list of phone numbers until you find one that looks local.**

   The numbers are listed in numerical order, so all the ones in your current area code (if any) are right next to each other. If you don't find a local number, you have two choices: You can choose a number that looks close enough and pay the long-distance charges, or you can call Netcom's 800 number. *The 800 number is not free.* It costs an extra eight cents a minute, in addition to your regular account charges, which is still cheaper than most long-distance calls.

4. **Click the number that you've chosen.**

   Or click the Use Netcom Dial-800 button.

5. **Adjust the dialing prefix.**

   NetCruiser assumes this call is local unless you tell it otherwise. If it needs to dial some prefix to get an outside line, dial the area code, or dial 1, you need to tell it so.

6. **Click OK.**

   The Phone Number dialog box returns with the new phone number displayed.

7. **Click OK again.**

   Unless you want to look at numbers again.

The new phone number is set up, and from now on you can log in normally.

Cruising with NetCruiser

When you log in, NetCruiser starts you off in the Web-browsing tool — specifically, at the Netcom Homeport (shown in Figure 12-1). All of NetCruiser's various applications are available from the icon bar just below the menu. By America Online standards, the icons are a bit amateurish, but they get the message across. Table 12-1 lists what the icons stand for.

Figure 12-1: The Netcom Homeport.

Table 12-1 Interpreting the Icons

Icon Description	*Application*
Question mark	Help
Inbox	Check mail
Letter coming out of computer screen	Write mail
Spider's web	Web browser
Buck-toothed animal	Gopher
Newspaper	Read newsgroup
Newspaper with a lightning bolt	Write to newsgroup
Telephone lines	FTP file transfer
Computers with telnet	Telnet
Pointing finger	Finger
Lips saying *IRC*	Internet Relay Chat

You can give yourself more room on the screen by removing the icon bar. The View⇨Toolbar command does the trick. You can access everything that was on the icon bar from the Internet menu.

Figure 12-1 contains a couple of icons that you won't see on your screen the first time that you log in: the Application Launcher icons. These are non-Netcom programs that you can access from within NetCruiser. (If you have any non-Netcom programs, that is — Netcom doesn't provide or maintain any of these programs.) The Application Launcher in Figure 12-1 contains icons for launching Eudora and Netscape. We'll explain how to configure NetCruiser to work with your favorite WinSock programs in the section "Using WinSock Programs with NetCruiser," later in this chapter.

The Help that you get by clicking the question mark icon isn't very helpful — it's just installation and registration Help. You can reach helpful Help via the NetCruiser button at the bottom of the Homeport page.

Sending and Receiving Mail

What would the Internet be without e-mail? You just can't have an all-in-one Internet software package without including a mail program. NetCruiser's e-mail program is simple and effective, but a little lacking in the bells-and-whistles department.

Addressing your mail

To send a message to another Netcom user, address the message to your friend's username (*newuser*, for example). To send a message to someone on the Internet, use the person's Internet address.

Your own Internet e-mail address is your username followed by `@ix.netcom.com`. If your user ID is *newuser,* for example, your e-mail address is `newuser@ix.netcom.com`.

Reading your mail

Check your mail by following these steps:

1. **Either click the inbox icon (the second from left on the toolbar) or choose Internet⇨Read Mail-In.**
2. **Double-click Inbox in the dialog box that appears.**

   The screen splits into two windows as shown in Figure 12-2.
3. **From the list of messages in the top window, double-click the name of the message that you want to read.**

   The text of the message appears in the bottom window.

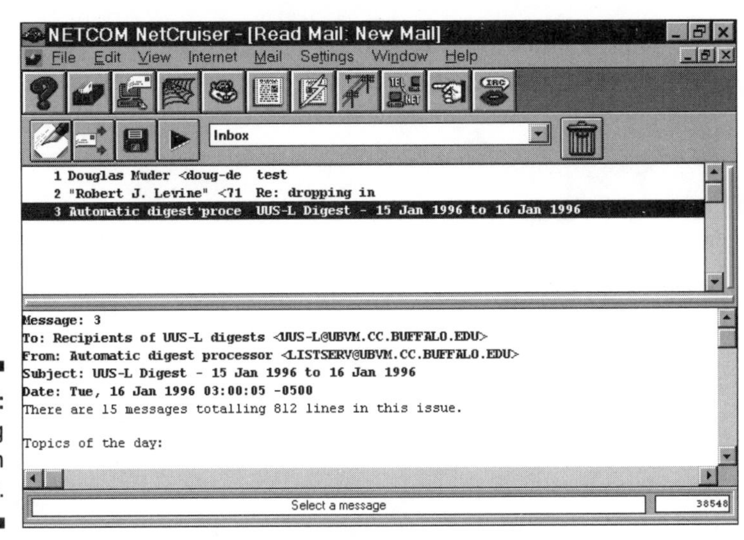

Figure 12-2: Reading your mail in NetCruiser.

Take that message and . . .

The icons at the top of the Read Mail window (shown in Figure 12-2) spell out all the things that you can do with a message. After you have a message displayed in the bottom half of the window, you can

- **Reply to it.** Clicking the fountain pen icon opens up a Send Mail window, with a new message addressed to the sender of the original message. Learn more about the powers of the Send Mail window in the section "Writing a new message," later in this chapter.
- **Forward it to somebody else.** The letter-with-two-arrows icon opens an Address Mail To dialog box and creates a Send Mail window that has the to-be-forwarded message.

- **Save it.** Clicking the disk icon saves the current message in the NETCOM\MAIL directory. Messages in this directory can be read offline by any word processor you may have, but figuring out which message is which will be a bear. The first message that you save is filed as 00000001.MSG, the second as 00000002.MSG, and so on. Your best bet is to resave them as word-processing documents with names and in directories or folders that give you a chance of finding what you want.
- **Get over it.** Selecting another message in the message list and clicking the arrow icon moves you to that message.
- **Trash it.** Clicking the trash can icon sends the current message into oblivion.

Writing a new message

To send e-mail to someone

1. **Click the computer-with-a-letter-coming-out-of-it icon or choose Internet⇨Send Mail-Out.**

   A Send Mail window opens, as shown in Figure 12-3, along with an Address Mail To dialog box.

2. **To address the message, type the address of a person whom you want to send mail to (or select an address from your address book) on the left side of the Address Mail To box and click the Use button.**

   The address shifts to the right side of the screen. When the right side of the box lists all the recipients you want, click OK.

3. **Type a subject in the Subject box.**
4. **Write the message.**

5. **Think about whether you really want to send it.**

   Many e-mails are written in haste and anger. Unlike with snail mail, you don't have all that cooling-off time while you look for a stamp and walk to the mailbox. If you decide the world is better off without this message, click the torn-letter icon to cancel.

6. **Send the message.**

   Click the computer-with-a-letter-coming-out-of-it icon on the Send Mail toolbar. Confusingly, this icon is identical to and sits below the icon that you clicked in step 1. Be sure that you click the lower one.

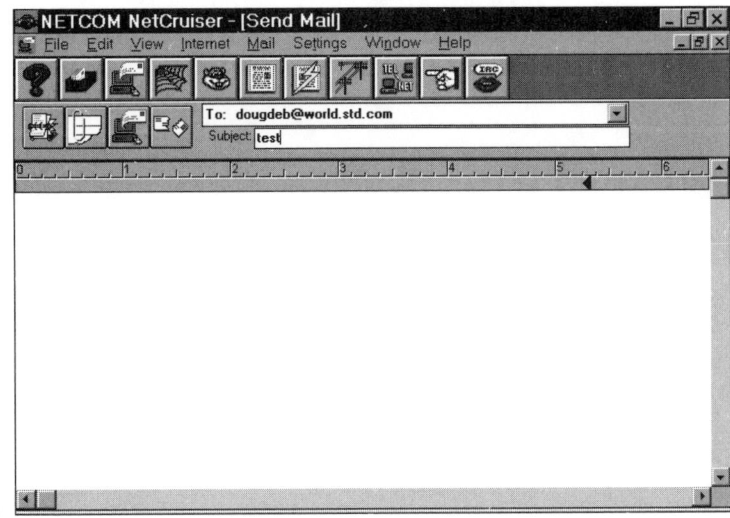

Figure 12-3: The Send Mail toolbar is an extra row of buttons below the regular toolbar.

If you want to test your command of e-mail, send a message to us at `moreint2@dummies.com`. You'll get a message back from our friendly mail robot, telling you what your e-mail address is.

Reading and sending attached files

When the message you are reading has a file attached to it, two new icons appear in the toolbar in the Read Mail window (shown in Figure 12-2). Click the eye icon to open the attached file. Click the disk-with-a-note-paper-clipped-to-it icon to save the attached file to your hard drive.

To attach a file to a message that you send

1. **When the message is ready to go, click the paper clip icon on the Send Mail toolbar.**

   An Open window appears.

2. **In the Open window, find the file that you want to attach.**
3. **Click OK.**

The location (on your machine) of the attached file appears in the Attachments window just below the subject line. Two extra icons appear in the Send Mail toolbar. Clicking the eye icon opens the attached file, so you can check that it is really the one you wanted. If it isn't, you can unattach it by clicking the paper-clipped-trash-can icon.

Keeping an address book

Nobody remembers all those crazy e-mail addresses. When you come across an address that you think you will need to use again, store it like this:

1. **Go to either the Send Mail or Read Mail window.**
2. **Choose Mail⇨Address Book.**
3. **Click the New Entry button.**
4. **Fill out the Edit Address Book Entry form.**

The form gives space not only for the person's name and e-mail address, but also for handy comments like "Bob's roommate's sister's husband."

Now whenever the Address Mail To window appears, the list of people in your address book appears as well (their real names, not the e-mail addresses). When you select a name from the address book and click the Use button, the corresponding e-mail address magically appears in the Email Recipients window.

Cruising the Web

NetCruiser has a nice Web browser built right in. You can access the NetCruiser Web Browser by doing any of the following:

- **Logging in.**

  The login process opens the Web Browser automatically to the Netcom Homeport as seen in Figure 12-1.
- **Clicking the spider's web icon on the toolbar.**
- **Choosing Internet⇨World Wide Web-Browser from the menu.**

The Web Browser toolbar provides the following tools for traversing the Web:

- **Jump to a bookmark.** Click the marked-book icon.
- **Go to the previous/next page.** Click the backward/forward arrows.
- **Return to the Homeport.** Click the house icon.
- **Go to another Web page.** Type the URL in the window.
- **Open a file on your computer.** Click the folder icon.

For more information about finding information on the Web, see Chapter 4 in *The Internet For Dummies,* 3rd Edition.

There's no port like home

The Netcom Homeport (see Figure 12-1) is not a bad place to start your Web wandering. The 12 category links (the little buttons labeled News, Sports, and so on) take you to other pages of links, and you can get to a lot of interesting information quickly.

Six useful buttons are also lurking at the bottom of the page. (You have to scroll down to see them.) In addition to the Homeport button, they are

- **NETCOM.** The Netcom home page. Mostly this is a list of products and services, but a couple of useful links are hidden near the bottom of the page. CruzInfo takes you to a page that lets you check on your account — like how many peak hours you have left this month. PopInfo lists Netcom's telephone numbers around the country and whether any of them are having technical problems.
- **NetCruiser.** Your path to some very good help files.
- **The Club.** A list of useful stuff on the NETCOM and NetCruiser pages.
- **Search.** Access to search engines for finding things on the Web.
- **New.** An infrequently updated list of what's new on the Netcom service.

Can you make your own Web page?

Not yet, but perhaps soon. A Netcom press release from November 1995 says, "Expected in the first quarter of 1996, individuals will be able to create their own Web pages using the NetCruiser service for personal publishing." The same announcement promises a "personal services portfolio," whatever that means. After you get online, you can go to the Netcom home page (at `http://www.netcom.com`) to see if a more recent announcement exists.

Cruising into Gopher Menus

Clicking the buck-toothed-cartoon-animal icon (or choosing Internet ⇨ Gopher-Browser) launches NetCruiser's Gopher browser, shown in Figure 12-4. The first menu you see is the home Gopher server `gopher.netcom.com`. From there, you can go anywhere by

- **Using a bookmark.** The book-with-bookmark icon opens the bookmark window. From there, you can either place a bookmark at the current location or jump to a previously marked location.
- **Opening one of the displayed folders or documents by double-clicking its icon.**
- **Typing a Gopher address in the address box.**

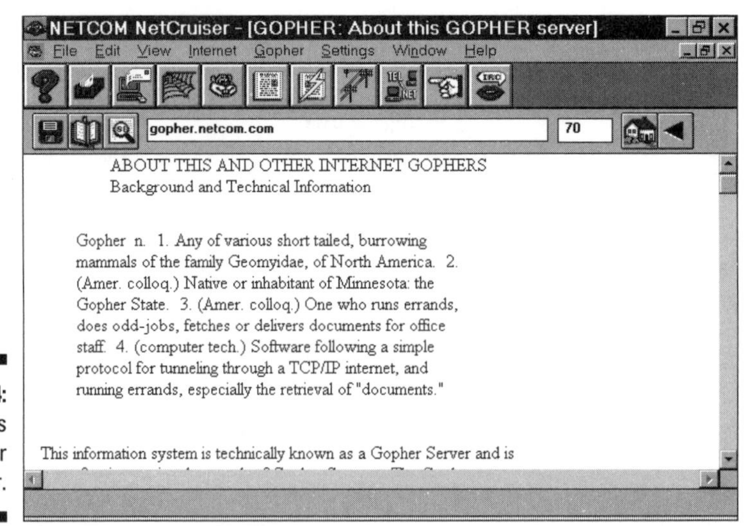

Figure 12-4: NetCruiser's Gopher browser.

A good *first place to go* is your local weather forecast. From the opening window, double-click the Weather folder and then find your state and town. Put a bookmark there.

After you find a document that you want to keep, you can save it by clicking the disk icon. Unlike in the mail or newsgroup parts of NetCruiser, the Save icon in the Gopher browser opens a genuine Windows-style Save As window. You can put some structure on your files and give them names that you hope to recognize in the future.

To go back to the previous Gopher menu, click the arrow icon on the far right of the Gopher toolbar. To go back to `gopher.netcom.com`, click the house icon.

For more information on using Gopher, see Chapter 20 of this book.

Cruising Usenet Newsgroups

Unknown to you, NetCruiser has already signed you up to subscribe to a few Netcom and new user newsgroups. The newsgroups are worth a look, particularly `news.announce.newusers`, which is a kind of Usenet primer. After you get the hang of the newsreader, you'll want to find newsgroups of your own to subscribe to, and you'll probably even start writing to them.

Reading a newsgroup you subscribe to

To read a Usenet newsgroups with NetCruiser

1. **Either click the newspaper-page icon or choose Internet⇨Read USENET-In.**

   The Select a Newsgroup window appears, containing a list of the newsgroups that you are currently subscribed to. If you were looking for something else, read the section "Finding and subscribing to newsgroups," later in this chapter.

2. **Click the name of a newsgroup in the Select a Newsgroup window.**

   The Retrieve Article Headers window appears to tell you how many articles are available.

3. **Move the sliders or type numbers into the boxes to select a range of articles. Then click OK.**

   After a brief delay, NetCruiser returns with a list of the articles, shown in Figure 12-5.

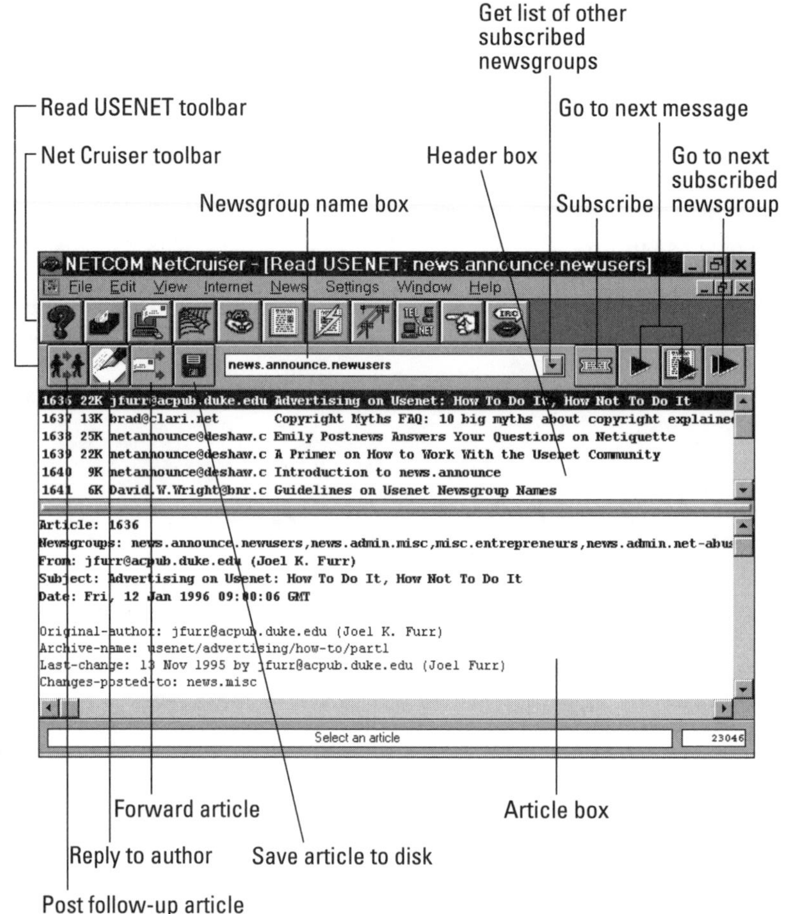

Figure 12-5: The Read USENET Window.

4. **Scroll through the list and select articles that look interesting.**

   You can change the order in which articles are displayed by choosing View➪Sort By. The options are to sort by article number (the default), by subject, or by sender. Select one article simply by clicking it. Select additional articles by holding down the Ctrl key and clicking them as well.

5. **Click the black-triangle icon to open the first selected message.**

   The message appears in the message window in the bottom half of the screen.

Now that a message is displayed, you have many options. See the section "What to do with a newsgroup article," coming up soon in this chapter.

If you want to get the most out of your online time (or you don't want to tie up your phone too long), you needn't read the messages online. Simply open them and save them one by one. You can read them offline using a word-processing program. Unfortunately, you cannot tell NetCruiser to save all the selected messages at once.

Finding and subscribing to newsgroups

If you could only read newsgroups about Netcom and Usenet, neither Netcom nor Usenet would be worth reading about. Thousands and thousands of newsgroups are out there. Most of them would bore you silly, but most likely you would really enjoy a few. How do you find them?

If you know the name of a newsgroup, you can simply type it into the box in the center of the newsreader toolbar. NetCruiser goes off to find the recent messages, and if you like what you see, you can click the ticket icon to subscribe to the newsgroup. From then on, that newsgroup will be one of the choices in the Select a Newsgroup window.

If you don't know the exact name of a newsgroup but you know it's out there somewhere, the easiest way to find it is to type a keyword into the FindNews program. From the Homeport, follow these steps:

1. **Click the NetCruiser button at the bottom of the page.**
2. **Click the FindNews link (highlighted in blue).**
3. **Type your keyword into the Find window.**

   We typed *magick* and found nine newsgroups.
4. **Press the Enter key.**

FindNews displays a list of newsgroups that contain the keyword somewhere in their names. Unfortunately, you have to copy down the names that look interesting. At present, FindNews can't connect you straight into the newsreader. Instead, you have to find the name in the Select USENET Newsgroup window, which we describe next.

If all you know is that you are interested in a topic and you *hope* that you can find a newsgroup devoted to it, choose Internet⇨Choose USENET Newsgroups. The Select USENET Newsgroups window appears.

The overall list of thousands of newsgroups is too long to wade through, so Netcom has created ten more focused lists that can take care of many (but perhaps not all) of your newsgroup needs. Clicking on one of the ten icons moves that list into the Newsgroup Mover window. Scan through the list to see if anything looks interesting.

From the Select USENET Newsgroups window, you can subscribe to a newsgroup by selecting its name in the Newsgroup Mover window and clicking the Subscribe button. Unsubscribe to a newsgroup by finding it in the My Reading List window and clicking the Unsubscribe button.

Anytime you are reading a newsgroup that you are not subscribed to, you can subscribe simply by clicking the ticket icon. If you are subscribed to the newsgroup that you are reading, you can unsubscribe the same way. In either case, NetCruiser asks you if you really mean it; if you click Yes, it's done.

What to do with a newsgroup article

The icons in the Read Mail window spell out your options. You can

- **Post a follow-up message.** Choose News⇨Followup or click the only icon that isn't obvious. The picture is of two arrows going from one person to another. Clicking on this icon opens a Post to USENET Newsgroups window. (Please think long and hard before you do this, because the newsgroups are clogged with an enormous number of trivial messages already. Do thousands of people really need to see what you're about to write? Wouldn't you do just as well to e-mail your reaction to two or three people?)
- **Send e-mail to the author.** Choose News⇨Reply or click the pen-on-paper icon. A Send Mail window opens with the author's address already inserted. If all you really want to say is "You tell them!" or "What a moron," this is your best choice. Actually, forgetting the whole thing and taking a short walk is your very best choice.
- **Forward the article to someone.** Choose News⇨Forward or click the letter-with-two-arrows icon. A Send Mail window opens with the article copied into the message window. Add your comments, address it, and off it goes.
- **Save the article to your disk.** Choose News⇨Save or click the disk icon. The current article is saved in the folder NETCOM\NEWS. Like mail messages, the articles are saved by number (00000001.MSG and so on). Once the messages are on your disk, you'd better do something with them quickly before you forget what they are.
- **Move on.** You have several ways to move on. The black-triangle icon moves to the next selected message in the newsgroup. The black-triangle-on-a-newspaper icon leaves the original message selected but moves to the next selected message. The double-black-triangle icon moves to the next newsgroup on your subscription list.

Posting your own article

For many of us, the day eventually arrives when we can no longer sit on the sidelines and watch other people dominate our favorite newsgroups with opinions and points of view far inferior to our own. (Those folks can't actually *like* that terrible actor whom you hate, can they?) The time has come to take up arms (light sabers included) against the Forces of Ignorance and shine our light in the faces of the Powers of Darkness. It is time, in other words, to post our own article to a newsgroup.

NetCruiser makes the fight pretty simple:

1. **Click the newspaper-with-a-lightning-bolt icon or choose Internet⇨Post to USENET-Out.**

   From the Read USENET Newsgroups window, you can either click the two-people-and-two-arrows icon or choose News⇨Followup.

2. **In the Newsgroups box, type the name of the newsgroup (or groups, separated by commas) that you want to post to.**

   If you got to this window from the Read USENET Newsgroups window, the group you were reading is shown here automatically.

3. **Fill in the Subject box with something appropriate.**

   If you got here by clicking the Follow Up icon on the Read USENET Newsgroups window, the subject line of the message you were reading is repeated here automatically with Re: in front of it.

4. **Type the message into the message box below the ruler.**

   Or (better) write the message offline in a word processor and paste the text into the message box.

5. **Click the Send button.**

Scary how easy it is. People all over the world can now read something that you may not have sent out at all if you'd thought another two seconds about it.

Newsgroups are a little bit like small towns. Most of the regulars feel like they know each other by now, and they don't take kindly to strangers who barge in and try to tell them what's what. In general, reading a newsgroup for a while before you post to it is a good idea.

Cruising in Other Ways

NetCruiser lets you use FTP to download files from FTP servers, telnet to log into other computers on the Internet, and IRC to chat with other users. Here's a quick roundup of these Internet services.

Cruising into FTP archives

To connect to an FTP server and download some files, here's what to do:

1. **In the Netcom NetCruiser window, either click the telephone-lines icon or choose Internet⇨FTP Download.**

   The FTP: Connect To window appears.

2. **Type the address of the FTP server that you want to connect to and press Enter.**

3. **Enter a username and password for the FTP server and then press Enter.**

   If the computer allows anonymous FTP, NetCruiser has already filled in what you need (*anonymous* for the name and your e-mail address for the password). Just press Enter. If you need more file permissions than this computer will give to anyone off the street, though, you'll need to fill in a real username and password.

That should be enough to get you in. The FTP window appears, with icons that allow you to upload, download, or erase files and create or delete directories.

For more information on what you can do with FTP, see Chapter 10 in *The Internet For Dummies,* 3rd Edition.

Using telnet

If you have an account on another computer, you can use NetCruiser's telnet program to log onto it. Here's how:

1. **Click the telnet icon or choose Internet⇨Telnet-Remote Login.**

   A Telnet: Connect To window appears.

2. **In the Site box, type the name of the computer that you want to log onto.**

3. **Click OK or press Enter.**

4. **Log in to the remote computer as you normally would.**

For information about telnet, see Chapter 19 of this book.

Chatting on the IRC

The lips icon launches NetCruiser's IRC application. Netcom offers EFNet or Netcom Private IRC networks. On EFNet, you encounter IRC users worldwide, while Netcom Private chat groups are limited to Netcom users. IRC, unlike Usenet newsgroups, happens in what computer-geeks call *real time,* which means that the messages you type are delivered immediately and other folks respond in just a few seconds.

To get to NetCruiser's IRC window, here's what to do:

1. **Choose Internet⇨IRC or click the IRC icon, the one with the lips saying "IRC."**

   You see the IRC Connection dialog box.

2. **Choose which IRC server you want to use.**

   You can choose EFNet if you want to chat with folks from throughout the Internet, or you can choose Netcom Private IRC to chat only with other Netcom users.

3. **In the Nickname box, type the nickname that you want to use when chatting.**

   Netcom assumes you want to use your username, but you can type in any name you want — maybe even your real name if you really want to be unique. (Most people on the IRC use an alias.)

4. **Click the Save Setting button.**

   NetCruiser saves the information in the IRC Connection dialog box, so you don't have to type it all the next time.

5. **Click the Connect button.**

   You see the IRC Control Panel, shown in Figure 12-6.

When you see the IRC Control Panel, you are ready to chat. In the IRC Control Panel, you can use the following six icons (listed in the order in which they appear on the toolbar, from left to right):

- **Join a Channel** (person walking into a doorway): Click to join a new channel.
- **Users and Channels** (Psst icon): Click to find out about the other people in the current channel.
- **Ignore User** (person crossed out): Click to tell NetCruiser not to display any messages from someone who is acting obnoxious.
- **About Yourself** (person sitting at computer): Click to enter information about yourself for other IRC folks to read.

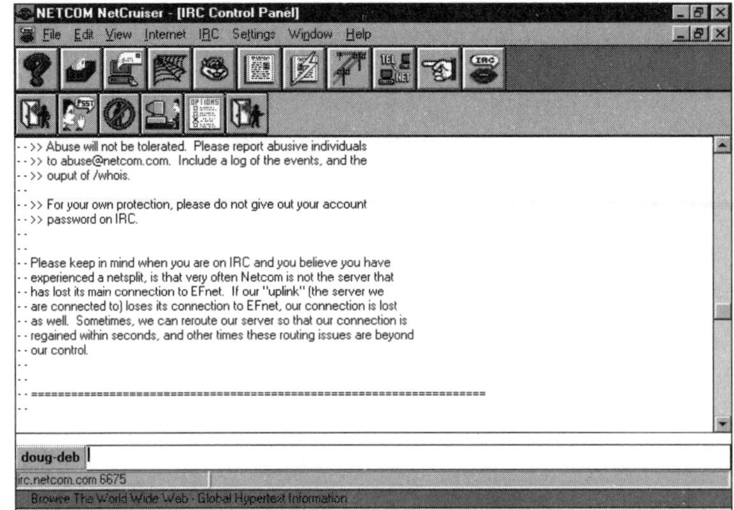

Figure 12-6: You're ready to chat using NetCruiser.

- **IRC Options** (options): Click to see the User Information dialog box, where you can set your IRC options.
- **Exit Channel** (person walking out of a doorway): Leave the current IRC channel (conversation).

That's all very interesting, but you're still not chatting with anybody. To plunge into the action

1. **Choose IRC⇨List⇨Channels.**

   The List Channels dialog box appears. The list of channels can be pretty long. (Though if you've already limited yourself to the Netcom chat groups, the list probably won't be. On a Wednesday afternoon, we got a list of eight groups.) By filling out the options on the List Channels dialog box, you can narrow down your choices. If you don't want to narrow your choices, leave the boxes blank and click OK. This gives you a list of all the channels that you might join.

2. **Look at the list until you find a channel you want to join and double-click its name in the list.**

   Now you see a Join dialog box with the name of the channel already filled in. Unless you know a password for this group (there may not be one), leave the password box blank.

3. **Click OK in the Join dialog box.**

   A chat window appears with the channel name and topic across the top (see Figure 12-7). This window has all the same icons as the IRC Control Panel, plus one more: the people-around-a-table icon. You can ignore it — if you were a channel operator you could use it to change the settings on the channel.

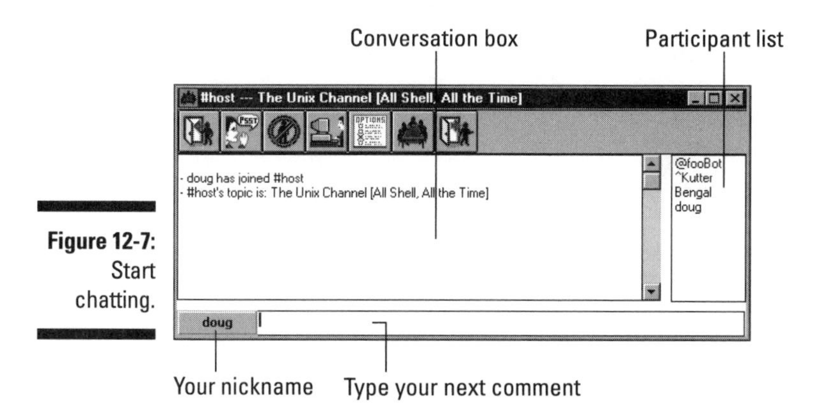

Figure 12-7: Start chatting.

Once you're in a channel, you can see the conversation in the channel scrolling by in the chat window. To make a comment of your own, type it in the box at the bottom of the window. What you type appears in the conversation box, preceded by your nickname.

If the conversation becomes too banal, too obnoxious, or fizzles out altogether, leave the channel by clicking the Exit Channel button on the toolbar.

For more information on IRC, see Chapter 18 of this book.

Using WinSock Programs with NetCruiser

If you don't like one or more of NetCruiser's applications, you aren't stuck with them. NetCruiser allows you to work with the 16-bit versions of any WinSock program. After NetCruiser knows about the existence of these other applications, NetCruiser adds their icons to a special toolbar called the Application Launcher. Clicking an icon in the Application Launcher toolbar is just like clicking the icon of a NetCruiser application — the corresponding program runs and does its thing.

Many programs written for Windows 95 are 32-bit applications. NetCruiser cannot add them to its Application Launcher. Most of these programs, however, are also available in 16-bit versions for Windows 3.1. Windows 95 can run them as well, and they *can* be added to the Application Launcher. This is how we got Netscape onto our Applications Launcher. (See that little window in the upper-right corner of Figure 12-1, with the ship's wheel button? That's a button for Netscape.)

Adding WinSock programs automatically to the Application Launcher

You can ask NetCruiser to scan your disk, look for the most popular Internet applications, and add them to the Application Launcher toolbar. Follow these steps:

1. **Choose File⇨Application Launcher.**
2. **From the menu bar of the Application Launcher window, choose Options⇨Configure.**
3. **Click the Auto Detect button.**

   NetCruiser now scans your hard disk and reports what it finds in the Select Applications window.
4. **Deselect any applications you *don't* want to add by clicking them. Then click OK.**

   The selected applications are added to the list of Current Applications in the Application Launcher Configuration window.
5. **Click the Done button.**

Now you can click the icons to run the WinSock programs that NetCruiser found.

Adding WinSock programs manually to the Application Launcher

The automatic process doesn't always find all the applications you would like it to. (When we asked NetCruiser to find WinSock applications, it missed Free Agent, a popular WinSock newsreader.) Don't interpret this to mean that NetCruiser can't work with these programs. Just add them to the Application Launcher manually, and they should work fine. Here's how:

1. **Return to the Application Launcher Configuration window by choosing File⇨Application Launcher, followed by the Options⇨Configure command.**
2. **Click the Add Manually button.**
3. **Either type the location of the application into the Complete Application Path window or (easier) click the Browse button, find the application on your hard drive, and double-click it.**
4. **Enter the application's name in the Menu Mnemonic window.**
5. **Click OK.**
6. **Click Done.**

Avoiding NetCruiser Entirely

As you accumulate an array of favorite WinSock applications on the Application Launcher, the day may come when you find that you only use NetCruiser to dial in to your account. Why stop there? You can configure your Netcom account to work with the Dial-Up Networking feature of Windows 95. This configuration has the added advantage of allowing you to use your favorite 32-bit applications again.

You might imagine that Netcom would discourage this desertion from its software, but you are wrong. (As long as you use the service, Netcom is happy.) You can find the best set of instructions for configuring Dial-Up Networking and Netcom from the Netcom Homeport.

1. **Click the NetCruiser button on the Homeport page.**
2. **Scroll down the page until you see the Dialer FAQ-Windows 95 link.**
3. **Click the link.**
4. **Follow the directions.**

For More Information

The NetCruiser Help Home Page is (surprise!) quite helpful. You can get there by typing this URL into the URL window of the Web Browser:

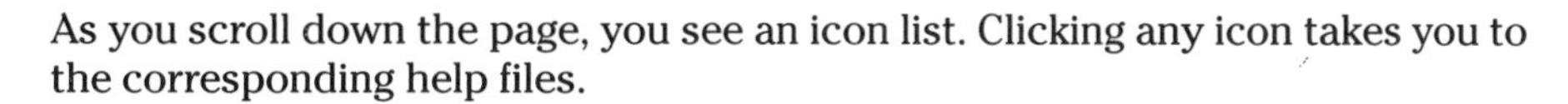

```
http://www.netcom.com/faq/win/2.1
```

Or you can get there from the Homeport:

1. **Click the NetCruiser button at the bottom of the Homeport page.**
2. **Click the V2.1 Help Files hotlink.**

As you scroll down the page, you see an icon list. Clicking any icon takes you to the corresponding help files.

The first time you visit the NetCruiser Help Home Page, put a bookmark there by clicking the book-with-bookmark icon and then clicking the Add button in the Bookmark window.

The newsgroup `netcom.netcruiser.general` is a worthwhile place to look for solutions to common problems. (Occasionally, you find a solution to something that you never realized was a problem until now.) If nothing else, be comforted to know that whatever strange thing is happening to you is also happening to a bunch of other people.

Chapter 13

Connecting to the Internet via GNN

In This Chapter

- Signing up for GNN
- Setting up your GNN program
- Typing commands
- Hanging up
- Sending e-mail
- Browsing the Web
- Reading newsgroups, including downloading uuencoded files
- Chatting live with other Internet users around the world
- Downloading files from FTP servers

GNN is the latest national Internet provider on the block. America Online owns and operates GNN, and if you are used to AOL's software, you'll find GNN very familiar. Signing up for an account is easy, and the software works fine. To use GNN, you need a Windows or Mac computer, 5MB of free space on your hard disk, a modem, and a major credit card. (Forget paying by check.)

This chapter describes GNN software version 1.2. If you have a different software version, your screen may not exactly match the figures in this chapter.

Signing Up for GNN

Signing up for GNN is easy. In fact, you have probably already gotten three free GNN sign-up diskettes or CDs in the mail. If for some reason you haven't, call 800-819-6112 and ask for a trial membership. Specify that you want the Windows version of the software (unless, of course, you have a Mac or a computer running DOS) and tell the folks at GNN whether you'd like a diskette or CD. You receive all the software you need to sign up for and use a GNN account. While you're on the phone, ask about pricing because, after you use your free introductory hours each month, you pay by the hour.

In this chapter, we describe how to use the Windows version of GNN with either Windows 3.1 or Windows 95. The Mac version is similar enough that you should be able to follow along and make a few adjustments for the Mac.

Installing GNN and setting up an account

To install the GNN For Windows software on a PC running Windows 3.1 and to register for your new GNN account, follow these steps:

1. **Start Windows and stick the disk or CD-ROM in the drive.**
2. **If you use Windows 95, click the Start button on the Taskbar and select Run. If you use Windows 3.1, choose File⇨Run from the Windows Program Manager's menu bar.**
3. **In the dialog box that appears, type**

   ```
   a:setup
   ```

   (If your disk is in drive B or D, substitute b or d for a.)
4. **Click OK.**

   The setup program is very friendly and tells you what to do.
5. **Choose Install.**

   Your disk drives whir for a few minutes as the setup program installs the GNN program on your hard disk in a directory called \GNN. The setup program also creates a program group in Program Manager called Global Network Navigator (which is what GNN stands for, if you are wondering). When the setup is done, you see a message telling you that you are ready to register for an account.

The pros and cons of GNN

GNN is easy to install and run because you get all the software you need on one diskette and an automated program signs you up. The Web browser works nicely and even lets you see several pages at once. GNN is cheaper than online services such as AOL.

On the other hand, the e-mail and newsreader programs aren't as good as WinSock programs you can use with an Internet SLIP or PPP account. And a GNN account is more expensive than an Internet account. (Netcom is cheaper, too.) In early 1996, GNN cost about $15 a month for 20 hours, plus about $2 for each additional hour.

6. **Click OK.**

   You see the GNN Registration dialog box, shown in Figure 13-1. As the directions instruct you, find the piece of paper that came with the disk, or the envelope that the disk came in. You are looking for the registration number (which has about ten digits) and the password (which is two words connected with a hyphen).

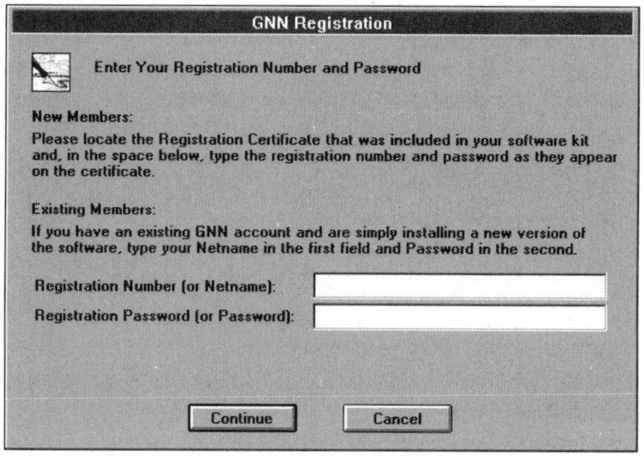

Figure 13-1: To register for a GNN account, you must type the secret passwords.

7. **Type your registration number and password into the boxes and click Continue.**

8. **Follow the instructions on-screen.**

   First, GNN calls up an 800 number to find out the closest local access number to you. You type your area code, GNN shows you the access phone numbers in your area, and then you choose the ones you want to use (in case you don't know, you should choose those numbers that are local calls). Click a number that is closest to you, or any number that is a local call, and click Select. Choose another number as your second choice.

   After you indicate what phone numbers to use, GNN connects using the phone number you specified. After displaying informational messages, you see the Registration Information dialog box, shown in Figure 13-2.

9. **Fill in your personal information so that GNN knows who you are and click Continue. Then tell GNN how you plan to pay for your account.**

   GNN strongly urges you to pay with a credit card. In fact, using a credit card is your only option.

   You get free hours when you sign up with GNN (as of this writing, you get ten free hours). If you cancel your account before using all your free hours, GNN doesn't charge you anything.

Registration Information

Registration Information

Please complete the following information. To move from one box to another, press the TAB key or move the cursor with your mouse and click on the next box.

First Name:

Last Name:

Street:

City:

State: Country code: USA

Zip Code:

Daytime Phone: (eg. 703-555-1212)

Evening Phone:

When you have accurately completed all of the above information, click "Continue" or press the ENTER key.

Continue Cancel

Figure 13-2: Who are you, and what do you want with GNN?

10. **When GNN displays the users agreement, read it and click Agree (assuming that you do).**

    If you don't agree, you're sunk; GNN is unlikely to change its users agreement just for you.

11. **Choose a netname (that is, an account name) for yourself and then click Continue.**

    Your netname can be as long as ten characters and can contain spaces. You can use a combination of capital and small letters, as in *MargyL* or *JLevine.* When GNN creates your account, it checks its list of existing netnames. If someone is already using that name (*JohnSmith*, for example), GNN lets you know on the spot, and you have to invent another one. You can use a fanciful netname, such as *DarkWolf* or *QueenBee,* if you like.

12. **Type your password (twice). Then click Select Password.**

    You may be asked to download new software, if GNN notices that your software isn't up to date. Don't worry — the new software is free. After you download new software, GNN tells you what to do to install it — usually, the program disconnects, installs the software automagically, and asks you to log in again.

    You're done when you see the GNNconnect window, shown in Figure 13-3.

If the netname you want is already taken, simply add a number to the end to make your netname unique. For example, if *Elvis* is taken (and we're sure that it is), you can be *Elvis326.*

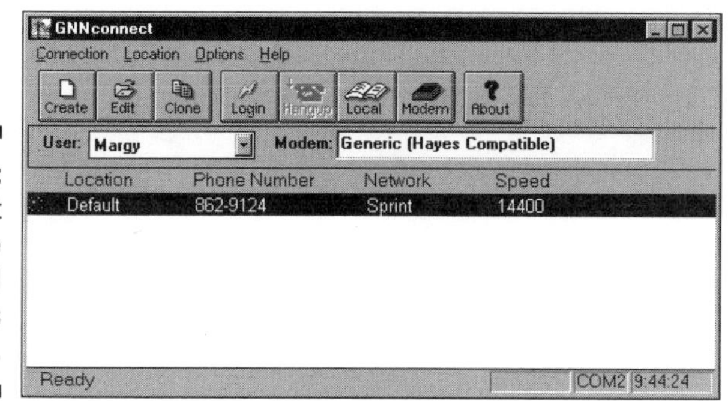

Figure 13-3: GNNconnect dials the phone and connects you to GNN.

The installation program creates a Program Manager program group, named Global Network Navigator, with two icons in it. You can copy the icons into another program group, if you prefer, so that you can minimize this one. To copy an icon, hold down the Ctrl key while you drag the icon into another program group.

If you have trouble installing the GNN software, call GNN at 800-819-6112 to get help.

Gee, It's GNN!

After you've got a GNN account, calling up and connecting is easy.

Online with GNN

To connect your computer to GNN:

1. **Double-click the GNNconnect icon, unless GNNconnect is already running.**

   The GNNconnect icon has a little picture of telephone wires. If GNNconnect is already running, you see either the telephone-wires icon at the bottom of your screen or the GNNconnect window, shown in Figure 13-3.

2. **Click the Login button on the toolbar.**

   Or choose Connection⇨Login or press Ctrl+L — your choice. You see the Login dialog box.

3. **Type your password in the Password box and click OK.**

   A window shows you the progress of the connection. After you are connected, you see the Welcome window, shown in Figure 13-4.

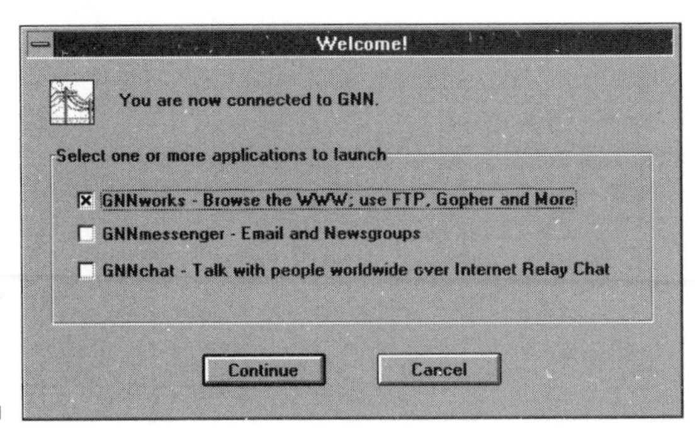

Figure 13-4: You're on GNN — what do you want to do?

4. **Choose which programs you want to run.**

   Click one, two, or three of these options, to run one, two, or all three programs and then click Continue.

   - GNNworks: to use the World Wide Web, FTP, Gopher, and other Internet services
   - GNNmessenger: to use e-mail and Usenet newsgroups
   - GNNchat: to use IRC (Internet Relay Chat)

   You see a window for each program you choose to run. Each program is described in its own section later in this chapter. "Mail It, GNN" describes GNNmessenger; "Globally Navigating the Net with GNN" describes GNNworks; and "Chatting on GNN" describes GNNchat.

If GNN runs into a problem connecting to a service, you may see an error message. If an error message appears, check whether you are logged into the system. Even if you see an error message, GNNconnect may have succeeded in logging in to GNN, and you may be paying for connect time. Be sure to log off, by following the instructions in the next section, to avoid racking up connect charges. Then try again later.

Hang me up!

With all the windows that appear on-screen, remembering how to hang up can be hard. But hanging up is important so that your GNN bill isn't astronomical.

When you connect to GNN, the GNNconnect program shrinks to an icon at the bottom of your screen, as shown in Figure 13-5.

Figure 13-5: GNNconnect is lurking on-screen.

To hang up, double-click the icon to bring GNNconnect back to life. Then click the Hangup icon, choose Connection⇨Hangup, or press Ctrl+H. GNN hangs up, but your GNN programs continue to run. Because GNN is conveniently still running, you can look at your e-mail or the last Web page you retrieved while you are offline, that is, without paying by the minute to do so. To close the GNN programs, choose File⇨Exit from each program.

Connecting from other GNN programs

You can connect to GNN from any GNN program, not just GNNconnect. For example, run GNNworks. When it notices that GNNconnect isn't running, GNNworks runs the program. When GNNconnect notices that you aren't online with GNN, the Login dialog box appears, asking for your password. When you click OK, you connect to GNN.

The same thing works for GNNmessenger and GNNchat — you can run these programs, and GNN knows to log you in.

Internet, Ho!

GNN provides access to all major Internet services, as listed in Table 13-1.

Table 13-1 Internet Services and How to Use Them

Service	*How to Use It*
E-mail	GNNmessenger
World Wide Web	GNNworks
Usenet	GNNmessenger
FTP	GNNworks
Gopher	GNNworks
IRC (Internet Relay Chat)	GNNchat

You can also create and publish your own Web pages using GNNpress, described in the section "Creating your own Web page," later in this chapter.

Mail It, GNN

Using GNNmessenger, you can send and receive e-mail to and from other GNN users in addition to folks on the rest of the Internet.

Your Internet address is your username (omitting any spaces) plus `@gnn.com`. If your username is John Smith, for example, your Internet address is `JohnSmith@gnn.com`.

Running GNNmessenger

To send or receive e-mail, run the GNNmessenger program. If you aren't already connected to GNN, GNNconnect runs and asks you to log in, as described in the section "Gee, It's GNN!" earlier in this chapter. When GNNmessenger is running and you are connected to GNN, you see the GNNmessenger window, shown in Figure 13-6.

The top part of the GNNmessenger window shows the list of messages with one highlighted message. The bottom part of the window shows the text of the highlighted message.

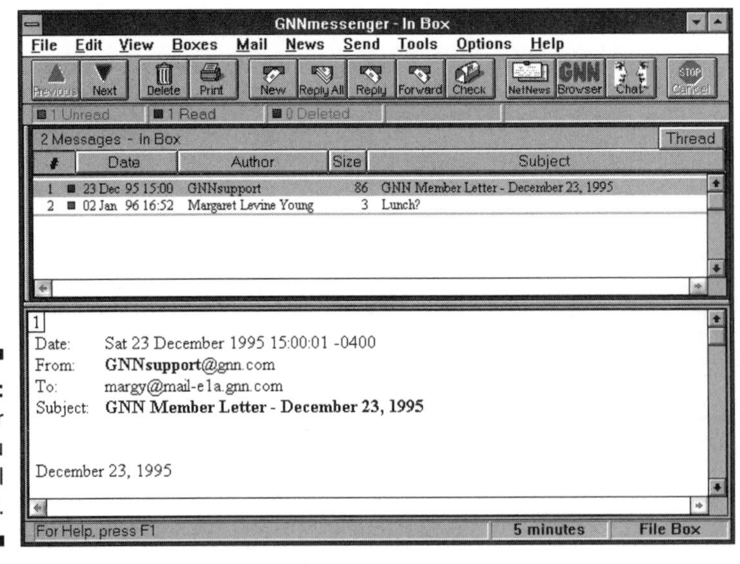

Figure 13-6: GNNmessenger shows you your e-mail messages.

If you want to switch to reading Usenet newsgroups, you don't have to hang up or even switch programs. Simply click the NetNews button on the toolbar. To switch to browsing the Web or getting files by FTP, click the GNN Browser button. To start chatting on IRC, click the Chat button.

Reading your mail

You probably *do* have mail, in fact, because every new member gets a nice note from GNN's technical support department (a nice touch). To read your unread mail, follow these steps:

1. **Click the Check button on the toolbar.**

   If you're not already connected to GNN, GNNconnect asks for your password, dials GNN, and logs in. Then GNN copies all your incoming mail onto your hard disk and lists the messages in the In Box list in the top of the GNNmessenger window. Each message appears as a single line with header information including the date, time, sender, message size, and subject. The little square to the left of each message tells you the message's status: red for a new message, blue for a message you've read, and gray for messages you've deleted.

2. **Select a message from the list in the top half of the window.**

   When you select a message, the text of the message appears in the bottom half of the window.

Here are things you can do with the selected message:

- Print the message by clicking the Print button on the toolbar, pressing Ctrl+P, or choosing File⇨Print.
- Delete the message by clicking the Delete button on the toolbar, pressing **d**, or choosing Edit⇨Delete Selection.
- Reply to the message by clicking the Reply button on the toolbar, choosing Send⇨Reply, or pressing Ctrl+R. See the section, "Composing a new message," for what to do next. If the message was addressed to other people, too, you can click Reply All if you want your reply to be addressed to everyone who got the original message.
- Forward the message by clicking the Forward button on the toolbar or choosing Send⇨Forward. See the section, "Composing a new message," for what to do next.
- Save the message in a text file by choosing File⇨Save Message. GNN asks for the directory and filename to save the message in.

When you are connected to GNN, GNNmessenger retrieves your e-mail every five minutes. If you get a new message, you see a dialog box saying `Retrieved one new lett`er from the Post Office`. Click OK to make the dialog box go away. You can change how often GNNmessenger checks your mail by choosing Options⇨Preferences.

Keeping your mail in boxes

If you use e-mail much, you end up wanting to keep messages for reference. Instead of leaving messages lying around in your in box, you can save them in your file box. GNNmessenger actually has five lists of messages:

- **In Box** — in which new incoming messages are stored
- **File Box** — in which you can save messages
- **Outgoing Box** — where messages live after you create them until GNNmessenger sends them
- **Out Box** — in which GNNmessenger stores copies of your outgoing mail
- **Wastebasket** — where your deleted messages go to die

To switch from one list to the next, choose Boxes from the menu. To move a message from one list to another (like from your In Box to your File Box), choose Edit⇨Move Selection to.

Real e-mail programs, such as Eudora, let you create lots of file boxes (usually called folders) so that you can store your messages in groups according to the subject, sender, or whatever.

Composing a new message

You don't have to reply to messages — you can start an exchange of messages, assuming that you know the e-mail address of the person you want to write to. To create a new e-mail message from scratch, click the New button on the toolbar, press Ctrl+N, or choose Send⇨New Message.

Alternatively, you may want to reply to a message or forward it along to someone else. Easy — simply click the Reply or Forward button on the toolbar.

Whichever method you use to start composing a message, you see the Send Mail window, shown in Figure 13-7. Here's what to do with the window:

1. **If the To line is blank, type the address to send the message to.**

   If you are replying to a message, GNNmessenger has already filled in the e-mail address of the person who wrote the original message. You can send the message to several people by separating their names with commas.

2. **If the Subject line is blank, type the subject of the message.**

   Make the subject as descriptive as possible. If you are asking a question, don't make the subject "Help!"

   If you are replying to or forwarding a message, GNNmessenger creates a subject, which you can edit.

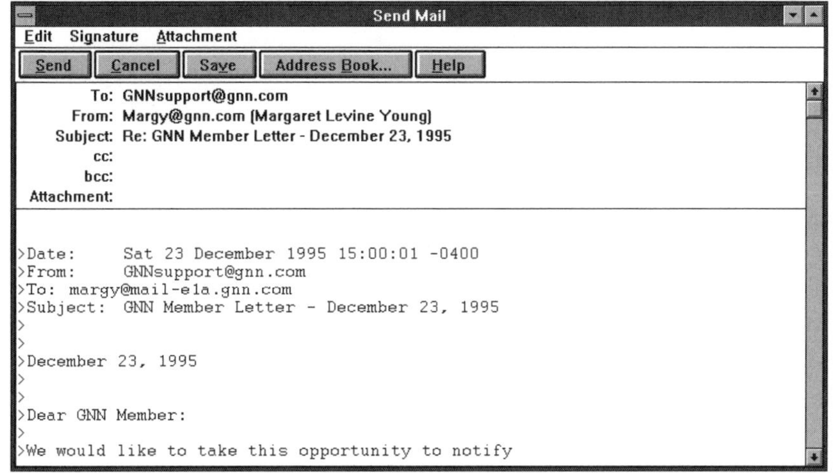

Figure 13-7: Simply fill in the blanks to send e-mail.

3. **To send copies of the message, type the e-mail addresses on the cc line. For blind copies (copies that are sent without the other recipients knowing), type the addresses on the bcc line.**

4. **Skip the Attachment line.**

   See the next section if you want to attach a file to your message.

5. **Below the line, in the bottom half of the Send Mail window, type the text of your message.**

   If you are replying to or forwarding a message, the text of the original message appears in your new message, with each line preceded by a >. Delete all the boring lines — just keep the lines that the recipient will be interested in. (Signatures and most headers should go.)

6. **When you are ready to send the message, click the Send or Queue button.**

   If you choose Send and you aren't connected to GNN, GNNconnect pops up, asking for your password so that it can log in to GNN and send your message. The Queue button appears if you have told GNN not to send your messages — see the section, "Working offline to save $$$," later in this chapter.

   If you change your mind about sending the message, you can click the Cancel button.

Attaching a file to your message

If you want to send a file from your PC to someone as an e-mail message, you can. The Internet has three standard ways of attaching a file to e-mail: uuencoded (the classic), MIME (new and improved), and BinHex (used mainly on Macs). The details of how these types of attachments work don't matter. The key thing is that GNNmessenger can handle all three methods.

To attach a file to your message, compose your text as usual. You can start a message from scratch, reply to a message, or forward one — what you do doesn't matter. When you see the Send Mail window, choose Attachment⇨Browse from the window's menu. Choose the directory and filename of the file you want to send along with the e-mail message.

If you don't tell it otherwise, GNNmessenger attaches the file using MIME. If the person who receives the file has an e-mail program that can't handle MIME attachments, you can change the attachment method to uuencoding by choosing Attachment⇨Uuencode.

What if someone sends you a message with a file attached? If the file was attached using MIME or uuencoding, GNN stores the file in the DOWNLOAD subdirectory of the GNN program directory (on most systems, this directory is C:\GNN\DOWNLOAD).

Working offline to save $$$

You don't have to be connected to GNN to read your mail. When GNNconnect asks for your password, simply click the Cancel button. GNNconnect gives up on the idea of connecting to your account, but GNNmessenger runs anyway.

Every five minutes (or whatever frequency you have told GNNmessenger to check for new mail), GNNconnect nags you about connecting to GNN. Simply click Cancel again. If you spend a lot of time in GNNmessenger offline, you may want to change how often GNNmessenger tries to connect and check for mail. Choose Options⇨Preferences, click the Mail tab, and change the number in the Check For New Mail Every box. If you don't want GNNmessenger to check automatically at all, click the box to the left of the setting so that no X appears in the box. Click OK to save your changes. Now you have to tell GNNmessenger when to get your mail by clicking the Check box on the toolbar, pressing **k**, or choosing Mail⇨Check for New Mail.

If you are connected to GNN and want to hang up so that you can read your message in peace, without worrying about the meter ticking, double-click the GNNconnect icon near the bottom of your screen and click the Hangup button on the toolbar.

You can also compose messages while offline — simply run GNNmessenger and refuse to provide your password when asked. You must tell GNNmessenger not to try to send each message you compose right away by choosing Mail⇨Pause Sending. The messages you have written are stored in the Outgoing Box, marked with little white status boxes to show that they haven't been sent.

When you are ready to send all the messages you've written, choose Mail⇨Resume Sending. Then choose Mail⇨Restart Connection to tell GNNconnect to log you in.

GNN's little black book

GNNmessenger keeps an address book for you so that you don't have to type e-mail addresses over and over. When you are sending a message, click the Address Book button on the Send Mail window to see the Address Book window, shown in Figure 13-8. You can also see the Address Book when you aren't composing a message by choosing Mail⇨Address Book.

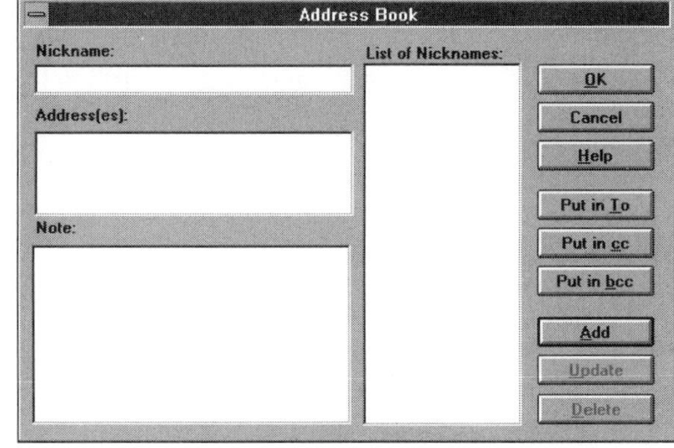

Figure 13-8: GNN's Address Book stores the e-mail address you plan to use.

To store an address in the Address Book, type the nickname (the person's real name or the name you'd like to type in the To part of the message) in the Nickname box and the e-mail address in the Address(es) box. Then click the Add button.

When you are composing a message, type the person's nickname on the To line of the message. Or click the Address Book button to display the Address Book, click the nickname you want to use, and click the Put in To button.

You can create a small mailing list by entering a list of e-mail addresses in the Address(es) box. For example, to send e-mail to all your relatives, you can type **Family** in the Nickname box and the e-mail addresses of your family members in the Address(es) box.

Exiting from GNNmessenger

When you are done reading and composing mail, you can exit from GNNmessenger. Be sure to use GNNconnect to hang up your connection with GNN, too, or you keep paying GNNconnect charges.

Globally Navigating the Net with GNN

GNN started life as a Web site, almost like a multimedia online magazine. When America Online bought GNN, it turned GNN into an Internet provider but kept the GNN Web pages.

Getting onto the Web

To browse the Web with GNN, double-click the GNNworks icon. If you aren't already connected to GNN, GNNconnect runs and asks you to log in. After you're connected, you see the GNNworks window, which looks like Figure 13-9. GNNworks automatically retrieves GNN's home page, also called Welcome to GNN (it is at `http:/gnn.com/`, if you are wondering).

To use the browser, click any picture that has a blue border or any button or text that appears underlined. (See Chapters 4 and 5 in *The Internet For Dummies,* 3rd Edition, for information about the World Wide Web. Or see Chapter 22 in this book for some interesting Web pages to look at.) When you are done, exit from GNNworks by choosing File⇨Exit. Be sure to log out from GNNconnect, too, if you are done using GNN.

If you decide not to see a page after GNN has started to download it, click the Cancel button (the one with the Stop sign). GNN stops downloading the page. To reload the current page by downloading it again, click the Reload button. If GNN *still* doesn't update the page, hold down the Ctrl button while you click the Reload button.

Getting around

Here are ways to get from page to page in GNNworks:

- To return to the previous page, click the Back button on the toolbar or press Ctrl+←.
- To see the GNN home page, click the Home button on the toolbar.
- If you know the URL of the page you want to see (for example, if you want to see a Web page described in Chapter 22), type the URL into the box near the top of the GNNworks window, the box that shows the URL of the current page. You have to erase the URL that's in the box and type the one you want to see. When you press Enter, GNNworks fetches that Web page.
- GNNworks shows you a row of *tabs* along the bottom of the GNNworks window. The tabs show you where you've been, and you can click a tab to return to that page. The Card Catalog tab displays your tabs in a vertical stack. To see a page, click the right-arrow button on the tab. The tabs also show information about the page, such as its URL and the date you retrieved the page.

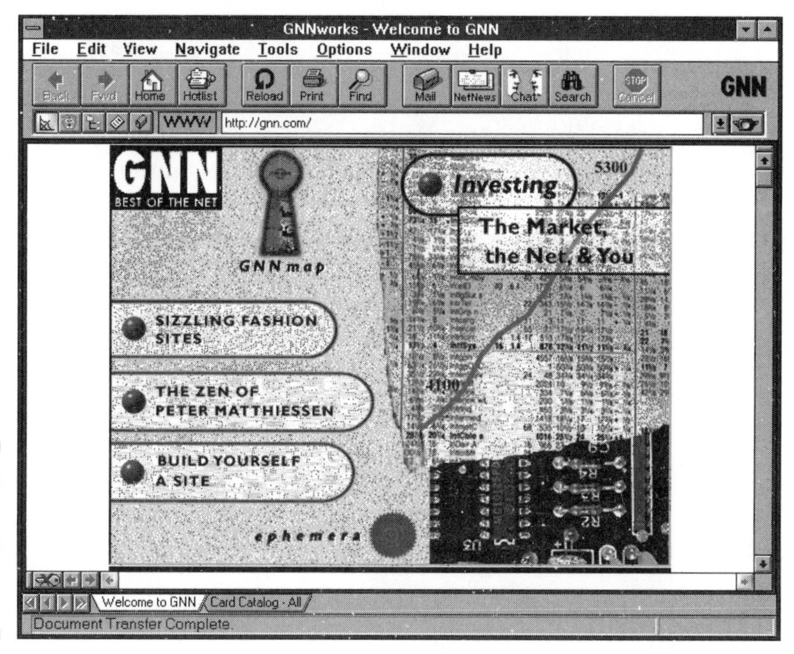

Figure 13-9: GNNworks is GNN's Web browser.

If you can't see any tabs at the bottom of the GNNworks window, choose View⇨Tabs.

- Like most Web browsers, GNN lets you create a *hot list,* that is, a list of the Web pages that you want to visit again. You add a page to your hot list by choosing Navigate⇨Add to Hotlist. To see your hot list, click the Hotlist button on the toolbar, choose Navigate⇨Hotlist, or press Ctrl+H. You see the GNNworks Hotlist window, shown in Figure 13-10. To return to a page that's listed on your hot list, double-click the page name or click the page name and click Go To. When you are done using your hot list, click the Close button.

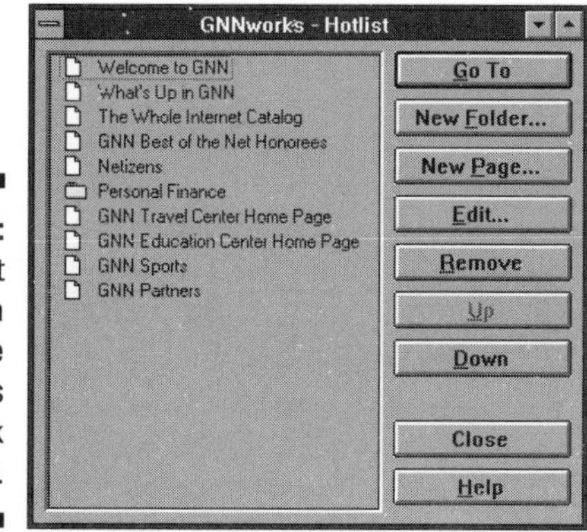

Figure 13-10: Your hot list contains a list of the Web sites you think are hot.

If you have had enough of the Web, you've got other options, too:

- To read your e-mail, click the Mail button on the toolbar or choose Tools⇨Mail. GNNmessenger fires up, and you can read and send e-mail as described in the section "Mail It, GNN" earlier in this chapter.
- To read Usenet newsgroups, click the NetNews button on the toolbar or choose Tools⇨NetNews. GNNmessenger shows you the Usenet newsgroups you've subscribed to, as described in the section "Reading Newsgroups" later in this chapter.
- To chat with other Internet users via IRC, click the Chat button or choose Tools⇨Chat. GNNchat runs, as described in the section "Chatting on GNN" later in this chapter.

Using the GNN pages

The GNN home page — the one you see when GNNworks starts up — has a list of interesting links near the top of the page:

- The **GNN Map,** shown in Figure 13-11, contains links to lots of GNN pages, as well as a Search link that lets you search for Web pages of interest. Clicking the Search link gives you the choice of several popular Web indexes. We don't really understand the difference between this page and the GNN home page, but you can use either or both.

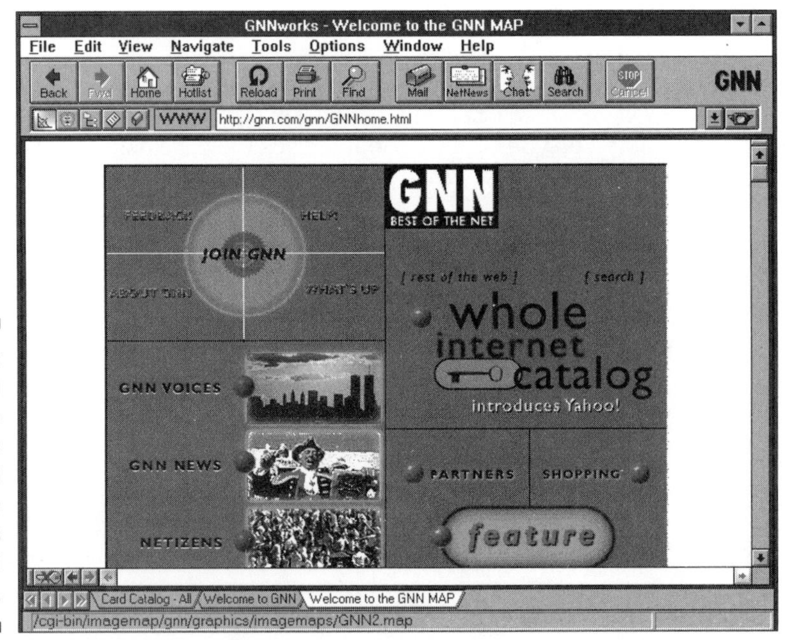

Figure 13-11: The GNN map contains links to all the Web services that GNN provides.

- The **Whole Internet Catalog** contains links to the most popular Web pages and other pages that GNN recommends.
- **GNN Voices** contains original writing, with stories about travel, literature, and other stuff.
- **GNN News** shows you news from the Reuters newsfeed, the Sports Network, and other sources.
- **Netizens** is where you can create your own Web pages and read Web pages by other GNNers.
- **GNN Help** provides information about GNN. Take a look at these Web pages if you run into trouble.
- **Ephemera** points to a different interesting Web site each day.
- **GNNdirect** is an online shopping mall, if you like that kind of thing.

Surfing two waves at once

GNNworks lets you look at two or more Web pages at the same time — a trick that most other browsers can't do. To see two pages, choose Window⇨Split Horizontally (or press Ctrl+2) or Window⇨Split Vertically (or press Ctrl+5). GNN splits its window, showing the same page in both halves. Each of these windows is called a *pane.* One pane is *active,* that is, it's the window you are currently working with. You can split the active pane again and again, although after you have more than about four panes, each pane is too small to do much with.

When you click a link in a pane, a new page appears in that pane — other panes are unaffected. You can also use the tabs at the bottom of the GNN window, the hot list, or other methods to display a Web page in the current pane. Figure 13-12 shows the screen split horizontally, showing different Web pages in each pane.

To get rid of all these panes, click the pane you want to discard, and choose Window⇨Close Pane or press Ctrl+0 (that's a zero). The current pane closes, and another pane expands to take its space.

If you type the URL of a Usenet newsgroup into the location box near the top of the GNNworks window, GNNworks runs GNNmessenger, GNN's e-mail and newsreader program — see section "Reading Newsgroups" later in this chapter. The URL of a newsgroup begins with `news://`.

Using GNNworks offline

GNNworks stores the pages that you have retrieved during the current GNN session, and you can take a look at these pages again even when you aren't connected to GNN.

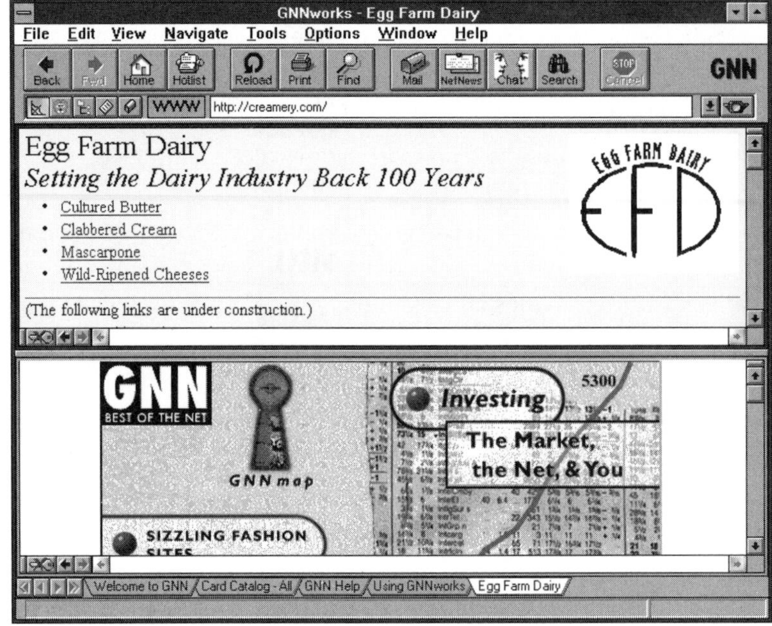

Figure 13-12: GNNworks can show two or more Web pages at the same time.

Creating your own Web page

Looking at Web pages that other people have created is fun, but what about making your own? GNN lets you create your own *home page* (a page about you). GNN also provides a place for you to store your home pages so that everyone on the Web can see them — GNN's Alphabet City.

GNN lets you download GNNpress, a program that helps you create a Web page. Look on the GNN Map to find it — the description is usually something like *Build Your Own Web Site*. Follow the instructions to download the program to your computer. As of this writing, the program is at

```
ftp://ftp.members.gnn.com/pub/press.exe
```

Double-click the filename PRESS.EXE in File Manager or Windows Explorer after you download it.

Reading Newsgroups

Usenet newsgroups are where the hot gossip is — see Chapter 9 in *The Internet For Dummies,* 3rd Edition. Thousands of newsgroups exist, so you aren't going to read all of them. The idea is to find the newsgroups that discuss subjects that interest you. After you've chosen one or more newsgroups, you still have to sift through the messages (also known as *articles* or *postings*) to find the ones you want to read — some newsgroups get hundreds of postings a day.

GNNmessenger, the same program you used for reading e-mail, is GNN's Usenet newsreader. You can use GNNmessenger to read Usenet articles offline, just as you can read e-mail when you are not connected to GNN.

To read Usenet newsgroups, click the NetNews button on the GNNmessenger toolbar. The GNNmessenger window changes to look like Figure 13-13. The window has three *panes* (sections of the window):

- The newsgroup index is in the upper-left section. You can click the Subscribed, New, or All tabs to display only the newsgroups you are subscribed to, only the new newsgroups, or all the newsgroups that GNN carries (thousands). Select a newsgroup from the index by clicking it.
- The message index is to the right of the newsgroup index and lists the messages that GNNmessenger has downloaded for the selected newsgroup. You can select one message by clicking it.
- The message pane is in the bottom half of the GNNmessenger window. This pane shows the text of the selected message.

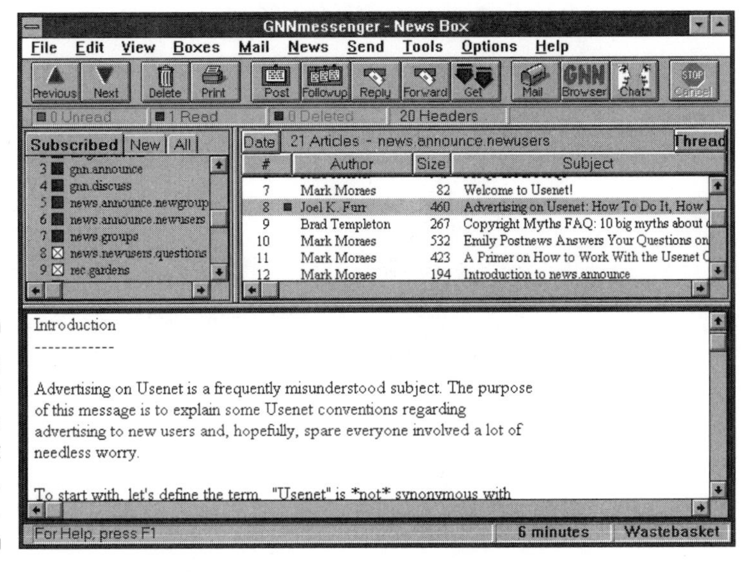

Figure 13-13: GNNmessenger lets you read Usenet newsgroups, too.

Subscribing to a newsgroup

In the newsgroup index (the upper-left part of the GNNmessenger window), the newsgroups you've subscribed to are shown with little Xs in the boxes to their left. When you open your GNN account, you are subscribed to a few of the most useful newsgroups for new folks, including a few GNN-specific groups. Reading these groups for a while, until you've read all the good pointers and advice they have to offer, is not a bad idea.

To subscribe to other groups, click the All tab in the newsgroup index. Then, to tell GNNmessenger to send you the latest list of newsgroups, click the Download button that appears. Thousands of newsgroups exist so that downloading can take a few minutes. However, you don't have to wait until the entire list has appeared: GNNmessenger shows you the top of the list right away, which you can start browsing through, looking for groups that interest you.

Browsing through all the groups can take hours, so you may want to choose Edit⇨Find (or press Ctrl+F) to search for a newsgroup whose name contains a particular word.

When you find a newsgroup you like, click in the box to the left of the newsgroup name so that an X appears in the box. Poof! You've subscribed.

Newsgroup names can get rather long so that you can't see the whole names in the newsgroup index. Using the mouse, drag the divider between the newsgroup index and the article index to the right to make the newsgroup index wider.

Reading newsgroup messages

To tell GNNmessenger to get the messages in one newsgroup, double-click the newsgroup name on the newsgroup index. Or select the newsgroup and choose News⇨Get Headers for Newsgroup. You can also tell GNNmessenger to get the

Where did all these newsgroups come from?

If you are familiar with Usenet newsgroups, you know that eight major *hierarchies* exist, and each has its own word that appears at the beginning of its newsgroup. These hierarchies are `alt` (alternative), `comp` (computing), `misc` (miscellaneous), `news` (Usenet administration), `rec` (recreation), `sci` (science), `soc` (social), and `talk` (just that). All but `alt` are tightly controlled (more or less) by the worldwide cabal of Internet host system administrators, and a good thing, too — Usenet is chaotic enough as it is!

So where did all these other groups come from? Well, each country that has many people on the Net has started its own sets of newsgroups, with names that start with the country code or other abbreviation (both `ca` and `can`, for example, for Canada). Some states have their own groups, such as `ny` and `il`. Several regions have newsgroups, such as `ba` for the San Francisco Bay Area and `ne` for the Northeast. Other organizations have set up their own groups, too — take a look at `ibm` and `utexas`.

And GNN's got 'em all — over 22,000 newsgroups at last count — even the dirty ones.

message headers for all the newsgroups you are subscribed to. First, click the Subscribed tab in the newsgroups index to see which groups you are subscribed to. Unsubscribe to those newsgroups that you don't actually care about. Then choose News⇨Get Headers for All Subscribed.

Either way, GNNmessenger doesn't download the complete text of the messages; it just downloads the headers, that is, the date, sender, and subject for each message. A list of the messages appears in the message index (eventually). A newsgroup can have lots of messages, so a delay may occur.

To read the messages in a newsgroup, select the newsgroup in the newsgroup index and look at the message headers in the message index. You can make the message index wider by dragging the divider to the left. Or maximize the whole GNNmessenger window to make it as large as possible by clicking the Maximize button (the upward-pointing triangle in the upper-right corner of the GNNmessenger window).

The messages make a lot more sense if you read them in the right order, that is, *threaded.* A thread is a message, all the replies to that message, all the replies to the replies, and so on. Click the Thread button to tell GNNmessenger to arrange the messages into threads so that you can read the articles in an order that makes sense.

When you double-click a message header, GNNmessenger downloads the text of the message and displays it in the message pane (the lower half of the GNNmessenger window). Downloading may take a few seconds (or longer for long messages). It's not always obvious that GNNmessenger is on the case, because GNN doesn't display anything to tell you that it's downloading. After the article is downloaded, a blue square appears next to the message header on the message index.

Here's other information about reading Usenet newsgroup articles:

- To delete the article, click the Delete button on the toolbar. The article doesn't disappear from Usenet, of course, only from your computer. In fact, the article doesn't disappear from your computer, either, until GNNmessenger decides to take out the garbage. You can encourage it to do so by choosing Mail⇨Empty Wastebasket from the GNNmessenger menu.
- To read the next message in the newsgroup, click the Next button on the toolbar or press **n**.
- To print the message, click the Print button on the toolbar, press Ctrl+P, or choose File⇨Print.
- To save the message in a file, choose File⇨Save Message.
- To send the text of the article to someone by e-mail, click the Forward button on the toolbar or choose Send⇨Forward. You see the Send Mail window — use this window just as you do for sending mail (see the section "Composing a new message," earlier in this chapter).

Getting the picture

Articles can contain *binary attachments,* that is, nontext information that came along for the ride. For example, the newsgroup `alt.binaries.pictures.fractals` has lots of cool *fractals,* which are mathematically generated pictures. An article with a binary attachment has a little blue triangle next to its name on the message index. The attached file is usually too large to fit into one article (the maximum article size in Usenet is about 25K), so you may see a series of articles with names like *Fractal rose (0/4), Fractal rose (1/4), Fractal rose (2/4), Fractal rose (3/4),* and *Fractal rose (4/4).* The zeroeth message is the description of the file, and the file itself is contained in the rest of the files.

Be sure to click the Thread button in the message index so that all the articles that make up one picture are listed together.

To read the file description, double-click message number zero in the group (nerds love to start numbering things with zero). To download the file, double-click any article in the group. GNNmessenger finds the rest of the messages that contain the picture, downloads them all, decodes the file, and stores it in the DOWNLOAD subdirectory of the GNN program directory (usually C:\GNN\DOWNLOAD). If the file is a picture, sound, or something else that GNNworks knows how to display or play, GNNworks fires up as if by magic and shows you what you just got.

GNNmessenger makes getting binary files from Usenet a snap, although the process is still not foolproof. Sometimes one of the messages that makes up the file is missing or has gotten garbled, and GNNmessenger can't decode the file you want.

Mouthing off

Always read a newsgroup for at least a week before you send anything. Newbies (new Internet users) have a reputation (well earned, unfortunately) of barging into newsgroups and having no idea of what the group is about or what people are discussing. So *please* restrain your creative impulses for a few days before contributing to a group. The rest of Usenet will thank you.

After reading a message, you can send a response. Make sure, however, that you read all the existing responses first. Someone may already have made the excellent point you want to make.

Instead of replying to the newsgroup, consider sending e-mail to the person who posted the original message. If the information in your response is of interest mainly to the original poster, send e-mail. If you are sure that your response interests lots of people in the newsgroup, post it to the newsgroup.

Reply by e-mail to the person who posted the message by clicking the Reply button on the toolbar. You see the Send Mail window, and you can compose and send your reply like any other piece of e-mail (see the section "Composing a new message" earlier in this chapter).

To post an article in response to the entire newsgroup, click the Follow Up button. You see the Post Article window, which looks suspiciously like the Send Mail window in Figure 13-7. Type your message and post the article by clicking the Send button.

In addition to making sure that you are not repeating what someone may have already said, be sure to write clearly, proofread your message, stay calm rather than get emotional (emotional responses don't work well in newsgroups), be polite (Net surfers are people, too), and keep your message brief. After all, tens of thousands of people are likely to read your posting, so don't waste their time.

If you begin to compose a reply and then think better of it, you can cancel sending the reply. Click the Cancel button in the Post Article window. If you are ticked off about an article, sometimes the best thing is to let off steam by composing a scathing reply, which you cancel. You can start a flame war (a long, pointless series of angry messages) by sending your reply.

Usenet offline

After you have downloaded a bunch of messages, you can hang up on GNN while you read them. After you have downloaded the lists of messages for each newsgroup you subscribe to (by choosing News⇨Get Headers for All Subscribed), you can hang up on GNN (by double-clicking the GNNconnect icon and clicking the Hangup button on its toolbar). Select articles you want to read at your leisure when you're not paying to be connected to GNN by clicking the first article you want and then Ctrl+clicking the other articles you want. Then choose News⇨Get Selected Article Bodies. You are prompted for your password so that you can reconnect to GNN, and the GNNmessenger gets all the messages you choose.

Chatting on GNN

Usenet is cool, but it's not immediate. After you post a message, someone can take hours or days before getting back to you. Those of you with short attention spans will want to try GNNchat, which gives you access to the Internet Relay Chat (IRC), an Internet service that's described in Chapter 18.

When you double-click the GNNchat icon, GNNchat checks whether you are connected to GNN. If not, GNNconnect runs, asks for your password, and logs you in to GNN. Unlike GNNmessenger and GNNworks, you can't do much with GNNchat if you are not connected to GNN. Because chatting occurs on the spot, you can't chat when you are offline.

What's on?

The GNNchat window looks like Figure 13-14. You can't see the window, though, because the first thing that GNNchat does when you connect to GNN is to get and display a huge list of the IRC channels that currently exist. A *channel* is like a room in which a conversation is taking place. To chat, you join a channel, which allows you to listen to and participate in the conversation on that channel. Channel names all begin with a # or & character. Thousands of channels frequently are active — most of them are pretty worthless.

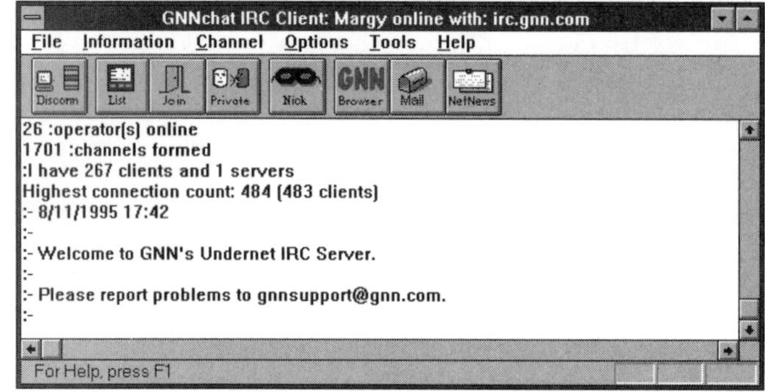

Figure 13-14: The GNNchat window.

GNNchat's list of channels looks like Figure 13-15. The channels are listed in alphabetical order, starting with the ones that begin with punctuation and numbers.

Channels present :1655

Channel	Members	Topic
#21plus	13	No love here!! just stone cold hearts!!!!!!!!!!!!!!!!!!!!!!
#25+	1	
#25+friends	7	Total Confussion
#25plus	21	The Friendliest Channel on the Net!
#26plus	2	The Snow if Finally Melting...Let's Have a Party!
#2hearts	2	
#30+4play	15	Everybody wish TSTORM a HAPPY BIRTHDAY!!!
#30+pinoy	1	
#30+sex	10	Hot Tub's hot...Bar is open...
#30deluxe	1	
#30plus	21	Cutieduc's sister had a baby girl Brianne Nicole. :)
#31plus	11	

OK Join Update Help

Figure 13-15: GNNchat lists the channels that you can join. Most look pretty unattractive, we think.

Join up!

To join a channel and begin chatting, double-click the channel name on the list of channels. You see a window for the channel. Figure 13-16 shows a window for the #gnn channel.

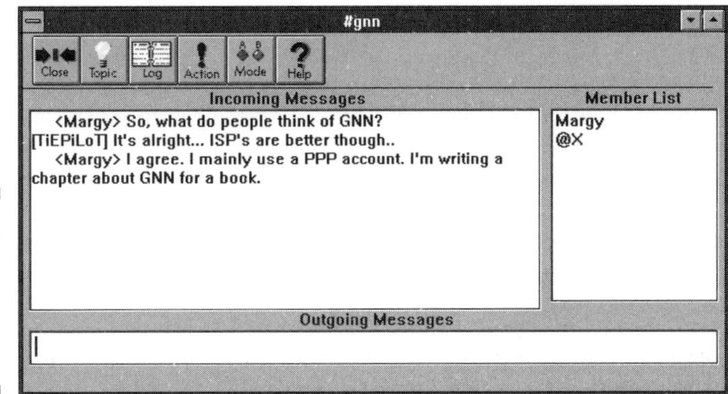

Figure 13-16: Here's the chat on the #gnn channel.

The list of people in the channel appears at the right side of the window in the Member List box. These folks aren't necessarily GNN users — they are folks from all over the Internet and all over the world.

The large box is where you see the conversation on the channel. Each comment starts with the username (or nickname) of the person "talking," followed by what they said.

For help with GNN, join the #gnnchat channel. It's got friendly people with advice about GNN.

If you want to join a channel without wading through the thousands of channels in the channel list, click the Join button in the GNNchat window. Then you can type the exact channel name and click OK to join.

OK, I'm in

After you are part of a channel, simply follow the conversation and act friendly. You can join several channels at once by double-clicking another name on the list of channel names. Each channel appears in its own window. But don't join more channels than you can read at the same time!

You can make the chat window bigger, if you want to be able to see more lines of conversation before they scroll off the top of the screen. Simply drag the bottom edge of the window downward.

Here are things you can do while chatting:

- To find out more about someone (maybe), click his username from the Member List. Then click his username with your *right* mouse button. A little menu appears where your mouse pointer is. Choose Whois (with your left mouse button). A screen with information about the person appears, though that information is not always revealing.

- If someone is annoying you, GNNchat can help you ignore her. Click her username from the Member List. Then click her username with your *right* mouse button. Choose Ignore from the little menu that appears. GNNchat won't display any messages from the person. To stop ignoring someone, do the same thing again.
- You can change your name by using a nickname. To change your name, click in the GNNchat window (not the window for a channel), and then click the Nick button on the toolbar. Or choose Information⇨Set Nickname. GNNchat asks for your new nickname.
- Sometimes actions speak louder than words (or so we hear). To tell people that you are doing something, like laughing or leaving for a minute, click the Action button in the channel window. *ACTION* appears in the window where you type. Then type the action, like *laughs* or *runs out for a minute to get another decaf latte*. What you type appears on other people's screens preceded by two asterisks and your name. If you click Action and type **laughs**, they see `**Elvis laughs`.
- You can send someone a private message that the rest of the channel can't see. In the GNNchat window, click the Private button on the toolbar. On the Private window that appears, type the person's username in the Recipient box and your message in the Outgoing Messages box. Press Enter or click Send to send the message. Your private conversation appears in the Incoming Messages box. When you are done whispering together, click the Cancel button.

If you need to see the channel list again, click the List button in the GNNchat window.

We want to be alone

For real privacy, you can use *DCC* (direct client connections) with another user. (DCC is described in Chapter 17.) DCC lets you send and receive files, too. Lots of IRC folks use DCC to send pictures of each other, so you know who you're talking to (assuming that you believe that's *really* what the person looks like).

To send a file to someone, choose Options⇨DCC Send from the GNNchat menu. You see the DCC Send dialog box, shown in Figure 13-17.

In the Send file box, type the filename you want to send or click the Browse button to search for the file. Type the intended recipient's username in the To box. (Remember, the person has got to be online and chatting at that very moment to send the file. IRC is live!)

When you click OK, GNNchat tries to send the file. When the person whose username you typed accepts the file, the file zings across the Internet.

If someone tries to send you a file using DCC, you see the DCC Receive dialog box. This dialog box shows the name of the file and who wants to send it to you.

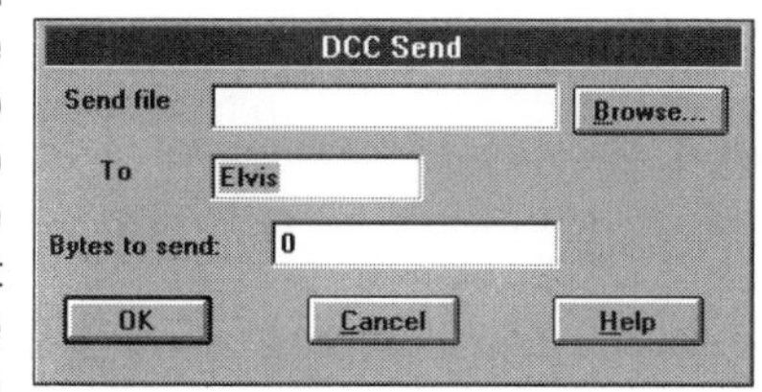

Figure 13-17: You can use GNNchat to send files to other people on the spot or receive files from them.

If you want the file, click the Accept button and tell GNNchat where you want to store the file.

You can also chat directly with someone using DCC. Choose Options⇨DCC Chat from the GNNchat menu. Type the username of the person you want to chat with and click OK. The DCC Chat window appears, with a big window at the top that shows the conversation and a little window at the bottom in which you can type. When you type something that you want to send, press Enter or click the Send button. When you are done chatting, click Cancel.

Get me out of here

When you are done chatting on a particular channel, click the Close button. The channel window closes, but you are still running GNNchat. If you are totally done chatting, close the GNNchat window by choosing File⇨Exit. (Wonder why the hot key for the Exit command is *E* instead of the Windows standard *X*? We do!) Be sure to tell GNNconnect to hang up, too, to avoid big GNN bills.

Grabbing Files with GNN

To download a file from an FTP server, you use GNNworks. Type the URL of the file you want in the location box near the top of the GNNworks window and press Enter. The URL of a file on an FTP server looks like

```
ftp://servername/pathname
```

See Chapter 5 for more information on URLs.

If you don't know the exact filename, you can type the URL for a directory. In Figure 13-18, GNNworks shows what's in the main *(root)* directory of `ftp.microsoft.com`, Microsoft's FTP server. To download a file, click its name. To switch to a subdirectory, click the directory name.

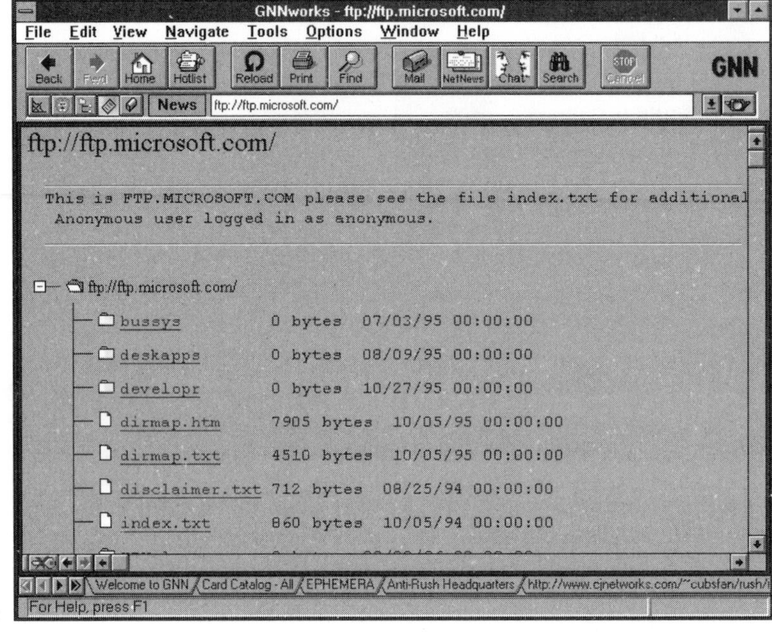

Figure 13-18: GNNworks can act like an FTP program, if you want to download a file.

Using WinSock Software with GNN

GNN's Web browser (GNNworks) is pretty good. But its Usenet newsreader isn't as good as a truly excellent newsreader like Agent. Luckily, you can use your favorite WinSock software — Netscape, Agent, or whatever — with your GNN account. These instructions apply only if you use a computer with Windows 3.1 or Windows 95 — not a Mac.

To use your favorite WinSock software, you have to use GNN's WinSock program. You need to put GNN's WINSOCK.DLL file into your Windows program directory. Here's how:

1. **In Windows File Manager or Explorer, see if you have a file named WINSOCK.DLL in your Windows program directory.**

   Look in C:\WINDOWS for the file. If you have a file named WINSOCK.DLL, it's probably part of the software for another online service or Internet software. Windows 95 comes with a WINSOCK.DLL program.

2. **Rename your existing WINSOCK.DLL, if you have one.**

   If you know where the WINSOCK.DLL in your Windows program directory came from, rename it accordingly. We named our America Online WINSOCK.DLL as WINSOCK.AOL, our CompuServe WINSOCK.DLL as WINSOCK.CIS (for CompuServe Information Service), and our Internet Chameleon WINSOCK.DLL as WINSOCK.CHA.

If you don't know where your WINSOCK.DLL came from, rename it as WINSOCK.OLD.

By renaming the WINSOCK.DLL file, you keep it around so that you can rename it back to WINSOCK.DLL file later if you need to.

3. **Copy the file WINSOCK.DLL from the GNN program directory to your Windows program directory.**

   Hold down the Ctrl key while dragging the filename to the Windows program directory.

   Now the WinSock program in your Windows directory is the one that works with GNN.

4. **Run WinSock software.**

   We find that WinSock runs a lot slower than with a regular Internet SLIP or PPP account, but it runs.

If you want to be able to use WinSock software with another account, like a SLIP or PPP account, you may need to put the original WINSOCK.DLL file back where you found it. When you are done using your GNN account, rename WINSOCK.DLL as WINSOCK.GNN and rename the file that was originally WINSOCK.DLL as WINSOCK.DLL again.

We like to keep copies of all the WINSOCK.DLL files that we may need in our Windows program directory. We give each one an extension that indicates what the file is for — CIS for CompuServe, AOL for America Online, GNN for GNN, and so on. We *copy* the one we want to use as WINSOCK.DLL. Copying means that the file named WINSOCK.DLL is always a duplicate of one of the other WINSOCK files in the Windows program directory. We don't have to worry about deleting the file and copying a different WINSOCK.DLL file for use with a different online service. On the other hand, you may not use as many different Internet and online accounts as we do!

For More Information

If you have questions about GNN, read its Web pages, starting at the GNN home page. Sending e-mail to `support@gnn.com` with questions about the service is also a good idea. If you want the complete scoop on GNN, get *Global Network Navigator For Dummies* (IDG Books Worldwide, Inc.), by John Kaufeld.

Thanks to ettil, D-In-Tx, Iggie, and the rest of the gang on the IRC #gnnchat channel for their help with this chapter!

Part IV

Home Page, Ho!

In this part . . .

Anyone who's anyone has a home page on the Web, right? We certainly do! You might want to join the hordes of people with home pages or (preferably) create Web pages for your company, school, church, or other outfit with information that may actually be of interest to people. Whatever your reasons for creating Web pages, this part of the book tells you how.

Chapter 14
Home-Page Bound

In This Chapter

- Making a Web page
- Understanding HTML
- Putting a page on the Web

Everyone who's anyone on the Net (and just about everyone else) has a World Wide Web home page. Sometimes they're interesting, sometimes they're exciting, sometimes they're pretty stupid. We're sure you fall into one of the first two categories, so in the next two chapters we tell you how to create your own Web pages.

The Big Picture

Here's what you have to do to put a home page, or any Web page, on the Net:

1. **Write the page on your own computer, inserting all the special codes that control the page's appearance in Web browsers.**

   Web pages are basically plain text files, so you can create them with any text editor you want, even Windows Notepad or WordPad. You can just type them in, using codes we explain in this chapter and the next one.

2. **Check that the page actually looks like what you envisioned.**

   Your page rarely looks the way you want it to on the first try. Fine-tune the page until you're happy with the result. You can use your regular Web browser to look at the page and then fix mistakes in the text editor.

3. **Copy the page to your Internet provider's computer, where the page will be available to everyone on the Net.**

4. **Repeat these steps forever, as you keep adding and updating your Web pages.**

The bad news about writing Web pages

To create a Web page, you need to wear three different hats:

- A writer, to create the text
- A graphic designer, to create the images and the overall appearance of the page
- A programmer, to create the special coding required to make the page look the way you want it to in a browser

Not many people can do even two of these things well, and only an exceedingly rare person can do all three well. That's why you find lots and lots of Web pages that are badly written, badly designed, and badly coded.

Big, rich companies solve this problem by hiring Web-building teams, which include professional writers, designers, and programmers. But if you're the only one making your pages, what are you going to do? Our answer is *don't try too hard.* For example, when we made the pages for Internet For Dummies Central at `http://dummies.com`, we figured that we knew a little about writing and programming (that's our job, after all) but practically nothing about graphic design. We kept the design of our pages simple, figuring that the less we tried to do, the less we could mess up.

We suggest that you start simple as well, because a simple page that's attractive and readable is going to attract a lot more fans than a complicated and ugly one.

Who Cares about HTML?

You do. HTML, short for *HyperText Markup Language,* is the language that makes the Web go. HTML codes tell your browser what's text, what's a heading, where the links go, where to put the pictures, and everything else about your page. HTML codes use a consistent syntax, with each code enclosed in angle brackets, such as `<P>`,to start a new paragraph. For example, the HTML in the file in Figure 14-1 makes Netscape display the page in Figure 14-2.

HTML in its full glory is, to put it mildly, rather complicated. Fortunately, you can create entirely respectable-looking pages using only a handful of simple HTML codes.

Gentlemen, Start Your Software

You can create files with HTML-coded documents in lots of different ways. In keeping with this chapter's philosophy of not trying overly hard, we suggest you start with something like Windows Notepad or Windows 95 WordPad, the simplest text editors around.

You'll probably have a bunch of Web pages, so before you start up your text editor, create a directory called `\WEB` in which to store them.

```
<HTML>
<HEAD>
<TITLE>Your Name Here's Home Page</TITLE>
</HEAD>
<BODY>
<H1>Welcome to Your Name Here's Home Page</H1>
<P>
I've been reading the most fabulous book ever written,
<I>MORE Internet For Dummies, 2nd Edition</I>.
I'll add more stuff to this page, but first I have to go buy
15 more copies of the book to give to all of my family and
closest friends.
</BODY>
</HTML>
```

Figure 14-1: A simple HTML file.

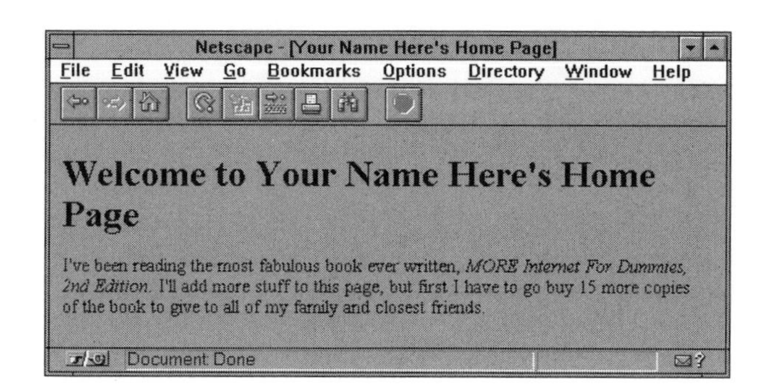

Figure 14-2: The same file, displayed in Netscape.

Web Page, Take One

Start with a really simple page, the one in Figure 14-2. Type the text from Figure 14-1 into your text editor, save it in your `\WEB` directory, and call the file `MYPAGE.HTM`. If you're feeling creative, go ahead and put in your own name.

Well, that should have been easy enough. How do you look at your new page as a Web page? Simply open the file in your Web browser. In Netscape, for example, you choose File⇨Open File and select the file. Poof! The Web page appears. (And it appears quickly, too, because the page is loaded from the disk, not over the network.)

Where did HTML and the Web come from?

An atomic physics laboratory in Switzerland, in fact. (Say this sentence with a mad scientist accent for the best effect.)

CERN is an international laboratory near Geneva, Switzerland, where atomic physicists do atomic physics-type experiments. These experiments generate mountains of data, to the extent that simply organizing and presenting the data is a big problem. So in 1990, Dr. Tim Berners-Lee, an English researcher who was then at CERN, built an online hypertext system inspired by Ted Nelson's Project Xanadu (see the next sidebar, "And where did hypertext come from?") that evolved into the World Wide Web that we know today.

HTML is a version of *SGML,* the Standard General Markup Language adopted as an international standard for encoding documents in computers. SGML is a high-level language, and any actual useful SGML requires what's known as a Document Template Description, or DTD, a template that describes what can actually be included in some category of documents. HTML is basically a DTD that is a template for Web pages.

The original Web system primarily handled text, not pictures or other data. But in the early 1990s, at the National Center for Supercomputer Applications, two student programmers, Marc Andreesen and Rob McCool, were working on their own Web software for the UNIX-based X Window system. (Legend says the two were supposed to be doing something else at the time.) An X Window program without graphics isn't much fun, so Andreesen and McCool added features to the Web's HTML language so that they could mix pictures into their Web pages. Their programs, Mosaic (for the user) and the NCSA HTTPD (for the server), quickly became the Web programs people wanted to use, partly because they were so cool and partly because they were free. Andreesen left NCSA to join a Web software startup now known as Netscape. You may have heard of it.

And where did hypertext come from?

Most people think that hypertext is a recent invention, but it's not. Our friend Ted Nelson first conceived of hypertext in 1965, in an era when most people who thought about computers at all thought of them as machines that turned stacks of punched cards into telephone bills.

Ted has labored on for years, trying to persuade people that hypertext is an important idea, and not getting very far. But during some 15-minute time period in the 1980s, hypertext metamorphosed from a cockamamy idea that nobody who *really* understood computers would take seriously into the inevitable framework for literature of the future. Ted's vision of hypertext has been wrapped up in his Project Xanadu, an online publishing concept which, after years of work and a lot of dead ends, may yet come to fruition on the Internet, using the Web as its underpinning.

Unless you have superhuman typing skills, the chances are pretty good that the page on-screen doesn't look quite right, because you've typed one of the codes wrong. (We know this problem, because we've never gotten a page right on the first try, either.) Look at your page in the browser and look for the first place where the page looks wrong. That place is usually pretty close to the mistake. Switch back to your text editor, find and fix the mistake, save the page again, switch back to your browser, and load the revised page by pressing the Reload button. After a few rounds of editing, browsing, and revising, you should be able to get your page looking okay.

Although this nit-picking is a pain, it's inevitable with any system like HTML. The *tags* in HTML, the stuff in angle brackets, are interpreted by computers, and those computers are, unfortunately, extremely dumb and unforgiving when it comes to coding errors. (In case you were wondering, this sort of error picking is what programmers spend about half of their time doing.) If you find you have a lot of trouble getting the tags right, *HTML editors,* which automate a lot of the tagging process, are available. We talk about HTML editors in the next chapter. (We don't actually find HTML editors worth the trouble, which is why we start you out with writing your own tags.)

What Are All These Tags, Really?

Take a closer look at all the tag glop in that Web page. A lot of different tags exist, but most have a pretty simple structure.

Each HTML tag is enclosed in angle brackets, like this: `<GLOP>`. A lot of tags bracket information that's supposed to be treated in a particular way, in which case the end of the material is marked with a tag that starts with a slash, like this: `</GLOP>`. For example, the EM tag means emphasized text, which you write as `<EM>stuff to emphasize</EM>`.

In most cases, spacing and indentation don't affect the your Web page's appearance, so arranging the material so that you can see the structure of the tags is a good idea. You can put in handy comments, which don't affect the page's appearance, to remind yourself of what you were doing when you come back after a month to look at your page.

```
<!– this is a comment. The two dashes at the front and end
are required–>
```

Your minimal set of tags

You write Web pages in HTML, so a Web page has to start with a tag that says, "Here comes some HTML," and end with a tag that says, "That's the end of the HTML," like this:

```
<HTML>
... contents of the page
</HTML>
```

(Computers, being extremely dim, don't find the fact that your HTML document consists of HTML obvious.)

Furthermore, within the HTML tags, you need two sections: the header and the body.

```
<HTML>
 <HEAD>
... header stuff here ...
 </HEAD>
 <BODY>
... actual contents of the page here ...
 </BODY>
</HTML>
```

You need to put only the page's title, which most browsers display in their title bar at the top of the screen, in the header. So here's a complete header section:

```
 <HEAD>
 <TITLE>The Combination to the Vault at Fort Knox</TITLE>
 </HEAD>
```

Note the <TITLE> and </TITLE> that bracket the text of the title.

How many kinds of HTML *are there*?

Too many, unfortunately. HTML has evolved at a furious rate over the years. The most recently standardized version is HTML 2.0, and every browser you're likely to come across can handle all tags defined in HTML 2.0. Lack of further standards hasn't slowed down browser writers, though, and every browser has features beyond what 2.0 offers. Netscape has been the most enthusiastic adder of features, but nobody can resist.

The World Wide Web consortium (W3) is working on a 3.0 update to the spec, and some new features will definitely be included (tables, for example), and some won't (blinking text — ugh). But a lot of details have yet to be decided.

Until 3.0 comes out, either you need to be sure you use only 2.0 features, which everyone's browser handles, or try your pages in lots of Web browsers to be sure they all look reasonable. You can do reasonable-looking pages with 2.0, so start with that version's features.

Do I really have to put in all these tags?

Well, since you ask, a lot of Web browsers let you get away with some pretty sloppy tagging. Even if you leave out a lot of the required tags, the browsers display something anyway.

But no browser *promises* to do the right thing if you have missing tags. Your page may look okay today, but when the next version of Netscape, or Microsoft's Internet Explorer, or whatever, comes out, your page may not work anymore. So put in all those tags — you'll be glad you did.

Body language

The actual contents of the page go between <BODY> and </BODY> tags. You can put any material you want in the body — HTML doesn't require that you structure your page's body in any particular way.

Look at the body of our sample page.

```
<BODY>
<H1>Welcome to Your Name Here's Home Page</H1>
<P>
I've been reading the most fabulous book ever written,
<I>MORE Internet For Dummies, 2nd Edition.</I>
I'll add more stuff to this page, but first I have to go buy
15 more copies of the book to give to all of my family and
closest friends.
</BODY>
```

The first thing is <H1>, a first-level heading, which is displayed at the top of the page. (The page's title repeated as a heading is pretty common, because not all browsers display the title.) The <P> code introduces a paragraph of plain text. In that paragraph, we italicize the book's name by putting the name inside <I> and </I> tags.

So that's what's required to make a Web page. You can put your newly–created Web page on a server for all the world to see. In the next chapter, we come back to making the page prettier.

Going Public

Okay, you have a Web page. You think your page is ready for prime time. How do you release your page to the world? In principle, showing off your page is easy, but in practice, a wee bit of confusion is possible.

For other people to see your Web pages, you have to load your handiwork onto a machine with a public Web server. Nearly every Internet provider has such a server, but no two providers handle the uploading process quite the same way.

You have to check with your provider to get the details, but the general strategy for loading your Web page is as follows:

1. **Run your FTP program.**

   We use WS_FTP (described in Chapter 10), but any FTP program will do.

2. **Log into your provider's Web server, using your own login and password.**

   Usually the server's name is something like `www.gorgonzola.net`, though providers differ. At TIAC, one of the providers we use, you log into `ftp.www.tiac.net` when you're uploading Web pages.

3. **Change to the directory where your Web home belongs.**

   Usually the name is something like `/pub/elvis`, `/pub/www/elvis`, or `/pub/elvis/www`. Your provider will tell you what to use.

4. **Upload your Web page.**

   Use ASCII mode, not binary mode, because your Web page is a text file.

Now, if your page on the server is called `mypage.htm`, its URL is something like

```
http://www.gorgonzola.net/~elvis/mypage.htm
```

Again, URLs vary by provider. Some providers don't follow the convention of putting a tilde in front of the name. Others name their users' pages something like `/user/elvis`, rather than `~elvis`. You have to check with your provider to find out its convention.

You should generally call your home page, the one that you want people to see first, `index.html`. If someone goes to your Web area without specifying a page name, like `http://www.gorgonzola.net/~elvis`, a nearly universal convention is to display the page named `index.html`. If you don't have a page by that name, most Web servers construct a page with a directory listing of the pages in your Web directory. This listing is functional enough, because it lets people go to any of your pages with one click, but it's not cool.

Sprucing Up Your Page

After you've gotten over the hurdle of creating and installing a Web page, you can add fancier contents. We finish this chapter with suggestions of ways to add more interesting text to your Web pages.

Pictures and hyperlinks are topics of their own, so we're saving them until the next chapter.

To update your page, edit the copy on your own computer, debug it using your Web browser, and then upload it to your Internet provider, replacing the previous version of the page.

Let's Get Organized

Web pages can be organized like an outline, with up to six levels of headings. You mark headings with tags like <H1>, <H2>, and so forth, up to <H6>. You mark the end of each heading with </H1> and the like. Figures 14-3 and 14-4 show some headings.

Be sure to put an end-of-heading tag at the end of each heading. The tag goes at the end of the heading itself, not after any material that may be under that heading.

Although you can use up to six levels of headings, we rarely use more than two or three. Usually a <H1> heading goes at the top of the page, and <H2> indicates any intermediate headings that you want.

```
<HTML>
<HEAD>
<TITLE>Headings</TITLE>
</HEAD>
<BODY>
<H1>This is a first level heading</H1>
<H2>And a second level heading</H2>
<H3>A third level heading, yet</H3>
<H4>Is anyone really organized enough to need a fourth level
heading?</H4>
Oh yeah, you can have some text, too.
</BODY>
</HTML>
```

Figure 14-3: A lot of headings.

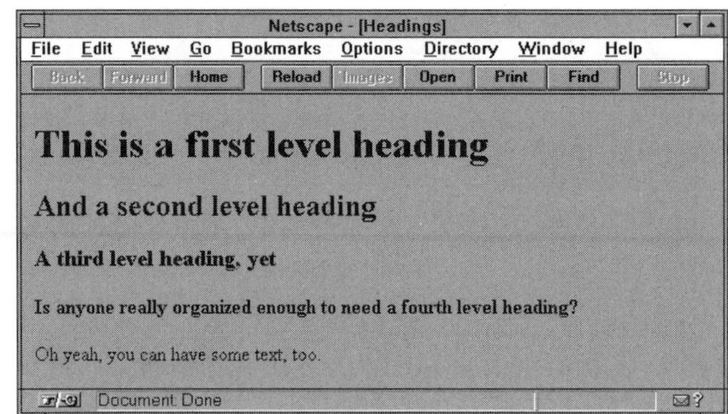

Figure 14-4: A lot of headings, displayed in Netscape.

Run, Text, Run

You usually have paragraphs of plain old text within your document. (We know people who've done entire pages as headers, but the result looks pretty brutal.) You use paragraph tags <P> to separate paragraphs of running text. You can also use <BR> to force line breaks without the extra space that the browser puts between paragraphs. Figures 14-5 and 14-6 show paragraphs and line breaks.

The Strong, the Bold, and Other Typography

HTML has quite a few codes for various kinds of text. Each code begins with an HTML tag and ends with the same tag preceded by a slash.

- <EM> for emphasized text
- <STRONG> for strong emphasis
- <CITE> for citations of book titles and the like
- <CODE> for examples of computer code
- <SAMP> for sample text of some sort
- <ADDRESS> for addresses, usually the page author's address
- <PRE> for preformatted text, which unlike all other text in a Web page, is displayed with spacing and line breaks unchanged

```
<HTML>
<HEAD>
<TITLE>Paragraphs</TITLE>
</HEAD>
<BODY>
<P>Here is a paragraph of running text. Run, text, run.
You'll notice that the Web browser moves the text from line
to line so that the lines it displays are all more or less
the same length.
<P>
This is a good thing, since when you write your Web page, you
can't tell how wide a user's screen will be when she displays
your page, so this lets the page look reasonable regardless
of the screen width.
<P>
Paragraphs are separated with white space. Line break tags
don't add any space, which can be useful when your material
should be displayed together, as in the lyrics of this song:
<P>
We knew a man whose name was Lang
<BR>
And he had a neon sign
<BR>
But Mr. Lang was very old
<BR>
So we called it Old Lang's Sign!
</BODY>
</HTML>
```

Figure 14-5: Some paragraphs.

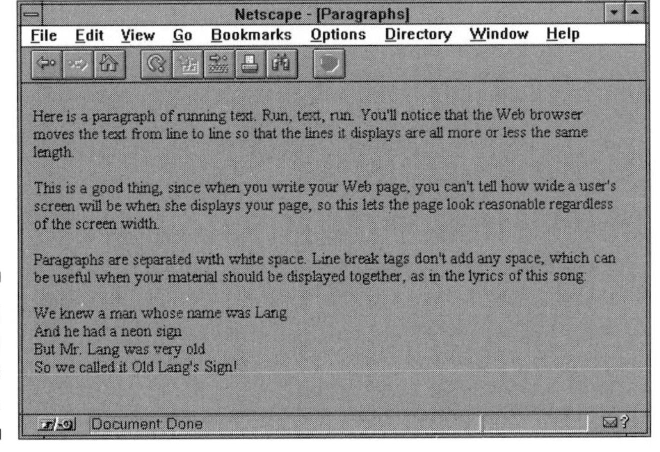

Figure 14-6: Some paragraphs in Netscape.

Most browsers don't actually have separate styles for all these tags but in fact display them in variations of bold, italic, and fixed-spacing text. You can also specify typography directly.

- <B> for bold text
- <I> for italic text
- <TT> for typewriter *(fixed pitch)* text

HTML also throws in one graphic element, <HR>, for a horizontal rule — that is, a line across the page.

Figures 14-7 and 14-8 show a badly designed Web page that displays all these typographic elements. We suggest keeping the fancy formatting to a minimum because a lot of formatting looks awful.

```
<HTML>
<HEAD>
<TITLE>A Ransom Note</TITLE>
</HEAD>
<BODY>
This text is <EM> emphasized</EM>, while this text has
<STRONG> strong emphasis</STRONG>.
<P>
My favorite book is <CITE>MORE Internet For Dummies, 2nd
Edition</CITE>.
<P>
It's hard to come up with a plausible example that has both
<CODE>examples of computer code</CODE> as well as <SAMP>
sample text</SAMP>, so we won't try. And examples of
<B>bold</B>, <I>italic</I>, and <TT>typewriter</TT> text are
just as hard.
<P>
<PRE>
If you FTP text files in binary rather than ASCII mode
you'll find that the
                    line breaks usually
                                        come out like this.
So don't do that.
</PRE>
<!— It's pretty common to put a horizontal rule above the
address—>
<HR>
<ADDRESS>
The Internet For Dummies Authors' Cabal<BR>
http://dummies.com/
</ADDRESS>
</BODY>
</HTML>
```

Figure 14-7: The HTML for a really ugly Web page.

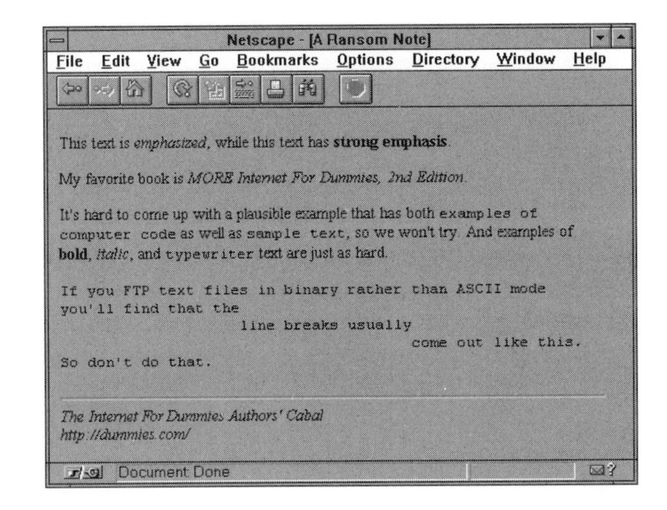

Figure 14-8: Netscape displays the really ugly Web page.

The absolute No. 1 error that novice typographers make — and that's what we all are when we begin designing Web pages — is to overformat material. Experienced users disparagingly refer to documents with too many fonts and other typographic elements as "ransom notes."

Chapter 15

Pretty as a Picture — and Well Connected, Too

In This Chapter

- Adding graphics to your Web pages
- And links
- And a few suggestions on announcing your Web page

Okay, in Chapter 14, you find out how to make Web pages. In this chapter, you can discover how to make *good* Web pages . . . or, at least, more aesthetically appealing pages.

Picture This

Most Web pages contain graphics of some sort. As usual where computers are concerned, adding graphics to your pages is easy in principle but a little more complicated in practice.

Even in Web pages that look like they're mostly text, you frequently find a lot of graphics "dressing up" the page. In Figure 15-1, for example, you certainly notice the graphic of the word art in the upper-left corner, but 29 other graphics appear in the figure as well. In front of the words `ABOUT` and `NEWS` are little ball icons, which appear in color on-screen, as well as the `N„EW!` icons and the arrow at the lower left corner. This sort of layout is pretty typical of Web pages these days.

The theory of putting graphics into your pages is easy enough: You put the graphic in a separate file and then add a reference to that file in your Web page so that your browser fetches the graphic and displays it in the page. The practice is complicated by the facts that pictures are stored in at least two common file formats and that some browsers understand pictures better than other browsers do.

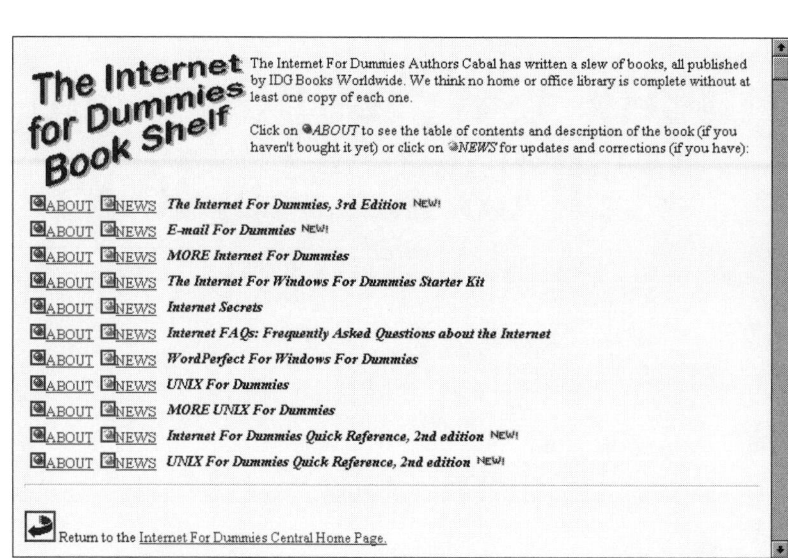

Figure 15-1: A typical Web page with more graphics than you may notice.

Format wars

"How many different ways can you have to store a picture in a computer?" you may ask. Dozens, maybe hundreds — that's how many. On your Windows machine, you may run into BMP, PCX, DIB, GIF, JPG, TGA, and other files, all of which contain various kinds of pictures. (If, for some reason, you want more details on this convoluted state of affairs, you probably aren't surprised that we suggest *Graphic File Formats,* 2nd Edition, by David Kay and John Levine [Windcrest, 1994], and *Programming for Graphics Files in C and C++* [Wiley, 1994], which John wrote by himself.)

Fortunately, only two picture formats are in common use on the Web. These formats are known as GIF and JPEG. Many lengthy . . . er, *free* and *frank* discussions have occurred on the Net concerning the relative merits of these two formats. Because John is an Official Graphics Format Expert (by virtue of having persuaded two otherwise reputable publishers to publish his books on the topic), Table 15-1 lists his opinions on the subject.

If you have a picture in any other format, such as BMP or PCX, you must convert it to either GIF or JPEG before you can use it in a Web page. Many graphics-wrangling programs are available; check out the Consummate WinSock Apps page at `http://cwsapps.texas.net` for some suggestions.

Table 15-1 JPEG and GIF Duke It Out

JPEG	*GIF*
Best format for scanned photographs	Best format for computer-drawn cartoons and icons
Handles "true color" better	Can have transparent backgrounds (which we discuss at the end of the chapter)
Files are usually smaller	Files are usually larger
Doesn't handle large areas of solid color or sharp edges well	Handles solid color areas well
Some older browsers don't handle JPEG	Most browsers handle GIF
Slower to decode	Faster to decode

So I've got some images already

After you have your image file, plugging it into your Web page is simplicity itself. You put a tag identifying the file to display at the place in your page where you want the image to appear. The following example is such a tag:

```
<IMG SRC="filename">
```

The following tag, for example, tells the browser to locate a file named `monalisa.jpg` on the Internet For Dummies Central Computer and display that file on your page:

```
<IMG SRC="http://www.dummies.com/greatart/italian/
monalisa.jpg">
```

Make sure that the file name ends with `gif` if the file's a GIF and `jpeg` or `jpg` if it's a JPEG file so that other browsers can determine how to decode the file.

The `SRC` value in the IMG tag is, in theory, a full Web Universal Resource Locator (URL), but 99 percent of the time, the image is actually in a file in the same directory as the Web page itself, or in a directory nearby, so you can abbreviate the URL to just the filename, along with the relative directory path if needed, similar to the following example:

```
<IMG SRC="icons/elbow.gif">
```

This tag tells the browser to display a file named `elbow.gif` in the `icons` subdirectory of the directory in which the Web page is stored. (Use forward rather than backward slashes, as UNIX servers understand only forward slashes as filename and directory separators.)

You should always put your image files either in the same directory with your Web pages or in a nearby directory that you call `icons` or `images` or something similar. That positioning enables you to check your pages and images locally on your own machine. Then you can upload all the pages and images to your Web server, and as long as the relative positions of the files don't change, your pages are sure to work.

Making your image fit into your pages

In the simplest cases, images are just spliced into your Web page as though they were large text characters. If your image is a tiny icon, such as the little balls and `NEW!` shown back in Figure 15-1, you can get away with this effect, but the process tends to produce rather unsatisfactory results with larger pictures. Figure 15-2 shows what happens when the following HTML splices in a graphic as text:

```
<HTML>
<HEAD><TITLE>An ugly picture</TITLE></HEAD>
<BODY>
<H1>This is my picture</H1>
Here comes my picture.
<IMG SRC="ugly.gif">
That was my picture. Bye.
</BODY>
</HTML>
```

Figure 15-2: This example isn't a very attractive Web page.

Fortunately, you can improve the layout of your page in several ways so that the images and text look reasonable. The most simple approach is to put the picture into a separate paragraph, as the following bit of HTML does:

```
<IMG SRC="pretty.gif">
<P>
This is a bunch of text ...
```

Now the text appears beneath the picture, which usually looks okay, rather than in the middle of a line of text, which doesn't.

Netscape has added options that enable you to "float" the image to the left or right side of the window, which in most cases results in a better look than positioning the picture by itself. You add the option ALIGN=LEFT or ALIGN=RIGHT inside the image tag, as in the following example:

```
<IMG ALIGN=LEFT SRC="filename">
```

The following HTML example results in the display shown in Figure 15-3:

```
<HTML>
<HEAD><TITLE>A less ugly picture</TITLE></HEAD>
<BODY>
<H1>This is my picture</H1>
<IMG ALIGN=LEFT SRC="pretty.gif">
<P>
This is a bunch of text that will be displayed along side
my picture and will flow around underneath it when it gets
long enough.
<P>
We've found that floating a picture to the left like this is
usually the easiest way to put a large image into a page and
have it look decent.
<P>
Remember that different browsers will use different sizes of
text and different sizes of window, so you can't count on
exactly where the text will flow under the picture.
</BODY>
</HTML>
```

The ALIGN=LEFT and ALIGN=RIGHT options aren't part of the HTML 2.0 standard, so although they're quite widely supported, some Web browsers still in use don't understand them. That's why we put the <P> tag right after the image; if someone's browser doesn't understand how to left-align the picture, the browser will place the picture in its own paragraph above the text so that the page doesn't look entirely stupid.

How about us text lovers?

Ah, yes. A fair number of users still use Lynx, the UNIX Web browser that handles only text. And to save time, many people who use Netscape or other graphical browsers set them up so that the browsers don't load the images in each page. Can you do something for them?

Yes, indeed. In each IMG tag, you can — and usually should — put an "alternative text" tag that tells the browser what to display if it can't display the picture.

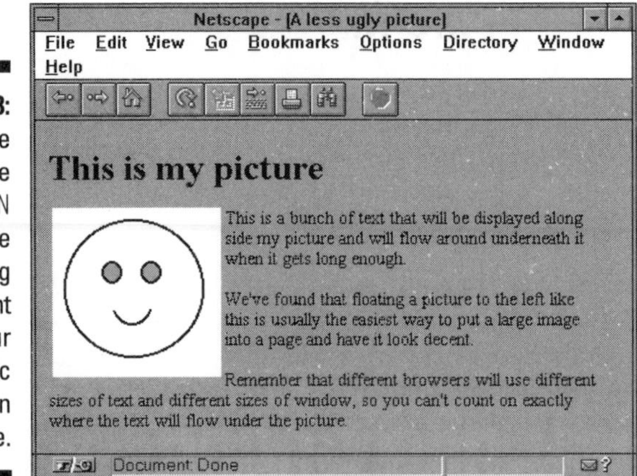

Figure 15-3: Using the Netscape `ALIGN` feature makes a big improvement in how your graphic appears on your page.

For example, we changed the IMG tag line in the preceding example as follows:

```
<IMG ALIGN=LEFT SRC="pretty.gif" ALT="The Mona Lisa">
```

Now if a user views this page without graphics, the page looks like the one shown in Figure 15-4.

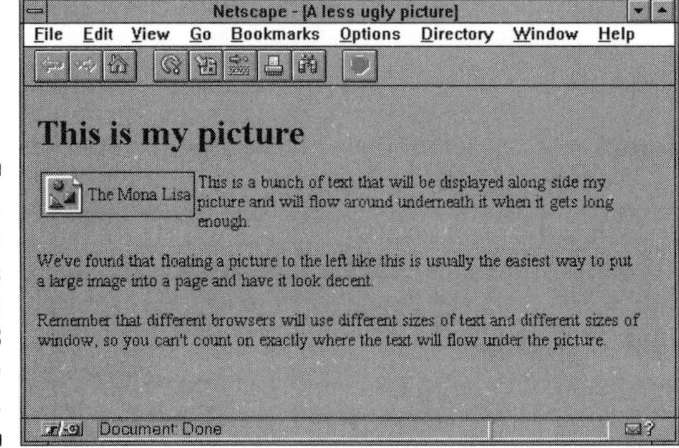

Figure 15-4: The same page as shown in Figure 15-3 without the graphic.

Where can I get some images?

That's a good question. You can always draw them yourself by using a paint program or scanning in photographs, but unless you're a rather good artist or photographer, your graphics may not appear as nice as you'd like. (See, for example, the images in Figures 15-2 and 15-3. Luckily for us, we don't claim to be artists.)

Fortunately, you can locate lots of sources of graphical material, as described in the following list:

- Plenty of freeware, shareware, and commercial clip art is available on the Net itself. See, for example, the nice collection put together by a member of the Yale computer science department at `http://www.cs.yale.edu/homes/sjl/clipart.html`. (She's the same person who created the world-famous Froggy Page.) Also try searching for `clip art` in any Web directory or index.
- If you see an image in a Web page that you'd like to use, you can write to the page's owner and ask for permission. More likely than not, the owner will let you use the image.
- Lots of regular old software programs totally unrelated to the Internet, such as paint and draw programs, presentation programs, and even word processors, come with clip art collections.
- You can buy CD-ROMs full of clip art, which tend to be of higher quality than the free stuff. These items usually aren't all that expensive, particularly considering how many images fit on one CD-ROM.

Clip art, like any art, is protected by copyright. Whether the art's been used in a Web page before or whether a copyright notice appears on or near the image doesn't matter. It's still copyrighted.

If you use someone else's copyrighted art, you must get permission to do so. Whether your use is educational, personal, or noncommercial is irrelevant. If you fail to secure permission, you run the risk of anything from a crabby phone call from the owner's lawyer to winding up on the losing end of a lawsuit.

Most people are quite reasonable whenever you ask for permission to use something. So if an image you want to use doesn't already come with a blanket permission to use it, just check with the owner before you decide to add it to your own Web page.

Sloooow loooading pages

Many Web pages we know are burdened with images that, although beautiful, take a long time to load — so long that many users may give up before the pages are completely loaded. (Our publisher offers a surprisingly good example of this at `http://www.idgbooks.com`.)

You can take a few steps to make your Web pages load more quickly. The main step, of course, is to limit the size of the images you use. A 20K image takes twice as long to load as a 10K image, which takes twice as long to load as a 5K image. You can estimate that images load at 1K per second (on a dial-up connection), so a 5K image loads in about 5 seconds, which is fast, while a 120K image takes 2 minutes to load, so that image had better be worth the wait.

If your images are in GIF files, images with fewer colors load faster than images with more colors. We find that, in many cases, if you use a graphics editor to reduce a scanned GIF from 256 colors to 32 or even 16 colors, the appearance hardly changes, but the file shrinks dramatically. And if you set up your graphics program to store the GIF file in *interlaced* format, browsers can display a blurry approximation of the image as it's downloading, which at least gives the user a hint of what's coming.

If your images are JPEG files, you can adjust the "quality" level in the JPEG with a lower quality making the file smaller. In our experience, because of the limited resolution of most computer screens, you can set the quality quite low with little effect on what actually appears on users' screens.

You can also take advantage of the *cache* that browsers use. The cache keeps copies of previously viewed pages and images. If any image in a page a user is downloading is already in the browser's cache, that image needn't be loaded again. So if you use the same icon several places in a page, the icon's file is only downloaded by the browser once, and the same image is used for all examples on the page. Although the page in Figure 15-1, for example, contains 29 images, only 5 different files actually are downloaded (the word art, the 2 balls, the `NEW!` icon, and the return to home page arrow), so the page loads relatively quickly. So in creating your Web page, you should try to use the same icons from one page to the next, both to give your page a consistent style and to speed up the process of downloading its images.

The Missing Link

We saved the best for last (or at least almost last): hyperlinks. Hyperlinks are the things that make the Web the Web. A *hyperlink* (which we call merely a *link* from here on, because we're lazy typists) enables a user to hop from one page to the next at the click of a mouse.

Plain links

You install links in your page by using HTML tags called *anchors*. An anchor performs two functions: It identifies the page to which your page is linked and displays some text or image in the page that the user can click on (or the keyboard equivalent) to tell the browser to follow the link. An anchor looks like the following example:

```
<A HREF="URL">text</A>
```

The `URL` in the anchor identifies where to jump after the user clicks the link. The `text` is the text of the link — that is, the text that appears blue and underlined on the Web page. You can see these components in the following example:

```
<A HREF="http://dummies.com">Internet for Dummies Central</A>
```

The link starts with an `<A>` tag, which contains an `HREF` with the URL of the page to link to. Following that is the text to display in the current page and an end tag `</A>`. The text `Internet for Dummies Central` thus appears on your Web page as a link. Following is the full HTML source that displays the text and link shown in Figure 15-5:

```
<HTML>
<HEAD><TITLE>A sample link</TITLE></HEAD>
<BODY>
<H1>Your Gateway to the Best Site on the Net</H1>
I've searched all over the net, and there's no question that
my favorite site of all is
<A HREF="http://dummies.com">Internet for Dummies Central</A>
<P>
See you there!
</BODY>
</HTML>
```

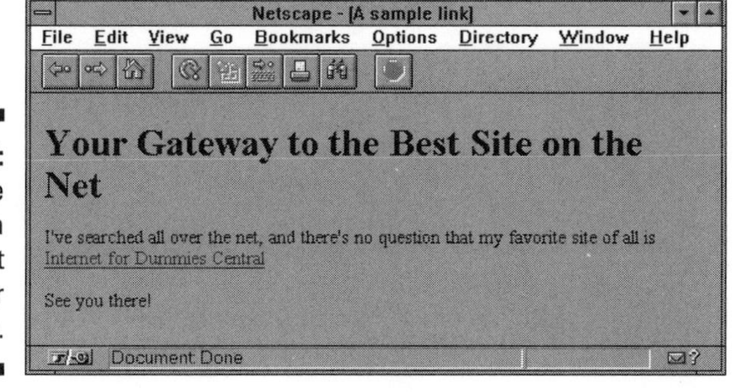

Figure 15-5: A Web page containing a link to yet another Web page.

If you link to a page of your own that is on the same server as the page containing the link, you can and should use the same kinds of abbreviated references for images — described in "So I've got some images already," earlier in this chapter — as in the following example:

```
<A HREF="poptart.htm">My favorite main course for dinner</A>
```

By using such abbreviated references, you can create and test your pages in a single directory on your own computer; then you can upload them as a group to your provider's server — and the references all still work.

Fancy links

You aren't limited just to using text in your anchors. You can also use an image or a combination of text and image in an anchor. You can even use an image as a link, as set up in the following example:

```
<A HREF="http://dummies.com"><IMG SRC="wow.gif" align=left></A>
```

And you can use all the fancy text formatting in an anchor that you can in any other place in your pages.

In theory, you can use images and text in a single link, but it looks strange if you do so. Use an image, or use text, but don't use both in the same link. You can make two separate links to the same place, one with an image and one with text.

For example, we added an additional link using an image and overformatted the existing text link (using **strong** and *italic* tags) as follows to create the Web page shown in Figure 15-6:

```
<HTML>
<HEAD><TITLE>A sample link</TITLE></HEAD>
<BODY>
<H1>Your Gateway to the Best Site on the Net</H1>
<A HREF="http://dummies.com"><IMG SRC="wow.gif" align=left
ALT="Wow! "></A>
I've searched all over the net, and there's no question that
my favorite site of all is
<A HREF="http://dummies.com">
<STRONG><I>Internet for Dummies Central</I></STRONG>
</A>
<P>
See you there!
</BODY>
</HTML>
```

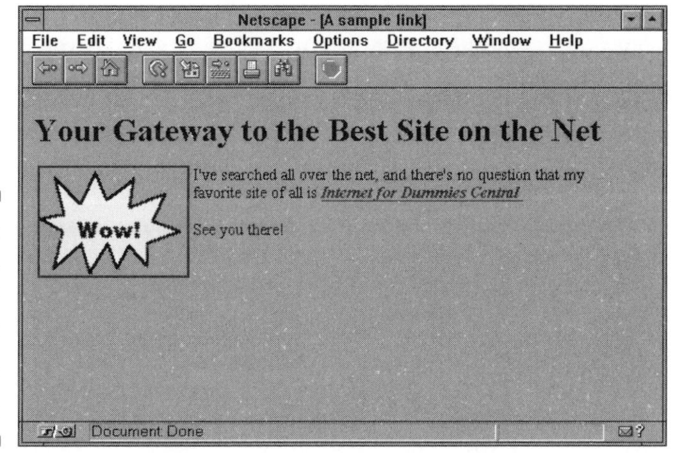

Figure 15-6: Links, beautified with an image and formatted text.

Colorizing Your Pages and Other Advanced Hackery

In case you're still with us, this section describes two more simple elements you can add to make your Web pages more attractive: transparent GIF images and Web page backgrounds with color.

Transparently better

One such element is *transparency.* In Figure 15-7, notice that the starburst on the left has an ugly white rectangle around it, while the one on the right has no border outside the star. That's because, in the GIF file for the right star, we made the white border transparent, which tells the browser to use the regular background color for that area. Whenever you have a GIF of an image that isn't really rectangular, making the area outside the image transparent always makes the image look better. Transparency adds only 10 bytes to the size of a GIF, so it doesn't affect the time to load or display the file at all.

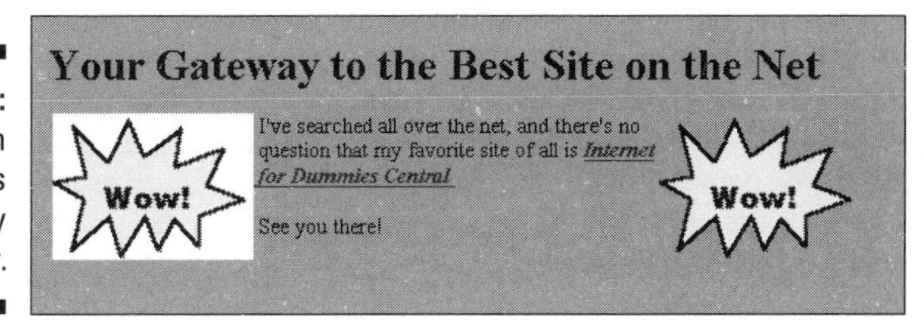

Figure 15-7: The star on the right is transparently better.

You need to use a graphics program that can mark one color in a GIF as transparent. In Windows, using the shareware program *Lview Pro* is the most popular way to do that. On UNIX systems, a little shareware program called *giftools* can mark one color as the transparent one. DOS users can use *GIFTRANS.* Some Web pages also can "transparentize" a GIF for you. The following pages are among those that can do so:

```
http://www.mit.edu:8001/tweb/map.html
http://www.vrl.com/Imaging
```

Colorful pages

Many Web pages have background patterns. We think that background patterns are almost without exception ugly and hard to read, however, so we don't intend to tell you how to use them.

Plain *background* and *foreground colors* on your pages look a lot better. They let you feature, for example, black text on a white background or vice versa — as long as a user's browser supports that effect, of course. (Colors are another Netscape addition but one that's very widely supported.)

You set the colors by adding `BGCOLOR` and `TEXT` fields to the `<BODY>` tag at the beginning of the body of your Web page, as follows:

```
<BODY BGCOLOR=#FFFFFF TEXT=#000000>
```

All set? Well, you do have to deal with the minor detail of that `#FFFFFF` glop, which is an extremely nerdoid way of identifying colors. A color is considered to consist of a mixture of red, green, and blue, with the amount of each color ranging from 0 (none) to 255 (the brightest). You convert each of the three amounts to a two-digit hexadecimal number (anywhere from 00 to FF, that is) and then glom the three numbers together.

If you find the preceding explanation less than obvious, Table 15-2 provides a list of some likely colors and their corresponding codes.

We find that you must always fiddle with colors to make them look good. Remember that many PC users can display only a limited number of colors on their screens at once. So if you use other than basic colors, Windows approximates your colors with "dithered" colors (using a geometrical pattern of basic colors) that is utterly illegible. Remember, too, that a lot of people are more or less color-blind, so make sure that you provide plenty of contrast between your text color and your background. White on black and black on white may seem boring, but these combinations have certainly stood the test of time.

Table 15-2 Web Page Color Coding

Code	Color
#FFFFFF	White
#000000	Black
#FF0000	Red
#00FF00	Green
#0000FF	Blue
#FFFF00	Bright yellow
#999999	Medium gray

Discovering More

Much, much more information on HTML and Web page design is available than we have room for here. We haven't even touched on tables, forms, VRML, or any of the other advanced Web features.

The Web itself is one of the best places to find out more about HTML. The following address takes you to a good Web page from which to start your quest — the HTML home page at the Web Consortium:

```
http://www.w3.org/pub/WWW/MarkUp
```

The following page is an excellent reference on HTML usage and low-level Web page design:

```
http://www.sandia.gov/sci_compute/html_ref.html
```

The address that follows is that of the HTML Specification page at the Web Consortium, which is far more readable than you may expect:

```
http://www.w3.org/pub/WWW/MarkUp/html-spec/html-spec_toc.html
```

Many books also are devoted to the topic of Web page design, such as *Creating Web Pages For Dummies,* by Bud Smith and Arthur Bebak, and *Creating Cool Web Pages with HTML,* by Dave Taylor (both available from IDG Books Worldwide, Inc.).

But nothing can substitute for direct hand-to-hand combat — building Web pages, looking at them, and throwing them away. And whenever you discover a Web page that you think looks particularly nice, instruct your browser to show you the source for the page so that you can examine the HTML that created the page.

In Netscape, for example, select View⇨Document Source to see the HTML.

HTML tags, yuck!

If you just hate the thought of writing HTML yourself, a bunch of HTML editors more or less automates the process for you.

Microsoft Word and WordPerfect both now have available free add-ons that enable you to edit documents and save them as HTML. Using one of these add-ons probably is the easiest way to go to create simple Web pages, although they're both really a pain to use for more complex formats. Word users should check out `http://www.microsoft.com/pages/deskapps/word/ia/default.htm`, which explains how to download and install the Microsoft Internet Assistant; WordPerfect users need to visit `http://wp.novell.com/elecpub/fawpip.htm`.

A number of stand-alone HTML editors also are available. Two that are well regarded are HoTMetaL (`http://www.sq.com/products/hotmetal/hfn.htm`), which comes in both a limited freeware version and a more complete commercial version, and HotDog (`http://www.sausage.com/index.htm`), a commercial product with standard and professional versions that you can download for a 30-day test.

We personally haven't found writing HTML tags all that difficult a process, so we've never found any of these editors worth the effort to use, but if you're less tag tolerant than we are, your opinion may well be different.

Much more elaborate and expensive Web-authoring systems also are available. These systems can help you keep track of the relationships among a group of pages, create the necessary server programs to process forms, and otherwise automate the maintenance of a Web site. These are big, expensive programs, however, that are severe overkill if all you want to do is put up a few personal pages of your own.

Part V
Online Odds and Ends

The 5th Wave
By Rich Tennant
In the end, it was Edward Scissorhands' cousin, Jonathan Hammerhead, who brought the group to a consensus on a domain name.
©RICHTENNANT

In this part . . .

This part of the book houses those odds and ends that didn't fit anywhere else. Several chapters are about Internet services that didn't get enough attention in *The Internet For Dummies,* 3rd Edition, such as Gopher and Internet Relay Chat. We've also thrown in some fascinating chapters on privacy, business, and how to register your own domain name (like `dummies.com`).

Chapter 16
Using the Net for Business

(Contributed by Carol Baroudi)

In This Chapter

- Setting up a Net presence
- Using e-mail for your business
- Providing information that attracts

Many people undoubtedly wish now that they'd been aware of the Internet and online services for the past 15 years. But, in fact, few people were. And very, very few people watched the commercial and sociological trends associated with these technologies for that length of time. Philippe Le Roux, entrepreneur and Internet expert of the first order, is among those few who have watched such developments with a close eye. He recently shared his insight and expertise with us in a personal interview. The remainder of this chapter conveys to you those insights, as well as the expertise of Mr. Le Roux, on using the Net for business purposes.

Presence of Mind — and Minding Your Presence

You may be tempted to go out and spend lots of money creating a "Net presence," investing big bucks on fancy graphics so that you can create the spiffiest home page on the Web, and then expect just to sit back and wait for the money to roll in. Before you do so, however, listen to what one of the world's experts on using the Net for business has to say.

According to one study, some 20 percent of companies with a Web presence are expected to dismantle their sites in 1996. Many companies do make money by using the Net, but doing so is not as easy as some would have you believe. The path to online success for your business may not lie in high-end graphical, multimedia Web pages — or even in having a Web site at all — but is, in every case, specific to *your* business. Here are some important ways to begin.

Almost every city hosts at least one Internet conference or forum a week. Self-proclaimed industry experts are ready to take your dollars and sell you a bill of goods. It's important not to get lost in the hype and hysteria as people flock to the Net as the latest gold rush. It's important to understand, from a business point of view, that people who know Net technology should not be confused with people who know how to use the Net to help your business.

To use the Net to help your business, you need to talk to people who understand Net culture and behavior: Who is on the Net? Why are they there? And what relevance — if any — can those on the Net have to your business? If you own a styling salon, for example, you're unlikely to find a Web site to generate much new business for you. On the other hand, your business *can* definitely benefit from strategic use of the Net in other ways.

If someone tells you that 50 million Internet users are all waiting to buy your product, that person's handing you a line. Many businesses have spent tens, if not hundreds, of thousands of dollars on Web sites but have realized no return at all on their investments. Other companies have experienced a ten- to twentyfold increase in sales. Still others say that their sites have saved them between $3 and $4 million.

What's the difference among these sites? The multimedia presentations, perhaps? Hardly. Some of the most lucrative sites are text based. And all sites need to pay attention to text-based browsers. Sophisticated software, known as *intelligent agent* software, is becoming more widely available, and these agents are all text based. Soon, everybody with access to the Net can tell these agents exactly what they want, and the agents can move out across the Web to find it for them. For a long time to come, you can expect this agent software to remain text dependent — which means that such software, in seeking out your Web site for potential clients, never even sees your fancy graphics.

No, the difference between the success of one Web site over another involves how effective the site is at providing what people actually want, *not* what you're trying to sell. You must begin to think of the Internet as an avenue that provides potential solutions to your business problems, not as an objective itself. If you start by identifying your own business problems, you begin to see how to use the Net to solve those problems.

For more information, see Chapter 4, "Doing Business on the Net," in our book, *Internet SECRETS* (IDG Books Worldwide, Inc.).

Saving Time and Money — Better Business with E-mail

You hear all the time about "surfing" the Net — especially Web sites and home pages — but the Web is not really the best place to start for a business new to the Net. Philippe recommends that you begin with e-mail. If you don't know how to use e-mail or haven't thought about the implications of using e-mail for your business, now is the time to begin both learning and thinking about it. E-mail predates the World Wide Web by more than 20 years and is a fundamental learning ground for understanding Net culture and potential.

E-mail opens an important new avenue of communication within and without an organization. Inside a company, e-mail becomes a powerful tool for company communication and project management. Using e-mail, people begin to communicate more easily with all levels of an organization, enabling information to flow much more freely. Those responsible for projects involving many people find that using e-mail facilitates group communications and heightens accountability. Because e-mail is almost free, sending a message to 245 people costs no more than sending a message to 3. Because people can read e-mail at their own convenience, using e-mail to communicate project information saves time otherwise spent in meetings and lessens the need to interrupt someone with phone or office chatting. We don't think e-mail replaces actually talking to people; we just know that it's difficult to get a lot of work done with a lot of interruptions, and e-mail can go a long way toward reducing interruptions.

E-mail is probably *the* cheapest way to communicate and is absolutely the cheapest way to reach a number of people around the world. E-mail often reaches its destination in a matter of seconds, and sending e-mail to Hong Kong, Lima, or New York City costs no more than sending it down the hall.

People who use e-mail find that the very technology itself changes how they work. Compared to a phone call, for example, e-mail communication is highly structured. Yet compared to traditional written communication, e-mail is quite versatile and easy to use. Every e-mail system includes a feature that enables the responder to include the original message in the text of the new, setting off the original text from the new by using special characters. Therefore, most people generally respond to e-mail point by point. This process enables e-mail recipients to clarify misunderstandings rapidly without requiring administrative aid to facilitate typing and without countless rounds of phone tag.

Simply compare the cost of e-mail with the cost of any other kind of express mail delivery — or even with the cost of overseas phone calls — and you begin to grasp the effect it can have. Suddenly, good communication with overseas offices and customers doesn't cost a lot of money. Suddenly, collaborative work is possible: People can easily and cheaply share files, pictures, and even video and sound. We know — we've been creating entire books for years by using e-mail.

(See our book, *Internet E-Mail For Dummies,* published by IDG Books Worldwide, Inc., for more suggestions on using e-mail effectively.)

Group Gatherings

Usenet newsgroups are an invaluable source of information — and, potentially, of customers as well. No, that's not to say, "Go advertise on the newsgroups." In fact, such advertising is a *really* bad idea. In fact, don't even *think* about it — you're just going to anger your potential customers. Instead, seek out all the newsgroups having anything to do with your field and begin reading them on a regular basis. In exploring what these newsgroups discuss, you can learn what people on the Net want — and maybe they want your service. Or maybe what they want is something that you could provide with a little work.

Begin to answer the queries of people who come to the newsgroups looking for answers. Many successful business relationships begin this way. Having wonderful products is nice, but having what people want is *much* nicer. You could spend considerable time and money attempting to attract customers to your product or service. Instead, why not go out to those places on the Net where people may be looking for your product or service? (In fact, we found the publisher who published our first book ten years ago through a Usenet contact.) See Chapter 9 of *The Internet For Dummies,* 3rd Edition, to get you started with newsgroups and Chapter 26 of *Internet Secrets* when you're ready to go pro.

Spinning the Web

Without putting your own site on the Web, you can gain a lot of strategic information quickly. You can often amass information in a few hours that could take months and cost hundreds of thousands of dollars to locate by using traditional information-gathering methods. Even information that's publicly available takes time and money to gather if you must write letters and make phone calls to obtain it. That same information now is often a few clicks away.

Value-Added Web Sites

Suppose, on the other hand, that you do identify a business problem you think can best be solved by creating a Web site. Here are some important ideas to bear in mind.

Come 'n get it

The Web is not a broadcast medium such as television or radio with a limited number of channels and a known audience. Television and radio advertisers know who watches and listens to what, and they spend their advertising dollars accordingly. The Web is *access on demand,* meaning that people see your Web site only if they choose to visit the site. Most people won't see it at all unless you can figure out how to get them there. You may have the coolest Web site on the planet, but without a *reason* to go there, no one is ever going to know about it. In determining how to make your Web site a *must-visit* kind of place, you need to distinguish between the following three categories of information:

- Information or a service that's really cool, fascinating, scintillating, enthralling, and otherwise unbelievable
- Information or a service that could really improve people's lives and that they *really need*
- Information or a service that people are *actually looking for*

Make sure that your Web site contains a healthy dose of the last category. Doing so is the *only* way to ensure that people visit your site.

Actively interactive

Just because your Web site links to other pages doesn't make your site interactive. *Interactive* means that the person using the site actually gets to *do* something — for example, buy train tickets, check the weather in Buenos Aires, or even determine whether they qualify for a mortgage.

Bangles, baubles, and beads

You may have something spectacular to tell everybody about, but at this point, no one even dreams of its existence. How do you get people to look at you, or *for* you, if they don't yet know that they want what you have to offer? One solution is to give them something they *do* want.

When they arrive at your site, you have a golden opportunity to show them even more than they're shopping for. For example, IBM has developed a reputation for great coverage of Internet news at its home page: `www.ibm.com`. People who've heard about it go there looking for the news and find out everything else IBM has to offer. By keeping its site current with current events, people have a reason to go there independent of any interest they have in product information — yet it's all in the same place.

Get before you give

If you give away something that people want, shouldn't you get something out of the deal as well? (Sure, you can *sell* your information, but that's a whole separate business itself.) You need, for example, to know exactly *who's* visiting your site. This information can be invaluable to you: It may be the basis of your next prospect list. It may also give you vital demographics on the people visiting your site. Knowing who's looking at your Web site may even help you understand what people on the Web want — and how you can provide to them what they want. Before allowing people to download your free demo, ask them to fill out a form. Get the data you need. Providing such information is a small price that most people are usually willing to pay.

Soliciting required

Ask for feedback on every page. Don't just think that you can put it on the last page — many people never get there. People need a way to communicate with you, and you need their input. Make feedback easy for people to give you, and acknowledge their feedback in a timely fashion.

Lovely Rita, meter maid

Measuring the success of your Web site is extremely important. Does your site solve the problem you set out to solve? Determine *how* you can measure the success of your site *before* you implement it. Such a success matrix may well guide the very design of your site. The number of hits a Web site gets is never a good matrix of success. If you want to increase your sales, for example, you need to determine how you can measure sales as related to your Web site. If you want to reduce calls to customer support, you must make sure that you have a way to track your calls.

Test the text

Remember that a considerable number of Web browsers are still text based and probably will remain so for a long time to come. Test your Web site by using text-only browsers to visit it. If you can't find your site with a text-only browser, your site isn't even there for many Web surfers.

Make a plan

Web sites need a plan. Understand exactly what you want to accomplish with the site. Look through the guidelines we've suggested. Plan your site with care. You're probably better off spending more resources on planning the site than on actually implementing it.

The Internet, of course, is not a universal medium. It does not reach everyone — nor, for that matter, does any other medium. The Internet is not likely to replace the phone or fax or television or radio, but the Net does have its own particular strengths and is likely to become the medium of choice for those who best know how to put it to strategic use.

French-born Philippe Le Roux is a founder of the Canadian Internet and online services consulting company VDL2, which is responsible for the interactive Web site and reservations system for Via Rail, Canada's Rail System. He is on the national board for Technology Watch and is the North American correspondent for Planete Internet. *His article, "Virtual Intimacy," can be found in* Internet Secrets *(IDG Books Worldwide, Inc., 1995). You can send him e-mail at* `leroux@vdl2.ca`.

Chapter 17

Have I Got a Secret?

(contributed by Arnold Reinhold)

In This Chapter

- Protecting your e-mail
- Responding to security problems

The Internet is big enough to have both good guys and bad guys, and what bad guys on the Net like to do is to spy on unsuspecting victims. Fortunately, in recent years, cryptographers have found surprisingly effective ways to let you send your messages in code so that even if a bad guy does intercept your messages, he can't figure them out.

Keeping Those Love Letters Private

As your e-mail message travels through the Internet, it goes through many different computers. Someone can intercept and read your message anywhere along the way without too much trouble. But some people on the Internet think they have solved this security problem.

Public key cryptography

The basic idea of encryption has been around for thousands of years — Julius Caesar used one of the earliest encryption schemes. You take the message that you want to keep secret and scramble *(encode)* it using a *key* that is, a secret password of some sort. You then send the scrambled version to the recipient, who then unscrambles *(decodes)* the message. Traditional codes use the same key for encryption and decryption, which causes two problems. One problem is the *key distribution,* which arranges for the sender and recipient of a secret message — but no one else — to have the secret key. The other problem is *key management,* which means having the right key to use for every message you want to send. To keep everything private, you'd need a separate key for each possible pair of users — with 10,000 users, you need 100,000,000 keys and some mighty big key chains.

The solution to both problems is *public key cryptography.* Invented in the mid-1970s, this technology simplifies encrypted communication by enabling the general public to exchange keys used to encode messages. Each user has two keys — a secret one (your private key) and a not-at-all-secret one (your public key). Here's how public key cryptography works:

If John and Arnold, for example, want to exchange encrypted e-mail, each must first have the other's public key in his computer.

- John encodes messages to Arnold by using Arnold's public key.
- Arnold decodes John's messages by using Arnold's secret key.
- Arnold encodes his reply to John by using John's public key.
- John decodes Arnold's reply by using John's secret key.

No one ever needs to give anyone else a secret code, yet everyone can communicate with privacy. Anyone can send you a secret message using your public key, but only you can decode those secret messages with your private key. You can tell anyone your public key without giving them the ability to read your mail.

You can also use public key cryptography in reverse to sign your messages in a way that cannot be forged — unless, of course, someone somehow manages to discover your secret key. That is, you can use your private key to encode a message. Because only your public key will decode this message, people will know it's from you.

Public key cryptography has been mired in hot political and legal controversy since its invention. Many governments around the world, including the U.S. government, wish that this technology had never been invented —because it makes it much easier for individuals and companies to use effective encryption — and are trying their best to control it. For example

- Export of strong cryptographic software is illegal in the United States.
- The European Union is considering restrictions on cryptography.
- France and Russia have banned cryptography outright.

PGP and Netscape Navigator 2.0 are two programs available on the Internet that use public key cryptography.

How secure is public key cryptography?

Pretty darned secure, we think, with a few ifs.

- If the program you are using is carefully written. In late 1995, for example, some students discovered several ways to break the encryption then used by Netscape, thanks to errors in the Netscape code. Those errors have been fixed, and we hope others don't exist. Encryption programs need to be scrutinized by cryptographic experts for a long time (months or years) before anyone believes that they're really secure.
- If your key is long enough — see the next section.
- If no breakthroughs in the mathematical knowledge needed to crack public keys occur — progress to date has been slow, but steady.

Although public key technology is good, you cannot rely on cryptology to keep your messages secret forever.

How big should my key be?

Public key encryption depends on arithmetic — lots of arithmetic. Your public key is the product of two large *prime numbers,* numbers that cannot be divided evenly by any other number. Your private key is one of those primes.

What makes public key cryptography work is that, while multiplying two prime numbers together is easy — if you're a computer, at least — figuring out what two primes create a particular product is hard. The larger the primes, or in computer-ese, the more bits the primes contain, the harder this task.

RSA, the company that owns the patents on this type of public key cryptography, recommends your public key be at least this long:

- For short-term security, 768 bits
- For medium-term security, 1,024 bits
- For long-term security, 2,048 bits

The largest public key that can be exported from the U.S. is a 512-bit key, which today's technology can break, albeit with considerable effort. Most PGP users (see the next section) choose at least 1,024-bit keys.

PGP

PGP, which stands for Pretty Good Privacy, is a freeware encryption program that has a strong following on the Internet. Here are things you should know about this program:

- PGP is free only for noncommercial use.
- A commercial version of PGP is available in North America from Viacrypt, 9033 N. 24th Avenue, Suite 7, Phoenix, AZ 85021; or send e-mail to viacrypt@acm.org.
- Most experts consider PGP to be very secure, if used properly.
- The current version of PGP, 2.6.2, is harder to use than Netscape Navigator, but a more user-friendly version, 3.0, should be released soon.
- PGP lets you make your own public and secret key pairs.

Public keys are distributed and certified via an informal network called "the web of trust," which is kind of like the letters of introduction popular in the preelectronic era.

The U.S. government threatened Philip Zimmermann, PGP's developer, with federal prosecution, because PGP had been exported from the U.S. (but not by him), before dropping the case in January 1996. So, for the moment, no legal challenge in the U.S. to PGP exists.

You can find out more about PGP — how to get it and how to use it — by following the Usenet newsgroup alt.security.pgp and, of course, reading that group's FAQ.

Netscape Navigator 2.0

Netscape Navigator 2.0 is available from Netscape at http://home.netscape.com/. Among the other 17,486 features included, Netscape Navigator supports encrypted e-mail through a version of public key technology called *SSL*.

Netscape Navigator shows a key icon on the bottom left of the screen. If the key looks broken, the connection is not secure.

Only the version of Netscape Navigator sold in North America offers full security. The export and free versions have been deliberately weakened to comply with U.S. export regulations. Even the fully secure version is believed to be less secure than PGP.

By using Netscape Navigator 2.0, you obtain your public and secret keys from a central key vendor. The only company authorized at the moment is VeriSign, which is at the Web address http://www.verisign.com. VeriSign calls the keys "Internet Driver Licenses." VeriSign offers these licenses in four levels:

- **CLASS 1:** Low level of assurance used for secure e-mail and casual browsing. Noncommercial and evaluation versions are offered for free, with a VeriSign-supported commercial version for $6 per year.
- **CLASS 2:** Next level of assurance for higher degree of trust and security. Used for access to advanced Web sites. Cost is $12 per year.
- **CLASS 3:** A higher level of assurance used for valued purchases and intercompany communications. Cost is $24 per year.
- **CLASS 4:** A maximum level of identity assurance for high-end financial transactions and trades. The price depends on what you plan to use this license for.

Netscape Navigator is new and is still being studied by cryptographic experts, but the full-strength version may offer easy-to-use encrypted e-mail with enough security for most users.

A Few Other Hot Topics

While we're on the topic of security, here are a couple areas that people often ask us about.

Should I give out my credit card number over the Internet?

This question always comes up. Several views on this practice exist.

One camp says that crooks can get credit card numbers in lots of other ways, so why worry about sending yours over the Net? Fishing a discarded paper receipt out of the trash is a lot easier than intercepting messages on the Net.

The other camp says that computer use allows fraud to take place on a much more massive scale than in the past. Therefore, the best available technology should be used to make cyberspace as safe as possible, and we should all insist on secure links before using the Internet for credit card and other financial transactions.

We think that, in general, the integrity of the outfit to whom you send your card number is more important than any possible theft en route. Indeed, to date, we've *never* heard of a credit card number actually being stolen while in transit over the Net. (We've heard of files on computers connected to the Net being broken into, but that problem is a separate issue — in one case, an Internet provider's entire user file, including credit card numbers that had been supplied over the phone and by paper mail, got swiped.)

What is key escrow?

Key escrow is a new kind of encryption technology where a master key that can read all your messages is split into pieces. The pieces are stored for safekeeping at two different *escrow agents,* organizations that promise not to give out your key information other than by court order. Key escrow appeals to

- Large organizations that fear an employee may abscond with the keys needed to decode vital data
- Law enforcement and intelligence agencies that want to be able to read the messages of people they consider a threat to society

Civil liberties groups and many people on the Net are horrified by the idea of key escrow encryption, likening the concept to the police demanding a key to your home in case a search is ever necessary.

The U.S. government's first attempt to push key escrow, the *Clipper chip,* has not caught on. A new software-only plan is in the works, and the European Union is working on a version. You can follow this debate on the Usenet newsgroup `talk.politics.crypto`.

Chapter 18

Internet Relay Chat: Worldwide Gossipmongering

In This Chapter

- How to connect to the Internet Relay Chat
- How to discover who's out there to talk to
- How to waste unlimited amounts of time exchanging pleasantries (or unpleasantries)

In theory, *Internet Relay Chat,* or *IRC,* is a way for individuals around the world to have stimulating, fascinating, online discussions. In reality, IRC is more often a way for bored undergraduates to waste time. But IRC, more than any other Internet service, is what you make it. If you can find interesting people to have interesting discussions with, IRC is wonderful. If not, kiss your free time good-bye or stay away from IRC.

Like every other Internet service, IRC has client programs and server programs. The *client* is, as usual, the program you run on your local machine (or perhaps on your provider's system) that you type at directly. An IRC *server* resembles a large switchboard, receiving everything you type and sending your messages to other users and vice versa. What's more, the different servers are all in constant contact with each other. As a result, stuff you type at one server is relayed to the other servers so that the entire IRC world is one big, chatty family.

To add a degree of coherence, IRC conversations are organized into *channels,* with each channel dedicated to a single topic, in theory at least. Any user can create a channel, so you get some funky ones (not to mention downright *dirty*).

Chatting in Theory and in Practice

You can use lots of different client programs for IRC that run on lots of different kinds of computers. But, fortunately, the steps to use the different client programs are practically identical:

Where did IRC come from?

Finland, actually, where Jarkko Oikarinen originally wrote IRC in 1988. IRC has since spread all over the world and is today one of the standard Internet services.

IRC's most notable hours were in the Gulf War and during the 1993 coup in Russia against Boris Yeltsin, when IRC users at the scene sent reports to thousands of other users around the world.

1. **Establish contact with an IRC server.**
2. **Tell the server who you are.**
3. **Pick a couple of channels.**
4. **Waste lots of time.**

Servers, Servers, Everywhere

If you're at a university or use a commercial Internet provider, a server is probably at or near your site. Users at The World, for example, our local Internet shell provider, use an IRC server that The World provides. Use a local server, if available, because using a local server is the polite thing to do and because a local server probably will respond faster than a server farther away.

If you use GNN, run the GNNchat program to connect to IRC. See Chapter 13 for how to use GNNchat.

If you're sure no local server is available, you can try one of the IRC servers listed in Table 18-1. Use the server closest to you. Several dozen public servers other than the ones in this table are available, but servers come and go frequently. Consult the Usenet group `alt.irc` for more complete and up-to-date lists. Unless otherwise specified, use port 6667 on any IRC servers.

Getting WinSock Ready to Chat by Using WSIRC

If you don't use WinSock programs, you can skip ahead to the section "Getting UNIX Ready to Chat."

Table 18-1 IRC Servers to Consider

Address	*Location*
cs-pub.bu.edu (also port 6666)	Massachusetts
irc.mit.edu, irc-2.mit.edu	Massachusetts
irc.umn.edu	Minnesota
irc.colorado.edu	Colorado
minnie.cc.utexas.edu	Texas
irc.stanford.edu	California
irc.funet.fi	Finland
cismhp.univ-lyon1.fr	France
disuns2.epfl.ch	Switzerland
sokrates.informatik.uni-kl.de	Germany
bim.itc.univie.ac.at	Austria
jello.qabc.uq.oz.au	Australia

Several Windows IRC programs are available, but we like WSIRC because it's a) easy to use, b) fairly reliable, and c) cheap. (You can imagine which of these factors was our most compelling reason.) Caesar M. Samsi wrote WinSock (be sure to read his bio in WSIRC's online help — click the Biography button at the end of the Contents page).

The WSIRC version we use is 2.0, so the archive file is called WSIRC20.ZIP. WSIRC's author improves the program from time to time, so a newer version may also be available. You can download WSIRC via FTP from one of the FTP servers in Table 18-2.

Table 18-2 FTP Servers with WSIRC

Host	*Directory*
oak.oakland.edu	/pub3/SimTel-win3/winsock
cs-ftp.bu.edu	/irc/clients/pc/windows
ftp.winsite.com	/pub/pc/win3/winsock

The ZIP file for WSIRC is *big*, so downloading takes a while. (The last version we grabbed was 686K.) See Chapter 10 in *The Internet For Dummies,* 3rd Edition, to learn how to download and install software via FTP.

Three versions of WSIRC are available: a registered version, a free version, and a shareware version. The differences are relatively minor: The registered version comes with a better help file, the free version limits you to two simultaneous IRC channels, and the other versions allow more channels. If you use WSIRC much, be a sport and register the program. The distribution of WSIRC includes `wsirc.exe`, the shareware version, and `wsircg.exe`, the free version. If you don't plan to use IRC enough to register the program, you can use `wsircg.exe` and delete `wsirc.exe`. If you're a more serious user, register and use `wsirc.exe` and delete `wsircg.exe`.

Connecting WSIRC to your IRC server

If you've just installed WSIRC, you have to go through a strange little ritual to get WSIRC set up (the figures show WSIRC running under Windows 95, but WSIRC works the same way using Windows 3.1):

1. **Start WSIRC or WSIRCG.**

   Before you can do anything else on IRC, you have to introduce yourself to your IRC server. Figure 18-1 shows the WSIRC Setup Options dialog box.

Figure 18-1: The WSIRC server setup window.

2. **In the IRC Server field, type your local server's name.**

   If you don't have a server locally, see the preceding section's suggestions.

3. **Leave the Port field set to 6667.**

   That's the magic number for IRC-ing.

4. **In the NickName field, type a nickname by which you will be identified to all other IRC users.**

   All IRC nicknames must be different from each other, so try a peculiar variation on your username.

5. **In the UserName and EMail fields, type your username on your provider's system and your e-mail address.**

6. **Click Ok.**

   A window appears, telling you that the changes will take effect the next time you connect to an IRC server. Click OK.

7. **Now connect to the server by clicking the open folder icon, the leftmost one in the row of icons at the top of the window.**

   If everything works okay, welcoming messages from your server appear (usually with threats about all the naughty things that will get you kicked off). If you get another linguistically challenged error message box, go back to step 2 and try another server.

After you're connected to a server, you're ready to try some real IRC chatting commands. When started in the future, WSIRC automatically connects to your server so that you don't have to go through this rigmarole again.

WSIRC's window on the world of IRC

The WSIRC window contains the Server Messages subwindow, which is divided into three parts. The largest part displays messages from the IRC server. At the bottom is a one-line window where you type commands. To the right is a tall, skinny window used for showing available IRC channels, as you see in a minute.

The next step is to choose a channel and begin typing. Skip ahead to the section "What Channels Are On?"

Getting UNIX Ready to Chat

The client program most commonly used by UNIX users is called *IRCII* (that's "IRC two"). You're most likely to run into IRCII if you type **irc** to a shell provider's system. Because IRCII is so popular, most other IRC client programs use the same commands. As a result, we can slay a multitude of avians with a single projectolith by telling you about IRCII commands in this book.

IRCII takes everything you type as lines of text. Two kinds of lines exist: commands to IRC and messages to other people. If a line begins with a slash, you have a command. If not, you have a message. (If only computers were this simple all the time.) The following command, for example,

```
/join #hottub
```

says to join the Hot Tub channel, a cheerful and usually crowded hangout.

What Channels Are On?

IRC discussions are organized (if you can call it that) into *channels*. Each channel has a name that begins with a sharp sign (#). We occasionally have a channel called `#dummies`, for example, for readers of the our books. To find out which channels are available, you can do one of the following:

- IRCII users can type **/list**.
- WSIRC users can click the LIST button (the tenth one from the left, which has four little lines and an open book). A box appears, in which you can type listing options. For the moment, just click OK.

Your IRC program gets the list of available channels, which is usually *very* long.

- In IRCII, the list of channels zoom by on-screen, probably faster than you can read the list. You can make a shorter list — see the next Tip icon.
- WSIRC displays the list of channels on the right side of the Server Messages window, and you can scroll up and down the list. Clicking the mouse once in the list of channels causes the list to fill the window, and you can see each channel's name, the number of users, and sometimes a channel description. Notice that most channels have only a single user, which means that one person is hanging out, hoping that someone talks to him. Generally, busier channels are more interesting.

In either WSIRC or IRCII, you can limit the list of channels to those with an interesting number of people. To see only channels with at least five people, type this line:

```
/list -min 5
```

(In WSIRC, you type this line in the one-line subwindow underneath Server Messages.) Typing this line should limit the list to a useful size.

If you use WSIRC and you don't see a list of channels in the screen's lower-right corner, click the List Channels icon (the one with the horizontal red lines).

Hey, Aren't We Ever Going to Do Some Chatting?

Oh, all right, we've stalled as long as we can. You can join a channel in the following ways:

How the heck can I remember what all those WSIRC buttons do?

You can't. Or more precisely, we can't. (You may well be smarter than we are and be able to memorize them all.) Fortunately, a built-in cheat sheet is available. If you move the cursor to any button without clicking, the button's name appears at the bottom of the WSIRC window. You can move the mouse back and forth until the button name you want appears.

But you must admit — WSIRC buttons are the most colorful bunch you've ever seen!

- IRCII users can type a **/join** command followed by the channel name (don't forget the #), as shown in the following example:

  ```
  /join #dummies
  ```

  IRCII lets you switch rapidly from one channel to another and even lets you join multiple channels, but the messages are jumbled together (which makes them hard to follow).

- WSIRC can let you do the same thing, by typing the **/join** command in the one-line subwindow underneath Server Messages. For lazy typists, WSIRC also lets you double-click the channel name in the list in the Server Messages window — much easier! WSIRC opens a new subwindow for every channel you join so that a dedicated IRCer can have several channels going at a time.

After you have joined a channel, everything that people on the channel type appears in the window, and everything you type is sent to these people. Whenever someone joins or leaves a channel, a message is sent to all remaining participants; when you join a channel, everyone else immediately knows that you're a participant. Stuff that people type is preceded by their nickname, as shown in this example:

```
[JoeBlow] But what do you do with the woodchucks once you
catch them?
```

Why do all IRC channel names begin with # ?

We don't know. Maybe # means something special in Finnish. In principle, although not common, channels can also begin with an ampersand (&) and be limited to a single server.

WSIRC displays a list of people in the channel on the right side of the channel's window so that you can tell whom you're up against.

As is so often the case on the Internet, naive users can easily make fools of themselves. When you join a channel, lurk for a while. Don't immediately begin typing — wait to see the tenor of the conversation. Then type away. If you find that you like IRC, you may stay up all night and well into the next day once you've joined the conversation.

Some other handy commands include the ones in this list:

- **/names:** Lists the people in a channel; plain /names lists all the channels, or you can follow /names by the name of a particular channel of interest.
- **/whois:** Followed by someone's nickname, tells you something about the person behind the nickname, usually the e-mail address and any other info that's been registered.

Enough, Already!

You can leave a channel you tire of in the following ways:

- IRCII users can type **/leave**.
- WSIRC users also can type **/leave** or close the channel's subwindow in the usual Windows manner (by double-clicking its upper-left corner).

Then you can join another channel or exit. To exit

- IRCII users can type **/quit**.
- WSIRC users can choose File⇨Exit from the menu.

Starting Your Own Channel

If you have nothing better to do, you can start your own IRC channel. Just make up a name and issue a **/join** command. IRC creates the channel automagically when you try to join it, as shown in the following example (remember that the name must begin with a #):

```
/join #cephalopods
```

In WSIRC, you can click the Join button (the ninth button from the left — the one with an arrow and an open book). A window appears, in which you type the channel name. That's all you have to do.

You can use the /topic command to display a topic line to other IRCers.

```
/topic Squid, cuttlefish, and their cousins
```

Then you wait, perhaps for a long, long time, until someone else joins your channel and begins talking. If you're the first person on a channel, you're considered to be the channel's operator, which gives you the greatly overrated privilege of kicking off your channel any people you don't like (see the nearby sidebar, "Operator, is this the party to whom I am connected?").

When you lose interest, you leave your channel in the same way as you leave any other channel, by typing **/leave** or by closing its window.

Can We Have a Little Privacy?

IRC lets you send messages directly to individuals and to channels. To send a message to an individual, assuming that you know her nickname, you type the following command:

```
/msg nickname your personal message here.
```

For example, a message to Johnny looks like the following:

```
/msg johnny Can you believe how dumb that guy is?!!!
```

You can also converse privately with someone. When you type **/query** followed by a nickname, the subsequent lines you type are sent to that person only. When you type **/query** with no nickname, you're back to normal, sending lines to your current channel.

Attack of the robots

Most participants on IRC are people. Some participants aren't — some are robots. Hooking up IRC clients to programs, usually known as *bots,* is not too difficult. Bots can participate like a person can (more exactly, like a very *stupid* person can). Some bots are inoffensive and do such things as hold a channel open and send a cheery welcome message to anyone who joins. Some bots are really obnoxious and send large numbers of annoying messages to people whom the bot's creator doesn't like.

In many parts of IRC Land, bots are considered to be terminally antisocial and aren't the least bit welcome. We don't tell you how to create a bot, but you should keep in mind that a particularly cement-headed user may actually have a microchip for a brain.

Operator, is this the party to whom I am connected?

IRC channels and IRC servers both have *operators,* people with particular authority to give some kinds of commands. The first person on a channel is considered the channel's operator, and the operator can anoint other users as operators, too. In the /names listing or the list in the WSIRC window, operators' nicknames are preceded by an at-sign (@).

The main command you get to use as a channel operator is /kick, which kicks someone off your channel, at least for the three seconds until he rejoins the channel. Kicking off someone is a thrill, but a rather small one, sort of like discovering that you've won 75 cents in the lottery. In WS!RC, the rightmost button is the Kick button.

People usually get kicked out of channels for being rude or obstructive, or for sending so many garbage messages that they make the channel unusable.

Server operators manage entire servers and can kick unruly users entirely off a server, permanently. Don't let that happen to you; be a ruly user, please.

Your private conversation can be routed through a dozen IRC servers, and the operators of any of these servers can log all your messages. So don't say anything that has to be *really* private.

It's a Jungle Out There

The Internet is pretty anarchic, and IRC is one of the more extreme parts of the anarchy. In particular, all you really know about the people you're chatting with are their nicknames and who they purport to be. Unfortunately, some IRC users have a sick sense of humor and delight in offering other chatters "helpful speed-up files" that in fact delete your files or let them crack into your account. Also, many users have a completely different persona in IRC than they do in real life: These users alter details of their age, interests, lifestyle, gender — you name it. In some cases, the make-believe is fun, and in others it's just strange. So chat all you want, but keep in mind that not all your IRC friends may be who or what they claim to be.

If someone on IRC tells you to type a command, don't do it. Nefarious people may suggest that you type commands that can make it possible for other people to use your Internet account. (No, we're not going to tell you the commands!)

Remember that IRC is a form of virtual reality and that some people find the IRC addicting. Students have been known to miss entire semesters of classes because they spent every minute on IRC. Remember that IRC can be fun, but it's no substitute for real life.

Chapter 19

How to Break In to Computers on the Net

In This Chapter

- Using telnet to log in to other computers
- Using WinSock telnet programs
- Some interesting computers to break into

Yes, indeed, it's true — while sitting at your own desk, you can quickly and silently log on to computers all over the world, without the owner of the computer even knowing! You can give commands, see information, and access files just like those teenagers in the movie *The Net.* How? By using *telnet.*

One proviso does exist, though — you can legally "break in" only to computers that specifically give you permission to do so. Bummer — but them's the breaks. When you use telnet, you either need to have an account on the computer you want to use or you need to telnet to computers that allow public access. Some Internet hosts, primarily libraries, do allow public access. For example, libraries let you search their catalogs for books in their collections.

Telnet, Telnet, Who's Got the Telnet?

When you use telnet, you log in to a remote *host* (telnet-ese for a computer) as though your *terminal* (workstation, PC, whatever) were attached directly to that host. Because all hosts on the Internet are officially equal, you can log in to a host on the other side of the world as easily as you can log in to a host down the hall; the only difference is that the connection to the distant host may be a little slower.

The key thing to remember when you're telnetting is that when you're logged in to another computer on the Internet, you have to use commands that the other computer understands. If you use a PC running Windows and you telnet to a computer that runs UNIX, you have to give UNIX commands. Luckily, most host computers that let the public telnet in provide menus rather than require you to know a bunch of commands. The following is the other key thing to remember: When you finish using the other computer, log out!

To use telnet to log in to a computer over the Internet, you need a telnet program. If you use a UNIX shell provider, you can use the `telnet` command. If you use WinSock or MacTCP software, you have to get a telnet program. Telnet programs come with popular Internet programs (such as Chameleon and Internet in a Box), or you can get telnet programs from the Internet via FTP.

The best way to get a good WinSock telnet program is to use your Web browser to download a program from the Consummate WinSock Apps List maintained by Forrest Stroud. The list is located at a bunch of URLs, including

```
http://cwsapps.texas.net/
http://cws.wilmington.net/
```

Choose the Terminal Apps section of the list and pick a telnet program that looks good to you. We happen to like these two:

- **NetTerm:** This shareware telnet program is also available via FTP from `ftp.neosoft.com` in the directory `/pub/users/z/zkrr01`. Download a file named `neterm28.zip` (the number may be larger for a later version).
- **EWAN:** You can also download this freeware telnet program from `ftp.best.com` in the directory `/pub/bryanw/pc/winsock`, in a file named `ewan1052.zip` (the number part may change).

Refer to Chapter 10 to find out how to download and install programs from the Net.

Among the commercial online services, only CompuServe offers telnet, although you can use WinSock telnet programs with AOL, GNN, and NetCruiser.

Telnetting, for You UNIX Users

In the following true-life example, John telnets to his home computer and logs in as himself (no, you can't have his password — sorry):

```
% telnet iecc.com
Trying 140.186.81.1 ... Connected to iecc.com.
Escape character is '^]'.
System V UNIX (iecc)
login: johnl
Password:
Terminal type (default VT100):
...
```

Notice the following points:

- Some telnet versions report the numeric addresses of the hosts they contact, as in 140.186.81.1 in the preceding example. If your version reports numeric addresses, take note of that number in case of later trouble with the network connection.
- The thing that's absolutely essential to note is the *escape character,* which is your secret key to unhooking yourself from the remote host if the host becomes recalcitrant and stops doing anything useful. WinSock telnet programs often use a Disconnect menu item rather than an escape character.
- In our example, the escape character is `^]`, which means that you hold down the Ctrl key and press `]` (the right-bracket character on your keyboard). This escape character is the most common escape character used on UNIX systems.

After you're logged in, you can work pretty much as though you were indeed directly logged in to the remote host. The primary difference is that characters take a little longer to appear on-screen — as long as a full second or more. In most cases, you can keep typing even when what you typed hasn't yet appeared; the remote host eventually catches up.

You're Not My Terminal Type

If you use a full-screen program, such as the UNIX text editors emacs and vi or the mail programs elm and Pine, you have to set your *terminal type.* This problem shouldn't exist in the first place. But because this problem does exist, you have to deal with it.

The problem is that about a dozen different conventions exist for ending screen control messages, such as Clear Screen, Move to Position (x,y), and so on. The program you're using on the remote host has to use the same convention as your terminal (if you're using a terminal) or as your local terminal program (if you're on a PC or a workstation).

If the conventions are not the same, you get garbage (funky-looking characters) on-screen when you try to use a full-screen program. In most cases, the remote system asks you which terminal type to use. The trick is knowing the right answer:

- If you're using a PC, the best answer is usually *ANSI* because most PC terminal programs use ANSI terminal conventions. ANSI stands for the American National Standards Institute. One of its several thousand standards defines a set of terminal control conventions that MS-DOS PCs — which otherwise wouldn't know an ANSI standard if they tripped over one — invariably use.

- If you're using an X Window-based system, such as Motif or Open Look, the answer is more likely to be *VT-100,* a popular terminal from the 1970s that became a de facto standard.
- In places in which a great deal of IBM equipment is used, the terminal type may be *3101,* an early IBM terminal that was also quite popular.

The ANSI and VT-100 conventions are not much different from each other, so if you use one of these conventions and your screen is only somewhat screwed up, try the other convention.

Depending on how well implemented your local version of telnet is, telnet may automatically advise the remote system about which kind of terminal you're using. So with luck, you don't actually have to set your terminal type, or perhaps you just have to reply **y** when telnet says something like `Terminal type VT100 OK?`.

Help! I've Telnetted and I Can't Get Out!

The normal way to leave telnet is to log out from the remote host. When you log out, the remote host closes its end of the telnet connection, which tells your local telnet program that the remote host is finished. Easy enough — normally. Sometimes, though, the other end gets stuck and pays no attention to what you type. Or the remote host doesn't get permanently stuck but responds so slowly that you have no interest in waiting for a response anymore. (This slowness sometimes happens when network congestion occurs between you and the other host.)

Some versions of host software, which we won't name for looking-gift-horses-in-the-mouth-type reasons, get hopelessly slowed down by congestion, much more than the congestion itself causes. So you have to know how to escape from telnet, which is where the magic escape character comes in handy.

- First, you have to get telnet's attention by pressing the escape character. (If nothing happens after a few seconds, try pressing Enter.) Telnet should come back with a prompt, telling you that it's there.
- Then type **quit** to tell telnet that you're finished. You should see something like the following:

```
^]
telnet> quit
Connection closed.
```

You can give telnet a dozen other commands (press **?** to see them), but none of the commands is anywhere near as useful as `quit`.

New, Improved Telnet, with Whiter Whites

If you use a Macintosh, a PC under Microsoft Windows, or some other windowing system, you start telnet differently than you do a UNIX system. You start the telnet program by double-clicking its icon, and a window pops up with menu choices at the top. Connect (or something similar) is usually a choice. Click Connect to get a Connect window. Figure 19-1 shows a typical window you get from the Connect menu item, using Internet Chameleon's Telnet program running under Windows 95. Type the name of the host you want or choose the host name from a list, click OK, and away you go.

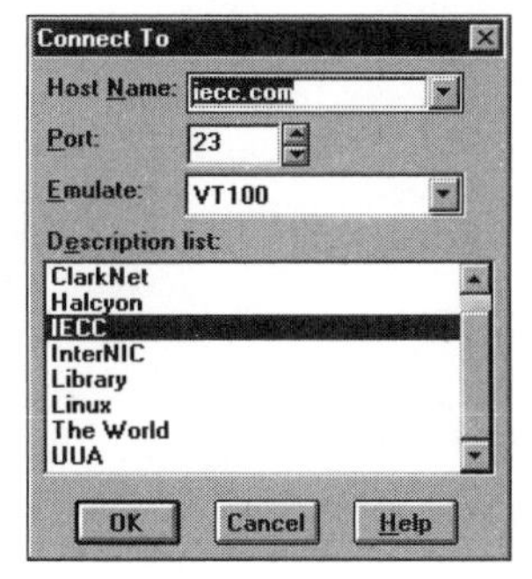

Figure 19-1: Connecting by running Internet Chameleon's Telnet program.

Figure 19-2 shows a connection to the same computer as shown earlier in this chapter, but this time from a Windows machine using Internet Chameleon's Telnet program. When you run a Windows or Mac telnet program, you don't need an escape character because you do all the escape-type stuff from the program's menu. To disconnect from a recalcitrant host, for example, click a menu item called Disconnect (or something similar).

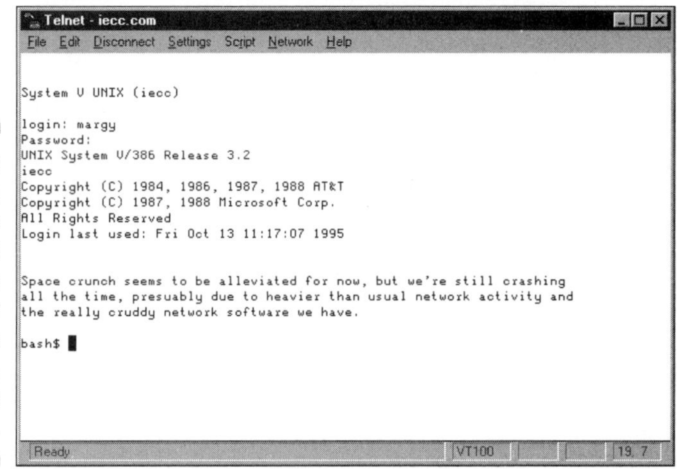

Figure 19-2: When you've finished using the computer you've telnetted to, choose Disconnect.

Any Port in a Storm

When you telnet in to a remote host, you have to choose not just the host but also a port on the host. The *port* is a small number that identifies which service you want. The usual port for telnet is (for obscure historical reasons) the number 23, which means that you want to log in to the host. If you use the UNIX `telnet` program, you choose another port by putting the port name after the host name.

```
telnet ntw.org 13
```

If you use a Windows or Mac telnet program, you type the port number in the same dialog box in which you enter the host name.

In case you were wondering, port 13 is the *daytime* port. Port 13 tells you the host's idea of the time of day and then disconnects. This exercise is not terribly useful, although occasionally you may want to see what time zone another host is in.

We're from IBM and We Know What's Good for You

All the terminals discussed earlier that are handled by telnet are basically souped-up teletypes, with data passed character by character between the terminal and the host. This kind of terminal interaction can be called *teletype-ish.*

IBM developed an entirely different approach to terminal use for its 3270-series display terminals. The principle is that the computer is in charge. These terminals work more like filling in paper forms. The computer draws what it wants on-screen, marks which parts of the screen the user can type into, and then unlocks the keyboard so that users can fill in whichever blanks they want. When the user presses Enter, the terminal locks the keyboard, transmits the changed parts of the screen to the computer, and awaits additional instructions from headquarters.

To be fair, the IBM 3270 terminal is perfectly reasonable for dedicated data-entry and data-retrieval applications. The terminals on the desks at your bank and electric company, for example, are probably 3270s — or more likely these days, cheap PCs *emulating* (pretending to be) 3270s. Because the 3270 terminal protocol squeezes a great deal more on a phone line than does teletype-ish, all 3270s in an office usually share the same single phone line, with reasonable performance.

The Internet is a big place, and plenty of IBM mainframes run applications on the Net. Some IBM mainframe applications are quite useful. Some library catalogs, for example, speak 3270-ish. If you telnet to a system that wants a

3270, the system usually converts from the teletype-ish that telnet speaks to 3270-ish so that you can use the system anyway. But some 3270 systems speak only 3270-ish, and if you telnet to these systems, they connect and disconnect without saying anything in between.

To log in to a 3270-ish host from a UNIX system, use a variant of telnet that speaks 3270-ish called *tn3270.* If you find that a system keeps disconnecting or if you see full-screen pictures, try using the command `tn3270` rather than `telnet`. Large amounts of UPPERCASE LETTERS and references to the IBM operating systems VM or MVS are also tip-offs that you're talking to a 3270. Even if a 3270 system allows regular telnet, you get a snappier response if you use tn3270 (shown in Figure 19-3).

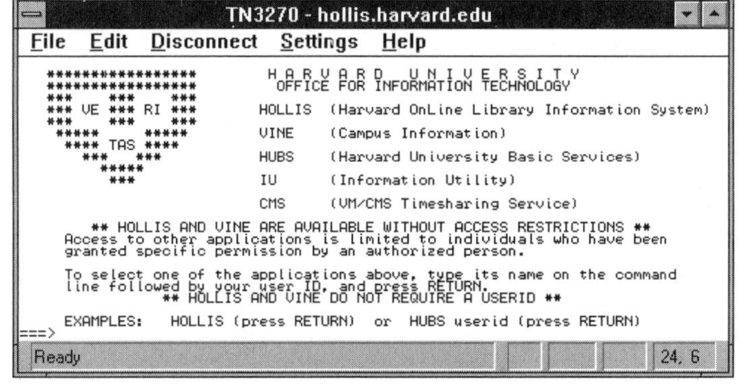

Figure 19-3: Using `tn3270` to log in to the Harvard University Catalog.

Fun Computers to Break In To

The Internet is a remarkably friendly place. Many systems let you telnet in with little or no prearrangement. Most systems just let you telnet in without restriction. Other systems require that you register the first time you log in but still don't ask you to pay anything. These systems simply want to have an idea who their users are.

In the list of services in this chapter, the code letters have the meanings shown in Table 19-1.

Table 19-1 Codes in the Listing of Telnet Sites

Code Letter	*Meaning*
T	Connect via regular telnet.
Port Number	Specify a port number after the host name in your telnet command (see Chapter 1 for details).

(continued)

Table 19-1 *(continued)*

Code Letter	*Meaning*
3	Connect via `tn3270`. Most `tn3270` systems listed in this chapter also allow regular telnet for people without `tn3270`.
R	Registration required. The first time you log in, you have to say who you are.
A	Account required. You have to sign up and arrange to pay money. (Not many of these accounts are listed.)

Libraries

Nearly every large library in the country (indeed, in the developed world) has a computerized catalog, and most catalogs are on the Internet. Most online catalogs also have other research info that is certainly more interesting than the catalogs themselves. This section lists the more prominent library systems and how to access them.

Library: Library of Congress
Address: locis.loc.gov
Access code: T3

The Library of Congress is the largest library in the world and certainly has the biggest catalog system, called LOCIS (your tax dollars at work, or maybe at play). Along with the regular card catalog, in which you can look up pretty much any book ever published in the United States, the Library of Congress has an extensive and useful congressional legislation system that you can use to look up the bills that are in Congress. You can find out what bills have been introduced; what's happened to them (getting a bill through Congress is somewhat more complicated than getting someone canonized as a saint); who sponsored the bills; and what the bills say (in summary).

Note: LOCIS is available only during library hours, generally 9 a.m. to 9 p.m. (Eastern time) on weekdays, with shorter hours on weekends. Other times, LOCIS disconnects immediately.

Library: Dartmouth College Library
Address: library.dartmouth.edu
Access code: T

Along with the card catalog, this service includes the full text of William Shakespeare's plays and sonnets and the works of other great authors. To search the plays, type **select file s plays**; for sonnets, type **select file s sonnets**.

Library: Yale Library
Address: orbis.yale.edu
Access code: 3

This large library is the only one where you can find a copy of John's thesis, "A Data Base System for Small Interactive Computers," which may not matter to you, but we think it's interesting. Type **orbis** to get started.

Many libraries are online. We generally find that the Library of Congress is the most useful for finding names of books, unless we are planning to physically visit one of the other libraries.

Geography databases

Even residents of cyberspace need to visit the physical world from time to time. Here are a few sites to help you find your way around.

Database: Earthquake info
Address: geophys.washington.edu
Access code: T

Log in as *quake* and use the password *quake*. Did you know that the United States has earthquakes almost every day? And you thought you were paranoid!

Database: GLIS
Address: glis.cr.usgs.gov
Access code: TR

GLIS is the government's *Global Land Use Info System*. An enormous amount of map data is available in computer form, which GLIS enables you to locate and order. Impress your friends by whipping out a computerized map of your town, state, and/or planet.

Outer space databases

Care to roam the far reaches of the universe (or talk to people who do)? Then the outer space databases are for you.

Database: Spacelink
Address: spacelink.msfc.nasa.gov
Access code: TR

Spacelink contains NASA news, including the shuttle launch schedule.

Database: European Space Agency
Address: esrin.esa.it
Access code: T

European Space Agency tells you what's new in the European part of outer space.

Other databases

As usual, you can find information about almost anything on the Internet, and telnet is no exception to this rule.

History databases
Database: University of Kansas
Address: ukanaix.cc.ukans.edu
Access code: T

You history buffs can find lots of good stuff in a variety of history databases around the Net.

Log in as *history* for databases on history, or as *ex-ussr* for databases on Russia and its neighbors. These databases list documents, bibliographies, and other info of interest to historians.

Aviation database
Database: DUATS
Address: duats.gtefsd.com
Access code: TR

Interested in the wild blue yonder? We've found someplace you can roam.

This database provides pilot info, briefings, and flight plans. If you're a real certified pilot, log into *duat.gtefsd.com* instead. Log in using your last name as the login name.

Book database
Database: CARL
Address: pac.carl.org
Access code: TA

CARL contains book reviews, magazines, and articles, including fax article delivery.

For many of the services, you need a library card (or at least the number of a library card) from a participating library in Colorado or Wyoming, such as the Denver Public Library. Type **pac** to get started.

WorldWindow
Gateway: WorldWindow, the Washington University Electronic Information Gateway
Address: library.wustl.edu
Access code: T

WorldWindow is the best place to start browsing if you like to telnet to far-off interesting places.

Log in as *services.* WorldWindow is a gateway to hundreds of other services around the Net. When you find an interesting service, make a note of its name (and port and login, if need be) so that you can telnet in directly next time.

Chapter 20

Welcome to Gopherspace!

In This Chapter

- What is Gopherspace, and where'd the name come from?
- Using Gopher from a UNIX shell account
- Using Gopher with a Web browser

As the Internet grew (not that it's done growing), users ran into two related problems. One problem was that so much information was available that nobody could find it all. The other problem was that umpteen different ways existed to get to different resources (telnet, FTP, finger, Archie, and so on), and remembering what you said to which program was getting difficult.

Welcome to Gopherspace

Gopher solved both problems by reducing nearly everything to menus. You start up Gopher, you see a menu. You pick an item, you see another menu. After a certain amount of wandering from menu to menu, you get to menus with actual, useful stuff. Some menu items are files that Gopher can display, mail to you, or (usually) copy to your computer. Some menu items are telnet items that start a telnet session to a host that provides a particular service. And some menu items are search items that ask you to enter a *search string* and the name or partial name of what you're looking for and then use the search string to decide what to get next — more menus, files, or whatever.

You can look at Gopher as directories on your disk, in which some entries are files of various sorts and other entries are other directories. Whether you think of it as a source for menus or for directories, Gopher gets much of its power from the fact that any item in any menu can reside on any host in Gopherspace. Having a menu on which every item refers to a different host is common. Gopher automatically takes care of finding whatever data you want, no matter the data's location. You can use a dozen or more different Gopher servers in a single session without knowing that you're doing so.

This extremely simple model turns out to be very powerful, and until recently Gopher was usually the fastest, easiest, and most fun way to wander around the Net looking for and frequently finding the information you needed. However, the World Wide Web has now eaten Gopher's lunch (in our modest opinions). The Web, like Gopher, is an easy-to-use method of accessing information from many different services. In fact, Web browsers can show you information from Gopher, too! But lots of Gopher information is still available on the Net, so it's worth knowing how to find and use Gopher.

The Good, the Bad, and the Ugly

You use Gopher by running a *Gopher client program* or by running a Web browser that can handle Gopher (most browsers do). If you use a UNIX shell provider, for example, you can use the UNIX `gopher` command. Gopher is moving into the multimedia era with a vengeance, however, and the classic UNIX Gopher program handles only text. For anything other than text, Gopher goes into what one may call *cruel joke mode,* in which Gopher tells you that a swell picture you would love to see is available, but you can't look. A good Gopher client, on the other hand, wastes no time in finding the picture, copying it to your computer, and popping it up in a window on-screen. Graphic Web browsers, such as Netscape and Mosaic, handle pictures from Gopher with aplomb.

These days most people who look at information from Gopher probably use a Web browser rather than a program designed just for Gopher. In this section, you see how to use the UNIX Gopher program and a Web browser to cruise around in Gopherspace.

If you use WinSock software and are bound and determined to run a Gopher program rather than use a Web browser, we can't stop you. If you spend a great deal of time Gophering, you may prefer a Gopher program — who knows? If you like, download WS Gopher from `dewey.tis.inel.gov` in the directory `/pub/wsgopher`. The filename begins with `wsg`. (You can also find this program at the Consummate WinSock Apps List, maintained by Forrest Stroud, at `http://cwsapps.texas.net/`. See Chapter 10 to learn how to download and install software via FTP.)

Among commercial online services, only AOL provides Gopher directly (go to the keyword **GOPHER**, of all things). If you use another online service, you're still in luck, though, because you can use the Web browser to see Gopher menus.

Why is Gopher called Gopher?

The folks at the University of Minnesota who created Gopher named it Gopher for two reasons: First, the gopher is an industrious little animal, always busy, scurrying about on behalf of its family. Second, Gopher is an obvious pun on "go fer" because Gopher "goes fer" your files.

The fact that a gopher is the mascot of the University of Minnesota, is, of course, *completely* irrelevant.

Gopher has been so successful that *Gopher+,* an improved version, has appeared. Fortunately, the main difference between the two is that Gopher+ can handle more and different kinds of information than plain Gopher can. Other than that difference, the two programs are so similar that they're interchangeable, and plain Gopher and Gopher+ items can intermix in the same menu.

Gophering Around in the Web

Enough of this Theory of Pure Gopherology — let's take Gopher for a test drive. These days the convenient way for people to use Gopher is by firing up their Web browser. As you may recall, the Web gives each Web page a *URL,* which is a horrible-looking address that begins with `http://`. The secret to using Gopher via a Web browser is that Gopher menus have URLs, too. Gopher URLs begin with `gopher://`. Simple enough?

Here's how to figure out a Gopher menu's URL if you know the name of the Gopher server the menu is on: Type **gopher://**, followed by the Gopher server name, followed by another slash. For example, for the University of Minnesota Gopher server (at `gopher.micro.umn.edu`), the URL is

```
gopher://gopher.micro.umn.edu/
```

This URL gets you to the main, or root, menu on the Gopher server. From there, begin choosing items until you get to the menu you want. Someone may give you the URL of a specific menu on a specific Gopher server. The URL looks like

```
gopher://mudhoney.micro.umn.edu:4325/7
```

The stuff following the Gopher server host name tells your Web browser exactly where the menu is stored. Don't worry about what this stuff means — we don't!

To see a Gopher menu with your Web browser, type the URL into the box just below the toolbar and press Enter. (If your browser doesn't let you type in that box, get a better browser! In the meantime, choose File from the menu and look for a command such as Open Location.) Your Web browser gets the Gopher menu and formats the menu as though it were a Web page, as shown in Figure 20-1.

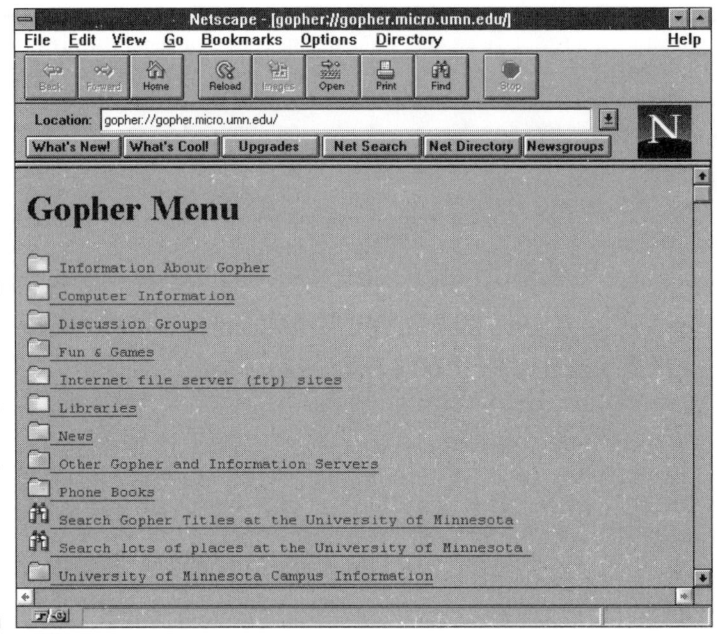

Figure 20-1: When a Web browser displays a Gopher menu, each menu item appears as a link.

Each item on the Gopher menu appears as a link (a connection to information elsewhere). To choose that item, click the link. Items on Gopher menus can be any of the following:

- **Another Gopher menu:** Some browsers display a cute, little file folder to the left of these menu items. When you click one of these folder icons, another menu appears.
- **A text file:** These items usually have a little sheet-of-paper icon to their left. When you click one of these icons, your browser displays the text.
- **A search item:** Some browsers display little binoculars by these items. When you click a search item, a Web page appears that enables you to search Gopher menus for information. For example, Figure 20-2 shows a Gopher search item in Netscape. When you enter a word to search for and press Enter, Gopher returns a menu of items that contains the word you searched for.

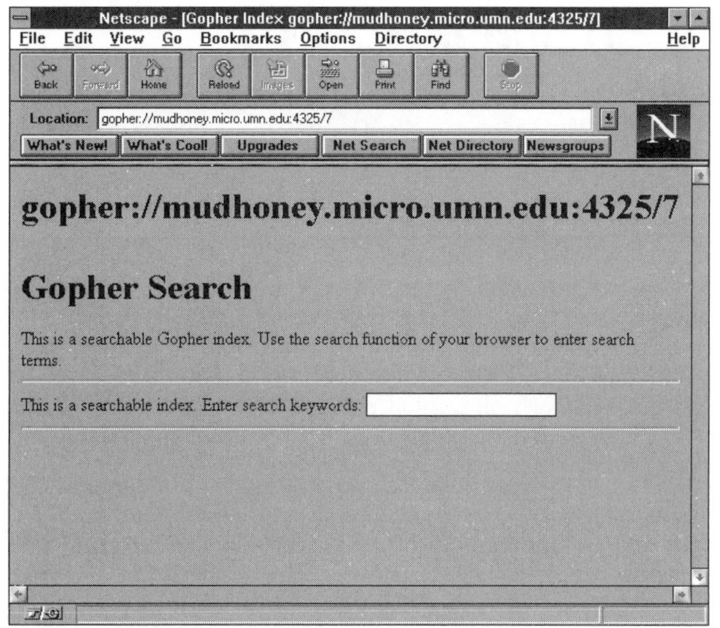

Figure 20-2: To find Gopher items that contain a certain word, type the word that you want to find.

- **A telnet item:** When you click telnet items (which have a little picture of a terminal to their left), you log in to an Internet host by using telnet (see Chapter 19). Most browsers run a separate telnet program. If clicking telnet items doesn't work, you may have to get a telnet program and configure your browser to work with it. If you use a commercial online service's built-in browser, you're out of luck. If you use WinSock software, refer to Chapter 19 to learn how to get a telnet program. To configure Netscape to use your telnet program, choose Options⇨General Preferences from the menu, click the Apps tab, and type the pathname of your telnet program in the Telnet Application box (or click the Browse button to the right of the box).
- **A graphics, sound, video, or other file:** These items are marked by a variety of adorable little icons. When you click one of these files, your browser downloads the file. If you click a graphics, sound, or video file that the browser knows how to display or play, your browser does so. Otherwise, the browser asks you where to store the file.

As you use your Web browser to surf the Net, you may find yourself looking at Gopher menus when you least expect it. Many Web pages contain links to items in Gopher menus. Now you know how to proceed when you see a Gopher menu on the Web.

Gophering Around in UNIX

If you use an Internet shell provider, you should have a Gopher client program named `gopher`. The section "Hello, Gopher?" describes how to use this program.

My Gopher is missing!

If your UNIX system doesn't have the Gopher program, you can telnet to a Gopher server and use its Gopher program. Telnetting to Gopher is much better than no Gopher at all. Fortunately, quite a few Gopher systems offer telnet access. Table 20-1 lists Internet host computers that offer telnet access to Gopher. Because nearly all Gopher servers have references to each other (or at least to the master *every Gopher in the world* list in Minnesota), you can get to any Gopher information from any Gopher system. So choose a Gopher close to you. ***Note:*** Unless otherwise instructed, if the system you telnet to asks you to log in, log in as `gopher`. If it asks for a password, just press Enter.

Table 20-1 Gopher Servers

Country	*Server Address*	*Special Instructions*
Australia	`info.anu.edu.au`	Log in as info
Austria	`finfo.tu-graz.ac.at`	In English, German, or Styrian; log in as `info`
Chile	`tolten.puc.cl`	In Spanish
Germany	`gopher.th-darmstadt.de`	In German
Japan	`gan.ncc.go.jp`	In English
Poland	`gopher.torun.edu.pl`	In Polish
Spain	`gopher.uv.es`	In Spanish
USA	`consultant.micro.umn.edu`	
	`sailor.lib.md.us`	Also provides Lynx
	`gopher.msu.edu`	Also provides Lynx
	`cat.ohiolink.edu`	Log in as `ohiolink`
	`sunsite.unc.edu`	
	`ecosys.drdr.virginia.edu`	
	`gopher.ora.com`	

The first thing most systems do when you telnet to them is to ask your terminal type. If you don't know, the correct guess is probably `vt100` (an extremely obsolete terminal that, for sentimental reasons, most PC and Mac terminal programs emulate) or `ansi`. If you guess wrong, your screen looks scrambled; press **q** and Enter to escape and try again.

Hello, Gopher?

Here's how to use the UNIX Gopher program:

1. **Type** gopher.

   You see a copyright screen. After you press Enter, you get a screen like the following:

   ```
    Internet Gopher Information Client v1.1
    Root gopher server: gopher.micro.umn.edu -
   > 1. Information About Gopher/
    2. Computer Information/
    3. Discussion Groups/
    4. Fun & Games/
    5. Internet file server (ftp) sites/
    6. Libraries/
    7. News/
    8. Other Gopher and Information Servers/
    9. Phone Books/
    10. Search Gopher Titles at the University of Minnesota <?>
    11. Search lots of places at the University of Minnesota <?>
    12. University of Minnesota Campus Information/
   Press ? for Help, q to Quit, u to go up a menu Page: 1/1
   ```

   If you don't have a local Gopher client, telnet to a system listed in Table 20-1. The items in the menu differ, but the screen's general appearance is the same for local client Gopher and telnet Gopher.

   The menu items differ depending on the program you use, but the screen's general appearance is the same.

   This particular menu contains two kinds of items. Items that end with / are other menus, and the items with <?> are search items, which we consider in the next section.

2. **Choose items from the Gopher menu by moving the cursor down to the item and pressing Enter or by typing the line number and pressing Enter.**

   If the item ends with a slash, you see another menu. If it's another kind of item, something else happens.

3. **Keep choosing things from menus until you find something interesting.**

   You can wade around in Gopher menus for hours!

4. **When you finish, press** q **to quit.**

That's all you have to do to use Gopher! Well, not all, but you've got the general idea.

Using Other Kinds of Gopher Items

In the preceding section, you saw the main (or *root*) menu of the Mother of All Gophers at the University of Minnesota. Although Minnesota is a swell place, gophers and all, let's look farther afield in this Gopher tour. This section shows what you might find in your hike through Gopherspace.

Choose number 8, Other Gopher and Information Servers, from the menu. That is, either move the cursor down to line 8 or go to line 8 directly by pressing **8** and then pressing Enter. When you press Enter, the next menu appears (we're leaving out the top and bottom headers to save space):

```
-> 1. All the Gopher Servers in the World/
   2. Search titles in Gopherspace using veronica/
   3. Africa/
   4. Asia/
   5. Europe/
   6. International Organizations/
   7. Middle East/
   8. North America/
   9. Pacific/
   10. South America/
   11. Terminal Based Information/
   12. WAIS Based Information/
```

Choosing North America and then USA displays a menu that lists all the states. The menu is too big to fit on a single screen, which Gopher tells you by putting `Page: 1/3` at the bottom (meaning that this page is the first of three pages). You move from page to page in the listing by pressing the + and – keys or move to a particular item by typing its number. If you know the name of the item you want, you can search for the item by typing / and part of the name and then pressing Enter, at which point Gopher finds the next menu item that matches what you typed.

Eventually (in this example) you end up at the National Bureau of Economic Research (NBER) because you're looking for a position paper the organization published. The menu looks like

```
-> 1. NBER Information.
   2. About this Gopher.
   3. Search for any NBER publication <?>
   4. Penn-World Tables v. 5.5/
   5. Phone books at other institutions/
   6. NetEc (Universal) Economics Working Paper Server/
```

These indexes are a mess

If you use Gopher much, you quickly notice a great deal of inconsistency from one menu to another. The inconsistency is because Gopher is a totally decentralized system, like the World Wide Web. That is, anyone who wants to can put up a Gopher server. Putting up a Gopher server is relatively easy; the system manager only needs to install a few programs and create some index files containing the text of the local menus. If one site wants to include in its Gopher menu a link to an item or menu somewhere else, the site can do so without requiring any cooperation from the manager of the item or menu linked to.

So the *good* news is that thousands of Gopher servers are on the Net, put up by volunteers who want data retrieval to be easier. The *bad* news is that because almost none of these people has any experience in indexing and information retrieval (for that experience, you need a degree in library science), the same item may appear on five different menus under five different names, and no two Gopher menus are quite the same.

Figuring out where people have hidden stuff can take some experimenting and poking around, but that poking around is invariably worth the effort.

Yoo-hoo, Gopher

Now take advantage of a search item in the NBER menu, indicated by <?>. When you choose this search item, Gopher provides a box in which you type words to search for. In this case, you type the name of the paper's author, and Gopher soon returns a menu of papers he has written:

```
Search for any NBER publication: Krugman –
> 1. |TI| Pricing to Market when the Exchange Rate Changes
  2. |TI| Industrial Organization and International Trade
  3. |TI| Is the Japan Problem Over?
  ...
```

Gopher search items are a very general feature. In this case, the search was done through a local database, but the interpretation of any particular search key is entirely up to the Gopher server that does the search. People have written extremely clever servers that do all sorts of searching (see Chapter 11 of *The Internet For Dummies,* 3rd Edition).

Finally, Some Files

Now you have a menu of file items, which in this case contains citations of the papers you want. When you choose any item, its file is displayed on-screen, a page at a time. When the entire file has been displayed (or after you press **Q** to shut it up), Gopher says

```
Press <RETURN> to continue, <m> to mail, <s> to save, or <p>
to print:
```

If you decide that you liked that file, you can get a copy of your very own. If you press **m**, Gopher asks for your e-mail address and mails you a copy. If you press **s**, Gopher asks for a filename and copies the file (invisibly, using FTP) to your computer. If you press **p**, Gopher sends a copy to the printer. If you're using telnet to access Gopher, your only option is m because the disk and the printer on the computer on which the Gopher program is running may be thousands of miles away.

If you've dialed in from a PC running a terminal program such as Crosstalk or Procomm, you can usually download files by using a scheme such as Kermit or Zmodem. At the end of a document, press Enter to get back to the menu and then **D** to download. Gopher pops up a box asking which download method to use. Accessing the Internet by way of a PC is by far the easiest way to get copies of files because doing so combines FTP retrieval and downloading in one step. (For more info about the mysteries of terminal programs, downloading, and the like, see Chapter 10 of *The Internet For Dummies,* 3rd Edition.) Gopher can download any file in its menus, even if the file isn't text, on the theory that you probably have a program to handle the file.

Leaping Tall Systems in a Single Bound

Menu items flagged with `<TEL>` are *telnet* items. When you choose a telnet item, Gopher automatically runs telnet (which is discussed in Chapter 19) to connect you with a system that provides a service. More often than not, you have to log in to the remote system — if so, just before it starts the connection, Gopher tells you the login name to use.

If your short-term memory isn't great, you may want to write down the login name the telnetted-to system requires because the system can take a while before it gets around to asking you for the login name.

To get back to Gopher, log out of the new system. If you can't figure out how to log out, press Ctrl+] and then, at the `telnet>` prompt, type **quit**. (***Note:*** If you have telnetted to Gopher instead of running the program directly, read the nearby sidebar, "How many telnets would a telnet telnet if a telnet . . . ," before trying this maneuver.)

When Gopher telnets to a system, Gopher is not doing anything magical — if Gopher can telnet somewhere, so can you. If you find one of Gopher's online systems to be interesting, make a note of its host name, which is displayed just before connection takes place. Next time you can telnet to the system yourself without Gopher's help.

Making Book (marks)

As you move through Gopherspace, you often come to a menu you want to revisit. One way to revisit a menu is to carefully note the menu sequence that led up to the menu you like — but doing so is exactly the sort of thing that computers do better than people. Gopher *bookmarks,* then, note your favorite places in Gopherspace.

We've come up with sets of bookmarks that are close to the items we regularly use. Using bookmarks lets us get to our regular Gopher haunts in only one or two keystrokes, starting from our bookmark menu.

How many telnets would a telnet telnet if a telnet . . .

Here's a problem that nobody had to worry about before computers existed: Suppose that you're working on your UNIX system and you telnet to a Gopher system. You use that Gopher to telnet to a *third* system, and your session on the third system is messed up, so you want to stop that session. As Gopher never tires of pointing out, you can interrupt its telnet session by pressing Ctrl+].

But wait a minute. Ctrl+] also interrupts the telnet session from your computer to the Gopher system. If you press Ctrl+], which process does the character interrupt — the first session (you to Gopher) or the second session (Gopher to third system)? Both? Neither?

The answer is that Ctrl+] interrupts the first session. But, in that case, how do you interrupt the second session? To do so, a trick is available: Press Ctrl+] to interrupt the first session and then, at the `telnet>` prompt, change your interrupt character by typing the following command: **set escape ^X.**

That last line ends with the two keys ^ (caret) and X. These keys tell the first telnet that henceforth you will press Ctrl+X to interrupt the first session. Now, if you press Ctrl+], you interrupt the second telnet session, which is what you wanted to do in the first place. If Gopher itself messes up, you can use Ctrl+X to get the local telnet's attention.

Incidentally, after you have telnet's attention, the command to tell telnet to quit is `quit`.

Attention Mac and Windows users: If you're using SLIP or PPP, you don't have to worry about this nonsense because your telnet version has a sensible way to disconnect. Pressing Ctrl+] interrupts the second session so that you can type **quit** and get back to Gopher. If you want to hang up on Gopher, you use, as usual, the menu item (usually called Disconnect) that your telnet provides.

If you use the UNIX Gopher client program, you can use the following commands:

- To remember the current item, press **a** (lowercase), for *a*dd a bookmark.
- To remember the entire current menu, press **A** (uppercase).
- To use your bookmarks, press **v** (for *v*iew), and Gopher constructs a menu that contains all your bookmarks. You can use that menu like any other menu.
- You can prune that menu by pressing **D** (uppercase) to *d*elete the current item.

If you're running the Gopher client directly, your bookmarks are saved in a file so that they're available every time you go Gophering. If you telnet in, the bookmarks are discarded (unfortunately) at the end of each session.

A UNIX Gopher Cheat Sheet

Table 20-2 contains all the keys for the basic UNIX Gopher. Except as noted, each key takes effect immediately, that is, as you type it.

Table 20-2 Basic UNIX Gopher Commands

Command	*What It Does*
Enter	Selects current item; same as cursor right
u	Moves up, goes back to preceding menu; same as cursor left
+	Moves to next menu page
–	Moves to preceding menu page
m	Goes to main menu
digits	Goes to particular menu item; type the item's number and press Enter
/	Searches menu for string
n	Searches for next match
q	Quits, leaves Gopher
=	Describes current item
Bookmark commands	
a	Adds current item to list
A	Adds current menu to list
v	Views bookmarks as a menu
D	Deletes current bookmark

Command	What It Does
m	Mails current file to user
s	Saves current file (not for telnet)
p	Prints current file (not for telnet)
D	Downloads current file

Move the cursor up and down to move up and down in the current menu. Moving the cursor to the left moves you back to the preceding menu. Moving the cursor to the right selects the current item.

Chapter 21

How to Register a Domain Name

In This Chapter

- How to find out whether the name you want is taken
- How to register the name
- How to use the name

Domain names have class, cachet, and style — having your own domain name shows the world that you are a classy dude (or dudette). Gee, IBM has ibm.com, Microsoft has microsoft.com, and Procter & Gamble has diarrhea.com. Wouldn't it be cool to have your own name as the domain name of your e-mail address, something like elvis@presley.com? We thought so too, and John registered dummies.com years ago.

Registering a domain name for just yourself doesn't make a great deal of sense — registering takes time and costs at least $50 a year. But if you have a business, club, or other organization, a domain name may be just the thing. If you registered, say, dummies.com, you can have a Web server named www.dummies.com and an FTP server named ftp.dummies.com, and you can receive e-mail addressed to info@dummies.com or sales@dummies.com. (Our Web server is named both www.dummies.com and dummies.com — either one works. We don't have info or sales addresses. Yet.)

What Kind of Domain Do You Want?

The Internet, being a fairly big place, has several different kinds of domains. You can have a full-fledged domain, which can contain lots of different computers, or you can have a simple domain that only works for e-mail. You also have choices about where to register your domain.

Do you have what it takes?

When you register a domain, you're actually asking to have your domain *delegated* to you. That is, when someone asks for a name in your domain, the name system passes the request to you so that you can answer the request

What's a domain, anyway?

A *domain* is a name given to a computer or group of computers on the Internet. In the smallest domains, the domain itself is used as a computer name, but in most cases, other names are assigned within the group. For example, all the computers at the White House are in the domain `whitehouse.gov`, such as `www.whitehouse.gov` and `ftp.whitehouse.gov`. All the computers at our Internet provider (TIAC) are in the domain `tiac.net`, such as `zork.tiac.net` and `challenge.tiac.net`.

The last part of a domain name is the *zone.* Three-letter zones, such as `com`, are used for mostly U.S. domains. The `com` zone is for commercial sites, `gov` is for the U.S. government, `edu` for educational institutions, `net` for network organizations, `int` for international bodies, `mil` for the U.S. military, and `org` for other groups, such as nonprofits. Two-letter zones are used for geographically organized domains: A two-letter zone exists for each country in the world. For example, `ca` is Canada's zone and `us` is the U.S.'s zone.

Domains and zones are described in more detail in Chapter 2, and the Appendix has a list of two-letter zones from around the world.

yourself. For this process to work, you need a *domain server,* a computer permanently attached to the Net that can respond to name requests. To make things work reliably, you actually need at least two separate servers, a main server and at least one backup server, in case the main server or its network link fails. (This two-server requirement is nonnegotiable. Name registries do not accept a registration request without verifying that the two servers for the new domain are working.)

Unless you have at least two separate machines with permanent Net connections, you'll have to get someone else to be your domain server. In most cases, your Internet provider will, for a modest fee, be your domain server.

If you ask your provider to be your domain server, you may as well ask your provider to handle the entire registration. Provider registration usually doesn't cost much and can save you a great deal of work.

What do you offer?

What do you plan to do with your domain? E-mail? Web pages? FTP archives? If you plan to do anything more than e-mail, you need a server permanently attached to the Net to provide the Web pages, FTP server, and so on. Again, if you don't have a machine permanently connected to the Net, your provider can host your Web pages and other services for you as well.

A way around registering new domains

If your organization already has a domain name, consider using subdomain names rather than registering additional domains. For example, say that you work at The Plebney Group and have registered `plebney.com`. If you open a new waxed-fruit division, rather than registering `waxedfruit.com`, you can create a second-level domain name as part of `plebney.com`—`waxedfruit.plebney.com`. The computers in this new division can have names like `www.waxedfruit.plebney.com`, `ftp.waxedfruit.plebney.com`, and `sales.waxedfruit.plebney.com`. Setting up subdomains is much easier than getting a new domain name; your organization's system manager can usually create a new subdomain in a few minutes, and you save fifty bucks a year.

If you only want to use your domain for an e-mail address, you can use a dial-up machine. You can use a special Domain Name Service feature called *mail exchange* (MX) to route all the mail for your domain to your provider's computer, where it can be stored until you call in to pick it up.

Where do you live?

Two kinds of domains are on the Net — geographic domains, which end with a two-letter country code, such as `us` for the U.S., and generic domains, which end with a three-letter code for the kind of organization, such as `com` for companies. People in the U.S. most often register a generic domain, and people in other countries most often register in their countries' domains. But no matter where you live, you can register either way.

Registration is a multistep process: first, pick a name; second, set up domain servers; and third, send an application to the registry that handles your desired domain. The InterNIC is the organization that registers generic domains that end with `com`, `edu`, `gov`, `org`, or `net`. For `com`, `org`, and `net` names, InterNIC charges $100 for the first two years and $50 a year thereafter for each domain you register. Table 21-1 lists the country registration contacts for the U.S. and most English-speaking countries. Drop a short e-mail note to your country's contact to find out your country's registration rules.

If you're in the U.S., names in the `us` domain are structured geographically. For example, because I.E.C.C. is in Trumansburg, New York, it has a geographic domain name of `iecc.trumansburg.ny.us`. If you only want to register a single machine or a name simply for e-mail, registering in the `us` domain is much easier than registering in any generic domain.

For one thing, you don't have to provide your own domain servers (the folks who manage geographical domains just add your entry to their master servers), and for another, the us domain registries still don't charge anything. We recommend using the us domain, unless you expect to have a lot of different computers in your domain. For more info on the us domain, aim your Web browser at http://www.isi.edu/in-notes/usdnr/.

Table 21-1 Country Registration Contacts

Country	*Contact*	*Address*
Australia	Elz, Robert	kre@munnari.oz.au
Bahamas	Ambrister, Barbara	ambri@cob.edu.bs
Bermuda	Coelho, Tom	tom@bercol.bm
Canada	Demco, John	demco@cs.ubc.ca
Fiji	Kumar, Sunil	postmaster@usp.ac.fj
Guam	Nguyen, Luan, Dr.	admin@ns.edu.gu
India	Ramani, Srinivasan	ramani@saathi.ncst.ernet.in
Ireland	Hostmaster Team	hostmaster@ucd.ie
Hong Kong	Ng, Nam	hcxcnng@hkujnt.hku.hk
Jamaica	Manison, Keith	manison@uwimona.edu.jm
New Zealand	Houlker, John Charles	j.houlker@waikato.ac.nz
Papua New Guinea	Bright, Graham	graham@ee.unitech.ac.pg
Puerto Rico	Moreno, Oscar	moreno@sun386-gauss.pr
Saint Lucia	Daniels, Albert	adaniels@isis.org.lc
Singapore	Tan, Marc	marctan@ncb.gov.sg
South Africa	Lawrie, Mike	mlawrie@frd.ac.za
Trinidad	Hosein, Patrick	hosein@ldc.uwi.tt
U.S.	Cooper, Ann Westine	us-domain@isi.edu
U.K.	Black, Dr. Willie	uk-admin-contact@ukerna.ac.uk
Vanuatu	Kenneth, Dorosday	kennethd@fisheries.gov.vu
Zambia	Bennett, Mark	mbennett@unza.zm
Zimbabwe	Sheppard, John	postmaster@zimbix.uz.zw

Somebody Took My Name!

Before you try to register, use the Whois service to make sure that the domain name you want isn't already taken. Here's how:

1. **Use your World Wide Web browser to see this Web page:**

   ```
   http://www.internic.net/
   ```

2. **Choose Registration Services and then Whois Query Form on the page that appears.**

   Alternatively, go directly to this URL:

   ```
   http://rs.internic.net/cgi-bin/whois
   ```

   You see a Web page that looks something like Figure 21-1.

3. **Type a domain name into the blank and press Enter.**

   For example, if you want to register `caviar.com`, type that name. (By the way, it's already taken.) When you press Enter, your request flies over the Internet back to InterNIC. You see a response like the one shown in Figure 21-2.

   If Whois can't find the domain name, then the name is not registered. You're in luck! If some lout has already taken the domain name you had set your heart on, click the Back button on your Web browser and try another name.

If your computer has a Whois program (nearly all UNIX shell systems have one, as do many Windows Internet packages, such as Chameleon), use that program, which is faster.

When you find a domain name that you like and that isn't already taken, bingo! You're ready to move along to the next step.

When choosing a domain name, if you decide to use a generic domain, remember to use the right zone for your domain name (the last part of the name). If you are a commercial organization, use `com`. If you are a nonprofit organization, use `org`. If you are an educational institution, use `edu`.

Where Will Your Domain Live?

A domain name has to be connected to a computer on the Internet. In fact, a domain can be used for one, two, or hundreds of Internet hosts — just imagine how many computers with names ending in microsoft.com or digital.com must be on the Net! But no matter what, you need at least one Internet host computer to which your new domain name can apply or at least can receive mail for your domain.

You can arrange to have at least one Internet host computer in two ways: do so yourself, or get your Internet provider to do so.

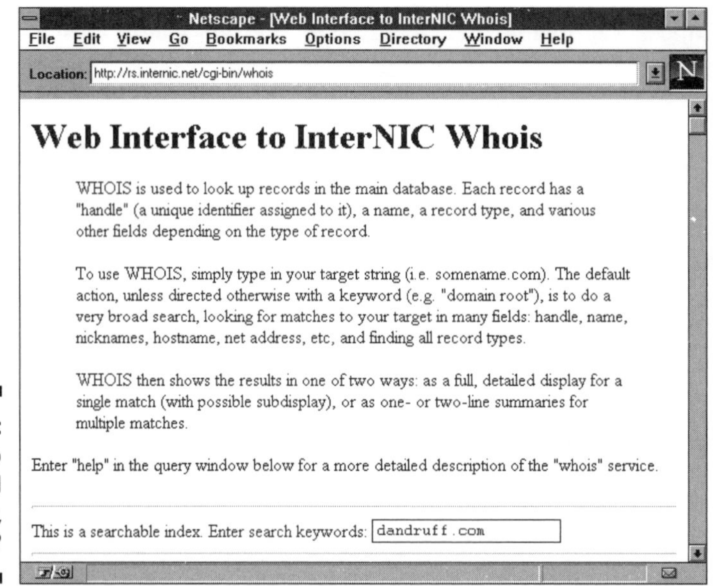

Netscape - [Web Interface to InterNIC Whois]
File Edit View Go Bookmarks Options Directory Window Help
Location: http://rs.internic.net/cgi-bin/whois
Web Interface to InterNIC Whois
WHOIS is used to look up records in the main database. Each record has a "handle" (a unique identifier assigned to it), a name, a record type, and various other fields depending on the type of record.
To use WHOIS, simply type in your target string (i.e. somename.com). The default action, unless directed otherwise with a keyword (e.g. "domain root"), is to do a very broad search, looking for matches to your target in many fields: handle, name, nicknames, hostname, net address, etc, and finding all record types.
WHOIS then shows the results in one of two ways: as a full, detailed display for a single match (with possible subdisplay), or as one- or two-line summaries for multiple matches.
Enter "help" in the query window below for a more detailed description of the "whois" service.
This is a searchable index. Enter search keywords: dandruff.com

Figure 21-1: Who registered dandruff.com, anyway?

Find your own domain name home

If your organization has its own permanently connected Internet hosts, talk to the system administrator to find out whether the new domain name can apply to an existing computer in your organization. One computer can have lots of domain names. For example, John has one computer named dummies.com, ivan.iecc.com, www.dummies.com, ftp.dummies.com, iecc.com, jclt.com, gurus.com, creamery.com, and a few other miscellaneous names.

You also need two permanently connected Internet hosts that agree to be Domain Name Servers for your domain. Your system administrator can probably help you with this too.

Take up (domain) residence with your Internet provider

Your commercial Internet provider can list your new domain on its domain name servers. Simply ask your provider to register your domain name (see the next section), and the provider handles the domain name server business.

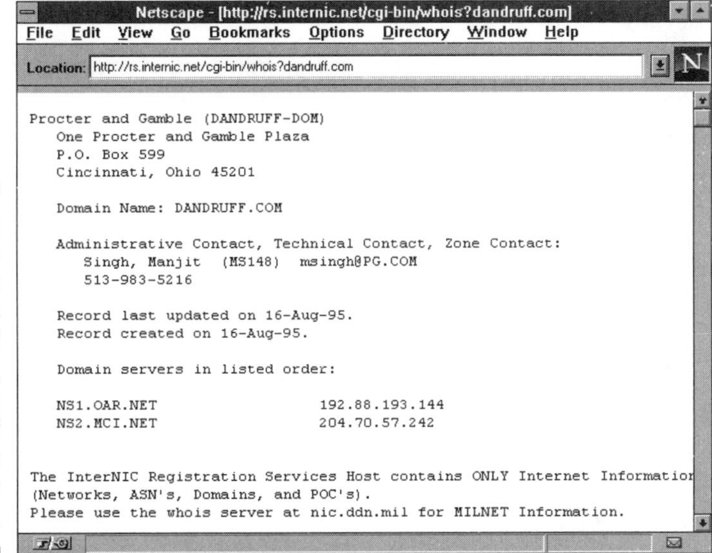

Netscape - [http://rs.internic.net/cgi-bin/whois?dandruff.com]
File Edit View Go Bookmarks Options Directory Window Help
Location: http://rs.internic.net/cgi-bin/whois?dandruff.com
Procter and Gamble (DANDRUFF-DOM)
One Procter and Gamble Plaza
P.O. Box 599
Cincinnati, Ohio 45201
Domain Name: DANDRUFF.COM
Administrative Contact, Technical Contact, Zone Contact:
Singh, Manjit (MS148) msingh@PG.COM
513-983-5216
Record last updated on 16-Aug-95.
Record created on 16-Aug-95.
Domain servers in listed order:
NS1.OAR.NET 192.88.193.144
NS2.MCI.NET 204.70.57.242
The InterNIC Registration Services Host contains ONLY Internet Informatio
(Networks, ASN's, Domains, and POC's).
Please use the whois server at nic.ddn.mil for MILNET Information.

Figure 21-2: Procter & Gamble is listed as the owner of dandruff.com, along with a bunch of other savory domain names.

Registering Your Name

After you have chosen a domain name that no one else has registered, found a computer to use the name on, and enlisted two domain name servers to list your new domain name, you are ready to register your name. Once again, you can either register your name yourself or get your Internet provider to do so. Our Internet provider (TIAC, in Bedford, Massachusetts) charges about $20 to do the job.

To register a generic domain yourself, send a form by e-mail to InterNIC. If you want to register within your country's domain, the process is similar, but you'll have to ask your country's registration contact (see Table 21-1) for the details.

Here's how to register a name at InterNIC:

1. **Use your Web browser or FTP program to get the form (a partial example is shown in Figure 21-3). The form is available on the Web at this URL:**

   ```
   ftp://rs.internic.net/templates/domain-template.txt
   ```

2. **Save the form to a text file. In most Web browsers, you choose File⇨Save As.**

3. **Using a word processor, text editor, or your e-mail program, edit the form, adding the information about your new domain name.**

   Detailed instructions for filling out the form are at the end of the form itself. Don't fool around with the form's format and don't delete anything.

4. **Send the form by e-mail to** `hostmaster@internic.net`.

   For the subject of the e-mail message, type **NEW DOMAIN**, followed by the domain name you want to register. Keep a copy, too, just in case.

   You will receive a reply from InterNIC's mail robot, including a tracking number. If you need to send any e-mail asking about your registration, be sure to include the tracking number in the subject of the e-mail. InterNIC can take days or weeks to process a domain registration, depending on its workload.

   Sooner or later, you get a response from InterNIC, confirming that your domain is registered. InterNIC may also reject the registration, for example, if someone else registered the same name minutes before you did or if your two domain name servers didn't list your new domain properly.

5. **Pay your bill.**

   You get an invoice from InterNIC for the domain. As of 1996, registering a domain name costs $100, which includes the first two years' fees. After that time, you're charged $50 per year.

Remember that InterNIC accepts these forms *only* by e-mail. Don't print the forms to complete by hand. Don't photocopy the form out of this book and type on it neatly. Only e-mail will do. And be sure to check InterNIC's home page (at `http://www.internic.net/`) for any changes in the registration instructions since this book went to press.

```
[ URL ftp://rs.internic.net/templates/domain-template.txt ]     [ 09/95 ]

******************* Please DO NOT REMOVE Version Number
 Domain Version Number: 2.0

**************** Please see attached detailed instructions ********
Only for registrations under ROOT, COM, ORG, NET, EDU, GOV

0.  (N)ew (M)odify (D)elete....:

1.  Purpose/Description........:

2.  Complete Domain Name.......:

Organization Using Domain Name

3a.  Organization Name..........:

3b.  Street Address.............:

3c.  City.......................:

3d.  State......................:

3e.  Postal Code................:

3f.  Country....................:

Administrative Contact

4a.  NIC Handle (if known)......:

4b.  Name (Last, First).........:

4c.  Organization Name..........:

4d.  Street Address.............:

4e.  City.......................:

4f.  State......................:

4g.  Postal Code................:

4h.  Country....................:

4i.  Phone Number...............:

4j.  E-Mailbox..................:
```

Figure 21-3: Domain registration form from InterNIC.

Now What?

After your domain is set up, you have to connect it to something. Again, your system administrator or your Internet provider is the first place to ask about setting up e-mail, a Web server, and other services in your new domain.

First, get your Internet provider or system administrator to set up the mail system so that you can get e-mail at your new domain. You need to specify what should happen to mail addressed to users with names like `info`, `postmaster`, `sales`, `help`, and the like at your domain, since people wanting to know about your domain are likely to send mail to those addresses. You must be able to handle mail to `postmaster`. All other mail addresses are optional.

Our Internet provider charges about $20 per month to maintain a Web address such as `http://www.whatever.com/` for your Web pages. Your Internet provider may also be willing to provide space on its FTP server for your files so that you can offer files with a domain name of `ftp.whatever.com`.

Chapter 22

Cool Stuff Is Out There!

In This Chapter

- Finding information about the Net on the Net
- Frequently asked questions (FAQs) and their answers
- The Usenet urban folklore quiz
- Weather, news, stock prices, and sports
- Fun, adventure, and total silliness

The Internet is such a huge place that no single book can possibly list all the resources and services available. And even if it did, the book would be out of date the day it was published. Fortunately, the Net itself is the ideal place to find out more about its resources. (Think of the Net as looking up the word *dictionary* in the dictionary, except that you're more likely to find something you didn't already know. By the way, have you heard that by lexicographer's tradition, the word *gullible* doesn't appear in any dictionary?)

In this chapter, we look at our favorite sources of information about the Internet itself, other useful information, and just plain silly stuff. For each service, we list the URL of the server — that is, its Uniform Resource Locator. Chapter 5 tells you how to use URLs to access stuff by using Gopher, WAIS, and — first and foremost — the World Wide Web. URLs that begin with *http* are World Wide Web pages. URLs that begin with *news* are Usenet newsgroups. URLs that begin with *ftp* are files available from FTP servers. And URLs that begin with *gopher* are Gopher items.

Yuck! I Hate Typing URLs!

This chapter is full of URLs, and they are a pain to type. Of course, *we* didn't have to type them, because we used cut-and-paste commands to copy the URLs from our Web browser to the word processor we used to write this chapter. But you are stuck typing them back into *your* browser. Or are you?

The Internet comes to the rescue! Simply type in this one URL:

```
http://dummies.com/
```

You see The Internet For Dummies Central, the home page about this book and other books by the same great group of authors. (Not to mention humble!) Follow the links to see the update page about *MORE Internet For Dummies,* and you see all the URLs that appear in this chapter. Instead of typing the URLs, simply click. We also update any URLs that have changed on this Web page.

The Net on the Net

We'll start with information about the Internet itself, including indexes to information on the World Wide Web.

The Usenet urban folklore quiz (Part I)

Face it — more interesting things exist than chapters full of lists. One of our fellow . . .*For Dummies* authors calls these kinds of chapters Ten Coffee Pot Chapters. So to perk things up, (direct from the world-famous Usenet group) `alt.folklore.urban`, it's the Usenet Urban Folklore Quiz.

Each section has ten true or false questions. The answers are at the end of this chapter. Don't cheat by looking at the answers first!

Part I: Science

True or false:

1. You can make ice much faster by starting with warmer water.
2. Boiled water freezes faster than ordinary water at the same initial temperature.
3. Daylight sky appears dark enough to see stars from the bottom of a deep well.
4. Fluorescent lamps light up when held near a high-voltage line.
5. Leather saddles used to be treated with llama dung to avoid scaring horses.
6. If the entire population of China jumped up at the same time: a) the Earth's orbit would be disturbed or b) the entire U.S. would be swamped by a tidal wave.
7. You can see glass flow in the windows of old buildings.
8. A newspaper once substituted "in the African-American" for "in the black."
9. Scientists once concluded that bumblebees can't fly.
10. The F-51D fighter plane can flip because of engine torque.

Indexes to the Net

```
http://www.yahoo.com/
http://www.lycos.com/
http://www.altavista.digital.com/
http://www.excite.com/
http://www.infoseek.com/
http://www.opentext.com:8080/
```

If you're looking for information and decide to see what the Web has to offer, any of these indexes works great. Most indexes contain a blank you can fill in to search for a word or phrase in almost any page on the World Wide Web. Yahoo! also contains a detailed topic list so that you can browse through the information on the Web. Lycos and Alta Vista let you search huge databases of Web pages, larger (we think) than Yahoo!'s database. (Lycos's database contains more than 16 million Web pages, as of December 1995.) Alta Vista indexes articles in Usenet newsgroups, too. Excite also reviews Web pages. InfoSeek provides a free Internet search service, or you can sign up for an account that allows you to search the text of wire service news stories, business magazines, and newspapers.

The Scout Report

```
http://rs.internic.net/scout_report-index.html
```

The Scout Report comes out more or less weekly and lists new resources the InterNIC scouts found during the preceding week. To join the Scout Report mailing list, send an e-mail message to `listserv@lists.internic.net`, with the line `subscribe scout-report yourfirstname yourlastname` in the text of the message.

Entering the World-Wide Web: A Guide to Cyberspace

```
http://www.hcc.hawaii.edu/guide/www.guide.html
```

This interesting introductory guide to the Web is chock-full of pictures and hyperlinks written by Kevin Hughes at the Honolulu Community College. The only problem is that this guide is large and can take 15 minutes to retrieve over a SLIP link. It's also a little dated (1993).

World Wide Web FAQs and Guides

`http://cuiwww.unige.ch/OSG/FAQ/www.html`

Oskar Stern, at the Centre Universitaire d'Informatique, University of Geneva, has thoughtfully created a Web page with references to just about every Web guide on the Net. So this page is a great place to start a Web walk.

Yanoff's List of Special InternetConnections

`http://www.uwm.edu/Mirror/inet.services.html`

Scott Yanoff has been compiling a list of Internet servers and addresses for several years. His list is the place we turn to first to find out how to get to a new service or to locate the most up-to-date list of servers that let you telnet to services such as Archie and Gopher.

Wow! It's Big!

`http://www.netgen.com/cgi/comprehensive`

A company called net.Genesis keeps a list of all domain names on the Internet — that is, all the sites that have computers on the Internet. (A domain name is the last two parts of an Internet host computer's name. For example, the Internet For Dummies Central Web server runs on a computer named `ivan.dummies.com`. It's in the `dummies.com` domain.)

You can use the Comprehensive List of Sites to find out all the American universities on the Internet (look for the names ending in `edu`) or sites in other countries (each country other than the U.S. has its own two-letter abbreviation, which is used as the last part of the domain name: for example, Brazil's is `br`).

Online Magazines

In a place as big and busy as the Internet, keeping up with what's new can be difficult because it changes every day. Fortunately, you're not on your own — lots of magazines, both on paper and online, can help keep you up to date. Paper magazines are hopelessly retro, so here we look at the online sources.

HotWired

```
http://www.hotwired.com
```

HotWired is the online edition of *Wired* magazine, that cool, '90s rag that is so graphically advanced that it's almost impossible to read. (Actually, the online edition is much easier on the eyes.)

The Global Network Navigator

```
http://gnn.com/
```

The *Global Network Navigator* also grew out of an Internet book and has become the best magazine on the Net. Unlike the other magazines, *GNN* is supported by advertising, which gives it a budget to pay writers to write real articles rather than to scrounge stuff or have the editor write everything. The difference is obvious: The writing is better and the breadth of coverage is much greater than in other online magazines.

GNN has sections of feature articles (usually with provisions for reader responses online), commentary, collections of clippings from both the Net and the regular media, and commercial sections. As *GNN* has evolved, it has grown new sections. In 1993, *GNN* gained a section on travel and in early 1994 a section on personal finance. New material appears nearly every day, so *GNN* is always worth a visit.

America Online bought *GNN* from O'Reilly & Associates, and an Internet service named GNN (described in Chapter 13) now exists, but the *GNN* magazine continues as before.

The Atlantic

```
http://www.theAtlantic.com
```

The Atlantic Monthly has been around for more than 100 years and concentrates on culture and politics. It's a top-class rag, and we'd say that even if we weren't friends with Corby Kummer, a senior editor and food columnist. Figure 22-1 shows Corby's Recipe-of-the-Month for December 1995.

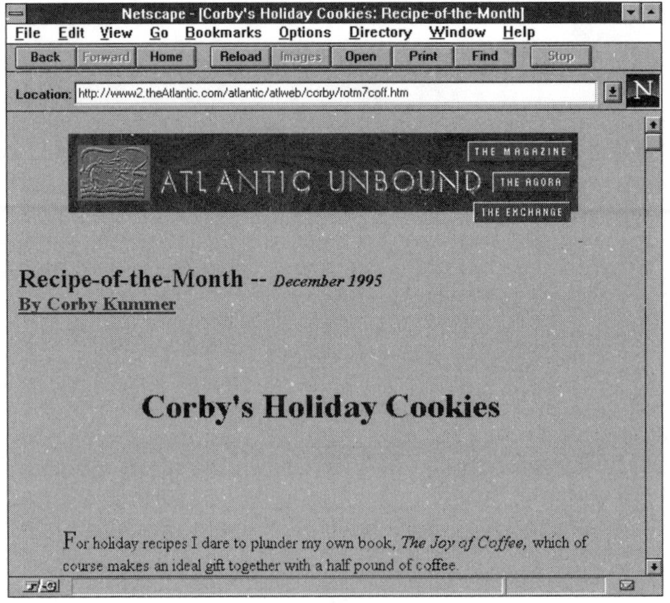

Figure 22-1: Here's a page from *The Atlantic Monthly's* online magazine. Cookies, anyone? (Web page designed by Charles Mann.)

The Electronic Newsstand

```
http://www.enews.com/
gopher://enews.com/
telnet://enews.com/ (login as enews)
```

The Internet Company (which, despite its grand name, consists mostly of two guys named Rob and Bill) has developed the Electronic Newsstand, which offers a wide variety of magazines and online information services. All magazines offer tables of contents and selected articles and let you order single issues or discounted subscriptions online. A few offer the entire magazine electronically. The magazines really run the gamut, from *American Demographics* to *Canoe & Kayak* to *The New Yorker* to *Yellow Silk*.

Rare Groove

```
http://rg.media.mit.edu/RG/RG.html
```

This magazine is about popular music, with playlists, charts, reviews, and even sound snippets of new songs. Signing up is free.

Put up or shut up on the Information Superhighway

Back at the dawn of electronic history, someone went around and asked people what they liked to watch on television. The answers were along the lines of classic movies and plays, educational lectures, concerts, and stuff like that. And what did we really watch? *I Love Lucy* and *Queen for a Day*.

So recently someone asked similar questions about what people would want access to on the coming information Superhighway (known in some circles as the Information Supercollider). What do you know: classic movies and plays, educational lectures — you get the idea. With the Internet Multicasting Service, we got what we asked for. Are we going to take advantage of it, or are we really waiting for Internet *Wheel of Fortune*?

Word

```
http://www.word.com
```

Word has nothing to do with Microsoft Word, the word-processing program. Instead, it's a quirky, independent pop-culture magazine put out by a few people in an apartment in New York. It's gotten excellent reviews for writing and reporting. *Word* has ads, which can be a bit annoying, but it's nice to get an interesting magazine for free.

Suck

```
http://www.suck.com
```

If you are interested in reading a daily magazine with a bad attitude, this Web site is for you. The magazine contains just one article, which changes every day.

And Now, the News

The online services (America Online, CompuServe, Prodigy, and Microsoft Network, among others) provide up-to-the-minute news from big, fancy new services like AP and Reuters. But don't be disappointed if you have an Internet account — the Web has lots of up-to-date news, too!

The Usenet urban folklore quiz (Part II)

Still with us? Amazing!

Part II: Computing and medicine

True or false:

11. Apple used a Cray supercomputer to design hardware systems; Cray used an Apple.
12. Bill Gates has a $750,000 Porsche 959 he can't use because it can't be made to comply with emission laws.
13. A Russian mechanical translator program translated "out of sight, out of mind" into "blind and insane," and "Spirit is willing, but the flesh is weak" as "the drink is good, but the meat is rotten."
14. In 1947 a moth was found in a relay of the Harvard Mark II computer and was taped in to the logbook as the "first actual case of bug being found."
15. Computing pioneer Grace Hopper coined the term "bug" as a result of this event.
16. A London doctor was fired for inveigling Turkish peasants to donate a kidney.
17. Flowers are bad in hospital rooms because they suck oxygen from the air.
18. Some people sneeze when they're exposed to bright light.
19. Drinking large quantities of deionized or distilled water over a long period of time can screw you up because of ion imbalances.
20. You can catch a cold by being chilled.

Yahoo!'s news

```
http://www.yahoo.com/headlines/news/
```

Yahoo!, the Web index described earlier in this chapter, also lists the day's top news stories, courtesy of Reuters NewMedia. You can even read news stories from the preceding seven days.

ClariNet

```
http://www.yahoo.com/News/Newswires/ClariNet/
news:groupname
```

ClariNet distributes news, features, and commentary in the form of articles in Usenet newsgroups. The newsgroup names all begin with `clari`, and we've listed some interesting newsgroups in Table 22-1. To read the newsgroup, use your newsreader or Web browser (if it can read newsgroups). The URL for a newsgroup consists of `news:` followed by the newsgroup name. For example, the URL for `clari.world.top` is `news:clari.world.top`.

Note: Not all Internet providers carry the ClariNet newsgroups because ClariNet charges providers for the news.

Table 22-1 ClariNet Newsgroups

Newsgroup Name	*Description*
`clari.bix.briefs`	Business news briefs
`clari.biz.urgent`	Late-breaking business news
`clari.nb.online`	Newsbytes about the Internet and online services
`clari.news.briefs`	Hourly news briefs about the U.S.
`clari.news.weather`	Weather news and reports
`clari.sports.briefs`	Sports scores
`clari.sports.features`	Sports feature stories
`clari.sports.top`	Top sports news
`clari.world.americas.canada`	General Canadian news
`clari.world.briefs`	News briefs from around the world
`clari.world.top`	Top world news stories

To see lists of all the ClariNet newsgroups, go to the Yahoo URL listed at the beginning of this section.

The New York Times

```
http://www.nytimes.com/
http://nytimesfax.com/
```

The *New York Times* has gone online in a big way, with all of each day's major stories on the Web, as well as some background material not printed in the wood pulp edition. You have to register to use it, but it's free, supported by unobtrusive advertising. (They say they may eventually charge users connecting from outside the U.S.)

Also, the *Times* has distributed an eight-page summary of the news by fax for several years, and now the same version is available online. To read the summary, you need an Adobe Acrobat reader, a program you can download from `http://www.adobe.com/`. A link to the Adobe page is right on *The TimesFax* page. (Acrobat is available for Windows, Macs, and a few kinds of UNIX workstations.)

This site can be really busy in the morning but clears up in the afternoon, after all those busy executives have gotten their news fix.

Let's Hear It

The global village even has radio stations. You can download sound files and play them on your computer. However, be warned that sound files are *large,* like many megabytes. Don't try downloading sound files unless you've got a fast Net connection. You can make yourself extremely unpopular if you download 15MB files in the middle of the day from a server on another continent. Check the list of sites to find a server close to you and do your heavy-duty downloading at off-peak times, like in the middle of the night or on weekends.

RealAudio takes a different approach, feeding your computer the data to play sound as needed. The sound quality isn't quite as good as a downloaded file, but the sound clips start up in seconds rather than hours. To listen to RealAudio sound files, you need a RealAudio player, which you can download from `http://www.realaudio.com/`.

National Public Radio

`http://www.npr.org/`

After NPR started giving out e-mail addresses on all its news programs, could a Web site be far behind? You can hear the day's newscast or its favorite story of the day in RealAudio format.

ABC News Reports

`http://www.realaudio.com/contentp/abc.html`

ABC provides hourly news, at 15 minutes after every hour, in RealAudio format. You can also hear sports, commentary, and special reports.

Air Force Radio

`http://www.brooks.af.mil/realaudio/`

This five-minute news broadcast is updated daily (see Figure 22-2).

How's the Weather?

Everyone talks about the weather, but nobody does anything about it, right? Well, you still may not be able to do anything about it, but at least you can be well informed.

See the "ClariNet" section earlier in this chapter for one source of up-to-the-minute weather reports.

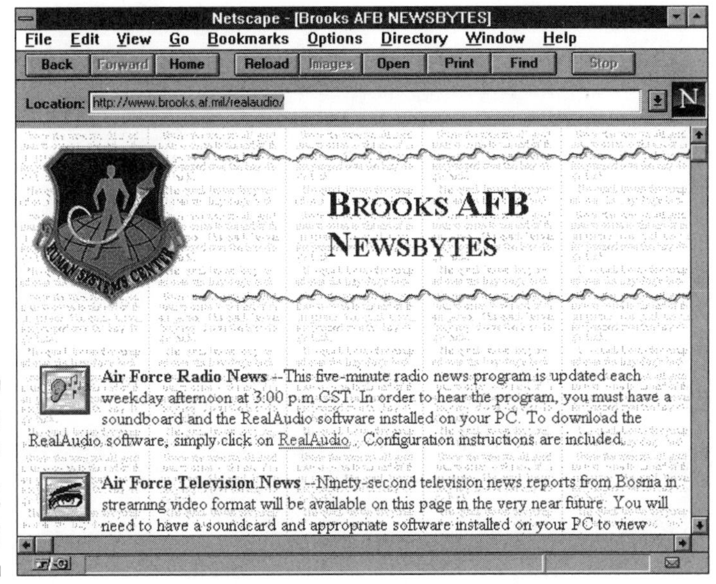

Figure 22-2: Internet to Air Force, come in, Air Force!

The National Weather Map

```
http://www.mit.edu:8001/usa.html
```

The WWW weather map, shown in Figure 22-3, shows the current national weather map. The weather info's up to date; the Weather Service issued the map in the figure only 45 minutes before we snapped a picture of it here at Internet For Dummies Central. When you click any point in the map, you get the forecast for that place. (We would show you the forecast, too, but the forecast is a little out of date.)

WWW Weather World

`http://www.atmos.uiuc.edu/wxworld/html/top.html`

Weather information has been available online from the University of Illinois for years. Weather World makes everything available at the click of a button. You can get weather maps, infrared satellite photographs, and visible light photographs. You can also get animations of the last several hours' photographs, just like they do on The Weather Channel. Real weather junkies can leave the map displayed in a window and then every hour or so press the Reload button to refetch the most current image.

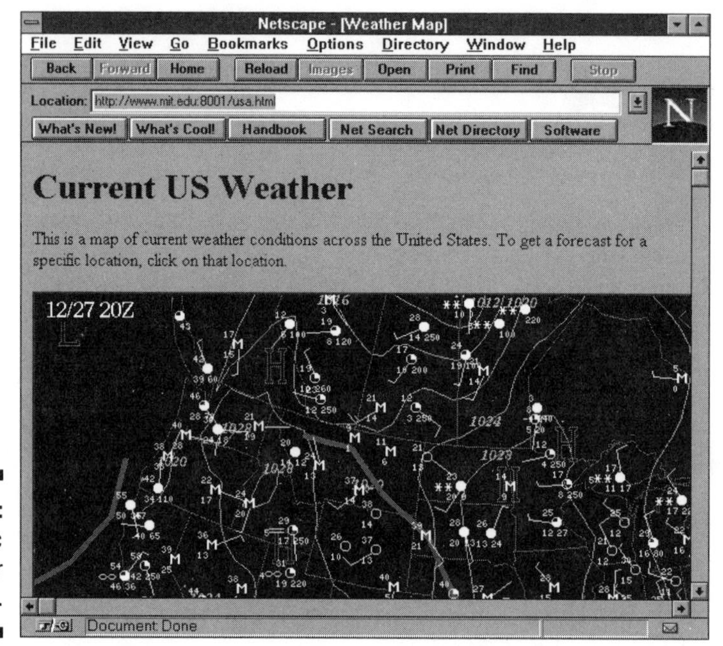

Figure 22-3: Your basic weather map.

Touchdown! Goal! Home Run!

Whatever your sport, you can find lots of information about it on the Net.

See the "ClariNet" section earlier in this chapter for one source of up-to-the-minute sports news.

The Tennis Server

`http://www.tennisserver.com/`

This page contains all kinds of information about tennis, from the rules of the game to current tennis news to pictures of the players. It's also got links to dozens of other tennis ties on the Web.

Sports Network

`http://www.sportsnetwork.com/`

Sports Network concentrates on scores and news, rather than background information about sports. If you want to see scores for today's games in baseball, football, basketball, tennis, hockey, golf, boxing, horse racing, and the Olympics (when they are on), this is the page for you. This page also has news, statistics, and odds for each sport.

ESPNet Sportszone

`http://espnet.sportszone.com/`

ESPN, the cable sports news network, has put together a Web service as well. This service is so popular that getting through to ESPN's Web server, though, can be tough — you may want to click the Mostly Text Front Page to see a version with fewer graphics. If you subscribe (for about $5 a month), you can also get more in-depth sports information.

Awesome Sports Web Sites

`http://www.awesomesports.com/`

If you want to find the most awesome sports Web pages around, this Web page tells you where to find them.

The Literary Life

Until the online revolution reaches its final victory, many old-fashioned books will still be made in the traditional way, by pressing ink on thin layers of dissolved, deceased trees. (You have one of them in your hands now.) In the meantime, many bookstores are on the Net, many with online catalogs, and all of which welcome online orders. (Wouldn't this be a good time to buy another dozen copies of this book to give to your friends? How about just one or two?) This section presents a selection of them.

Amazon Books

`http://www.amazon.com/`

Amazon Books exists only online (that is, it doesn't have a retail store) and claims to carry over one million titles. Its goal is to carry every book in print (good luck!). You can search for a book by keyword, title, or author, and you can even ask it to notify you when a book is available in paperback or when an author publishes a new title.

Wordsworth

`http://www.wordsworth.com/`

Wordsworth is a large, general-interest bookstore in Cambridge, Massachusetts, that sells most books at a discount. It carries all . . .*For Dummies* books (IDG Books Worldwide, Inc.), many autographed by us. (Its book buyer said of one of your authors: "I have to buy all of his books. He's friends with my dog.") Wordsworth's search system isn't as complete as `amazon.com's`, but it does carry a lot of books in stock, so you can probably get them sooner.

Future Fantasy Bookstore

`http://futfan.com/`

This specialty sci-fi store in Palo Alto, California, holds readings and events in addition to selling books. An extremely cool logo appears on its WWW page. This tiny, little store gets a large fraction of its orders from the U.S. and overseas by way of the Internet.

Computer books, anyone?

```
http://internet-plaza.net/softpro/
http://www.quantumbooks.com/
http://www.nstn.ca/cybermall/roswell/index.html
http://www.clbooks.com/
```

Softpro has stores near Boston and in Denver. Quantum has stores in Cambridge, Massachusetts, and Philadelphia. Roswell is a large, Canadian computer bookstore located in Halifax, Nova Scotia. Computer Literacy Books is the premier computer bookstore chain in the country, with three stores in Silicon Valley and one near Washington, D.C. All are computer specialty bookstores with extensive catalogs of computer books, including all the . . .*For Dummies* books, of course, and all accept orders over the Internet.

The Usenet urban folklore quiz (Part III)

Hey, don't you have anything better to do than take quizzes? Well, if you insist:

Part III: The groves of academe

True or false:

21. A professor listed a famous unsolved math problem; a student thought that it was homework and solved it.
22. At some colleges, if a roommate commits suicide, it gets you an automatic *A* for all your courses.
23. A student got his tuition money by asking in a newspaper ad for a penny from each person.
24. A professor allowed students to "bring in what they can carry for the exam"; one student carried in a grad student.
25. A student submitted a 20-year-old paper for a class. The professor gave it an *A,* saying that he always liked it but that he got only a *B* when he wrote it.
26. Eminent Stanford professor Donald "Art of Computer Programming" Knuth's first publication was in *MAD* magazine.
27. A philosophy professor's one-word exam was "Why?" He gave an *A* to a student who replied, "Why not?"
28. A low-grading professor graded the same exam in successive semesters; he gave it a higher grade each time. The fourth time around, he wrote, "Like it more each time."
29. Science class students took a swab from the inside of their cheeks and examined it under a microscope. One group saw odd organisms and called the professor, who looked and declared that it was sperm.
30. Albert Einstein did poorly in school.

I don't like Spam!

A few businesses, unfortunately, have taken to blanketing the Net with obnoxious advertisements. Early in 1994, a pair of Arizona lawyers caused an enormous furor by blanketing Usenet newsgroups with thousands of copies of an electronic advertisement offering to file applications in an upcoming U.S. immigration lottery, known as a "Green Card" lottery. They claimed, not very plausibly, that nothing was wrong with what they had done and that people who objected were just fuddy-duddies who hated all advertisements. For their troubles, the pair managed to get their pictures in *The New York Times* and to get interviewed on CNN.

The lawyers also got many, many megabytes of online complaints, enough that their Internet provider (which had no advance notice of their plans) had to disconnect from the Net for a while. To put it mildly, the lawyers didn't make themselves popular. Internauts all over the world ground their teeth in fury for weeks.

Their technique was quickly dubbed *spamming,* from an old *Monty Python* skit of actors in Viking costume who, with almost no provocation, would break into a song about Spam. (Yes, it's the same stuff that comes in little, blue cans and sort of resembles meat.) With luck, as commercial providers become more sophisticated, spamming will be nipped in the bud and attempted spammers booted off the Net.

Let Your Mouse Do the Walking

More and more normal businesses are getting connections to the Net, usually with Gopher or WWW pages, where you can find out about their wares and, usually, order them.

The Internet Mall

```
http://www.internet-mall.com/
```

The Internet Mall is an extensive list of cybershops on the Net, selling everything from culinary herbs to fossils to computer books.

The Internet Shopping Network

```
http://shop.internet.net/
```

This WWW page points you to thousands of hardware and software items for personal computers and workstations, in addition to reprints from *InfoWorld.* It has snazzy graphics as well, though they take a while to appear unless you have a fast modem. Most products are sold at a discount.

You have to be a member to order, but membership is free. Anyone can browse and look at prices, descriptions, and even reviews of the products.

The Branch Mall

```
http://branch.com:1080/
```

This URL is another WWW mall, offering a florist, gift food baskets, and other goodies.

We're from the Government, and We're Here to Help You

The U.S. government maintains hundreds of Web sites in an effort to make information available to Joe Average Citizen. Here are a few sites that you may find useful.

Edgar, Prince of Profit

```
http://www.sec.gov/edgarhp.htm
```

Interested in money? We thought so. The U.S. Securities (World Almanac) and Exchange Commission, the government agency that regulates stock markets, has a system called EDGAR that contains data filed by all the thousands of publicly-held companies it regulates. Every time a company sneezes, it has to file stuff with the SEC, so you can find out a great deal about your favorite company from EDGAR. Check out companies in which you hold stock, companies in which you might like to hold stock, the company where you work, and the company where you plan to work next. (For those last two, it wasn't us who suggested that you do that.)

It's Patently Obvious

```
http://patents.cnidr.org:4242/
```

There's been much excitement (and anger) in the computer business about patents issued for software. You can find out about recent software patents and any other patents issued since 1994.

The Census Bureau

```
http://www.census.gov/
gopher://gopher.census.gov
ftp://ftp.census.gov/pub
```

The Census Bureau, repository of far more information than it is healthy to have in one place, has a comfortable home in cyberspace. (As it should, because the Census Bureau has among the best records of government agencies for protecting personal privacy.)

You can find statistical and financial data of many varieties. You don't find detailed statistical data (too bulky, evidently), but statistical briefs (beautifully formatted in PostScript form so that you have to retrieve them and then print them by using a PostScript viewer) full of interesting info are available. We found out from one brief, for example, that although Americans of Asian and Pacific Island backgrounds are only slightly more likely to graduate from high school than are whites, they're almost twice as likely to complete college and go on to a graduate degree. At certain kinds of cocktail parties, that sort of factoid can be darned handy.

Stock Prices, Almost Live

Everyone wants to know if you can get live, up-to-date stock price quotations on the Internet. The answer is yes, but not for free. You can get prices that are delayed by less than an hour, though. Here's how:

Quote.com

```
http://www.quote.com
```

This site provides lots of financial information online, including end-of-day prices for stocks, commodity futures, mutual funds, money market funds, and indexes. Some balance sheet data are available, too. You have to subscribe to use `quote.com`, but subscribing is free.

Search for your stock

```
http://www.secapl.com/cgi-bin/qs
http://www.pathfinder.com/money/quote/qc
http://www.dbc.com/quote.html
http://www.lombard.com/PACenter/index.html
```

A number of Web pages allow you to enter the stock ticker symbol for a stock and get its stock price, usually delayed by about 15 minutes. Some companies require you to register, but they don't charge for the quotes.

Arts and Crafts

Culture is alive and well on the Net. Here are some sites to browse.

The Smithsonian Institution

```
http://www.si.edu/
```

The Smithsonian Institution (which, because it's supported by U.S. tax money, you've probably already paid for) includes a bunch of interesting museums (our favorite is the National Air and Space Museum). A lot of stuff from the museums is available on its Web site.

The Usenet urban folklore quiz (Part IV)

Holy petunias, you're still here.

Part IV: The entirety of human knowledge

True or false:

31. The song "Happy Birthday" is copyrighted.
32. Studies indicate that the majority of U.S. currency has traces of cocaine.
33. A woman had epileptic seizures after hearing *Entertainment Tonight* anchor Mary Hart's voice.
34. Some parents got a video for their children and found that it was recorded over an old porn tape.
35. Unless fast food shakes are marked "dairy," they aren't milk; instead, they're mostly carrageenan (seaweed extract) gel.
36. Lead leaches from lead crystal decanters into drinks, which is not good for you.
37. People have been poisoned by eating food cooked on burning oleander branches.
38. A woman removed the label from a "tuna" can and found a cat-food label underneath.
39. There is a basketball hoop at the top of the Matterhorn replica at Disneyland.
40. There were (are?) Japanese soldiers hiding out on islands in the Pacific who believed that WWII was still on.
41. Gerbils are illegal in California.

The Metropolitan Museum of Art

```
http://www.metmuseum.org/
```

You want culture? This place has got plenty!

The Louvre

```
http://www.Louvre.fr/
```

The Louvre Museum's Web site is currently in French, but English and Spanish versions should appear any day now. The Web pages contain news and information about the museum and its programs, but it doesn't have any images of the art itself — maybe because Bill Gates has bought the copyright to all of them!

The WebMuseum

```
http://sunsite.unc.edu/wm/
```

The WebMuseum is a project of Nicolas Pioch, a French Web consultant, and includes images of art from every imaginable period. If you aren't in the eastern U.S., choose the mirror site (that is, Internet host that stores exactly the same set of Web pages as the original site) that is nearest you.

Travel

Internauts are a peripatetic crowd, always on the move. More information is about travel than about anything else (except for information about the Net itself). Because the Net is truly global, it has tons of information about specific countries available from the countries themselves.

The Global Network Navigator

```
http://gnn.com/gnn/meta/travel/index.html
```

The Global Network Navigator, which was mentioned earlier in this chapter, has an entire section dedicated to travel, including various running series written by people traveling slowly around the world, filing reports by modem from a laptop. As of January 1996, two guys were winding their way around Africa and had just sent a report from Ghana.

The Navigator also has travel tips, country features, and ads from travel-related businesses.

U.S. State Department travel advisories

```
http://www.stolaf.edu/network/travel-advisories.html
```

Wondering how dangerous it is to go to Djibouti? The U.S. State Department publishes for every country in the world (except, for some reason, the United States) a travel advisory that discusses travel facilities, entry requirements, political instability, medical facilities, and availability of U.S. embassies and consulates. (As developing African countries go, Djibouti's not particularly unsafe.)

This WWW page, at Saint Olaf College, has links to all the current travel advisories, so you can Know Before You Go. Many experienced travelers find these advisories to be a bit alarmist (Egad! You can't get Big Macs in Timbuktu!), so you may also want to take them with a grain or two of salt.

The page also has links to the CIA's *World Fact Book,* which has political and economic information for countries all over the world, and links to home pages for a few countries.

If you travel a lot, you can subscribe to the travel-advisories mailing list. To be added to the mailing list, send a message containing the word "subscribe" to `travel-advisories-request@stolaf.edu`.

The Railroad Page

```
http://www-cse.ucsd.edu/users/bowdidge/railroad/rail-
        home.html
```

This page displays mailing lists, FTP archives, commercial services, online maps — everything for the well-informed rail fan.

The Metro Server

```
telnet://metro.jussieu.fr:10000/
```

Are you troubled by getting lost on the subway? As long as you live in Vienna, Hong Kong, Montreal, Palermo, Toronto, Mexico City, Lille (France), Amsterdam, Lyon (France), Madrid, Marseilles, London, Paris, Boston, Toulouse (France), New York, Frankfurt (Germany), San Francisco, Munich, Washington, D.C., or Athens, today is your lucky day. The Metro server figures out your route for you. Telnet in, and you immediately are in the Metro system. You tell it the name of the city and the departing and arriving stations, and it gives you the best route and the travel time.

When the server asks whether you want to use the X Window system, say no. You can abbreviate stations to the shortest amount of the name that isn't ambiguous.

The Funnies

Enough travel. Let's relax and read the funnies.

Dr. Fun

```
http://sunsite.unc.edu/Dave/drfun.html
news:alt.binaries.pictures.misc
```

The Internet has its own daily cartoon, Dr. Fun, in the tradition of *The Far Side*. It ranges from the strange to the extremely strange; one caption was "Silly String and Crazy Glue — a Deadly Combination." (The picture was not unlike what you would expect.)

The Doctor appears every weekday as an attractive, full-color graphic. Don't miss him.

Dilbert

`http://www.unitedmedia.com/comics/dilbert/`

United Media, the company that distributes *Dilbert,* puts it on the Web, too. *Dilbert* is every nerd's favorite strip (because everything he says about us is true). In addition to the *Dilbert* strip of the day, you can see the preceding two weeks of *Dilbert* cartoons, an interview with Scott Adams (the creator of *Dilbert*), and even a photo tour of the very room in which Scott draws the strips.

Yahoo!, there are lots of comics!

`http://www.yahoo.com/News/Daily/Entertainment/Comics/`

Yahoo!, the index to the World Wide Web described earlier in this chapter, lists a bunch of comics — well, five, anyway, as of this writing. As more comics appear on the Net, Yahoo! will list them.

Um, It's Personal

Lest we forget that even nerds have personal lives, read on.

Match.com

`http://www.match.com/`

With over 45,000 registered members, this site is a good place to meet other singles and look for Ms. or Mr. Right.

Virtual MeetMarket

`http://vmm.ravenna.com/`

Because people in cyberspace are as sociable as those in real life, sometimes, it was just a matter of time until the personals column appeared, so here it is. Each ad gets a page. There aren't many ads yet, so they're free both to place and to respond to.

Fun and Games

And now for something completely different!

The Spot — An Online Soap Opera

```
http://www.thespot.com/
```

Figuring out what you're supposed to do to participate in this online free-for-all is a little tricky. Simply click things until you get a feeling for what's going on. Then go to the SpotBoard and send e-mail to The Spot to tell the soap opera characters what they should do next.

Attention, klutzes!

```
http://www.hal.com/services/juggle/
```

Ever want to learn how to juggle? The Juggling Information Service features news, advice, pictures, vendors of juggling equipment (flaming Indian clubs have to come from somewhere), software, and lots of gossip.

Puzzle of the Week

```
http://www.webcom.com/~clong/mensa/forvm.html
http://www.csua.berkeley.edu/~mikechu/PuzzleOfTheWeek/
http://www.wam.umd.edu/~panthera/pow.html
```

Several sites post a new puzzle every week (some even post one every day!). The first site on the list is a monthly puzzle for Mensa members, so you'd better be smart to get near it.

Anagrams (A ram sang?)

```
http://www.ssynth.co.uk/~gay/anagram.html
http://mmm.mbhs.edu/~bconnell/anagrams.html
http://www.wordsmith.org/awad-cgibin/anagram
http://www.infobahn.com/pages/anagram.html
http://csugrad.cs.vt.edu/~eburke/anagrams.html
```

Want to find out some cool anagrams for your name? These anagram generators are just the trick. The first one listed will also turn them out in Dutch.

We submitted the phrase *Zac Young* (the name of a charming one-year-old of our acquaintance), and got

- a cozy gnu
- a cozy gun
- can guy oz
- gay cun oz
- agy cun oz
- zag cun yo

(Since when is *cun* a word?)

Food, Food, Wonderful Food

Finally, we get to something we all can agree is interesting and important.

Like to cook?

```
http://www.gulf.net/~vbraun/food.html
```

Vicki Braun maintains a vast list of food- and drink-related Web sites, which is well worth browsing if you are looking for a recipe or general cooking information.

Where to eat in the hub of the universe

```
http://genoa.osf.org:8001/boston-food/
news:ne.food
```

Hungry in Boston? This page lists hundreds of restaurants, with reviews constantly updated by readers' messages to Usenet. Most listings are linked to longer reviews, as shown in this example:

```
Emporio Armani Express [Italian] — Back Bay
More a scene than anything else, though the food is rather
good. For the men: dress like you're in advertising; for the
women: wear either no makeup or way too much. Feign an atti-
tude. They hired the most obsequious waiter I've _ever_ had,
but you already guessed that. Have a drink in the bar down-
stairs first. If you don't feel too alienated, have dinner
upstairs. (4/94)
```

Online soda machines

```
http://www.cc.columbia.edu/~pepsi/
http://www.cc.columbia.edu/~cocacola/
http://nomad.comtech.com.au/cgi-bin/coke
```

Soda machines have been on the Net for almost as long as there's been a Net. Nothing annoys a hard-hacking nerd more than walking down the hall to get a life-sustaining carbonated sugar beverage, only to find out that the machine is empty or, worse, was just filled and the soda is warm. To avoid this unspeakable horror, machines were quickly networked for the benefit of local users. Of course, the Net being the Net, querying a machine from 10,000 miles away is as easy as querying one from 10 feet away.

To check on the status of a soda machine, you used to have to master the esoteric `finger` command, found mainly on UNIX systems. Thank heavens, soda machines are now found on the World Wide Web. All soda machine Web pages tell you the basics, that is, whether the soda is sold out. Some machines also add other crucial details, such as the soda's temperature — in Celsius, naturally — and whether change is available.

Figure 22-4: About half full.

The Trojan Room

```
http://www.cl.cam.ac.uk/coffee/coffee.html
```

In England, hackers evidently drink coffee rather than Coke, and going down the hall is pointless if the pot's empty. So in the finest hacker tradition, they pointed a video camera at the coffee pot with some extremely complicated software to digitize the picture once a second and send the image to their Web server. Now people all over the world can tell — if they happen to fly to Cambridge — whether the coffee is ready (see Figure 22-4).

Sometimes the picture is pitch black. Nothing's wrong, but it's probably the middle of the night and they've turned out the lights.

Answers to the Usenet urban folklore quiz

For much, much more information about these and other topics of vital interest, visit the Usenet groups `alt.folklore.urban` and `alt.folklore.suburban`.

1. False

2. True

3. False

4. True

5. True

6. Both false

7. False

8. True, but it was a reporter's prank

9. False

10. True

11. True

12. True

13. False

14. True

15. False

16. True

17. False

18. True; doctors call this the "photic sneeze effect"

19. True

20. False (take that, Mom)

21. True; the student was mathematician George Dantzig

22. False

23. True

24. False

25. False

26. True (*MAD* #33, "The Potrzebie system of weights and measures")

27. False

28. False

29. False

30. True

31. True

32. True

33. True

34. True

35. True

36. True

37. True

38. True

39. True

40. True

41. True [CA Reg. Title 14, Sec. 671 (c)(2)(J) 1]

Appendix

Countries on the Internet

This table lists all the countries and countrylike areas in the world along with their official two-letter code and their level of Internet access as of early 1996. The two-letter codes are the same as are used in geographically based domain names.

The codes are

- I: Full Internet access
- M: E-mail (and maybe Usenet) only
- X: No connection

Access	*Code*	*Country*
X	AF	Afghanistan (Islamic Republic of)
X	AL	Albania (Republic of)
I	DZ	Algeria (People's Democratic Republic of)
X	AS	American Samoa
X	AD	Andorra (Principality of)
M	AO	Angola (People's Republic of)
M	AI	Anguilla
I	AQ	Antarctica
I	AG	Antigua and Barbuda
I	AR	Argentina (Argentine Republic)
I	AM	Armenia
M	AW	Aruba
I	AU	Australia
I	AT	Austria (Republic of)
M	AZ	Azerbaijan
M	BS	Bahamas (Commonwealth of the)
M	BH	Bahrain (State of)

Access	*Code*	*Country*
M	BD	Bangladesh (People's Republic of)
I	BB	Barbados
I	BY	Belarus
I	BE	Belgium (Kingdom of)
M	BZ	Belize
X	BJ	Benin (People's Republic of)
I	BM	Bermuda
X	BT	Bhutan (Kingdom of)
M	BO	Bolivia (Republic of)
M	BA	Bosnia-Herzegovina
M	BW	Botswana (Republic of)
X	BV	Bouvet Island
I	BR	Brazil (Federative Republic of)
X	IO	British Indian Ocean Territory
X	BN	Brunei Darussalam
I	BG	Bulgaria (Republic of)
M	BF	Burkina Faso (formerly Upper Volta)
X	BI	Burundi (Republic of)
X	KH	Cambodia
M	CM	Cameroon (Republic of)
I	CA	Canada
X	CV	Cape Verde (Republic of)
X	KY	Cayman Islands
X	CF	Central African Republic
X	TD	Chad (Republic of)
I	CL	Chile (Republic of)
I	CN	China (People's Republic of)
X	CX	Christmas Island (Indian Ocean)
X	CC	Cocos (Keeling) Islands
I	CO	Colombia (Republic of)
X	KM	Comoros (Islamic Federal Republic of the)
M	CG	Congo (Republic of the)

Access	*Code*	*Country*
M	CK	Cook Islands
I	CR	Costa Rica (Republic of)
M	CI	Cote d'Ivoire (Republic of)
I	HR	Croatia
M	CU	Cuba (Republic of)
I	CY	Cyprus (Republic of)
I	CZ	Czech Republic
I	DK	Denmark (Kingdom of)
X	DJ	Djibouti (Republic of)
X	DM	Dominica (Commonwealth of)
I	DO	Dominican Republic
X	TP	East Timor
I	EC	Ecuador (Republic of)
I	EG	Egypt (Arab Republic of)
M	SV	El Salvador (Republic of)
X	GQ	Equatorial Guinea (Republic of)
M	ER	Eritrea
I	EE	Estonia (Republic of)
M	ET	Ethiopia (People's Democratic Republic of)
X	FK	Falkland Islands (Malvinas)
I	FO	Faroe Islands
I	FJ	Fiji (Republic of)
I	FI	Finland (Republic of)
I	FR	France (French Republic)
M	GF	French Guiana
M	PF	French Polynesia
X	TF	French Southern Territories
X	GA	Gabon (Gabonese Republic)
M	GM	Gambia (Republic of the)
M	GE	Georgia (Republic of)
I	DE	Germany (Federal Republic of)
M	GH	Ghana (Republic of)

Access	*Code*	*Country*
X	GI	Gibraltar
I	GR	Greece (Hellenic Republic)
I	GL	Greenland
M	GD	Grenada
M	GP	Guadeloupe (French Department of)
I	GU	Guam
M	GT	Guatemala (Republic of)
M	GN	Guinea (Republic of)
X	GW	Guinea-Bissau (Republic of)
M	GY	Guyana (Republic of)
M	HT	Haiti (Republic of)
X	HM	Heard and McDonald Islands
I	HN	Honduras (Republic of)
I	HK	Hong Kong
I	HU	Hungary (Republic of)
I	IS	Iceland (Republic of)
I	IN	India (Republic of)
I	ID	Indonesia (Republic of)
I	IR	Iran (Islamic Republic of)
X	IQ	Iraq (Republic of)
I	IE	Ireland
I	IL	Israel (State of)
I	IT	Italy (Italian Republic)
I	JM	Jamaica
I	JP	Japan
M	JO	Jordan (Hashemite Kingdom of)
I	KZ	Kazakhstan
M	KE	Kenya (Republic of)
M	KI	Kiribati (Republic of)
X	KP	Korea (Democratic People's Republic of)
I	KR	Korea (Republic of)
I	KW	Kuwait (State of)

Access	*Code*	*Country*
M	KG	Kyrgyz Republic
X	LA	Lao People's Democratic Republic (Laos)
I	LV	Latvia (Republic of)
M	LB	Lebanon (Lebanese Republic)
M	LS	Lesotho (Kingdom of)
X	LR	Liberia (Republic of)
X	LY	Libyan Arab Jamahiriya (Libya)
I	LI	Liechtenstein (Principality of)
I	LT	Lithuania
I	LU	Luxembourg (Grand Duchy of)
I	MO	Macau (or Ao-me'n in Chinese)
I	MK	Macedonia (Former Yugoslav Republic of)
M	MG	Madagascar (Democratic Republic of)
M	MW	Malawi (Republic of)
I	MY	Malaysia
X	MV	Maldives (Republic of)
M	ML	Mali (Republic of)
M	MT	Malta (Republic of)
M	MH	Marshall Islands (Republic of the)
X	MQ	Martinique (French Department of)
X	MR	Mauritania (Islamic Republic of)
M	MU	Mauritius
X	YT	Mayotte
I	MX	Mexico (United Mexican States)
X	FM	Micronesia (Federated States of)
I	MD	Moldova (Republic of)
I	MC	Monaco (Principality of)
M	MN	Mongolia
X	MS	Montserrat
M	MA	Morocco (Kingdom of)
I	MZ	Mozambique (People's Republic of)
X	MM	Myanmar (Union of)

Access	*Code*	*Country*
M	NA	Namibia (Republic of)
M	NR	Nauru (Republic of)
M	NP	Nepal (Kingdom of)
I	NL	Netherlands (Kingdom of the)
M	AN	Netherlands Antilles
X	NT	Neutral Zone (between Saudi Arabia and Iraq)
M	NC	New Caledonia
I	NZ	New Zealand
I	NI	Nicaragua (Republic of)
M	NE	Niger (Republic of the)
M	NG	Nigeria (Federal Republic of)
M	NU	Niue
X	NF	Norfolk Island
X	MP	Northern Mariana Islands (Commonwealth of the)
I	NO	Norway (Kingdom of)
X	OM	Oman (Sultanate of)
M	PK	Pakistan (Islamic Republic of)
X	PW	Palau (Republic of)
I	PA	Panama (Republic of)
M	PG	Papua New Guinea
M	PY	Paraguay (Republic of)
I	PE	Peru (Republic of)
I	PH	Philippines (Republic of the)
X	PN	Pitcairn Island
I	PL	Poland (Republic of)
I	PT	Portugal (Portuguese Republic)
I	PR	Puerto Rico
X	QA	Qatar (State of)
I	RE	Réunion (French Department of)
I	RO	Romania
I	RU	Russian Federation
X	RW	Rwanda (Rwandese Republic)

Access	*Code*	*Country*
X	SH	Saint Helena
X	KN	Saint Kitts and Nevis
M	LC	Saint Lucia
X	PM	Saint Pierre and Miquelon (French Department of)
M	VC	Saint Vincent and the Grenadines
M	WS	Samoa (Independent State of)
X	SM	San Marino (Republic of)
X	ST	São Tomé and Principe (Democratic Republic of)
M	SA	Saudi Arabia (Kingdom of)
M	SN	Senegal (Republic of)
M	SC	Seychelles (Republic of)
M	SL	Sierra Leone (Republic of)
I	SG	Singapore (Republic of)
I	SK	Slovakia
I	SI	Slovenia
M	SB	Solomon Islands
X	SO	Somalia (Somali Democratic Republic)
I	ZA	South Africa (Republic of)
I	ES	Spain (Kingdom of)
I	LK	Sri Lanka (Democratic Socialist Republic of)
X	SD	Sudan (Democratic Republic of the)
M	SR	Suriname (Republic of)
I	SJ	Svalbard and Jan Mayen Islands
M	SZ	Swaziland (Kingdom of)
I	SE	Sweden (Kingdom of)
I	CH	Switzerland (Swiss Confederation)
X	SY	Syria (Syrian Arab Republic)
I	TW	Taiwan, Province of China
M	TJ	Tajikistan
M	TZ	Tanzania (United Republic of)
I	TH	Thailand (Kingdom of)
M	TG	Togo (Togolese Republic)

Access	*Code*	*Country*
X	TK	Tokelau Islands
M	TO	Tonga (Kingdom of)
M	TT	Trinidad and Tobago (Republic of)
I	TN	Tunisia
I	TR	Turkey (Republic of)
M	TM	Turkmenistan
X	TC	Turks and Caicos Islands
M	TV	Tuvalu
M	UG	Uganda (Republic of)
I	UA	Ukraine
I	AE	United Arab Emirates
I	GB	United Kingdom (Domain name is UK rather than GB)
I	US	United States (United States of America)
X	UM	United States Minor Outlying Islands
I	UY	Uruguay (Eastern Republic of)
I	UZ	Uzbekistan
M	VU	Vanuatu (Republic of, formerly New Hebrides)
X	VA	Vatican City State (Holy See)
I	VE	Venezuela (Republic of)
M	VN	Vietnam (Socialist Republic of)
X	VG	Virgin Islands (British)
I	VI	Virgin Islands (U.S.)
X	WF	Wallis and Futuna Islands
X	EH	Western Sahara
X	YE	Yemen (Republic of)
M	YU	Yugoslavia (Socialist Federal Republic of)
X	ZR	Zaire (Republic of)
I	ZM	Zambia (Republic of)
I	ZW	Zimbabwe (Republic of)

Index

• Numbers •

• A •

• B •

• C •

• D •

• E •

• F •

• G •

• J •

• K •

• L •

• M •

• O •

• P •

• R •

• S •

• T •

• U •

• Y •

• Z •

IDG BOOKS WORLDWIDE REGISTRATION CARD

RETURN THIS
REGISTRATION CARD
FOR FREE CATALOG

Title of this book: MORE Internet For Dummies®, 2nd Edition

My overall rating of this book: ❑ Very good [1] ❑ Good [2] ❑ Satisfactory [3] ❑ Fair [4] ❑ Poor [5]

How I first heard about this book:

❑ Found in bookstore; name: [6] ❑ Book review: [7]

❑ Advertisement: [8] ❑ Catalog: [9]

❑ Word of mouth; heard about book from friend, co-worker, etc.: [10] ❑ Other: [11]

What I liked most about this book:

What I would change, add, delete, etc., in future editions of this book:

Other comments:

Number of computer books I purchase in a year: ❑ 1 [12] ❑ 2-5 [13] ❑ 6-10 [14] ❑ More than 10 [15]

I would characterize my computer skills as: ❑ Beginner [16] ❑ Intermediate [17] ❑ Advanced [18] ❑ Professional [19]

I use ❑ DOS [20] ❑ Windows [21] ❑ OS/2 [22] ❑ Unix [23] ❑ Macintosh [24] ❑ Other: [25] ______ (please specify)

I would be interested in new books on the following subjects:
(please check all that apply, and use the spaces provided to identify specific software)

❑ Word processing: [26] ❑ Spreadsheets: [27]

❑ Data bases: [28] ❑ Desktop publishing: [29]

❑ File Utilities: [30] ❑ Money management: [31]

❑ Networking: [32] ❑ Programming languages: [33]

❑ Other: [34]

I use a PC at (please check all that apply): ❑ home [35] ❑ work [36] ❑ school [37] ❑ other: [38] ______

The disks I prefer to use are ❑ 5.25 [39] ❑ 3.5 [40] ❑ other: [41] ______

I have a CD ROM: ❑ yes [42] ❑ no [43]

I plan to buy or upgrade computer hardware this year: ❑ yes [44] ❑ no [45]

I plan to buy or upgrade computer software this year: ❑ yes [46] ❑ no [47]

Name: Business title: [48] Type of Business: [49]

Address (❑ home [50] ❑ work [51]/Company name:)

Street/Suite#

City [52]/State [53]/Zipcode [54]: Country [55]

❑ **I liked this book!** You may quote me by name in future IDG Books Worldwide promotional materials.

My daytime phone number is ______

IDG BOOKS®
THE WORLD OF COMPUTER KNOWLEDGE

YES!

Please keep me informed about IDG's World of Computer Knowledge. Send me the latest IDG Books catalog.

NO POSTAGE
NECESSARY
IF MAILED
IN THE
UNITED STATES

BUSINESS REPLY MAIL

FIRST CLASS MAIL PERMIT NO. 2605 FOSTER CITY, CALIFORNIA

IDG Books Worldwide
919 E Hillsdale Blvd, STE 400
Foster City, CA 94404-9691